TABLE B Measures of U.S. Income, Prices, and Federal Debt

Year	GNP	Net National Product	National Income	Personal Income	Disposable Income	GNP Deflator (1982 = 100)		CPI (1982–1984 = 100)		Federal Budget Deficit	Federal Debt
						Index Number	Percent Change	Index Number	Percent Change		
	Billions of Dollars									Billions of Dollars	
1929	103.9	94.0	84.7	84.3	81.7	14.6	–	–	–	0.7	16.9
1933	56.0	48.4	39.4	46.3	44.9	11.2	– 2.2%	–	– 5.1%	– 2.6	22.5
1939	91.3	82.3	71.2	72.1	69.7	12.7	– 0.8%	13.9	– 1.4%	– 2.8	48.2
1940	100.4	91.1	79.6	77.6	75.0	13.0	2.0%	14.0	0.7%	– 2.9	50.7
1941	125.5	115.3	102.8	95.2	91.9	13.8	6.2%	14.7	5.0%	– 4.9	57.5
1942	159.0	147.7	136.2	122.4	116.4	14.7	6.6%	16.3	10.9%	– 20.5	79.2
1943	192.7	181.1	169.7	150.7	132.9	15.1	2.6%	17.3	6.1%	– 54.6	142.6
1944	211.4	199.4	182.6	164.5	145.6	15.3	1.4%	17.6	1.7%	– 47.6	204.1
1945	213.4	201.0	181.6	170.0	149.2	15.7	2.9%	18.0	2.3%	– 47.6	260.1
1946	212.4	198.2	180.7	177.6	158.9	19.4	22.9%	19.5	8.3%	– 15.9	271.0
1947	235.2	217.6	196.6	190.2	168.8	22.1	13.9%	22.3	14.4%	4.0	257.1
1948	261.6	241.2	221.5	209.2	188.1	23.6	7.0%	24.1	8.1%	11.8	252.0
1949	260.4	238.4	215.2	206.4	187.9	23.5	– 0.5%	23.8	– 1.2%	0.6	252.6
1950	288.3	264.6	239.8	228.1	207.5	23.9	2.0%	24.1	1.3%	– 3.1	256.9
1951	333.4	306.2	277.3	256.5	227.6	25.1	4.8%	26.0	7.9%	6.1	255.3
1952	351.6	322.5	291.6	273.8	239.8	25.5	1.5%	26.5	1.9%	– 1.5	259.1
1953	371.6	340.7	306.6	290.5	255.1	25.9	1.6%	26.7	0.8%	– 6.5	266.0
1954	372.5	340.0	306.3	293.0	260.5	26.3	1.6%	26.9	0.7%	– 1.2	270.8
1955	405.9	371.5	336.3	314.2	278.8	27.2	3.2%	26.8	– 0.4%	– 3.0	274.4
1956	428.2	390.1	356.3	337.2	297.5	28.1	3.4%	27.2	1.5%	3.9	272.7
1957	451.0	409.9	372.8	356.3	313.9	29.1	3.6%	28.1	3.3%	3.4	272.3
1958	456.8	414.0	375.0	367.1	324.9	29.7	2.1%	28.9	2.8%	– 2.8	279.7
1959	495.8	451.2	409.2	390.7	344.6	30.4	2.4%	29.1	0.7%	– 12.8	287.5
1960	515.3	468.9	424.9	409.4	358.9	30.9	1.6%	29.6	1.7%	0.3	290.5
1961	533.8	486.1	439.0	426.0	373.8	31.2	1.0%	29.9	1.0%	– 3.3	292.6
1962	574.6	525.2	473.3	453.2	396.2	31.9	2.2%	30.2	1.0%	– 7.1	302.9
1963	606.9	555.5	500.3	476.3	415.8	32.4	1.6%	30.6	1.3%	– 4.8	310.3
1964	649.8	595.9	537.6	510.2	451.4	32.9	1.5%	31.0	1.3%	– 5.9	316.1
1965	705.1	647.7	585.2	552.0	486.8	33.8	2.7%	31.5	1.6%	– 1.4	322.3
1966	772.0	709.9	642.0	600.8	525.9	35.0	3.6%	32.4	2.9%	– 3.7	328.5
1967	816.4	749.0	677.7	644.5	562.1	35.9	2.6%	33.4	3.1%	– 8.6	340.4
1968	892.7	818.7	739.1	707.2	609.6	37.7	5.0%	34.8	4.2%	– 25.2	368.7
1969	963.9	882.5	798.1	772.9	656.7	39.8	5.6%	36.7	5.5%	3.2	365.8
1970	1015.5	926.6	832.6	831.8	715.6	42.0	5.5%	38.8	5.7%	– 2.8	380.9
1971	1102.7	1005.1	898.1	894.0	776.8	44.4	5.7%	40.5	4.4%	– 23.0	408.2
1972	1212.8	1104.8	994.1	981.6	839.6	46.5	4.7%	41.8	3.2%	– 23.4	435.9
1973	1359.3	1241.2	1122.7	1101.7	949.8	49.5	6.5%	44.4	6.2%	– 14.9	466.3
1974	1472.8	1335.4	1203.5	1210.1	1038.4	54.0	9.1%	49.3	11.0%	– 6.1	483.9
1975	1598.4	1436.6	1289.1	1313.4	1142.8	59.3	9.8%	53.8	9.1%	– 53.2	541.9
1976	1782.8	1603.6	1441.4	1451.4	1252.6	63.1	6.4%	56.9	5.8%	– 73.7	629.0
1977	1990.5	1789.0	1617.8	1607.5	1379.3	67.3	6.7%	60.6	6.5%	– 53.6	706.4
1978	2249.7	2019.8	1838.2	1812.4	1551.2	72.2	7.3%	65.2	7.6%	– 59.2	776.6
1979	2508.2	2242.4	2047.3	2034.0	1729.3	78.6	8.9%	72.6	11.3%	– 40.2	828.9
1980	2732.0	2428.1	2203.5	2258.5	1918.0	85.7	9.0%	82.4	13.5%	– 73.8	908.5
1981	3052.6	2704.8	2443.5	2520.9	2127.6	94.0	9.7%	90.9	10.3%	– 78.9	994.3
1982	3166.0	2782.8	2518.4	2670.8	2261.4	100.0	6.4%	96.5	6.2%	– 127.9	1136.8
1983	3405.7	3009.1	2719.5	2838.6	2428.1	103.9	3.9%	99.6	3.2%	– 207.8	1371.2
1984	3772.2	3356.8	3028.6	3108.7	2668.6	107.7	3.7%	103.9	4.3%	– 185.3	1564.1
1985	4014.9	3577.6	3234.0	3325.3	2838.7	110.9	3.0%	107.6	3.6%	– 212.3	1817.0
1986	4231.6	3771.5	3412.6	3526.2	3013.3	113.8	2.6%	109.6	1.9%	– 221.2	2120.1
1987	4515.6	4028.6	3660.3	3766.4	3194.7	117.4	3.2%	113.6	3.6%	– 149.7	2345.6
1988	4873.7	4359.4	3984.9	4070.8	3479.2	121.3	3.3%	118.3	4.1%	– 155.1	2600.8
1989	5200.8	4646.4	4223.3	4384.3	3725.5	126.3	4.1%	124.0	4.8%	– 153.4	2867.5
1990	5463.0	4887.4	4417.5	4645.6	3945.8	131.5	4.1%	130.7	5.4%	– 220.4	3206.3

Source: *Economic Report of the President*, February 1991.

Third Edition

Macroeconomics

Intermediate Theory and Policy

Third Edition

Macroeconomics
Intermediate Theory and Policy

William J. Boyes
Professor of Economics
Arizona State University

COLLEGE DIVISION South-Western Publishing Co.

Cincinnati Ohio

Sponsoring Editor: James M. Keefe
Developmental Editor: Brigid M. Harmon
Production Editor: Rebecca Roby
Production House: Bookman Productions
Cover/Internal Design: Craig LaGesse Ramsdell
Cover/Internal Photographer: Alan Brown/Photonics © 1991
Computer Illustrator: Alan Brown/Photonics © 1991
Marketing Manager: Scott D. Person

HD70CA
Copyright © 1992
by SOUTH-WESTERN PUBLISHING CO.
Cincinnati, Ohio

ISBN: 0-538-81282-6

2 3 4 5 6 7 8 9 0 D 0 9 8 7 6 5 4 3 2

Printed in the United States of America

Library of Congress Cataloging-in-Publication Data

Boyes, William J.
    Macroeconomics : intermediate theory and policy / William J.
Boyes, — 3rd ed.
        p.   cm.
    Includes bibliographical references and indexes.
    ISBN 0-538-81282-6
    1. Macroeconomics.   I. Title.
HB172.5.B68   1991
    339—dc20   91-34467
                                                                              CIP

Preface

The pace of change throughout the world in the early 1990s has been incredible. The collapse of the Iron Curtain, the emergence of market systems in Eastern Europe and the Soviet Union, the changes in the European Economic Community, the Gulf War, and the meetings between Israel and Arab states are events that were not anticipated by most people in the 1980s. More than ever before, today's economic environment is a global one. Decisions made by individual firms are influenced by events in remote corners of the world. Government actions must take into account the reactions of other governments. We can no longer study macroeconomics in the context of a single isolated country.

Macroeconomists today cannot assume that any economy operates in isolation from the rest of the world. The impact of the United States on its trading partners and the effects of events abroad on the U.S. economy are important parts of our study. During the period from 1945 to 1980, the U.S. economy was relatively insulated from events elsewhere. This is no longer the case. Net exports are now a larger part of the U.S. gross national product than are private savings, and direct foreign investment here more than doubled during the 1980s.

This third edition of *Macroeconomics* responds to these developments by stressing the global nature of macroeconomics early and throughout the text. The balance of payments and exchange rates are introduced in the first chapters, and discussions throughout the text incorporate these topics. Complete chapters are devoted to the macroeconomic links among nations and to open economy macroeconomics.

The theory of macroeconomics has also evolved rapidly. In the past decade, the causes and characteristics of business cycles have surged to the forefront of macro research. In addition, business cycles and economic growth are more closely linked than at any time since the Great Depression. The new macroeconomics of cycles and growth takes up a major portion of this third edition. Business cycles are the subject of two full chapters, and another chapter is devoted to economic growth.

▼
Focus on Applications

Albert Einstein once said that everything should be made as simple as possible, but not more so. This edition has been written with that warning in mind. The length, coverage, and style of the book have been influenced by the author's many years of teaching intermediate and M.B.A. students who have a wide range of interests and talents. Such students are not interested in spending several hundred pages on theoretical developments before they can move on to real-world issues. The objective of this book continues to be holding the interest of all students without losing the theoretical foundations necessary to understand macroeconomics. In this third edition, the practical realities of global macroeconomics, the business cycle, and economic growth are brought to the fore. For instance, the practice and institutions of monetary policy in a global setting are the focus of two chapters. The business cycle is discussed not only by considering the new classical and new Keynesian theories, but also by examining the *actual* behavior of economic variables. In fact, the last section of Chapter 15 shows how a student can follow the pattern of important economic variables by reading the newspaper.

The realities of policymaking are clearly distinguished from the theory of policymaking. Chapter 18 is the first chapter written about public choice in a macro text; it shows how policy decisions are actually made in the United States. Rather than assuming that government spending and taxation are used in the public's interest to control the economy, and solve special problems, this chapter considers why policymakers prefer deficits and inflation to recession and unemployment and why government deficits and inflation have existed for the past two decades.

▼
Structure of the Chapters

Each chapter begins with a What to Expect section that introduces an interesting example of that chapter's topic. The section is followed by a list of Key Questions that focus the discussion. The answers to these questions are provided in the chapter's Summary section. Key Terms are indicated throughout the text in bold type, are listed at the end of each chapter (along with the page number where they first appeared), and are collected in a Glossary at the end of the book.

Review problems and exercises are provided at the end of each chapter. The exercises are constructed so that the early ones help the student review the material. The later exercises require extension and applications of that material.

▼
Chapter-by-Chapter Organization

Part 1 (Chapters 1 and 2) is introductory. It explains why people study macroeconomics and discusses the relationship of macroeconomics to individual lives. These chapters introduce the topics of inflation, unemployment, business cycles, growth, exchange rates, and the balance of payments. Part 2 (Chapters 3–7) develops the basic aggregate demand–aggregate supply model. Chapter 3 covers the fixed-price, aggregate expenditures framework, while Chapter 4 develops the IS–LM model. In Chapter 5, those two models are incorporated to generate the aggregate demand curve. Aggregate supply is the subject of Chapter 6, which covers expectations, efficiency wages, and other topics related to labor markets. Aggregate demand and supply are then combined in Chapter 7 to discuss inflation, unemployment, and output determination.

Part 3 (Chapters 8 and 9) is devoted to controversies and schools of thought. The relationship between the Phillips curve and the AD–AS model is examined, along with the debate over whether there is an exploitable inflation–unemployment tradeoff.

Part 4 of the text (Chapters 10–13) covers business cycles and economic policy. Purchasing power parity, arbitrage, interest rate parity, exchange rate determination, and exchange rate regimes are discussed, along with monetary and fiscal policy in an open economy. Part 5 (Chapters 14 and 15) considers economic growth and business cycles, while Part 6 is devoted to extensions of topics treated in the first fifteen chapters. Consumption and investment theories are reconsidered in Chapters 16 and 17 and in Chapter 18 the government and public choice are examined.

▼
Student Study Guide

A Study Guide has been prepared by Barbara M. Yates and Raymond J. Farrow of the Albers School of Business at Seattle University. For each text chapter, the Study Guide includes an overview, review questions, and problems. Answers are provided for all questions and problems.

▼
Instructor's Manual

The Instructor's Manual contains, for each chapter, an outline, suggested answers to the review questions, and multiple-choice questions.

▼
Acknowledgments

Many people contributed to this third edition. The following friends and colleagues provided suggestions and guidance along the way:

Steve Anders	Grace College
Art Blakemore	Arizona State University
Peter Clark	University of California at Davis
John Dundar	University of Kentucky
Duane Eberhardt	Missouri Southern State College
Carl Enomoto	New Mexico State University
James Fackler	University of Kentucky
Fred Graham	University of Texas, Arlington
Loren Guffey	University of Central Arkansas
Jan Hansen	University of Wisconsin, Eau Claire
James Holmes	State University of New York, Buffalo
Max Jerrell	Northern Arizona University
Jon Knight	Florida Institute of Technology
Kishore Kulkarni	University of Central Arkansas
Wolfgang Mayer	University of Cincinnati
Michael Melvin	Arizona State University
Stephen Russell	Weber State University

Don Schlagenhauf	Arizona State University
Paul Semonian	University of Richmond
Paul Smith	University of Missouri
David Smyth	Louisiana State University
Scott Thompson	Weber State University
Harland Whitmore	University of Cincinnati
Jeff Wrase	Arizona State University

Comments received in response to the second edition were very useful and contributed to the changes made in the third edition. I also benefited from very insightful reviews of the third edition manuscript. For this help, I wish to thank

Ali Akarca	University of Illinois, Chicago
Lee Bender	Temple University
Steven Cobb	Xavier University
B. F. Kiker	University of South Carolina
Leonard Lardaro	University of Rhode Island
Michael McElroy	North Carolina State University
Harlan Platt	Northeastern University
John Trapani	Tulane University
Moosa Valinezad	Western Kentucky University

The students in my M.B.A., intermediate macroeconomics, and honors principles courses provided many lessons that are reflected in this text.

William J. Boyes

Contents in Brief

Contents

Part One

Introduction

Chapter 1

Introduction and Overview

What to Expect

This book takes you from a knowledge of the principles of macroeconomic theory to an understanding of the real-world complications facing macroeconomic policymakers. In this chapter, we examine the fundamental themes of macroeconomics, the basic questions for which macroeconomics seeks answers, the basic framework of analysis—aggregate demand and aggregate supply, and the role of models in economic analysis. These are some of the questions considered in the chapter:

1. *What are the two main topics of macroeconomics?*

2. *What major macroeconomic variables does macroeconomic analysis seek to explain?*

3. *What is the basic framework of analysis in macroeconomics?*

4. *In what area of analysis do most disagreements among economists occur?*

5. *How are various macroeconomic models used to develop a framework of analysis?*

▼
Why Study Macroeconomics?

Macroeconomics should be of interest to you because it is about you; it affects you daily. You can't pick up a newspaper or magazine, watch television, or do virtually anything without confronting some macroeconomic issue. The prices of goods and services, the possibility of obtaining a job or moving to a better-paying job, incomes, the value of an education or specific job training, the unfortunate circumstances of poverty, the pleasant or unpleasant aspects of the welfare system, taxes, the environment, health care, social security, and military excursions all are topics of study in macroeconomics.

Macroeconomics gives you the big picture. It helps you understand the behavior of economies and how the economies of different nations affect each other. The big picture includes the entire world. You could lose your job in New York because a manager in Tokyo decides to decrease his or her firm's prices, or you could find that your degree in Soviet studies has become very valuable because U.S. companies are trying to expand into the Soviet economy as it moves from communist to capitalist. In many ways, you are now closer to the people in Amsterdam or Hong Kong than your grandparents were to people in a neighboring state. If you think that a global economy is just an abstract economic idea, look at the labels on your clothes and see how many countries are represented. Your tennis shoes may have been manufactured by a German company, but assembled in Italy, India, or China. When you bought them, did you pay in marks, lira, rupees, or yuan? No, you paid for them with dollars. Yet countries have their own currencies—they don't all rely on the U.S. dollar. Germany uses marks, Italy uses lira, India uses rupees, and China uses yuan. So for you to purchase these goods, their prices must be converted to U.S. dollars. How do the currencies get exchanged, and at what rates are they exchanged? Does it matter whether $1 exchanges for 1,000 lira or 1 million lira?

Conditions in the United States affect firms and people elsewhere; conditions elsewhere affect U.S. firms and citizens. In March 1991, U.S. mortgage interest rates rose even though the domestic economy was mired in a recession. Reasons given for the rise included the expected boost to the U.S. economy as U.S. firms worked to rebuild Kuwait after the Iraq war, the anticipated impact of the reunification of Germany on U.S. financial capital, and the role of the U.S. government budget deficit in channeling funds to government projects and away from housing. As a citizen, an employee, a manager, or a business owner, you need to understand the global economy.

The world's governments are at the center of the macroeconomics picture. A government plays many roles: providing national defense, issuing money, employing thousands of workers, enacting and administering income support programs, overseeing banking activities, and so forth. U.S. government activities can affect standards of living in the United States. U.S. foreign aid and economic policies can affect standards of living in Latin America or other parts of the world. U.S. residents don't think much about inflation when it's in the 3 to 5 percent range, but when it exceeds 10 percent, as it did in the early 1980s, they demand the government do something about the problem.

Americans who feel their jobs are secure often don't have the same concerns with economic trends and indicators as those whose jobs are susceptible to the fluctuations of the economy. Many are content to raise families and pursue their own versions of the American dream. But when the security disappears and unemployment ruins that dream, then the public demands the government do something. Unexpected or unanticipated events can affect the economy and you personally in a dramatic fashion. The invasion of Kuwait by Iraq raised oil and gas prices; the freezing weather in January 1991 raised citrus prices; and the collapse of communism in Eastern Europe in 1990 shook the world's economies. Americans and other citizens call for government actions to soften the blow from these shocks to their economies. In short, the government is a key player in the economy. The government's role, why it has an important role, and whether or not it *should* have that role are all subjects of study in macroeconomics.

Although all economies go through periodic bouts of inflation and unemployment, the basic fact of macroeconomics is that economies grow over the long run. On average, each successive generation in the United States and other developed countries have had higher standards of living than the previous generation. Will your standard of living be higher than your parents? Recent polls suggest that many of you do not think so. The causes of sustained or long-term economic growth and whether such growth will continue are also the subjects of macroeconomics.

At the same time that people in developed countries generally experience high standards of living, many people in the world barely eke out a living. For instance, many people in Sub-Saharan Africa live in abject poverty, scraping for anything that might keep their children from starving or their spouses from being consumed by disease. What accounts for the differences in the economic performance of different countries? This too is a subject of macroeconomics.

▼

What Are the Primary Topics of Study in Macroeconomics?

The two principal topics of macroeconomics are *business cycles* and *economic growth.* As students of macroeconomics, our objectives are to understand business cycles: what causes them, what their consequences are, and whether we or our government can or should do anything about them. In addition, we need to learn what causes economic growth and whether or not we or our government can alter the rates of economic growth.

Figure 1-1 shows the path taken by the U.S. economy since 1920. U.S. total output and income each year is called *real GNP.* You can see that according

FIGURE 1-1 *Growth and cycles of the U.S. economy. The path taken by the U.S. economy since 1920. U.S. total output and income each year is called* real GNP. *You can see that according to real GNP the U.S. economy has grown. The upward slope of the real GNP curve illustrates the growth. You can also see that the growth is not a steady upward process. Economies go through cycles: periods of expansion followed by periods of contraction. These cycles, called* business cycles, *have a major impact on people's lives, incomes, and standards of living.*

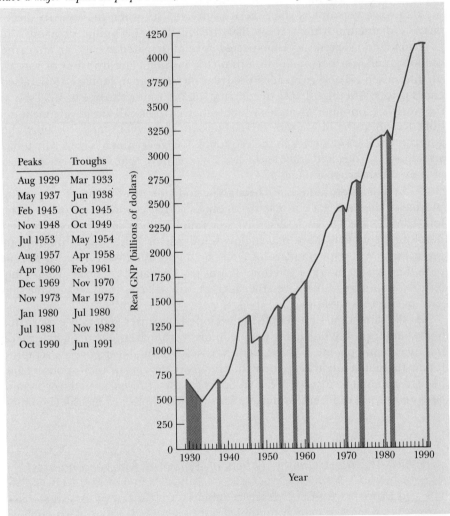

Peaks	Troughs
Aug 1929	Mar 1933
May 1937	Jun 1938
Feb 1945	Oct 1945
Nov 1948	Oct 1949
Jul 1953	May 1954
Aug 1957	Apr 1958
Apr 1960	Feb 1961
Dec 1969	Nov 1970
Nov 1973	Mar 1975
Jan 1980	Jul 1980
Jul 1981	Nov 1982
Oct 1990	Jun 1991

Source: Economic Report of the President, 1991 (Washington, DC: U.S. Government Printing Office, 1991).

to real GNP the U.S. economy has grown. The upward slope of the real GNP curve illustrates the growth. You can also see that the growth is not a steady upward process, but occurs in spurts. Economies go through cycles: periods of expansion followed by periods of contraction. These cycles, called **business**

cycles, have a major impact on people's lives, their incomes, and standards of living.

Why Care About Business Cycles?

Business cycles affect people's lives. Economic stagnation and recession throw many—often those who are already relatively poor—out of their jobs and into real poverty. **Economic growth** is an increase in the output produced in an economy. Economic growth increases the number of jobs and draws people out of poverty and into the mainstream of economic progress. In 1990, approximately 30 million U.S. residents were officially in poverty. Poverty is defined as income below some specified level. The income level selected is based on the cost of meals that meet certain nutritional standards. In 1959, the poverty level for a family of four in the United States was an income of $2,973 per year. In 1990, the poverty income level was about $13,000. As large as the number of people officially in poverty is, the incidence of poverty (the percentage of the total population in poverty) in the United States is smaller than in 1960 when poverty information was first collected. Figure 1·2 compares the percentage of the total population living in poverty year to year from 1960.

A major factor accounting for the incidence of poverty is the health of the economy. From 1960 to the late 1970s, the incidence of poverty in the United States declined rapidly as the economy experienced growth. However, the recessions since 1960 have strongly affected the numbers of people thrown into poverty. The recession of 1969–1970 was relatively mild. Between 1969 and 1971, the unemployment rate rose from 3.4 to 5.8 percent, and the total number of people unemployed rose from 2,832,000 to 5,016,000. The recession halted the decline in poverty rates that had been occurring since 1960. When the economy once again began to expand, the poverty rate again began to drop. The 1974 recession brought on another bout of unemployment that threw people into poverty. The 1974 recession was relatively serious, causing the unemployment rate to rise to 8.3 percent by 1975 and the number of unemployed to rise to 7,929,000. Once again, the poverty rate declined as the economy picked up after 1975. The recession of 1980–1982 threw the economy off track again. From the late 1970s until the early 1980s the incidence of poverty rose; it then began to decline again after 1982 as the economy picked up steam. In 1979, the total number of people unemployed was 6,137,000; by 1982, a whopping 10,717,000 were without jobs. As the economy came out of this recession, the poverty rate continued to decline as the economy continued to grow throughout the 1980s. In 1990, a recession again altered the pattern.

The official dating of a recession or expansion in the United States is the responsibility of a private research organization, the National Bureau of Economic Research (NBER). The NBER has identified the shaded regions in Figure 1·1 as recessions, the unshaded regions as expansions. **Recessions** are periods between peaks and the troughs that follow. A recession is defined as at least two consecutive quarters (at least 6 months) of decline in real GNP.

FIGURE 1-2 *The percentage of the total population living in poverty year to year from 1960 for the United States is shown. A major factor accounting for the incidence of poverty is the economic health of the nation. From 1960 to the late 1970s, the incidence of poverty in the United States declined rapidly as the economy grew. From the late 1970s until the early 1980s — a recessionary period — the incidence of poverty rose; it then began to decline again after 1982 as the economy picked up steam. Small upswings in the incidence of poverty occurred in 1968 and 1974, and a large rise occurred between 1978 and 1982, both associated with economic conditions.*

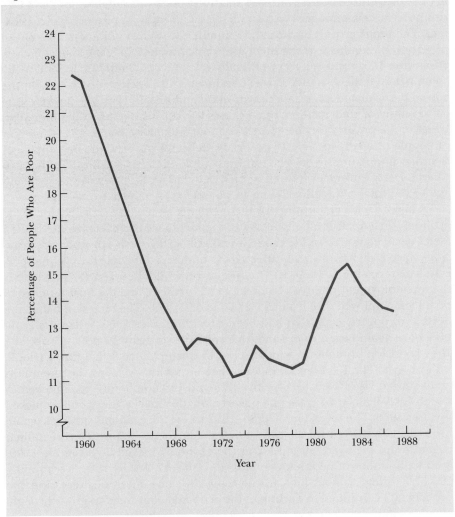

Source: U.S. Bureau of the Census, *Current Population Reports,* series P-60, no. 161 (Washington, DC: U.S. Government Printing Office, 1988).

Expansions are periods between troughs and the peaks that follow. Since 1929 there have been 12 recessions. The most severe was the Great Depression of the 1930s; a **depression** is a prolonged period of severe recession.

Over the course of a business cycle, unemployment and inflation typically move inversely to each other; as inflation rises, unemployment drops, and vice versa. When the economy is growing, the demand for goods and services tends to increase, firms hire more workers, and the unemployment rate falls. Expansion also has an impact on inflation. As the demand for goods and services rises, the prices of those goods and services also tend to rise. Conversely, during periods of recession the unemployment rate typically rises and inflation slows down. You can see in Figure 1-3 how U.S. civilian unemployment[1] and

FIGURE 1-3   *U.S. inflation and unemployment in the post-World War II period. U.S. inflation and civilian unemployment rates are plotted over the years since 1940. Typically, when the inflation rate increases, the unemployment rate decreases, and vice versa. That inverse relationship doesn't always hold, however. For instance, notice that during the late 1960s through the 1970s the two moved upward together.*

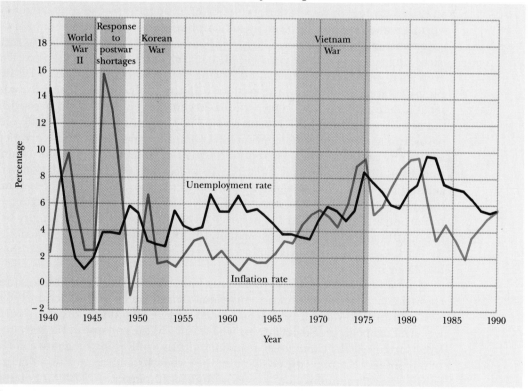

Source: Economic Report of the President (Washington, DC: U.S. Government Printing Office, various years).

1   The *civilian* unemployment rate excludes all members of the armed forces.

inflation rates are related. For instance, in 1961 a 1 percent rate of inflation occurred with a 6.7 percent civilian unemployment rate. By 1969, the inflation rate had risen to the relatively high figure of 5.5 percent while the civilian unemployment rate had declined to 3.5 percent. You can also see that the inverse relationship between inflation and unemployment rates doesn't always hold; at times, the inflation and unemployment rates rise together. For instance, throughout the 1960s and 1970s, inflation and unemployment both climbed, until in 1980 the civilian unemployment rate was 7.1 percent and the inflation rate was 13.5 percent.

Economies are linked. In Figure 1-4A, the paths of real output are illustrated for several nations. You can see how they tend to rise and fall together. As shown in panels B and C of Figure 1-4 the inflation and unemployment rates in different countries also tend to move together.

Although nations are linked economically, in some instances one country experiences a much more rapid inflation rate or significantly larger unemployment problems than the rest of the world. The term **hyperinflation** refers to an extremely high rate of inflation. Hyperinflation makes a country's currency worthless and often leads to the introduction of a new currency or even a new government. Chile experienced hyperinflation in 1974, with an inflation rate exceeding 500 percent per year. People couldn't carry enough cash to pay for even small purchases; registers and calculators ran out of digits. As a result, Chile replaced its currency, the escudo, with the Chilean peso. The peso was set at a value of 1 peso = 1,000 escudos. Argentina replaced its old peso with the peso Argentino in June 1983 at a value of 1 peso Argentino = 10,000 old pesos. But because inflation continued, Argentina again replaced its currency in 1985 by setting the new currency, the austral, equal to 1,000 pesos Argentino. Even that did not deter inflation. As a result of continuing inflation, Argentina began in 1991 to allow its citizens to use the U.S. dollar rather than the austral as currency. The most dramatic hyperinflation in history occurred in Europe after World War I. The price level in Germany rose so rapidly between 1914 and 1924 that it was virtually impossible to carry out transactions. By 1924, German prices were more than 100 trillion times higher than they had been in 1914.

Unemployment rates tend to move in concert but, as with inflation, some countries experience much worse problems than others. For instance, in 1989, Soviet President Mikhail Gorbachev stated that he would not forcefully keep Eastern Europe in the Soviet system. The result was the collapse of the so-called Iron Curtain. As the communist economies of Eastern Europe sought to change into freer, more capitalistic economies, they went through a transition that involved severe unemployment—rates as high as 40 percent in 1991 in Poland, Hungary, and even the former East Germany. During the Great Depression of the 1930s, massive unemployment was experienced throughout the world. Unemployment in the United States and the United Kingdom approached one-quarter of the labor force.

FIGURE 1·4 *Economies are linked. Panel A shows the path of real industrial output for several industrial nations. Panel B shows the inflation rates for these countries. As with real output, the inflation rates of the countries tend to rise and fall together. Panel C shows the civilian unemployment rates for these countries. They too tend to move in concert.*

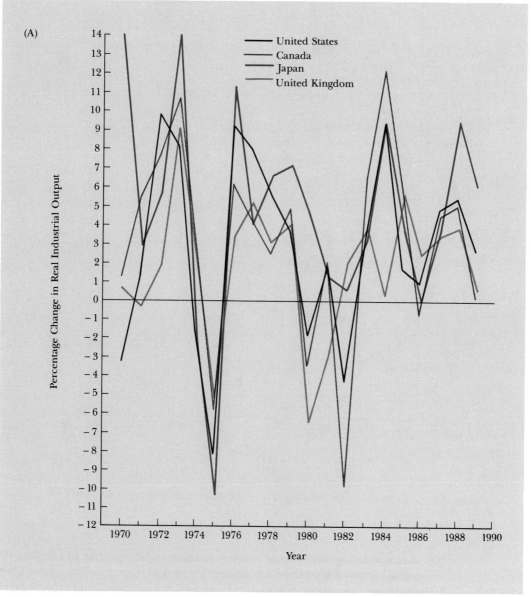

Source: Economic Report of the President, 1991 (Washington, DC: U.S. Government Printing Office, 1991).

FIGURE 1-4   *(continued)*

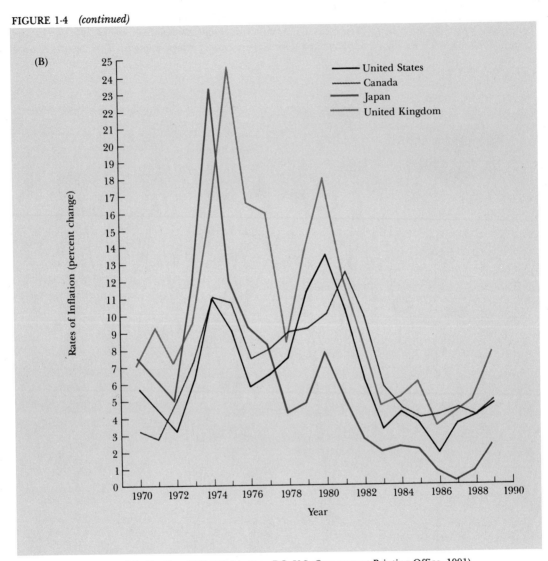

Source: Economic Report of the President, 1991 (Washington, DC: U.S. Government Printing Office, 1991).

Economic Growth

Standards of living differ from country to country irrespective of whether the economies are in a growth or a recessionary period. One measure of standard of living is per capita income. Figure 1-5 shows that the per capita income levels vary tremendously among nations. In 1990, Switzerland had a per capita income level of more than $27,000, while the level in Ethiopia was only $130. How can nations experience such vastly different standards of living?

FIGURE 1-4   *(continued)*

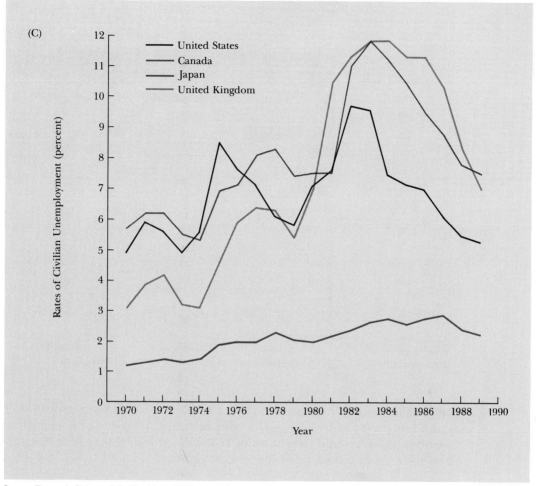

Source: Economic Report of the President, 1991 (Washington, DC: U.S. Government Printing Office, 1991).

During the past 20 years, the Japanese economy has grown at a significantly faster rate than the U.S. economy. Is it because Japanese workers are more diligent or more highly motivated? Is it because Japanese students study more than U.S. students? Is it because Japanese firms are more concerned with developing new products and new production techniques than U.S. firms? Is it because Japanese monetary and fiscal policies are more conducive to growth than U.S. policies? Although much of macroeconomics is aimed at understanding business cycles, the fact that most economies grow over time should not be forgotten. Different rates of growth can lead to vastly different living standards. If one country grows at a 3 percent rate per year and another at a 4 percent rate, it will take 24 years for the real GNP in the first economy to double but only

FIGURE 1-5 *Per capita income levels in several nations. The per capita income levels vary tremen-*
dously among nations. In 1990, Switzerland had a per capita income level of more than $27,000
while the level in Ethiopia was only $130.

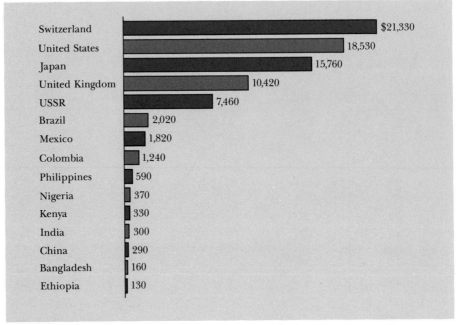

Switzerland	$21,330
United States	18,530
Japan	15,760
United Kingdom	10,420
USSR	7,460
Brazil	2,020
Mexico	1,820
Colombia	1,240
Philippines	590
Nigeria	370
Kenya	330
India	300
China	290
Bangladesh	160
Ethiopia	130

Source: World Bank, *World Development Report,* (New York: Oxford University Press, 1989).

18 years for real GNP in the second to double. Different rates of growth over
just a few years can lead to significantly different standards of living. Thus,
we need to understand the causes of economic growth if we are to discover
how to improve standards of living most rapidly.

▼
How Do We Study Business Cycles and Economic Growth?

Economic growth characterizes all economies over long periods of time, and
business cycles are a fairly common event in all economies. What causes economic growth and business cycles? Suppose we represent the economy in a simple demand and supply graph, as shown in Figure 1-6. When speaking of the
entire economy, we refer to total planned spending at various price levels as
aggregate demand *(AD)* and total output supplied at various price levels as **aggregate supply *(AS)*.** In Figure 1-6, the level of national income and output in
1991 is represented on the horizontal axis as Y_{1991} and the price level is shown
on the vertical axis P_{1991}. These levels are determined by the intersection between the aggregate demand curve, AD_{1991}, and the aggregate supply curve,

FIGURE 1-6   AD–AS *and a recession. The level of national income and output in 1991 is represented as* Y_{1991} *and the price level is* P_{1991}. *These levels are determined by the intersection between the aggregate demand curve,* AD_{1991}, *and the aggregate supply curve,* AS_{1991}. *A shift in either the aggregate demand curve or the aggregate supply curve can lead to changes in output, employment, and prices. Suppose the aggregate demand curve shifts in, to* AD_{1992}. *The new intersection between AD and AS is given by* Y_{1992} *and* P_{1992}. *The economy's output and income has fallen, as has the price level. The lower level of output means that firms will need fewer employees—unemployment will rise. Thus, in this case, the shift of the aggregate demand curve led to a recession. A shift of the aggregate supply curve could have done the same thing. Suppose that the aggregate supply curve shifts in from* AS_{1991} *to* AS_{1992}. *The intersection with the original AD curve occurs at a lower level of output. In addition, both aggregate supply and aggregate demand could have shifted and led to a recession.*

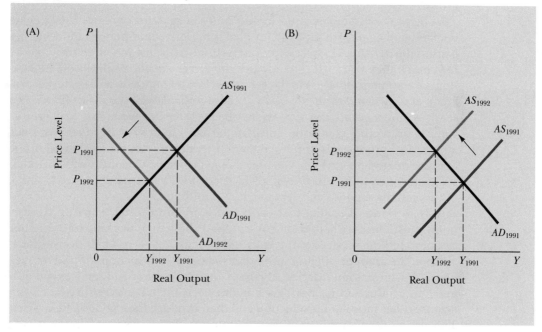

AS_{1991}. A shift in either the aggregate demand curve or the aggregate supply curve can lead to changes in output, employment, and price. Suppose the aggregate demand curve shifts in, to AD_{1992}. The new intersection between AD and AS results in Y_{1992} and P_{1992}. The economy's output and income has fallen, as has the price level. The reduced level of output means that firms need fewer employees—so unemployment rises. Thus, in this case, the shift of the aggregate demand curve has led to a recession.

A shift of the aggregate supply curve could have done the same thing as the shift of the aggregate demand curve. Suppose that the aggregate supply curve shifts in, from AS_{1991} to AS_{1992}. The intersection with the original AD curve occurs at a lower level of output—a recession. A business cycle can be started by either a change in aggregate demand or a change in aggregate supply, or even by a change in both aggregate demand *and* aggregate supply curves.

By examining what lies behind aggregate demand and aggregate supply, we can learn about the causes of business cycles. We also are able to learn about economic growth from studying aggregate demand and supply. Economic growth can be represented as a series of outward shifts of aggregate supply. Notice in Figure 1-7A that both the aggregate demand and aggregate supply curves are shifting out over time. The outward shifts lead to increasingly larger levels of real output, Y. This translates into Figure 1-7B, a pattern of economic growth.

The basic framework used in our study of macroeconomics is aggregate demand and aggregate supply. Our goal is to derive and understand what lies behind the *AD* and *AS* curves; to understand what causes them to shift and by how much they will shift. The *AD* and *AS* curves are the result of the interactions of four major players in the economy: households, businesses, the government, and the foreign sector. Each of these four players purchases goods and services. These goods and services may be produced in the home, or domestic, country or in other countries. The planned amount of spending on final goods and services produced in the domestic country determines the level of aggregate demand in an economy. Thus, to understand aggregate demand, we must understand the spending behavior of each of the four participants.

To purchase goods and services, households must obtain income. They do this by working or selling the services of land and capital they own. Households must decide whether or not to spend their time working and whether or not to sell the services of the land and capital they own. Their decisions determine the amount of labor and other factors of production offered to businesses. Businesses must decide whether to produce goods and services and how much to produce. Once having made this decision, businesses hire labor and acquire other factors of production and then produce their goods and services. The decisions of households and businesses define aggregate supply—the amount of final goods and services produced in an economy. Thus, to understand aggregate supply, we must understand why households and businesses make the choices they do.

The simple process of determining where aggregate demand and aggregate supply intersect defines the levels of output, income, employment, and the price level. It determines the quantity of transactions made and the price level of those transactions. As aggregate demand and/or aggregate supply change, the levels of output, income, employment, and prices change.

The economy is analyzed by considering the interaction of the four participants in three markets: the market for goods and services, the labor market, and the money market, as illustrated in Figure 1-8. The goods and services market is represented by the *AD* and *AS* curves. The labor market defines (1) the household's work–nonwork choice, (2) businesses' hiring decisions, and (3) the level of income households have. The money market defines the amount

FIGURE 1·7 *The AD–AS curve and economic growth. Economic growth can be represented as a series of outward shifts of aggregate supply. Notice in panel A that both the aggregate demand and aggregate supply curves are shifting out over time. The outward shifts lead to increasingly larger levels of real output, y. This translates into panel B, a pattern of economic growth.*

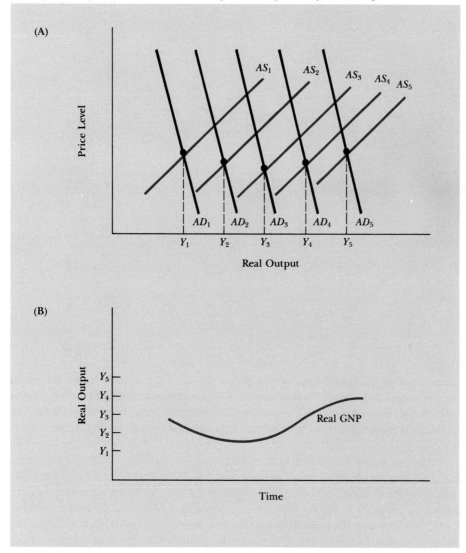

of money available for making transactions and money's influence on those transactions.

The three markets affect and are affected by each other. The demand for and supply of labor determines the level of employment and income. The amount of income influences the quantity of goods and services that can be

FIGURE 1-8   *The study of macroeconomics. The three markets discussed are the market for goods and services, the labor market, and the money market. The goods and services market is represented by the AD and AS curves. The labor market defines (1) the household's work–nonwork choice, (2) business's hiring decision, and (3) the level of income households have. The money market defines the amount of money available for making transactions and money's influence on those transactions.*

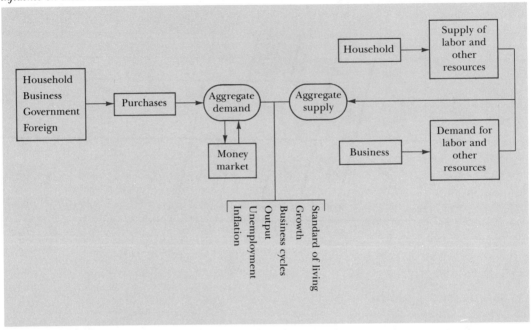

purchased — aggregate demand. The quantity and price of labor affects the quantity of goods and services businesses are willing and able to produce — aggregate supply. Wealth, interest rates, money, and people's attitudes or expectations influence their spending and working decisions. In short, the markets are interrelated.

We study macroeconomics in a step-by-step process of building from a very simple representation of an economy to an *AD–AS* framework that more realistically illustrates the behavior of an economy. The step-by-step approach is illustrated in Figure 1-8. We begin with the demand side of the economy, looking at the purchasing decisions of households, businesses, governments, and the foreign sector. We then examine the role of money in these purchasing decisions. Once we have studied aggregate demand, we turn to the supply side of the economy. We look at the household decision to work, to provide funds that business firms can use to expand and create new products, or to rent land. We also look at the business firm's decision to produce goods and services, to set prices, and to hire and fire workers. These decisions define aggregate supply. Once the *AD–AS* framework is constructed, we use it to discuss business cycles, economic growth, and all the issues involved in these two main themes.

The structure of this book is illustrated in Figure 1-9. Chapter 2 provides some definitions and terminology used to study macroeconomics. Chapters 3–5 focus on the demand side of the economy. Chapter 6 introduces aggregate supply, and Chapter 7 puts demand and supply together. With the full model developed, the remainder of the book relies on the *AD–AS* framework to examine debates among economists (Chapter 8), business cycles (Chapter 9), links among nations (Chapter 10), government policy (Chapters 11–13), growth and cycles (Chapters 14–15), and other aspects of macroeconomics (Chapters 16–18).

▼

The Economic Approach

As economics has evolved—at least since Adam Smith's 1776 publication of *The Wealth of Nations*—it has taken on a specific form. To analyze issues, economists apply what is known as the *scientific method* and rely primarily on positive analysis. Analysis that does not impose the value judgments of one individual on the decisions of others is called **positive analysis**. If you demonstrate that unemployment in the United States rises when people purchase goods produced in other countries instead of goods produced in the United States, you are undertaking positive analysis. However, if you claim there ought to be a law to stop people from buying foreign-made cars, you are imposing your value judgments on others and thus are undertaking **normative analysis**.

In most circumstances, the economic approach is to rely on positive analyses. However, normative analysis often plays an important role in economics. For instance, it is the basis for evaluating government programs and policies. A norm is defined, and then a program is judged in terms of that norm. Suppose the norm is that a program is beneficial if it helps more people than it hurts. A program that taxes the richest 30 percent more than it taxes the rest of the population might meet this norm. However, if the norm is changed the evaluation of the program could make at least one person better off without harming anyone else. The tax-the-rich program would not measure up because the rich are made worse off by it. The point here is that the outcome of normative analysis depends on the norms or value judgments being applied; positive analysis, in contrast, is free of value judgments, so its outcome does not vary as norms change.

There are many jokes about every profession. Those about economists tend to focus on their disagreements. There's one joke about how you can lay all the economists end to end and still not reach a conclusion. Economists are always disagreeing primarily because their normative approaches differ. Suppose one economist believes government programs should not reallocate income from the rich to the poor, and another economist believes incomes should be equalized. Clearly, these two will disagree about most government programs. It is when normative analysis becomes part of the discussion that economists are most likely to disagree. This does not mean that economists agree unani-

FIGURE 1-9   *The structure of the text. Chapter 2 provides some definitions and terminology used in the study of macroeconomics. Chapters 3–5 focus on the demand side of the economy. Chapter 6 introduces aggregate supply, and Chapter 7 puts demand and supply together. With the full model developed, the remainder of the book relies on the AD–AS framework to examine debates among economists, business cycles (Chapters 8–9), links among nations (Chapter 10) government policy (Chapters 11–13), growth and cycles (Chapters 14–15), specific international aspects of macroeconomics (Chapters 15–16), and other aspects of macroeconomics (Chapters 16–18).*

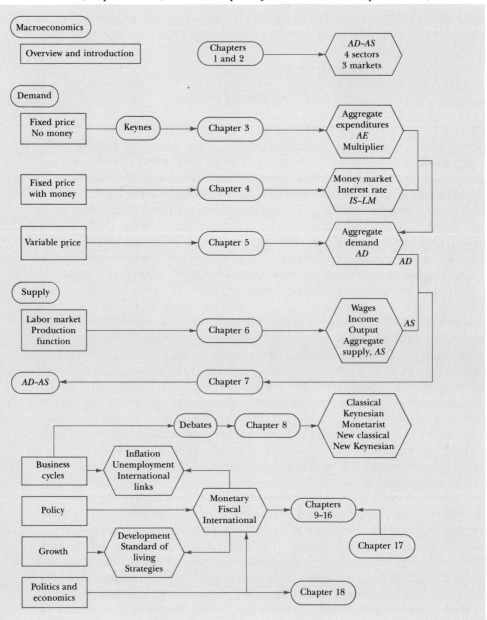

mously with how the economy behaves or how markets function—the positive aspects. But their disagreements over positive factors are relatively minor compared to the disagreements over normative issues.

Models

Economists develop theories or models to help them explain the complex behavior of economies. A theory or model is a simplified, logical story based on positive analysis that is used to explain an event. Often when people hear the words *model* and *theory,* they think of complex mathematical formulas. Some economic models are complex equations, but others are more likely to be simple stories that relate the main aspects of the issue at hand.

The development of a model is part of the scientific methodology. There are five steps in the **scientific method** as shown in Figure 1-10: (1) recognize the problem, (2) make assumptions in order to cut away unnecessary detail, (3) develop a model of the problem, (4) present a hypothesis, and (5) test the hypothesis. The role of assumptions is to reduce the complexity of a problem. We want to get to the center of an issue, so we use assumptions to cut away unnecessary detail. To understand why you purchase fewer books when the price of the books rises, we do not need to know the color of your hair, whether you wear socks, and your height. These might influence your decision in some way, but they are unnecessary details to the central issue.

One of the most commonly used assumptions in economics is *ceteris paribus.* This Latin phrase means "other things being equal," or everything else held constant. Thus, we might say that, *ceteris paribus,* the quantity of gasoline that people purchase declines when the price of gasoline rises. This means that if only the price and quantity demanded of gasoline are allowed to change, then as the price rises the quantity demanded falls.

A model enables us to develop a hypothesis, an explanation that accounts for a set of facts and allows us to make predictions in similar situations. For instance, the statement that Earth is the center of the universe is a hypothesis. The validity of the hypothesis must be tested to see if the model is substantiated by the facts. The model in this case lasted for several hundred years un-

FIGURE 1-10   *Development of a model. Economists use the scientific method illustrated in this figure to develop models that help explain the complex behavior of economies.*

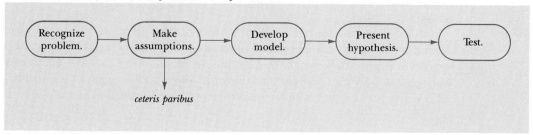

til tests could not validate the hypothesis. A simple demand and supply model might yield the hypothesis that the price of oranges will rise when a freeze occurs in Florida, all other events being constant. A test of this hypothesis is to determine what occurred to the price of oranges during those periods when a freeze occurred and to control for all other relevant variables. For instance, it would not be much of a test if during one freeze period in Florida a huge new crop of oranges from Brazil had been imported to the United States and that influx was not taken into account.

Common Errors of Analysis

Errors can be made in science even when proper methodology is followed. Two common mistakes in macroeconomics are the **fallacy of composition** and the **fallacy of interpreting association as causation**. The fallacy of composition is the error of attributing what applies to one to the case of many. If one person in a theater realizes that a fire has begun and races to the exit, that one person is better off than the theatergoers who stay in their seats. Running to the exit is appropriate. If we assume that a thousand people behaving just as the single individual did is the best approach, we would be committing the fallacy of composition. The mistaken interpretation of association as causation occurs when unrelated or coincidental events that occur at about the same time are believed to have a cause and effect relationship. If the stock market declines when the economy enters a recession, can we say that the stock market decline causes a recession? If the economy declines in years when skirt lengths are long and rises in years when skirt lengths are short, can we say that the length of skirts causes the economy's behavior?

As we proceed in our study of macroeconomics, keep in mind that we are developing a model of the behavior of economies. We want a model that can accurately describe how the economy will behave under various conditions. When the model fails to predict results that match reality, the model must be revised. Throughout the history of macroeconomics, the model has been under constant revision. In the beginning there was classical economics, predicting automatic full employment and continuous market clearing. The Great Depression of the 1930s led to a major revision—Keynesian economics. When the predictions of the Keynesian model ran into trouble in the 1970s, revisions occurred again. Monetarism took its place in macroeconomic thought and economic policy, as did rational expectations, new classical, and new Keynesian schools of thought.

Although there have been several schools of thought or approaches to macroeconomics, all the schools can be illustrated with the aggregate demand and aggregate supply framework. In fact, the development of the AD–AS framework in a step-by-step process lends itself nicely to a discussion of the historical revision process that occurs in macroeconomics. We begin with the demand side and what is referred to as **aggregate expenditure, AE**. This view of the economy assumes a fixed price level in order to focus on output and employment. In the *AE* model, we introduce money and interest rates via a framework known as the *IS–LM* model, in which *IS* represents the goods and services market and *LM* represents the money market. We then relax the fixed-price assumption and move from the *AE* and *IS–LM* models to *AD* and finally, we add *AS* to the analysis.

▼ ▼ ▼ ▼ ▼ ▼ ▼ ▼ ▼ ▼ ▼

Conclusions

Inflation, unemployment, recession, trade effects, budget deficits, monetary policy, fiscal policy, and free trade are just a few of the many topics discussed in this book. Discussing these topics appropriately requires that we employ the scientific method. We recognize a problem—understanding the behavior of the economy. We make simplifying assumptions and develop a model—the *AD–AS* framework. And we use the *AD–AS* framework to develop hypotheses about the behavior of the economy. We test our model by seeing if its predictions match our observations.

Now let's now turn to the task of examining the macroeconomy.

▼ ▼ ▼ ▼ ▼ ▼ ▼ ▼ ▼ ▼ ▼

Summary

1. What are the two main topics of macroeconomics?
The two main topics of macroeconomics are business cycles and economic growth.
2. What major macroeconomic variables does macroeconomic analysis seek to explain?
Within the two main topics lie the subtopics of inflation, unemployment, standards of living, poverty, recession, booms, exchange rates, and government activities.
3. What is the basic framework of analysis in macroeconomics?
Business cycles can be represented as shifts of the *AD* and/or *AS* curves. Economic growth can be represented as a series of shifts in the *AD* and *AS* curves.
4. In what area of analysis do most disagreements among economists occur?
Economists may disagree about positive aspects of macroeconomics such as the appropriate model, but these disagreements are quite small compared to their disagreements over normative aspects of macroeconomics.
5. How are various macroeconomic models used to develop a framework of analysis?
Macroeconomics involves a building process, proceeding from the simple model of fixed price without money, to one with fixed price but including money, to one of variable price. The models are known as the *AE* model or Keynesian model in the fixed-price case without money; *IS–LM* model in the "fixed price with money" model; and *AD–AS* model in the variable-price model.

▼
Key Terms

macroeconomics   4
business cycles   7
economic growth   7
recessions   7
expansions   9
depression   9
hyperinflation   10
standards of living   12
aggregate demand, *AD*   14

aggregate supply, *AS*   14
positive analysis   19
normative analysis   19
scientific method   21
ceteris paribus   21
fallacy of composition   22
fallacy of interpreting association as
   causation   22
aggregate expenditure, AE   23

▼
Problems and Exercises

1.   Define each of the key terms as used in the text.
2.   Using the *AD–AS* curves, show what the fixed price model would look like.
3.   Using the *AD–AS* curves, illustrate a business cycle, moving from one point through a recession and then through a boom.
4.   Using the *AD–AS* curves, illustrate economic growth. Explain why one economy might grow more rapidly than another.
5.   Given your reading of this chapter, what could you say might be the single most effective strategy against poverty?

Chapter 2

Measuring Key
Macroeconomic Variables

What to Expect

The U.S. economy has grown at an average annual rate of 3.5 percent since World War II, but this is only slightly more than half the growth rate of Japan. Still, the U.S. economy is twice as large as the Japanese economy and larger than the fifty largest developing countries combined. How do we compare these economies and their growth rates, and what do they mean? The national income accounts provide a standard of measurement. This chapter discusses the national income accounts. In addition, it discusses the accounts in which the exchange of goods and services between nations is measured, called the *balance of payments*. Also, in virtually any discussion of economics the topics of unemployment, inflation, and foreign exchange arise time and time again. To discuss macroeconomics, you must have a working knowledge of those terms, and you'll acquire that knowledge in this chapter. Some of the questions considered in this chapter include

1. What is GNP?

2. What is GDP?

3. How are economic transactions among nations measured?

4. What is unemployment?

5. How is inflation measured?

6. What are some of the currencies other nations use?

▼
Gross National Product

In national economies, many goods and services are produced in a variety of circumstances. It is, therefore, a very complex undertaking to seek to explain or predict the impact of events on the economy by looking at each individual market. Economists have simplified their analysis of the national economy by combining all goods and services into a single measure of total output known as the *gross national product (GNP)*.

It is unambiguous to state that in the United States the quantity of output of a single product has increased 5 percent since the same time last year, or that the price of the product has risen 3 percent. However, it is not clear what is meant by saying that the total output of the United States has risen 5 percent since the same time last year, or that the price of total output has risen 3 percent. If the quantity of every product rose by 5 percent, then obviously total output rose by 5 percent. But more typically output in some industries rises while in others it falls. How do we combine a 6 percent decrease in auto production, an 8 percent increase in housing construction, a 5 percent increase in the quantity of golf balls produced—and the variations in innumerable other goods and services in the economy—and then say there's been a 5 percent increase in total output?

To combine the many different goods and services into one measure of aggregate output, we find a common denominator in which all goods and services can be expressed. Because the common measure per unit for every good sold in the United States is dollars, we can measure the total production of each good by summing the market value of that good; that is, the total quantity of the good that is produced, multiplied by its price. We then add the total market value of all final goods and services to measure the economy. This measure is **gross national product (GNP)**.

Definition of GNP

Gross national product is the market value of all final goods and services produced during one year. Goods and services included in GNP are measured at market values or market prices. However, retail prices often include sales and excise taxes, so the price paid by the consumer is not always the price the seller actually receives. Determining GNP at market values also means that GNP cannot be compared from year to year unambiguously. Changes in GNP can be the result of price changes rather than of changes in the quantity of goods produced. And, finally, perhaps the most important implication of valuing output at current market prices is that any good that does not have such a value is excluded.[1] For instance, illegal transactions are not counted. Thus, activities in illicit drugs, prostitution, and illegal gambling are not included in GNP. In addition, most goods and services that are not traded in a market are not included. For example, unpaid production that takes place in households, like the value of a homemaker's services or do-it-yourself activities, are not counted. Barter and cash transactions in the underground economy also do not make it into the GNP measure. If a lawyer has a broken faucet and a plumber needs some legal work, the two might exchange work. This *barter* transaction (exchange of goods or services for goods or services without an exchange of money) often is not recorded by either party as income, because then the parties might have to pay income taxes. Unrecorded transactions do not usually end up in GNP. There are a few exceptions, such as the value of food output consumed by a farm household or the value of the imputed rent of owner-occupied housing, but most nonrecorded transactions are not part of GNP.

Another aspect of the definition of GNP is that only final goods and services are counted. A **final good or service** is one not used up in producing another product. **Intermediate goods** — those goods used up producing another product — are not counted as part of GNP. For example, producing a microwave oven begins with the purchase of inputs such as steel and glass. Suppose these inputs cost $100 and the microwave oven, once produced, is sold to a dealer for $175. Finally, the dealer sells this oven to a consumer for $200. If the three separate sales of the oven were added together, output would be valued at $475. However, $475 overstates the production value because the value of the steel and glass — intermediate goods — are included more than once. They were counted in the original purchase of inputs, in the sale to the dealer, and again in the sale to the consumer. This double-counting problem can be avoided by using the value of the final sale, $200, as the measure of current production.

An alternative approach to measuring aggregate output that avoids the duplication problem is to sum only the value added at each production stage — *value added.* The value added to a good at a particular manufacturing stage equals the value of the good sold minus the cost of the intermediate materials. In the microwave example, value added by the producer ($75) and by the dealer ($25) is added to the price of steel and glass ($100) to find a measure of current production. The value-added approach, although much more difficult to calculate, yields the same value as the final sales price.

1   There is one exception to the valuation at market prices. Government services have no market price. Because of the importance of these services, they cannot be excluded from GNP. Therefore, these items are valued at their cost, which usually means the wages of the government employees who produce them.

Only currently produced goods are included in GNP. Sales of old baseball cards, used cars, and secondhand clothing are not included. These goods were included in the GNP value at the time they were originally produced. To include them again would overstate GNP in the present period. What if a good produced this year is not sold? It is measured as a final good *produced* but not as a final good *sold* (which would give GNP two different values, depending on whether it was measured as expenditures or as production). Unsold goods are counted in this year's GNP as *change in inventories*.

Since the national income accounts are intended to measure goods and services, they exclude any transaction in which only money is transferred. Therefore, transfer payments such as social security, unemployment benefits, and welfare benefits are not included in GNP. These transactions are merely monetary transfers that do not change the total value of output.

Alternative Approaches to Measuring GNP

GNP is a measure of a nation's total output during a year. Intuition suggests that the total value of goods and services produced should be the same as the total value of goods and services purchased. Moreover, the value of output produced and purchased and the income generated in producing that output should be equal, because the receipts from the sale of output must accrue to someone as income. For businesses to produce goods, factors of production—land, labor, capital, and entrepreneurship—must be employed. In return, the owners of the factors of production receive payments for their services, respectively, rents, wages, interest, and profits. And with their income they purchase goods and services. Let's briefly consider the three approaches to measuring GNP: as output, as purchases or expenditures, and as income.

GNP Measured as Output. Figure 2-1 indicates who produced the U.S. GNP in 1990. Privately owned firms account for the great majority of U.S. output; about 85 percent of 1990 U.S. GNP was produced by private firms. Government produced 10.6 percent of GNP, households 4.1 percent, and only 0.7 percent of U.S. GNP was produced by the international sector.

Including goods and services produced by the international sector might seem a bit strange, because U.S. GNP is a measure of the output of the United States and these goods and services are produced outside the United States. U.S. residents can own production facilities located abroad, however, and the value of output produced by foreign resources owned by U.S. residents is counted as part of U.S. GNP. For example, if a U.S. factory in Germany earns a profit, the profit is counted as part of U.S. GNP, because it is received by U.S. households (the owners of the factory). The value of German labor and resources is counted as part of Germany's GNP.

FIGURE 2-1 *Who produces the U.S. GNP (billions of dollars)? Privately owned firms account for the great majority of U.S. output; almost 85 percent of 1990 U.S. GNP was produced by private firms. Government produced 10.6 percent of GNP, households 4.1 percent, and only .7 percent of 1990 U.S. GNP was produced by the international sector.*

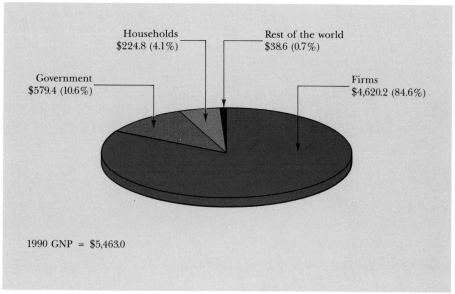

Source: *Economic Report of the President, 1991* (Washington, DC: U.S. Government Printing Office, 1991).

GNP Measured as Expenditures. The amount spent on each final good and service purchased is equal to the total value of all goods and services produced. Household spending is *consumption, C;* the spending of firms is *investment, I;* the government's purchases of goods and services are called *government spending, G,* and spending by the foreign sector is known as *net exports, X.* Investment includes purchases of new plant and equipment, new residential construction, and changes in business inventories. Net exports consists of the value of goods and services produced in the United States and sold to the rest of the world minus the value of goods and services produced in other nations and purchased by the United States.

GNP = consumption + investment + government spending + net exports

or

$$GNP = C + I + G + X$$

Data for GNP as total expenditures for the year 1990 are shown in Figure 2-2. Consumption is about two-thirds of national expenditures; government spending is about 20 percent; business investment spending is about 14 per-

FIGURE 2-2   *1990 U.S. GNP as total expenditures (billions of dollars). Data for GNP as total expenditures for the year 1990 are shown. Consumption is about two-thirds of national expenditures; government spending is about 20 percent; business investment spending is about 14 percent; and net exports are negative, meaning that imports exceeded exports.*

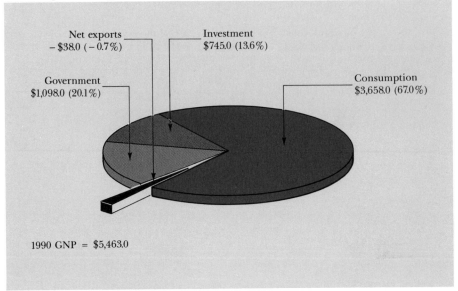

Net exports
– $38.0 (– 0.7%)

Investment
$745.0 (13.6%)

Government
$1,098.0 (20.1%)

Consumption
$3,658.0 (67.0%)

1990 GNP = $5,463.0

Source: Economic Report of the President, 1991 (Washington, DC: U.S. Government Printing Office, 1991).

cent; and net exports are negative, meaning that imports exceeded exports. Because imports are purchases of foreign goods and services by U.S. consumers, firms, and government, imports represent the use of U.S. income to purchase the output of other countries. Only by subtracting these purchases from U.S. GNP will an accurate measure of the total expenditures on U.S. goods and services be obtained.

GNP Measured as Income. One sector's expenditures is another's revenue or income. The income earned by resources is classified into four groups: wages, interest, rent, and profits. U.S. GNP in 1990 measured as income is shown in Figure 2-3. Wages accounted for about 60 percent of GNP. Rent was very small while interest and corporate profits accounted for 8.6 percent and 5.4 percent of GNP respectively.

There are three additional income categories shown in Figure 2-3 we have not discussed: capital consumption allowance, indirect business taxes, and proprietors' income. Capital consumption allowance is not a payment to a resource or factor of production. It is the estimated amount of capital goods worn out in production plus the value of accidental damage to capital goods. Capital goods, such as machines, tools, and buildings, wear out over time. The reduction in the value of the capital stock due to its being used or wearing out over

FIGURE 2-3   *1990 U.S. GNP measured as income (billions of dollars). Wages accounted for about 60 percent of GNP. Rent was very small while interest and corporate profits accounted for 8.6 percent and 5.4 percent of GNP respectively. In addition, measured on the income side are three additional income categories:* capital consumption allowance, indirect business taxes, *and* proprietors' income. *Capital consumption allowance is the estimated amount of capital goods worn out in production plus the value of accidental damage to capital goods. Indirect business taxes are taxes collected by business firms that are turned over to the government. Proprietors' income is the earnings of unincorporated businesses.*

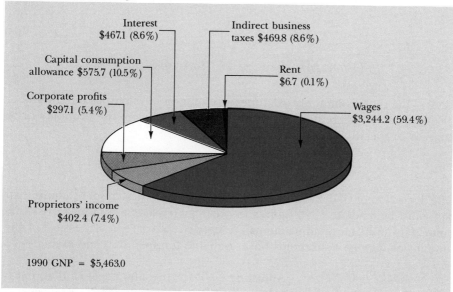

Source: Economic Report of the President, 1991 (Washington, DC: U.S. Government Printing Office, 1991).

time is called *depreciation.* Even though the capital consumption allowance does not represent income received by a factor of production, it must be accounted for in GNP measured as income. Otherwise, the value of GNP measured as output will be higher than the value of GNP measured as income.

Indirect business taxes, like capital consumption allowances, do not represent payments to a factor of production. These taxes are collected by business firms and are turned over to the government. For example, a consumer who stays in a motel room in Florida may be charged $90. Of that $90, $10 may be an excise tax. The motel received $80 as the value of the service provided; the other $10 is the indirect tax. The value of the income received is $80, but the payment made is $90. Unless indirect business taxes are taken into account, the expenditures and income sides to GNP will not match. Figure 2-3 also includes some additional minor adjustments in its value for indirect business taxes.

Proprietors' income includes earnings of individuals and partnerships from unincorporated businesses, such as professional associations, farms, and so forth. It includes elements of wages, rent, interest, and profit payable to the owners who provide labor services, land, capital, and entrepreneurship to the firm. It is impossible to divide proprietors' income into its four components.

There are several lessons to be taken from this first section, but for our purposes, the most important is that the levels of national income, national output, and national expenditures are equal—each sums to GNP.

▼
Other Measures of Output and Income

GNP is the most commonly used measure of a nation's output but a number of other measures are used to highlight specific areas of the economy or to emphasize specific developments.

From GNP to Disposable Personal Income

The discussion of GNP measured as income already indicated some adjustments that must be made to GNP figures in order to arrive at a true measure of income. However, more adjustments are needed to arrive at a measure of the amount of income households have available for spending and saving.

Net National Product (NNP). Adjusting GNP for the amount of capital that is worn out or made obsolete results in **net national product (NNP)**. NNP is equal to GNP minus capital consumption allowance. The investment measure included in GNP is called *gross investment.* Gross investment includes investment expenditures required to replace capital goods consumed in current production. NNP includes only new investment in excess of depreciation, or *net investment.* Net investment is equal to gross investment less capital consumption allowance.

National Income (NI). NNP minus indirect business taxes, plus or minus a couple of additional minor adjustments, yields *national income (NI).* NI measures the costs of factors of production used to produce output—the income earned by the factors of production.

Personal Income (PI). NI adjusted for income that is received but not earned in the current year and income that is earned but not received in the current year equals *personal income (PI).* Social security and welfare benefits are examples of income received but not earned in the current year. These are called *transfer payments,* because income is transferred from one citizen, who is earning income, to another citizen, who may not be. The government achieves this transfer of income by taxing one group of citizens and using the tax payments to fund the income given to the other group. An example of income earned but not currently received is corporate profits that are retained by the corporation to finance current needs within the firm rather than paid out to stockholders. Another example is social security or FICA (Federal Insurance Corporation of America) taxes.

Disposable Personal Income (DPI). The income that people can choose to spend or save is *disposable personal income (DPI).* PI minus personal taxes (income taxes, excise and real estate taxes on personal property, and any additional personal taxes) yields DPI.

Gross Domestic Product (GDP)

Gross domestic product (GDP) is a measure of the purely domestic output of a country. GNP is the total output produced by and total income received by a nation's residents. This measure includes income earned by domestic residents who own foreign factors of production. A U.S. citizen who works in Japan receives income from a Japanese firm. This income is part of U.S. GNP but not U.S. GDP. Similarly, Procter & Gamble, a U.S. firm, has factories throughout the world. The P&G factory in Brussels produces and sells output and generates profits. The value of P&G's output is part of U.S. GDP but the payments made to Belgian residents who are employees of P&G are not part of U.S. GNP. The difference between GNP and GDP is net factor income from abroad. *Net factor income from abroad* is income received from other nations by domestic residents less income payments made to foreign residents. By subtracting net factor income from abroad from GNP, we are left with GDP.

The difference between GNP and GDP for several countries is illustrated in Table 2-1. In some cases, like the United States, GNP exceeds GDP because the factor income received from abroad exceeds the factor income paid to foreigners. In other cases, like New Zealand, GDP exceeds GNP because more is paid to foreign factor owners than is received from abroad by domestic factor owners.

TABLE 2-1   *Gross National Product and Gross Domestic Product*

Country	GNP	GDP	Percent Difference
United Kingdom (billion pounds)	467	462	1.08%
United States (billion dollars)	5,234	5,189	0.86
Japan (billion yen)	367.4	365	0.66
New Zealand (billion N.Z. dollars)	56.5	59.3	− 4.72

Source: International Monetary Fund, *International Financial Statistics,* January 1991.

▼
Real and Nominal GNP

One reason for measuring output is to evaluate the health of the economy. This frequently means comparing the values of income and output at different times. For example, in 1990, U.S. GNP was $5,463 billion, while in 1974 it was $1,434 billion. Can we say we were better off in 1990 than in 1974? Are we more than four times better off?

Price Increases and GNP

Because goods are valued at current market prices in GNP, there is more than one way GNP can increase over time: (1) more goods can be produced at the same prices; (2) the same quantity of goods can be produced at higher prices; or (3) a combination of changed prices and changed quantities of goods can be produced. As an example, consider a hypothetical country producing one good—golf balls. Suppose this economy produced 1,000 golf balls in 1980 and 2,000 golf balls in 1990. If the price of golf balls remained at $1 a ball, GNP in this country would have increased from $1,000 to $2,000. If this economy produced the same quantity of golf balls in 1990 as it did in 1980, but the price of golf balls increased from $1 to $2 a ball, then GNP doubled. Price increases may inflate the measure of output and thus invalidate comparisons of GNP measured in current prices.

Calculating Real GNP

In order to compare measures of output at different times, we must isolate changes of the actual or physical output produced in the economy from changes in price. **Real GNP** measures the physical output produced, whereas **nominal GNP** measures the "value" of the output at prices prevailing in the year that output was produced. Because the nominal value of every good produced in a period of time is known and the price of each good is also known, real GNP can be calculated quite simply. To evaluate whether the physical quantity of goods and services produced has risen or fallen, we must choose a base year. Real GNP is currently measured in 1982 prices; that is, the base year is 1982. The choice of 1982 as the base year is arbitrary. Any year could be chosen as a base year. The base year is selected for purposes of comparison and convenience. Traditionally, a new base year is used every ten years: 1962, 1972, and 1982 for instance. In some cases, the base year is actually a number of years. For example, the current base year in use for U.S. consumer price data is an average of the years 1982–1984. The objective of selecting a base year is to choose a period in which unusual circumstances or events did not occur, events such as a recession or hyperinflation.

Having chosen a base year, we can calculate real GNP without too much difficulty. The value of each good and service is divided by its current price. This is then multiplied by the base year price, and the values are summed. The behavior of U.S. nominal and real GNP since 1960 is traced in Figure 2-4. Note that real and nominal GNP were equal in 1982. This is due to the use of 1982 as the base year. Also note that the growth of nominal GNP has been much greater than that of real GNP. Why? The reason is that prices have risen. If nominal GNP is denoted as PY, the current price level, P, times the output level, Y, then nominal GNP can increase if P rises even if Y declines. Real GNP is nominal GNP divided by the current price level, or $PY/Y = Y$, and it can rise only if Y rises. U.S. real GNP has declined only a few times since 1960: during

FIGURE 2-4   *The behavior of U.S. nominal and real GNP since 1960. Real and nominal GNP were equal in 1982. This is due to the use of 1982 as the base year. Also note that the growth of nominal GNP has been much greater than that of real GNP.*

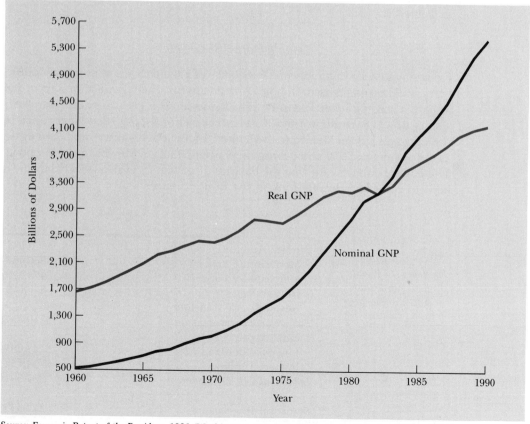

Source: Economic Report of the President, 1991 (Washington, DC: U.S. Government Printing Office, 1991).

1970, it fell 0.2 percent; from 1973 to 1975, it dropped 1.81 percent; it fell slightly in 1980, 0.2 percent; and it declined about 2.4 percent in 1982. Nominal GNP has not declined since 1960.

▼
The International Sector

If we wanted to know the size of an economy or to compare economies, we would probably look at the national income accounts. If we wanted to know how a country's trade with the rest of the world had changed over time, we would examine the **balance of payments**. The balance of payments is a record of a country's trade in goods, services, and financial assets with the rest of the world. This record is divided into two main categories: the current account and the capital account. A simplified balance of payments statement is shown in Table 2-2.

Double-Entry Bookkeeping

One thing to keep in mind with the balance of payments accounts is that double-entry bookkeeping is used. Double entry means that each transaction is recorded as both a credit and a debit entry. For instance, suppose a Mexican store sells a shirt to a U.S. resident for $30. The transaction is recorded twice: once as the shirt going from Mexico to the United States (a debit entry), and then again as the payment of $30 going from the United States to Mexico (a credit entry). The double entry means that the balance of payments is always in balance — it adds to zero. Let's briefly look at the BOP accounts.

TABLE 2-2 *Simplified Balance of Payments (1989 data for the United States, millions of dollars)*	**Current Account**
	Merchandise exports — $360,465
	Merchandise imports — ($475,329)
	Net services — $19,549
	Net unilateral transfers — ($14,720)
	Balance on current account — ($110,034)
	Capital Account
	Financial outflows — ($127,061)
	Financial inflows — $214,652
	Balance on capital account — $87,591
	Statistical Discrepancy — $22,443

Source: Economic Report of the President, 1991 (Washington, DC: U.S. Government Printing Office, 1991), p. 402.

The Current Account

The current account portion of the balance of payments includes all transactions involving goods, known as the *merchandise account*, and all transactions involving services, known as the *services account*.

- *Merchandise.* This account records all the transactions involving goods. Imports of foreign goods by U.S. residents are compared to exports of U.S. goods to foreigners. If the exports exceed the imports, then there is a surplus on the merchandise, or trade, account. If the imports exceed the exports, then this account has a deficit. In 1989, there was a merchandise trade deficit of almost $115 billion.
- *Services.* Included in this category are travel and tourism, royalties, transportation costs, insurance premiums, and other immediately consumed items. The largest component of the services account is the payment for the services of capital called the *return on investments,* which includes interest and dividends. In 1989, the services account posted a surplus of over $19 billion.

The sum of the merchandise and service balances is the net export value recorded in the U.S. national income accounts.

- *Net unilateral transfers.* Transfers are flows of goods or money where nothing is given in return, such as gifts and retirement pensions. The United States runs a large deficit on these items due to foreign aid given by the U.S. government and the large number of U.S. residents who send money to relatives living in a foreign country.

The sum of merchandise, services, and net unilateral transfers is called the *current account.* The current account is a useful summary measure of international transactions because it contains all the activity involving goods and services, yet excludes trade involving financial assets. In 1989, the U.S. current account was equal to a deficit of $110 billion.

The Capital Account

In the terminology of the balance of payments, *capital* represents financial flows associated with purchases and sales of assets. In the balance of payments, capital includes bank deposits, purchases of stocks, bonds, and loans. In 1989, the capital account of the United States had a surplus of $87.6 billion.

The final category listed in Table 2-2 is the statistical discrepancy. This could be called "errors and omissions." It occurs because the government cannot measure accurately all transactions that occur. In 1989, the statistical discrepancy was equal to $22.4 billion. The statistical discrepancy is usually considered as part of the capital account because most errors of measurement occur in the financial assets area.

Debtor and Creditor Nations

Adding the balance of payments accounts, we find that the sum is zero: the payments are in balance. When someone refers to a "balance of payments deficit or surplus," he or she is actually talking about one of the accounts in the balance of payments, usually the merchandise account or the current account. Often you hear about the "trade deficit," which is the merchandise portion of the current account. The merchandise trade account can be in deficit or surplus, as can the current account; the balance of payments cannot. The balance of payments is zero by definition: $BOP = 0$.

Because the balance of payments must balance, a deficit on the current account requires that, on net, everything below the current account must have a surplus that just offsets the current account deficit. This is how the current account indicates whether a country is a net borrower from or lender to the rest of the world. A current account deficit implies that a country is attracting sufficient buyers of its capital to offset or pay for the current account deficit. This is really no different from the case of an individual person. For instance, you might sell more assets than you purchase by obtaining a mortgage on your house and a loan on your car. In doing this, you acquire the money to pay for these assets but the lending institution owns the assets. You are a borrower. Similarly, the nation is acquiring the money to pay for the current account deficit, but it is selling assets to other nations—the country is a *net borrower* from the rest of the world.

The current account balance for the United States since the 1960s is shown in Figure 2-5. The United States was a net international creditor from the end of World War I until the mid-1980s. The United States experienced large current account deficits in the 1980s. These large current account deficits were financed by the U.S. borrowing from the rest of the world. As a result, the United States became a net international debtor in 1985 for the first time since World War I.

▼
Measures of Inflation

Inflation is defined as a sustained upward movement in the general level of prices. In the United States, three price indices are typically relied on as measures of inflation: the **consumer price index (CPI)**, the **producer price index (PPI)**, and the GNP **implicit price deflator**. Perhaps the most closely followed of these indices is the CPI. The reason for this attention is that the CPI is considered a measure of the cost of living. The CPI measures the cost of a given "basket" of goods produced by a typical urban household. The PPI focuses on the cost of a basket of goods at the level of the first significant commercial trans-

FIGURE 2-5   *The U.S. current account balance since the 1960s. The United States was a net international creditor from the end of World War I until the mid-1980s. The United States experienced large current account deficits in the 1980s. These large deficits were financed by the U.S. borrowing from the rest of the world. As a result, the United States became a net international debtor in 1985 for the first time since World War I.*

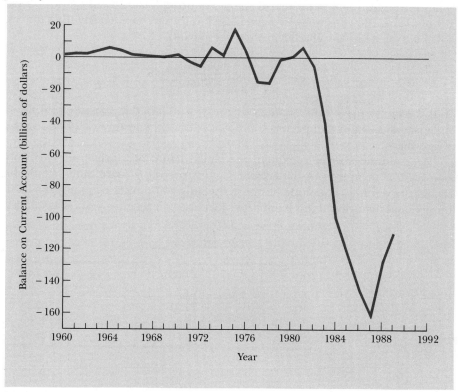

Source: Economic Report of the President, 1991 (Washington, DC: U.S. Government Printing Office, 1991).

action. Thus the prices of raw materials and semifinished goods are included in the PPI. The prices of these items enter the CPI only after they have been used to produce a final good included in the CPI "basket." The implicit price deflator is the broadest measure of prices, including all items measured in the gross national product.

If the CPI, PPI, and implicit price deflator are converted into percentage changes, measures of inflation are obtained. Although all measures are generally consistent, there are differences. For instance, in 1991 the implicit price deflator rose 4.1 percent, the CPI 5.4 percent, and the PPI 4.9 percent. The differences result from the way the indices are constructed.

Calculating the CPI and the PPI

The method used to calculate the CPI and PPI is to weight the various items in the market basket by the quantity of each good purchased in the base year. This method assumes that the quantities purchased in the base year are the quantities purchased in all years. The assumption lets us focus on how much it would cost the consumer in a given period to purchase exactly the same assortment of items purchased in the base period.

$$\text{price index}_t = \frac{\Sigma \, p_t^i q_0^i}{\Sigma \, p_0^i q_0^i} \times 100$$

In this equation $p_t^i q_0^i$ is the quantity of good i purchased in the base year times the price of this good in period t, and $p_0^i q_0^i$ is the expenditure on good i in the base year.

An example may help explain the construction of a price index. If only one good is produced in the economy, constructing a price index would be straightforward. For example, suppose the only good in the economy is a hamburger, and the price of this hamburger for three consecutive years is as follows:

Year	Price	Price Index (base = year 2)
1	$0.25	62.5
2	0.40	100.0
3	0.50	125.0

Because a price index compares prices over time, one year is chosen as the basis of comparison. This year is the *base period*. Although the selection of the base period is arbitrary, it is important that the base period be normal (no extremely high or low prices). In our one-good economy, we choose year 2 to serve as the base year. Then a price index for years 1 and 3 is constructed by dividing the price of hamburgers in years 1 and 3 by the price level in the base year. That is, the price index for year 3 is 0.50/0.40 or 1.25 and for year 1 is 0.25/0.40 = .625. It is traditional to multiply by 100 to get rid of the decimals, which makes the third-year price index 125 and the first year index 62.5. Notice that the price index for the base year is 100. Why?

Expanding our example, suppose only five goods are consumed—hamburgers, cola, bread, gasoline, and automobiles. These goods constitute the "market basket" of goods. Table 2-3 presents the prices and quantities of the goods in our market basket in the base year (year 0) and a later period (year 1). As can be seen, a total of $193.70 was spent on these goods in the base year.

TABLE 2-3   *Price Index Data*

Good	p_0 Price	q_0 Quantity	$p_0 q_0$ Total Spending
	Base Period (Year 0)		
Hamburger	$ 0.65/lb	60	$ 39.00
Cola	1.65/pack	10	16.50
Bread	0.35/loaf	52	18.20
Gasoline	0.40/gallon	50	20.00
Automobile	100.00	1	100.00
		Total	$193.70

Good	p_1 Price	q_0 Quantity	$p_1 q_0$ Total Spending
	Later Period (Year 1)		
Hamburger	$ 0.70/lb	60	$ 42.00
Cola	1.95/pack	10	19.50
Bread	0.40/loaf	52	20.80
Gasoline	1.00/gallon	50	50.00
Automobile	110.00	1	110.00
		Total	$242.30

If the same quantity of goods was purchased in the later period, they would cost $242.30.

The price index for our five goods in period 1 is

$$\text{price index}_1 = \frac{\Sigma\, p_1^i q_0^i}{\Sigma\, p_0^i q_0^i} \times 100$$

$$= \frac{\$242.30}{\$193.70} \times 100 = 125.09$$

This indicates that a basket of these five goods costs over 25 percent more in the second year.

Problems with Price Indices

Figure 2-6 shows the behavior of the implicit price deflator in relation to the CPI and PPI. As would be expected, all three indices increased over the period, reflecting the fact that aggregate prices were rising. However, the actual measure of inflation depends on the price index employed. Between 1985 and 1990, the inflation rate averaged 3.24 according to the implicit price deflator, 3.58 according to the CPI, and 2.42 according to the PPI. The differences are directly attributable to the different commodity baskets and methods used to calculate the indices.

FIGURE 2-6   *The behavior of the implicit price deflator in relation to the CPI and PPI. The graph plots the annual percentage change in the implicit price deflator, the CPI, and the PPI. As would be expected, all three indices increased over the period, reflecting the fact that aggregate prices were rising. However, the actual measure of inflation depends on the price index employed. Between 1985 and 1990, the inflation rate averaged 3.24 according to the implicit price deflator, 3.58 according to the CPI, and 2.42 according to the PPI. The differences are directly attributable to the different commodity baskets and methods used to calculate the indices.*

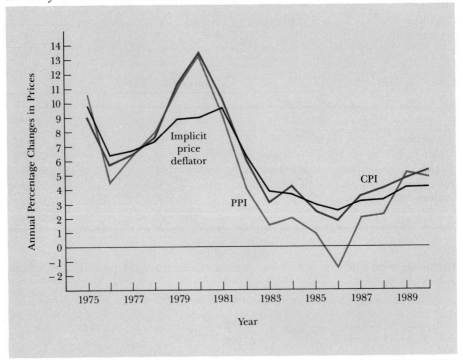

Source: Economic Report of the President, 1991 (Washington, DC: U.S. Government Printing Office, 1991).

For example, by assuming that goods and services are purchased in the same quantities as in the base year (as is done with the CPI), important biases in the index can develop. The CPI is biased upward in periods of rising prices because the consumer is assumed to go on buying the same basket of goods as in the base year. This can be a serious defect, because a basic fact of economics is that as the relative price of an item increases, the quantity of that item demanded decreases, *ceteris paribus.* Assuming a fixed market basket of goods doesn't let the law of demand play a role. Moreover, assuming a fixed market basket does not include either new products introduced into an economy over time or quality changes that might occur.

In addition to the problems associated with the weighting of goods, price indices are subject to sampling and measurement problems. In calculating the value of a price index, it is too costly to measure every item and every consumer. Hence, a sample must be used, and of course the design of the sample crucially affects the quality of the index. Even a correctly designed sample is susceptible to sampling error. This is why the Bureau of Labor Statistics (BLS) often cautions that a small change in an index may merely be a statistical artifact.

In principle, the actual prices at which transactions are made should be used in constructing the index. However, the BLS uses the list price, which creates problems if the transaction price differs from the list price. For instance, if discounts, special offers, and price shading are extensive, a price index will suggest a higher price level than is actually occurring. The *Wall Street Journal* of February 8, 1991, p. 1, noted that there was a great deal of discounting during the 1991 recession. It compared the indices during the worst years of the Great Depression, when average consumer prices dropped as much as 10 percent in a year to 1990 when inflation (as measured by the CPI) still ran at a 5.4 percent rate even during a recession. The difference suggested by the article was that in 1990 the CPI did not measure the fact that retail stores were selling goods for significantly less than the list price.

▼

The Unemployment Rate

Perhaps the most frequently used statistic to measure labor market conditions is the **unemployment rate**. This statistic indicates the extent to which available labor resources are being used.

Calculating the Unemployment Rate

If asked how to define the unemployment rate, you might guess that it is simply the number of unemployed people, divided by the total number of workers available. In principle, this response is correct. However, several questions arise. For instance, to calculate the unemployment rate, the number of workers available for work must be known. Is the number of workers available equal to the total population or to the number of workers actively seeking work? If the latter, then what does it mean to be "actively seeking work"? Are children and senior citizens to be counted as part of the labor force?

The BLS calculates the unemployment rate from surveys taken around the middle of each month. According to the BLS, individuals are *employed*

if they are 16 or older and (1) are in the armed forces; (2) did any work at all as paid employees in the survey week; (3) worked at their own business or farm; (4) worked fifteen hours or more during the survey week as unpaid workers in an enterprise run by a family member; or (5) spent the survey week absent from work because of illness, bad weather, vacation, or some personal reason.

Unemployed individuals are people who

are 16 or over, did not work at all during the survey week, were available for work, and were (1) looking for work during the last four weeks, (2) waiting to be called back to a job from which they had been laid off, (3) had a job to which they were going to report within thirty days, or (4) would have been actively looking for work if they had not been ill.

In December 1990, the BLS reported that the number of workers employed (including members of the armed forces) was 119,191,000 while 7,600,000 workers were unemployed. The unemployment rate for that month was 6.0 percent, which was found by dividing the total number of workers by the number unemployed: 7,600,000/(119,191,000 + 7,600,000).

The *civilian unemployment rate* is found by dividing the total number of civilian workers by the number unemployed. In December 1990, the BLS reported 117,574,000 employed civilian workers. Consequently, the civilian unemployment rate for that month was 7,600,000/(117,574,000 + 7,600,000), or 6.1 percent. Since all members of the armed forces are considered employed, the civilian unemployment rate will always be higher than the all-workers unemployment rate that includes members of the armed forces.

Problems with the Unemployment Rate

The unemployment rate alone may not present an accurate picture of the labor market situation. For example, when the unemployment rate is calculated, people are considered employed if they did any work for pay during the survey week. Thus, the unemployment rate does not distinguish between full- and part-time work. A person working only twenty hours a week is considered to be as fully employed as a person working forty hours a week. Another problem with the unemployment rate is *underemployment*. The difficulty stems from the formal definition of employment. Consider a trained geologist working as a janitor, or a music teacher employed as a short-order cook. No consideration is given for the worker who is employed but has skills for a higher-level job. To the extent that underemployment exists, the unemployment rate understates the true amount of unemployment.

The formal definition of an unemployed individual may also be misleading. Frequently, after a number of months, or even years, of looking for a job, a worker becomes frustrated and simply stops looking. Such people are not counted either in the number of workers employed or in the labor force, because they are not actively seeking work. Because these workers, whom labor economists describe as *discouraged workers,* are not counted as unemployed, the unemployment rate can be thought of as understating the amount of hardship. This problem is especially apparent in a prolonged recession, during which the average duration of unemployment increases.

Perhaps the most important problem in using the unemployment rate to measure labor market conditions results from institutional changes. Specifically, the rates at which women entered the labor force (began seeking jobs outside of the home) increased tremendously in the 1970s and has remained high. The female percentage of the labor force was 38 percent in 1972, 41 in 1977, and 43 in 1990. Many economists asserted that the unemployment rate increased simply because some of these new participants in the labor force did not have the experience and job skills required by employers and thus had more difficulty finding employment.

Several economists argue that the biggest drawback to using the unemployment rate as an indicator of labor market health is the availability of unemployment benefits. To be eligible to receive these benefits, people must register as unemployed with the U.S. Employment Service or must register for labor training. These people are counted among the unemployed. However, because high levels of unemployment compensation enable longer periods in which to search for a job or simply to enjoy leisure activities, much measured unemployment may be voluntary.

▼

Exchange Rates

Different countries use different currencies or monies as shown in Table 2-4 where several nations, their currency name, and the symbol for the currency are listed. When goods and services are exchanged across international borders, national monies are also traded. To make buying and selling decisions in the global marketplace, people must be able to compare prices across countries, to compare prices quoted in Japanese yen with those quoted in Mexican pesos. In most instances, when you buy a foreign product you see only the U.S. dollar price. You don't see the yen or pound price. Usually the U.S. business must trade dollars for yen to purchase the Mitsubishi TV or VCR. The business must carry out a transaction in the foreign exchange market in order to acquire the foreign products you purchase.

Foreign exchange is foreign money, including paper money and bank deposits such as checking accounts denominated in foreign currency. When someone with U.S. dollars wants to trade those dollars for Japanese yen, the trade takes place in the *foreign exchange market,* a global market in which people trade one currency for another.

An **exchange rate** is the price of one country's money in terms of another country's money. Exchange rates are needed to compare prices quoted in two different currencies. A shirt manufactured in Tijuana sells for U.S. $30 in San Diego and for 90,000 pesos in Mexico. Where would you get the better buy, Tijuana or San Diego? Unless you know the exchange rate between U.S. and Mexican monies, you can't tell. The exchange rate allows you to convert a foreign currency price into its domestic currency equivalent, which can then be compared to the domestic price. For example, on January 14, 1991, the exchange rate between the Mexican peso and the U.S. dollar was $1 to 2,947 pesos. This

TABLE 2-4
Currencies and Their
Symbols

Country	Currency	Symbol
Australia	Australian dollar	A$
Austria	schilling	Sch
Belgium	Belgian franc	BF
Canada	Canadian dollar	C$
China	yuan	Y
Denmark	Danish krone	DKr
Finland	markka	FM
France	French franc	FF
Germany	deutsche mark	DM
Greece	drachma	Dr
India	rupee	Rs
Iran	rial	RI
Italy	lira	Lit
Japan	yen	¥
Kuwait	dinar	KD
Mexico	peso	Ps
Netherlands	guilder	FL
Norway	Norwegian krone	NKr
Saudi Arabia	riyal	SR
Singapore	Singapore dollar	S$
South Africa	rand	R
Spain	peseta	Pts
Sweden	krona	SKr
Switzerland	Swiss franc	SF
United Kingdom	pound	£
United States	U.S. dollar	$
USSR	ruble	Rub

means that 90,000 pesos is equivalent to $30.50. Thus the shirt is $0.50 less expensive in San Diego than in Tijuana.

Exchange rates between the U.S. dollar and currencies for most other nations are listed daily in the *Wall Street Journal*'s "Money and Investing" section. If you open up section C of the *Wall Street Journal,* you will find exchange rates presented in a form similar to Table 2-5. The rates quoted are those occurring at a specific time, 3 P.M. Eastern time. The time is listed because the rates fluctuate throughout the day as the supply of and demand for currencies change. Each country for which foreign exchange is traded is noted, along with its currency name in parentheses, such as "Argentina (austral)." In the first column is the U.S. dollar equivalent of the nation's currency — austral, for instance — for the previous and current days. In the third and fourth columns are the exchange rates, the number of australs necessary to purchase one U.S. dollar for the current and previous days.

TABLE 2-5   *Exchange Rates (Friday, January 11, 1991)*

| | U.S.$ equiv. | | Currency per U.S.$ | |
Country	Fri	Thurs	Fri	Thurs
Argentina (austral)	0.0001727	0.001753	5,792.06	5,703.60
Australia (dollar)	0.7743	0.7740	1.2915	1.2920

Conclusions

To study the macroeconomy, we must have a common framework or foundation and a common language. To discuss macroeconomic issues requires at least a general understanding of terms such as output, inflation, unemployment, and exchange rates. This chapter discussed these terms and also defined gross national product, gross domestic product, the balance of payments, inflation, unemployment, and exchange rates. As we examine various macroeconomic theories throughout the text, we will refer often to the key concepts discussed in this chapter.

The government's methods of measuring these variables are not perfect, but because the same methods are used year after year the statistical trends do provide a fairly accurate picture of year-to-year changes in a given economy. However, it is important to remember that comparisons between countries are more difficult. Different countries often use different definitions of these key variables and different methods of collecting the data. Therefore, international comparisons of output, unemployment, inflation, and so forth should be viewed with caution.

Summary

1. What is GNP?
Gross national product, or GNP, is the sum of total expenditures or total income, or total production that occurs in an economy during the course of a year.
2. What is GDP?
Gross domestic product, or GDP, is the purely domestic expenditures, income, or production that occurs in an economy during the course of a year.
3. How are economic transactions among nations measured?
The *balance of payments* provides a measure of a country's trade with the rest of the world. The *current account* is a measure of all transactions between nations involving goods and services. The *capital account* is a measure of the financial transactions between nations. Together, the current and capital accounts must balance, hence the name *balance of payments*.

4. How is inflation measured?

Inflation is a sustained upward movement in the general level of prices. The prices can be measured in several ways. Three of the most commonly used measures in the United States are the consumer price index (CPI), the producer price index (PPI), and the implicit price deflator.

5. What is unemployment?

Unemployment is a measure of the number of people looking for work who do not have work as a percentage of the total number of people who could work.

6. What is foreign exchange?

Different countries have different currencies or money. The exchange of different currencies is referred to as a *foreign exchange transaction*. Foreign exchange is foreign money.

▼

Key Terms

gross national product (GNP)   26
final good or service   27
intermediate goods   27
net national product (NNP)   32
gross domestic product (GDP)   33
real GNP   34
nominal GNP   34
balance of payments   36

inflation   38
consumer price index (CPI)   38
producer price index (PPI)   38
implicit price deflator   38
unemployment rate   43
foreign exchange   45
exchange rate   45

▼

Problems and Exercises

1.   Consider the following table, which contains data for a hypothetical economy:

Item	Amount (in billions)
Indirect business tax *(IBT)*	$ 215
Government purchases of goods and services *(G)*	625
Disposable income	2,000
Net private domestic investment	175
Business transfer payments	10
Personal income taxes	400
Capital consumption allowances *(CCA)*	225
Corporate profits and inventory valuation adjustments	140
Compensation of employees	1,625
Net exports of goods and services *(X)*	− 5
Personal consumption expenditures *(C)*	1,750

Calculate the values of gross investment, GNP, net national product, national income, and personal income.

2.   The following table contains prices and quantities of the three goods produced in an economy in three different years:

	1990		1991		1992	
	Price	*Quantity*	*Price*	*Quantity*	*Price*	*Quantity*
Food	$1.00	10	$1.50	5	$0.50	15
Movies	4.00	10	4.00	10	4.25	9
Gasoline	1.15	50	1.30	48	1.50	45

Compute a price index from the preceding table. Use 1991 as the base year.

3.   Why does a price index such as the implicit price deflator understate price changes?

4.   Using the information in the following table, calculate the civilian unemployment rate for each of the years.

	1950	1960	1970	1980	1990
Civilian population	105	117	137	168	188
Civilian labor force	62	70	83	107	125
Civilian employment	59	66	79	99	118

5.   A value-added tax imposes a tax on each stage of processing. Suppose a 10 percent value-added tax was implemented in the United States in 1992. What would be the effect on the CPI? Is this inflation?

6.   "The more open an economy is, the greater is its GNP relative to GDP." Is this statement true or false? Explain.

7.   Look at a copy of the *Wall Street Journal*. The "Money and Investing" section contains a listing of exchange rates. List the date of the paper you use and then indicate the exchange rate between the U.S. dollar and each of the following:

• German mark
• U.K. pound
• Argentine austral
• Australian dollar
• Canadian dollar

Part Two

The Basic Macroeconomic Model

Chapter 3

Aggregate Expenditures

What to Expect

Aggregate demand and aggregate supply curves can be used to show an economy's behavior. For instance, an economic downturn or a boom period can be pictured as a shift or series of shifts of either or both the aggregate demand and aggregate supply curves. The effects of the shifts on national income, employment, and prices depend on the shapes of the curves and on the amount by which the curves shift. To understand why the economy behaves as it does, we must delve into why aggregate demand and supply curves shift and what factors define the shapes of the curves. Aggregate demand and aggregate supply curves are derived and discussed in Chapters 3–7.

This chapter focuses attention on the purchases of goods and services by each of the four sectors—households, business, government, and the foreign sector. The analysis proceeds by focusing in turn on each component of expenditures: consumption, C, investment, I, government purchases, G, and net exports, X; and by describing the most important determinants of spending in each case. Then C, I, G, and X are summed to describe the behavior of aggregate expenditures. Questions considered in this chapter include the following:

1. What is the difference between aggregate expenditures and aggregate demand?

2. What is the aggregate expenditures function?

3. What are the components of AE?

4. What are the determinants of each component of spending?

5. What causes the AE curve to shift?

6. What is the multiplier?

▼

Aggregate Expenditures (AE)

We begin our examination of the demand side of the economy by focusing on aggregate expenditures. Aggregate expenditures (AE) are the total *planned* spending on domestically produced final goods and services that takes place in the economy at various income levels during some period of time; this spending is the expenditures that households, businesses, the government, and the foreign sector together plan to make, during the next period, on domestically produced goods and services. Perhaps you have noticed the change in terminology from *aggregate demand* to *aggregate expenditures*. The distinction between these terms is relatively important; it specifies whether we are assuming that the price level is fixed or not. When we use the fixed price assumption, we refer to total expenditures as *aggregate expenditures;* when we relax the assumption of a fixed price, we refer to total expenditures as *aggregate demand.*

We assume a fixed price primarily because it lets us focus on the nonprice determinants of spending. As we shall see, this provides some special insights into the behavior of the economy. The fixed price assumption also lets us explain what is called the *Keynesian* approach to describing the behavior of the economy. The Keynesian model was developed in the 1930s, a time period when output and unemployment determination were the crucial issues. In the mid-1930s, the unemployment rate in the United States was approaching nearly one-quarter of the work force. Understandably, the goal of most economists at this time was to discover the causes of this depression. They cared relatively little about price determination. Thus, the Keynesian analysis, which focused on unemployment and output and essentially assumed a fixed price level, appealed to a large segment of the economics profession. The analysis presented in this chapter can be considered the first or simple Keynesian model of the economy. In it, the price level plays absolutely no role—it is fixed.

Notice also the term "planned" spending. Planned expenditures play a key role in determining output, employment, and inflation. Actual spending is what *has* occurred; planned spending is what people *expect* to occur and therefore what determines how people behave.

▼
Consumption

The first component of aggregate expenditures we study here is **consumption**, the quantity of spending households plan to make over a period of time. What is the most important determinant of the total amount that households plan to spend? You can answer this question by asking yourself, "What determines the amount I spend or consume?" Most likely you answer that your disposable income (*YD*) determines the amount you spend.

Consider someone who is contemplating how much to consume over a period of one week. Let's carry out an experiment by giving this person—let's say she's called Meg—various income levels (assuming there are no taxes) and finding out how much she chooses to consume. For example, with no income how much will Meg consume? Your initial reaction might be that with no income she couldn't buy anything. But this is not correct. Even if she believes that during the next week her income will be zero, she still will be consuming. Consumption can still go on (be positive) when income is zero because people can borrow or can use savings. Such behavior is called **dissaving**. So when Meg says her consumption will be $100 even though her income is zero, we need not be surprised.

Now, suppose Meg anticipates that her income over the week will be $1,000. She reasons she can consume better-quality products (steaks instead of beans) and can fulfill some new desires. Therefore, she might plan to spend the entire $1,000.

Now consider one other income level. Suppose our consumer's anticipated income over the week is $1,200. Because she can satisfy most of her wants with $1,000 per week, the extra $200 lets her make some additional, perhaps more frivolous, purchases and lets her save for a rainy day, for a period of reduced income. So when her income is $1,200 per week, she will spend $1,180 for consumption and save $20.

The Marginal Propensity to Consume (MPC)

We can continue this process for a large number of income levels. The result is a specific consumption schedule, such as shown in columns 1 and 2 of Table 3-1, showing that consumption increases as disposable income (or just income, because we assume there are no taxes) increases. Notice that for each additional $100 of income, consumption increases by $90. The relationship between the additional income (change in income) and the additional consumption (change in consumption) listed in column 6 is known as the **marginal propensity to consume (MPC)**. In our example, the *MPC* is a constant 0.9.[1]

1   Another insight can be reached by examining the fraction of income consumed at various income levels. This fraction is known as the *average propensity to consume (APC)*. At the income level of $100, the *APC* is 1.90; when income is $1,000, the *APC* falls to 1.0; at an income level of $1,200, the *APC* is 0.98. Therefore, the *APC* falls as income increases. This relationship exists because, as income increases, people save a larger share of their total income.

TABLE 3-1   *Consumption and Saving Schedules*

(1) Income (Y)	(2) Consumption (C)	(3) Saving (S)	(4) ΔC	(5) ΔY	(6) MPC = ΔC/ΔY	(7) MPS = ΔS/ΔY
$ 0	$ 100	– $100	90	100	0.90	0.10
100	190	– 90	90	100	0.90	0.10
200	280	– 80	90	100	0.90	0.10
300	370	– 70	90	100	0.90	0.10
400	460	– 60	90	100	0.90	0.10
500	550	– 50	90	100	0.90	0.10
600	640	– 40	90	100	0.90	0.10
700	730	– 30	90	100	0.90	0.10
800	820	– 20	90	100	0.90	0.10
900	910	– 10	90	100	0.90	0.10
1,000	1,000	0	90	100	0.90	0.10
1,100	1,090	10	90	100	0.90	0.10
1,200	1,180	20	90	100	0.90	0.10

How can we illustrate the relationship between consumption and income graphically? The *AD–AS* diagram does not let us do that because price and output are measured on the axes. Thus, we switch to a diagram where expenditures are measured on the vertical axis and output or income, *Y,* is measured on the horizontal axis. We use this diagram instead of the *AD–AS* diagram because we assume that the price is fixed. This assumption reduces the aggregate supply curve to a fixed horizontal line, as shown in Figure 3-1. With a horizontal aggregate supply curve, all changes in output occur because of changes in aggregate demand. The *AS* curve plays no role and provides no information. In addition, because the price level is fixed the vertical axis provides no information. By switching to the *AE* graph when we use the fixed price assumption, we can better illustrate the relationship between expenditures and income.

Based on the hypothetical data of columns 1 and 2 of Table 3-1, Figure 3-2 shows the relationship between aggregate income and aggregate consumption. At an income level of $0, consumption is $100. So the consumption function begins at $100 on the vertical axis. As we move by $100 increments out the horizontal axis, we move up in $90 increments. In other words, for each $100 increase in income, consumption increases by $90.

In algebraic form, the consumption function can be written as $C = C_0 + c_y YD$ or $C = C_0 + c_y[Y - T]$ where T refers to net taxes. C_0 is the intercept of the consumption function (if there are no lump-sum taxes) and represents the amount of consumption that occurs independently of the level of disposable income, called *autonomous consumption.* All determinants of consumption except income and taxes are reflected in C_0. In our example, $C_0 = 100. The other part of the consumption function is the term $c_y YD$. This portion of consumption spending varies with disposable income or depends on disposable

FIGURE 3-1 *The fixed price assumption. The fixed price assumption reduces the aggregate supply curve to a fixed horizontal line, so all changes in output occur because of changes in aggregate demand. The AS curve plays no role and provides no information. In addition, because the price level is fixed the vertical axis provides no information. By going from the AD–AS to the AE graph, we can better show the relationship between expenditures and output under the fixed price assumption.*

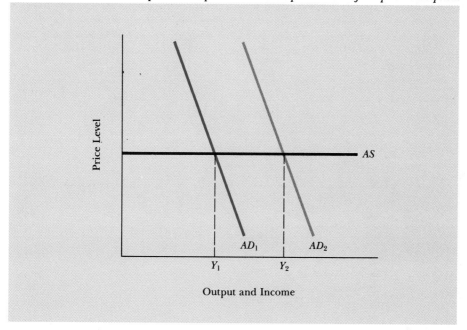

income. It is called *induced consumption.* The value of c_y is calculated by dividing the change in consumption by the change in income. Graphically, c_y is shown as the "rise" over the "run" along the consumption graph—the slope of the consumption function if there are no taxes. Also, c_y is the value of the marginal propensity to consume. In other words, the slope of the consumption function is the marginal propensity to consume, $c_y = MPC$, when there are no taxes. In our example, $c_y = 0.90$.

If net taxes vary as income varies—for example, an income tax specified as $T = t_y Y$—then the consumption function is written algebraically as

$$C = C_0 + c_y(Y - t_y Y)$$
$$= C_0 + (c_y - c_y t_y)Y$$

Here, the slope of the consumption function is the term in parentheses, $c_y - c_y t_y$. If the tax is a lump sum tax, a tax that does not vary as income varies, $T = T_0$, the consumption function is

$$C = (C_0 - c_y T_0) + c_y Y$$

FIGURE 3-2   *The consumption and saving functions. Based on the hypothetical data of columns 1 and 2 of Table 3-1, Figure 3-2 shows the relationship between aggregate income and planned consumption. At an income level of $0, consumption is $100. Thus, the consumption function begins at $100 on the vertical axis. As we move by $100 increments out the horizontal axis, we move up in $90 increments. In other words, for each $100 increase in income consumption increases by $90.*

Panel B shows the relationship between saving and income. In panel A, any point on the 45-degree line is a point at which consumption and income are equal because the 45-degree line lies exactly in the center of the two axes. Thus, the vertical distance between the consumption line and the 45-degree line at each income level in panel A measures saving. If this distance is plotted on a diagram with saving on the vertical axis and income on the horizontal axis, the saving function of panel B is traced.

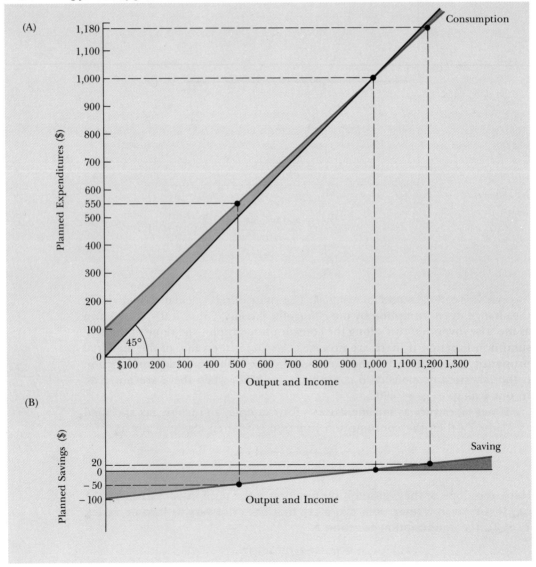

Here the slope of the consumption function is the *MPC,* or c_y, and the intercept is $C_0 - c_y T_0$, which reflects the net tax.[2]

Saving

Households can use their income to purchase goods and services, to pay taxes or to save.[3] After paying taxes, there are only two things that disposable income, *YD,* can be used for—consumption and **saving**. Thus, $YD = C + S$, so $S = YD - C$. This simple manipulation is important, for it tells us that once we know the consumption function, we know the saving function. We need not formulate an independent explanation of saving behavior.

Reconsider Table 3-1 *where we have assumed no net taxes.* At the zero income level, consumption is $100. This spending can come only from borrowing or from savings. Thus saving, listed in column 3, is – $100 when income is zero. At the income level of $1,000, consumption is $1,000, so saving must be zero. Other saving levels can be found by using the fact that saving plus consumption must equal income.

The relationship between the additional income (or change in income) and additional saving (change in saving) is known as the **marginal propensity to save (MPS)**. It is listed in column 7 of Table 3-1. If the *MPC* is 0.9, the *MPS* is 0.1. The *MPC* is defined as the fraction of an additional dollar of disposable income spent on goods and services. The *MPS* is defined as the fraction of an additional dollar of disposable income not spent on goods and services. Because an additional dollar of disposable income must be either spent on goods and services or saved, the *MPC* and *MPS* must sum to unity.[4]

Panel B in Figure 3-2 shows the relationship between saving and income. To simplify the explanation, a 45-degree line is added to the consumption function diagram of panel A in Figure 3-2. You can see the notation "45°" near the origin of Figure 3-2. In panel A, any point on the 45-degree line is a point at which consumption (measured on the vertical axis) and income (measured on the horizontal axis) are equal, because the 45-degree line lies exactly in the center of the two axes. Consider the income level $1,200. At this income level, con-

---

2   The term *net taxes* refers to taxes minus transfer payments. Whereas taxes reduce disposable income, transfer payments increase disposable income. Consequently, increased lump sum taxes reduce the intercept of the consumption function, but increased lump sum transfer payments increase the intercept of the consumption function. Similarly, if taxes and transfer payments vary as income varies, an increased tax rate reduces the slope of the consumption function, but an increased transfer payment rate increases the slope of the consumption function.

3   Notice the difference between the terms *saving* and *savings*. Saving occurs over a unit of time—a week, a month, a year. For instance, you might save $100 a week or $400 a month. Saving is a flow concept. Savings are an amount accumulated at a particular point in time— today, January 15, your sixty-fifth birthday. For example, you might have savings of $10,000 on January 15. Savings is a stock concept.

4   The average propensity to save *(APS)* increases as income increases. This makes sense, because as income rises most people save a higher percentage of their incomes.

sumption is $1,180. Therefore, saving must be $20. And $20 is precisely the vertical distance between the consumption line and the 45-degree line at the income level of $1,200. At a lower income level—say, $500—consumption is $550. In this case, the vertical distance between the 45-degree line and the consumption line represents the amount of dissaving, savings used for consumption, a dissaving of $50. Thus, the vertical distance between the consumption line and the 45-degree line at each income level in panel A measures saving. If this distance is plotted on a diagram with saving on the vertical axis and income on the horizontal axis, the saving function of panel B is traced out. When the consumption line lies above the 45-degree line, then the saving line lies below zero; when the consumption line lies below the 45-degree line, the saving line lies above the horizontal axis; when the consumption line intersects the 45-degree line, the saving line intersects the horizontal axis. As noted earlier, once we know what the consumption is we also know the saving level. Thus, let's now turn back to the determinants of consumption, knowing that these also are the determinants of saving.

▼

Other Determinants of Consumption

Disposable income is just one determinant of planned household spending. Other economic variables that affect household spending are wealth, expectations, demographics, interest rates, and the price level.

Real Wealth

Real wealth is the value of all the assets owned by a household. Real wealth is a stock variable; it includes homes, cars, checking and savings accounts, and stocks and bonds. Real wealth affects spending positively. The wealthier a person is, the more that person is likely to spend at every income level.

We emphasize *real* wealth here, not just wealth, because real wealth is the purchasing power of wealth. For instance, if we have $100,000 in assets (house, cars, savings accounts) and the price level is $P = 1.0$, we can buy twice as many goods and services as when the price level is $P = 2.0$. Thus, an increase in real wealth means that consumption increases at every level of income. You can see this in Figure 3-3 as a shift of the consumption function from C to C_1. The autonomous increase in consumption (caused by an increase in real wealth) shifts the intercept of the consumption function from $100 to $140, so consumption increases by $40 at every level of income. A decrease in real wealth has just the opposite effect: an autonomous drop in consumption, like the shift from C to C_2 in Figure 3-3. The new consumption functions, C_1 and C_2, parallel the old one, C; consumption is $40 more along C_1 and $40 less along C_2 at every income level than it previously was along C.

FIGURE 3-3   *Shifts of the consumption function. A decrease in real wealth results in an autonomous drop in consumption, like the shift from* C *to* C_2. *The new consumption functions,* C_1 *and* C_2, *parallel the old one,* C; *consumption is $40 more along* C_1 *and $40 less along* C_2 *at every income level than it previously was along* C.

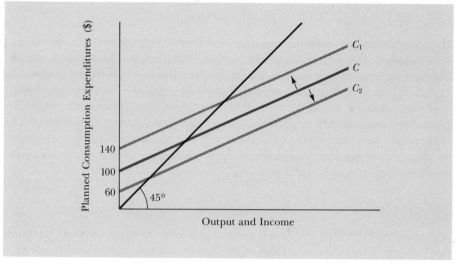

Expectations

Another important determinant of consumption is consumer expectations about future income, prices, and real wealth. When consumers expect a recession, when they are worried about losing jobs or cutbacks in hours worked, they tend to spend less and save more. This means an autonomous decrease in consumption and increase in saving—a downward shift of the consumption function. Conversely, when consumers are optimistic, we find an autonomous increase in consumption and decrease in saving—an upward shift of the consumption function.

Demographics

Other things being equal, the level of consumption should rise with increases in population. The greater the size of the population, *ceteris paribus,* the higher the intercept of the consumption function because more people are spending at each aggregate income level. In addition, the age of the population affects aggregate spending. People tend to have different values about saving when they are younger than when they are older; their rate of time discount is higher. Young households also are accumulating durable consumer goods (refrigerators, washing machines, automobiles), while older households already have these items. Thus, young households typically spend a greater fraction of their disposable income. This means that the intercept is higher and the *MPC* is probably higher (the slope of the consumption function increases) for a population with a large percentage of young households compared to a population with a large percentage of older households.

Interest Rates

Households can put their savings into interest-earning accounts or use the savings to buy stocks, bonds, land, art, or some other asset. Their choice will depend on the return they expect. The higher the interest rate or the greater the expected rate of return on a specified asset, the greater the incentive to buy that asset—to save. Using their income for consumption means that the households are forgoing any returns they might get from saving the income. The higher the opportunity cost of consumption is, the less consumption occurs. So, households tend to reduce consumption when the interest rate rises—the consumption function shifts down.

Prices

A change in the price level, *ceteris paribus,* can affect consumption. If the price level change alters the real wealth of the household sector, it affects household consumption as well. For instance, if a price level increase reduces real wealth (household wealth can buy fewer goods and services), then consumption declines. If the price level increases evenly on all goods, services, and assets, then household wealth does not decline in real terms, and consumption is not affected.

To summarize, increases in real wealth, consumer optimism, and population and decreases in interest rates and the price level shift the consumption function upward, while decreases in real wealth, consumer optimism, and population and increases in interest rates and the price level shift the consumption function downward.

▼
Investment

Spending on new capital goods, new residential construction, and changes in business inventories is **investment**. The buildings and equipment businesses need to produce their products are *capital* goods. Final goods or goods in process that have not been sold are **inventories**. Inventories can be planned or unplanned. For example, a retail department store wants to have enough sizes and styles of the new fall clothing lines to attract customers. Without a large inventory, sales will suffer. The goods the firm buys are *planned* inventory, based on expected sales. But by February the store wants to have as few fall clothes left unsold as possible. Goods not sold at this stage are *unplanned* inventory.

They are a sign that sales were not as good as expected and that too many goods were acquired by the firm last year. Both types of inventories—planned and unplanned—are called *investment,* but only planned inventories are part of planned investment or planned expenditures. Unplanned and unwanted inventories are simply the leftovers of what has recently gone on in the economy.

Investment and Income

The primary determinants of planned investment are interest rates, profit expectations, technological change, and the cost of capital goods. Because income is not a primary determinant of investment, we make the simplifying assumption that all investment is autonomous. This assumption means that the investment function is horizontal, as shown in Figure 3-4. No matter the income level, I is \$20, according to Figure 3-4. Changes in the determinants of investment shift the investment function up or down. Algebraically, the autonomous investment function is written as $I = I_0$.

The Determinants of Investment

The Interest Rate. Business investment is made in the hope of earning profit. The greater the expected profit, the greater is investment. Anything that affects businesses' profitability also affects their investment. A primary deter-

FIGURE 3-4   *The investment function. Because income is not a primary determinant of investment, we make the simplifying assumption that all investment is autonomous. This assumption means that the investment function is a horizontal line. No matter the income level, I is \$20. Changes in the determinants of investment shift the investment function up or down.*

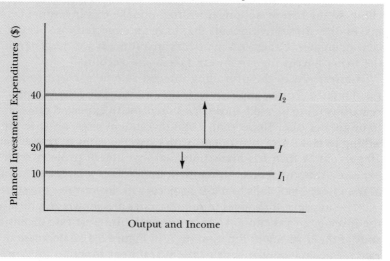

minant of whether or not an investment opportunity is profitable is the interest rate. Much business spending is financed by borrowing, so the interest rate represents the cost of borrowed funds. The interest rate also represents an opportunity cost of retained earnings. A firm could take its earnings and buy interest-earning assets. So by retaining its earnings, the firm is forgoing the interest it could earn.

As the interest rate goes up, fewer investment projects offer enough profit to warrant undertaking them. In other words, the higher the interest rate, the lower the level of investment. As the interest rate falls, there are more opportunities for earning a profit, so investment rises; the investment function shifts up.

Consider a simple example where a firm can buy a machine for $1,000 that is expected to yield $120 in net revenue each year. The net revenue is the profit after paying all expenses associated with operating and maintaining the machine. The firm's willingness to make this investment depends on whether it expects to earn a sufficient rate of return on its investment. The **expected rate of return** is the annual profit expected from the investment divided by the initial cost of the investment, or $120/$1,000 = 0.12.

If the firm must borrow $1,000 for the investment, it must pay interest to the lender. Suppose the lender charges 10 percent interest. The 12 percent expected rate of return exceeds the interest expense, so the firm is willing to buy the machine. In fact, the firm is willing to make any investment that can cover the cost of borrowing — any investment with an expected rate of return equal to or greater than 10 percent.

As the prevailing interest rate rises, the firm's cost of borrowing rises. The higher interest rate discourages investment. For example, if the interest rate rises to 15 percent, *ceteris paribus,* the cost of borrowing $1,000 to purchase the machine in our example now exceeds the expected rate of return from the machine, so the firm is no longer willing to make this investment. The firm now makes only those investments that have an expected rate of return of 15 percent or higher. Otherwise the firm's investments would generate a loss after the firm's borrowing costs were taken into account.

Conversely, as the prevailing interest rate falls, *ceteris paribus,* investment is stimulated. For example, even if the interest rate falls to 8 percent, the firm remains willing to make those investments with expected rates of return equal to or greater than 10 percent. Total investment rises, because the firm is also willing to make any investments with expected rates of return between 8 and 10 percent. A firm has many potential investment projects, with a variety of expected rates of return, so the firm undertakes a larger number of projects as the interest rate falls to make projects with lower rates of return profitable.

The impacts of changes in interest rates are shown graphically as shifts of the investment function. An increase in the interest rate means a downward shift of the investment function (to I_1 in Figure 3-4); a decrease in the interest rate means an upward shift of the investment function (to I_2 in Figure 3-4).

Profit Expectations. Firms invest in the expectation of earning a profit. Obviously, they cannot know exactly how much profit they will earn. So they use forecasts of future after-tax revenues and costs to calculate expected rates of return for each investment project. Only projects with sufficient expected rates of return are undertaken. Many factors can affect a firm's expectations of profit and therefore change expected rates of return and the firm's level of investment. Among them are new competitors, political change, new laws, taxes, or subsidies from government, and the overall economic health of the country or world. For example, a new competitor might be expected to reduce the existing firm's sales. Revenue projections would then drop, leading to lower expected rates of return on potential investments and a lower level of investment.

The impacts of changes in profit expectations are shown graphically as a shift of the investment function. For instance, a more optimistic forecast tends to increase investment, as shown by an upward shift of the investment function; a more pessimistic forecast tends to reduce investment and is shown by a downward shift of the investment function.

Cost of Capital Goods. The cost of capital goods also affects investment spending. As capital goods become more expensive, *ceteris paribus,* the expected rates of return from investment in them drop and the amount of investment falls. One factor that can change the cost of capital goods is government tax policy. For example, several times in the past the U.S. government has imposed and then removed investment tax credits. These credits let firms deduct part of the cost of capital gains from their tax bill. When the after-tax cost of capital gains drops, *ceteris paribus,* investment increases and the investment function shifts up. When the after-tax cost of capital goods increases, the level of investment falls and the investment function shifts down.

Technological Change. Technological change often drives new investment. New products or processes can be crucial to a firm's ability to remain competitive in a technological industry. The computer industry, for example, is driven by technological change. As faster and larger-capacity memory chips are developed, computer manufacturers must use them in order to stay competitive. The introduction of gasoline-powered tractors in the early 1900s spurred an agricultural boom; the introduction of microchips in the 1950s spurred the electronics industry boom.

The investment function shifts when a determinant of investment changes. The function shifts up when the interest rate declines, profit expectations rise, or cost of capital goods declines, or when technological change occurs. Conversely, the investment function shifts down when the interest rate rises, profit expectations fall, or cost of capital goods rises, or when a technological change generates additional costs.

▼
Government Purchases

Government purchases of goods and services constitute the second largest component of aggregate expenditures in the United States. Later chapters in this book focus on how politics and economics interact to determine the levels of spending and taxes. For now we can assume that government spending is set by government authorities at whatever level they choose, independent of current income. In other words, we assume that government purchases, like investment and autonomous consumption, are independent of income. The government spending function, like the investment function, is a horizontal line, as shown in Figure 3-5; the algebraic equivalent is $G = G_0$. Changes in government spending on goods and services lead to shifts of the government purchases function; such as to G_1.

▼
Net Exports

The last component of aggregate expenditures is **net exports**, which equal a country's exports of goods and services (what it sells to the rest of the world) minus its imports of goods and services (what it buys from the rest of the world). When net exports are positive, there is a surplus in the merchandise and ser-

FIGURE 3-5　*The government purchases function. The government purchases function, like the investment function, is a horizontal line. Changes in government spending on goods and services lead to shifts of the government purchases function.*

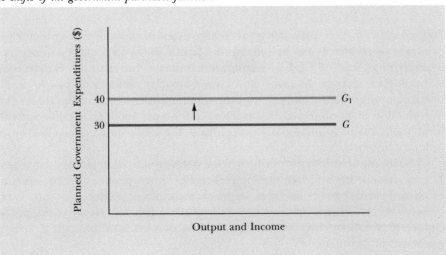

vices accounts. When net exports are negative, there is a deficit in these accounts. Positive net exports mean the United States is selling more to other countries than it is buying from other countries. This means that aggregate expenditures on U.S.-produced goods and services are higher than would be the case without net exports. Negative net exports mean that expenditures in the United States by foreign residents are less than U.S. spending on foreign goods and services. As a result, aggregate expenditures on U.S. goods and services are lower than would be the case without net exports.

Exports

Many factors determine the actual value of sales by domestic firms to the rest of the world (**exports**). Among these factors are foreign income, consumer tastes, government trade restrictions, relative price levels, and exchange rates. We assume that, like investment and government spending, exports are autonomous; that is, not affected by current *domestic* income. Exports depend on foreign income, not domestic income. Algebraically, exports are expressed as $EX = EX_0$.

As foreign income increases, foreign demand for all normal goods and services (both foreign and domestic) increases. Thus, domestic exports increase at every level of domestic income. Conversely, decreases in foreign income lower domestic exports at every level of domestic income. Similarly, changes in consumer tastes or government restrictions on international trade can cause the level of exports to shift autonomously. When foreign consumer tastes change in favor of domestic goods, domestic exports go up. When foreign consumer tastes change to favor foreign goods, domestic exports go down. When governments impose restrictions on international trade, exports fall. When restrictions are lowered, exports rise. In addition, when the domestic price level falls relative to the foreign price level, making domestic goods cheaper in foreign countries, domestic exports rise. Conversely, when the domestic price level rises relative to foreign price levels, making domestic goods more expensive in foreign countries, then domestic exports fall.

The rate at which two currencies are exchanged also affects exports. If U.S. $1 exchanges for DM2 (German marks), then a shirt costing U.S. $30 in New York is equivalent to a shirt costing DM60 in Berlin. If the exchange rate changes, *ceteris paribus*, to U.S. $1 = DM1, then the U.S. $30 shirt suddenly costs DM 30. The Germans would buy more U.S. shirts, and U.S. shirt makers would sell more shirts to Germany. U.S. exports rise autonomously. Conversely, if the U.S. dollar becomes more expensive, in terms of German marks, *ceteris paribus*, U.S. exports to Germany tend to fall.

Imports

Domestic purchases from the rest of the world (**imports**) also are determined by consumer tastes, trade restrictions, relative price levels, and exchange rates. However, domestic income plays a role too. As domestic income rises, domestic demand for all normal goods and services (both foreign and domestic) rises, so domestic imports rise. The relation between domestic income and imports is shown in Table 3-2, where spending on foreign goods and services rises as domestic income rises. The sensitivity of changes in imports to changes in income is measured by the **marginal propensity to import (MPI)**. It is the change in imports divided by the change in income. In Table 3-2 the *MPI* is 0.10. Every time income increases by $100, imports increase by $10. Algebraically, imports are written as part autonomous and part dependent on (or induced by) income:

$$IM = IM_0 + im_y Y$$

where im_y is the marginal propensity to import, or *MPI*.

How do other factors such as consumer tastes, government trade restrictions, relative price levels, and exchange rates affect imports? When domestic tastes change to favor foreign goods, imports rise at each income level. When domestic tastes change in favor of domestic goods, imports fall at each income level. When the government tightens restrictions on international trade, imports fall at each income level. Conversely, when restrictions are loosened, imports rise. In addition, when the domestic price level falls relative to foreign price levels (making foreign goods more expensive to domestic residents) imports fall, and, conversely, when the domestic price level rises relative to foreign price levels, imports rise.

Finally, exchange rate changes also affect imports. If the domestic currency falls in value relative to foreign currencies, *ceteris paribus*, domestic imports tend to fall. For example, if the U.S. dollar initially exchanges for DM2 (German marks) and then drops in value to DM1, German products become more expensive to U.S. residents. They then reduce their purchases of German products. Conversely, if the domestic currency rises in value relative to foreign currencies, domestic imports tend to rise.

Net Exports

Subtracting imports from exports at each income level gives *net exports* at each income level. This is the net exports function, shown as column 4 in Table 3-2

TABLE 3-2   *Export and Import Schedule*

(1) Domestic Income	(2) Exports (EX)	(3) Imports (IM)	(4) Net Exports (X)	(5) MPI $= \Delta IM / \Delta Y$
0	$40	$20	$20	0.10
$100	40	30	10	0.10
200	40	40	0	0.10
300	40	50	− 10	0.10
400	40	60	− 20	0.10
500	40	70	− 30	0.10
600	50	80	− 40	0.10

FIGURE 3-6   *The net exports function. Subtracting imports from exports at each income level gives net exports at each income level. This is the net exports function, shown as column 4 in Table 3-2 and plotted here. Because imports rise as domestic income rises while exports remain unchanged, net exports decline as income rises. Thus, the net export function slopes downward and eventually becomes negative.*

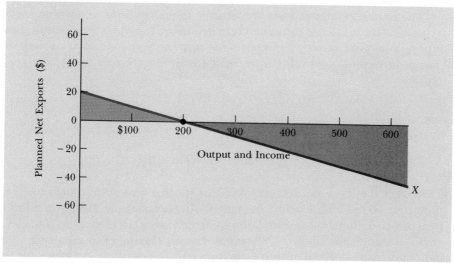

and plotted in Figure 3-6. Because imports rise as domestic income rises while exports remain unchanged, net exports decline as domestic income rises. Thus the net export function slopes downward, eventually becoming negative. The algebraic representation of net exports is $EX - IM = X$. Subtracting $IM = IM_0 + im_y Y$ from $EX = X_0$ yields

$$EX - IM = EX_0 - IM_0 - im_y Y.$$

Rewriting, we have the net exports function: $X = X_0 - X_y Y$. In other words, X represents $EX - IM$, or net exports; X_0 represents $EX_0 - IM_0$, the autonomous part of net exports; and X_y represents im_y, the induced part of net exports.

The net export function shifts whenever one of the determinants of net exports, other than domestic income, changes. For instance, the net export function shifts up when foreign income rises, or when changes in consumer tastes or exchange rates favor domestic goods and services. The net export function shifts down when foreign income falls, or when changes in consumer tastes or exchange rates favor foreign goods and services. In addition, net exports depend on the price level of goods and services in the domestic economy relative to the price level in foreign economies. A higher U.S. price level, *ceteris paribus*, raises the relative cost of U.S. goods. As a result, both U.S. and foreign residents buy fewer U.S. goods and more foreign goods. This shifts the net export function down as U.S. exports fall and imports rise. Conversely, a fall in the U.S. price level, *ceteris paribus*, makes U.S. goods relatively less expensive than foreign goods. Thus, both domestic residents and foreign consumers buy more U.S. goods and fewer foreign goods. The net exports function shifts up to show that more spending on U.S. goods occurs at each domestic income level.

The impact on net exports of a change in government restrictions on international trade is less clear. When restrictions are loosened, for example, both exports and imports rise. Net exports rise if the change in exports exceeds the change in imports and fall if the change in imports exceeds the change in exports.

▼
Determination of Real Output

The larger the level of a society's national income and output, the more employment occurs and, usually, the better off the society is. How is a nation's level of real national income and output determined? What happens if the level entails a significant amount of unemployment? Having examined each component of aggregate expenditures, we now can answer these questions for the simple Keynesian, or fixed price, model.

The AE Function

The aggregate expenditures function is the sum of the individual functions for each component of planned spending. Aggregate expenditures (AE) equals consumption (C) plus investment (I) plus government purchases (G) plus net exports (X):

$$AE = C + I + G + X$$

Table 3-3 lists aggregate expenditures data for a hypothetical economy. The aggregate expenditures function can be derived by summing columns 2–5. Notice that as income rises, consumption rises (the *MPC* is 0.9 and there are no income taxes), net exports fall (the *MPI* is 0.1), and investment and government spending are constant, or autonomous. Adding these components of planned spending together, we see that the quantity of aggregate expenditures rises as income rises. How much it rises depends on the *MPC* and *MPI*. In column 6, you can see that as income rises by $100, the quantity of aggregate expenditures increases by $80. The $100 increase in income means that consumption rises by $90 (the *MPC* is 0.9) and imports rise by $10 (the *MPI* is 0.1). Because *C* rises by $90 but $10 of that $90 is spent on foreign goods and services, only $80 of additional spending on domestic goods and services occurs as income

TABLE 3-3
Aggregate Expenditures

(1) Y	(2) C	(3) I	(4) G	(5) X	(6) AE
0	100	20	30	20	170
100	190	20	30	10	250
200	280	20	30	0	330
300	370	20	30	– 10	410
400	460	20	30	– 20	490
500	550	20	30	– 30	570
600	640	20	30	– 40	650
700	730	20	30	– 50	730
800	820	20	30	– 60	810
850	865	20	30	– 65	850
900	910	20	30	– 70	890
1,000	1,000	20	30	– 80	970
1,100	1,090	20	30	– 90	1,050

rises by \$100.[5] Graphically, the aggregate expenditures function is the vertical sum of all the individual spending functions, as shown in Figure 3-7. The consumption function slopes up. The investment and government spending functions are just constant amounts at each income level and so, when added to the consumption function, produce lines parallel to the consumption function. The net exports function slopes down, so that when added to C, I, and G, net exports make the aggregate expenditures function less steep. The AE function slopes up (because the MPC exceeds the MPI, so planned spending continues to increase as income rises), but is flatter than the consumption function, due to the influence of the net exports function. Recall that the net exports function in Figure 3-6 intersects the horizontal axis when income equals \$200. At income levels below \$200, net exports are positive. Consequently, the $C + I + G + X$ or AE function in Figure 3-7 is above the $C + I + G$ line. At income levels above \$200 in Figure 3-6, net exports are negative. Consequently, the AE function in Figure 3-7 is below the $C + I + G$ line. The AE function intersects the $C + I + G$ line when income equals \$200.

Income and Output

People do not change their behavior when everything is consistent with what they expect; that is, with their plans. However, when plans and reality do *not* match, people adjust their behavior to make them match. In Figure 3-8, only one output level corresponds to the AE_1 function where plans and reality match.

5   Make the simplifying assumption that all imports are purchased by households.

FIGURE 3-7   *The aggregate expenditures function. The aggregate expenditures function is the vertical sum of each of the individual spending functions:* AE = C + I + G + X. *The consumption function slopes upward. The investment and government purchases functions are just constant amounts at each income level and so when added to the consumption function produce lines parallel to the consumption function. The net exports function slopes down so that when added to C + I + G, net exports make the aggregate expenditures function less steep. C + I + G + X intersects C + I + G at the income level where exports equal imports so net exports are zero. The AE function slopes up but is flatter than the consumption function, due to the influence of the net exports function.*

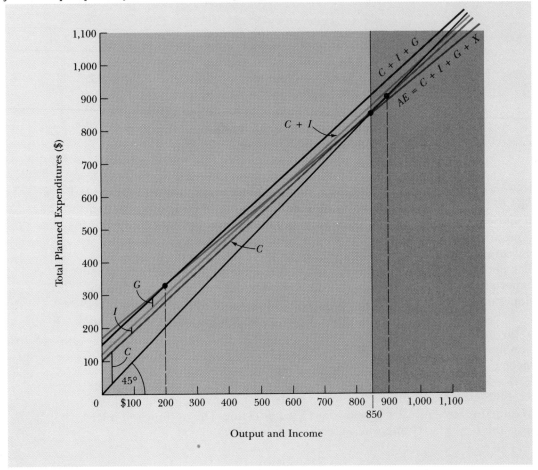

That output level occurs where the *AE* function intersects the 45-degree line—the output level where spending and income are equal, $850.

The intercept of the AE_1 function is the sum of C_0, I_0, G_0, and X_0. It is $100 + 20 + 30 + 20 = 170$. The slope of the AE_1 function is the difference between c_y and X_y or $0.9 - 0.1 = 0.8$. The level of output at which total planned spending and output are equal can be derived by setting $Y = AE$ and solving for Y. For instance,

FIGURE 3-8   *Determination of output. Notice that at $850, the* AE₂ *function lies above the 45-degree line. The distance of $30 is the amount of unintended sales of inventories. Because of the increase in government purchases, production rises and the level of income or output at which planned expenditures and output are the same increases from $850 to $1,000.*

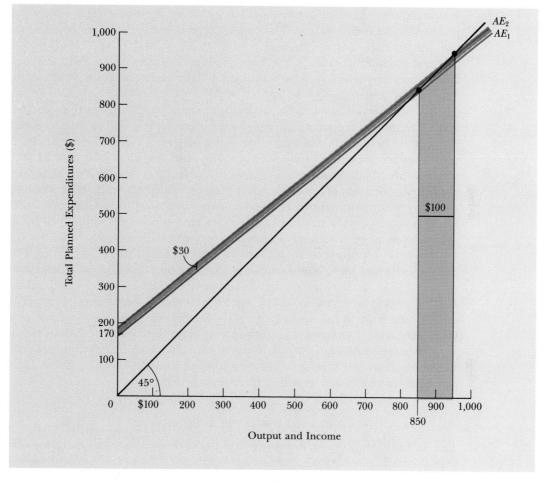

$$Y = 170 + 0.8Y$$
$$0.2Y = 170$$
$$Y = 850$$

What happens when planned spending and output are not equal? When planned spending on goods and services exceeds the current value of output, firms must sell their stocks of inventories. To replenish these stocks, firms must increase production. As more workers are hired and output rises, the level of national output also increases. This is the situation for all output levels below

$850 in Figure 3-8 and Table 3-3. At these levels, total planned spending is greater than output, which means that more goods and services are being bought than are being produced. The only way this can happen is for goods produced in the past to be sold. As inventory stocks begin to decline below desired levels, manufacturers increase production to replenish the stocks. The additional production increases output. Thus, when aggregate expenditures exceed output, output rises. For instance, at $Y = \$300$, AE_1 is $410. The $110 of excess planned expenditures must come from goods and services produced in the past. Inventories are reduced, which induces businesses to increase production. Production continues to rise until $Y = AE_1$ in Figure 3-8.

At output levels above $850, aggregate expenditures are less than output. Here, inventories are accumulating above planned levels, and more goods and services are being produced than are being bought. As inventories rise, businesses reduce the output they produce. For example, when output is $1,000, the quantity of aggregate expenditures in Table 3-3 is only $970. The $30 of produced goods that are not sold are measured as unplanned inventory investment. As the unplanned inventories increase, firms cut production and lay off workers, which causes output to fall. And output continues falling until there are no unplanned inventory accumulations—until $Y = AE_1$.

There is only one level of output in Figure 3-8 and Table 3-3 where output does not change: $850. When output is $850, the quantity of aggregate expenditures is $850, so there are no unplanned inventory accumulations or decumulations. This is referred to as the *equilibrium level of output and income*. It is equilibrium only in the sense that aggregate expenditures equal output and thus there are no *unintended* accumulations or decumulations of inventories. It is not an equilibrium in the sense of demand and supply being equal. Equilibrium, in this case, is simply the level of national income, output, and aggregate expenditures at which plans match reality.

Changes in Spending and the Determination of Output

The *AE* function is drawn assuming that all the determinants of spending (except domestic income) are fixed or held constant. Whenever one of these determinants of spending changes, the aggregate expenditures function shifts. For instance, if government purchases rise by $30, the *AE* function shifts up. The function shifts up because aggregate planned spending is $30 higher at each income level. When this happens, the $850 level of output is no longer the equilibrium level because firms find unintended decreases in their inventory stocks and therefore increase their production. Notice in Figure 3-8 that at $850 the AE_2 function lies above the 45-degree line. The distance of $30 is the amount of unintended sales of inventories. Because of the increase in government expenditures, production rises and the level of income or output at which planned expenditures and output are the same increases from $850 to $1,000.

A change in any determinant of planned spending (other than domestic income) affects the equilibrium level of aggregate output. The same type of change that we just saw with government purchases occurs if a determinant of autonomous consumption, investment, or net exports changes. These determinants are real wealth, expectations, demographics, taxes, the interest rate, the cost of capital goods, technological change, foreign income, consumer tastes, government trade policies, exchange rates, and foreign and domestic price levels.

The Multiplier

Although determining an economy's real output and income level now seems relatively straightforward, back in the 1930s it was a major breakthrough in macroeconomics. By showing how the national output level is determined, Keynes built a case for showing how the level could be changed. The Keynesian analysis gave policymakers an active part in directing the behavior of an economy. For instance, if an economy were mired in a deep recession, it need not remain in that recession for long, according to Keynesian analysis. The economy could be driven out of the recession by appropriately increasing autonomous spending. The increase in autonomous spending would shift the AE function up and increase the level of real output (equilibrium output). It seemed the only question was how much would autonomous spending need to be increased?

You may have noticed, in the illustration of how a change in government purchases affects output and expenditures, that government purchases rose by $30 and pushed the nation's income and output up $150. What accounts for this effect of a change in autonomous spending? The answer is the multiplier.

Let's look at an example, using Table 3-4. Suppose the government spends an additional $20 to improve highways. What happens to output and income?

TABLE 3-4   *The Multiplier Effect*

	(1) Change in Income	(2) Change in Domestic Expenditures	(3) Change in Saving	(4) Change in Imports
Round 1	$ 30.00	$ 24.00	$ 3.00	$ 3.00
Round 2	24.00	19.20	2.40	2.40
Round 3	19.20	15.36	1.92	1.92
Round 4	15.36	12.29	1.54	1.54
Round 5	9.83	7.86	0.98	0.98
	•	•	•	•
	•	•	•	•
	•	•	•	•
Totals	$150.00	$120.00	$15.00	$15.00

The autonomous increase in government purchases increases the income of highway construction crews by $30. As their income increases, their spending rises. Let's say they spend more money on groceries. In the process, they are raising the income of the grocery store employees and owners, who in turn increase their consumption.

Table 3-4 shows how the single $30 change in government purchases leads to more changes. Round 1 is the initial increase in government spending to improve roads. That $30 expenditure increases the income of construction crews by $30 (column 1). As income increases, those components of aggregate expenditures that depend on current domestic income—consumption and net exports—also increase by some fraction of the $30. Consumption changes by the MPC multiplied by the change in income; imports change by the MPI multiplied by the change in income. To find the total effect of the initial change in spending, we must know the fraction of any change in income that is spent in the domestic economy. In our hypothetical economy, the MPC is 0.90 and the MPI is 0.10. So for each $1 of new income, consumption rises by $0.90 and imports rise by $0.10. As a result, planned purchases of *domestic* goods and services rise by $0.80.

In round 1 of Table 3-4, the initial $30 increase in income induces an increase in spending on domestic goods and services of $24 (0.80 × $30). Of the $6 not spent on domestic goods and services, $3 is saved because the MPS is 0.10. The other $3 is spent on imports, because the MPI is 0.10. Only $24 of the workers' $30 of new income is spent on goods produced in the domestic economy. That $24 becomes income to the grocery store's employees and owners. When their income increases by $24, they spend 80 percent of that income ($19.20) on domestic goods (round 2, column 2). The rest of their income is saved and spent on imports.

Each time income increases, planned expenditures increase. But the increase is smaller and smaller with each new round of spending. The reason is that 10 percent of each change is saved and another 10 percent is spent on imports. These are the *leakages* out of the stream of spending on domestically produced goods and services. Saving and import purchases are not purchases of domestic goods and services.

To find the total effect of the initial $30 change in spending, we could keep on computing the change in income and spending round after round and then sum the total of all rounds. Fortunately, we don't have to do that. If we know the percentage of additional income that "leaks" from domestic spending at each round, we can determine the total change in income. Here we mean the additional income not passed on as additional spending on domestic goods and services: **leakages** include savings and imports. To find the total change in output resulting from a change in autonomous expenditures, all we do is (1) find the reciprocal of the percentage of additional income that leaks from the domestic spending stream at each round and (2) multiply this reciprocal times the initial change in autonomous spending. For instance, when the MPS is 0.1 and the MPI is 0.1, the total fraction of leakages is 0.2. The reciprocal is 1/0.2 or 5. Thus, an initial change of spending of $30 would result in a total change in income of 5 × $30 = $100. The number by which the initial change in spending is multiplied is called the **multiplier**. The multiplier is the reciprocal of the fraction of new income that is not passed on as spending on domestic goods and services.

$$\text{Multiplier} = \frac{1}{MPS + MPI}$$

When the *MPS* is 0.10 and the *MPI* is 0.10, the multiplier is 5. If the *MPS* were 0.20 (*MPC* = 0.80) and the *MPI* were 0.30, then the multiplier would be 2. In this case, the initial spending change of $30 would result in a total change in income of $60. The larger the leakages from the spending stream, the smaller the multiplier. The smaller the multiplier, the smaller is the total income change that results from a change in autonomous spending.

The multiplier is related to the slope of the *AE* function. You can see in Figure 3-9 that the steeper the slope of the *AE* function, the greater is the impact of any given change in autonomous expenditures on national output and income. Compare the solid-line *AE₁* function with the dashed-line *AE₃* function. The slope of the dashed *AE₃* function is larger; the curve is steeper. Initially, output is $400. As autonomous spending increases by $30, the new output according to the solid (less steep) *AE₂* function rises to $500. But according to

FIGURE 3-9   *The multiplier and the slope of the* AE *function. The multiplier is related to the slope of the* AE *function. You can see that the steeper the slope of the* AE *function, the greater is the impact of any given change in autonomous expenditures on national income and output. Compare the* AE₁ *and* AE₂ *functions (solid line) with the* AE₃ *and* AE₄ *functions (dashed line). The slope of the dashed* AE *functions is larger and steeper. Initially, output is $400. As autonomous spending increases by $30, the new output according to the (less steep)* AE *functions (solid line) rises to $500. According to the (steeper)* AE *functions (dashed line), the new output rises to $600.*

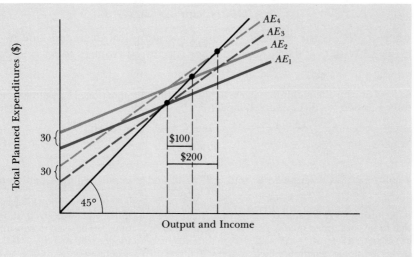

the dashed (steeper) AE_4 function, the new output rises to \$600. The multiplier can be written as

$$\frac{1}{1 - \text{slope of } AE}$$

This formula shows that as the slope of the AE function rises, the quantity (1 − slope) falls and thus the reciprocal of (1 − slope) rises. Because the slope of the AE function in our model is $MPC - MPI$, then the multiplier is the reciprocal of $1 - \text{slope} = 1 - MPC + MPI$; and because $1 - MPC$ in the model without income taxes is just MPS, the multiplier is the reciprocal of $MPS + MPI$.

Real World Complications

The multiplier we have just derived is a simplification of reality. Other factors beside the MPS and MPI determine the multiplier in an economy. For instance, if investment rises as domestic income rises, then the fraction of spending that leaks from the spending stream in each round is smaller and the multiplier is larger. If there is *induced investment*, I_y, the multiplier is

$$\frac{1}{MPS + MPI - I_y}$$

where I_y represents the fraction by which investment increases as income increases. If I_y is 0.10 and the MPS and MPI are each 0.10, then the multiplier is 10. Without I_y, the multiplier is 5.

Also, if net taxes increase as income increases, then the fraction of income that leaks from the spending stream in each round is larger and the multiplier is smaller. If net taxes rise by \$0.05 for each \$1 of income, $t_y = 0.05$, then the multiplier is

$$\frac{1}{1 - MPC + t_y MPC + MPI - I_y}$$

where $t_y MPC$ is the amount by which consumption decreases due to tax increases.[6] With $t_y = 0.05$, the multiplier is reduced from 10 to 6.67. Recall that,

---

6   Solving for the multiplier algebraically clarifies this equation. The aggregate expenditures function for this expanded model is

$$AE = C_0 + c_y Y(1 - t_y) + I_0 + I_y Y + G_0 + X_0 - X_y Y$$

or

$$AE = C_0 + I_0 + G_0 + X_0 + Y(c_y - c_y t_y + I_y - X_y).$$

Equilibrium Y is determined by setting $Y = AE$ and manipulating the equation to find

$$Y = (C_0 + I_0 + G_0 + X_0)/(1 - c_y + c_y t_y - I_y + X_y).$$

Substituting MPC for c_y and MPI for im_y yields the multiplier equation given above. Note that in this expanded model, each additional dollar of income can be used to consume, save, or pay taxes: $\Delta Y = \Delta C + \Delta S + \Delta T$. Consequently, it is no longer true that $1 - MPC = MPS$ in this multiplier equation, which assumes MPC and MPS are defined in terms of gross income.

in contrast to taxes, if transfers from the government to households vary with income, then the multiplier increases as the transfer rate rises. Transfers are payments such as social security, unemployment compensation, welfare, and Medicare. These payments tend to rise as income falls, because more people are unemployed and are eligible for the transfers. An increased tax rate reduces the slope of the aggregate expenditures function. An increased transfer rate increases the slope of the aggregate expenditures function.

Another factor altering the real-world multiplier stems from imports. We have assumed that whatever is spent on imports is permanently lost to the domestic economy. For a country whose imports are a small fraction of the exports of its trading partners, this assumption is realistic. But for a country whose imports are very important in determining the export volume for the rest of the world, this simple multiplier understates the true value of the multiplier. Such is the case for the United States. When a U.S. resident buys goods from another country, that purchase becomes income to foreign residents. If Paul in Miami buys art from José in the Dominican Republic, Paul's purchase increases José's income. So the import of art into the United States increases income in the Dominican Republic. Because the income in the Dominican Republic increases, the residents of the Dominican Republic buy more goods and services produced in their country and more from other countries, principally the United States. Thus, the *MPI* overstates the leakage that the United States experiences.

Because the value of the multiplier defines the amount by which national output changes as a result of autonomous spending changes, estimates of multipliers for various countries and various regions of countries have been developed to help policymakers formulate policies. From these estimates, we can get a sense of how much the simple multiplier formulas just listed underestimate the true values of the multiplier. Consider, for instance, Table 3-5 in which

TABLE 3-5
The Multiplier Effects Between the United States and Canada

Multiplier Effects of U.S. Government Purchases	
Country	*Multiplier*[a]
United States	2.0
Canada	0.5

Multiplier Effect in the United States of Canadian Government Purchases	
Country	*Multiplier*[a]
Canada	0.2

[a]Based on first year after increase in spending.
Source: Hali J. Edison, Jaime R. Marquez, and Ralph W. Tryon, *The Structure and Properties of the FRB Multicountry Model,* International Finance Discussion Paper, no. 293 (Washington, DC: Board of Governors of the Federal Reserve System, 1986).

multiplier estimates for the United States and Canada based on the Federal Reserve's multicountry model are listed. The first section of the table gives the multiplier effect of an increase in U.S. government purchases. The U.S. effect is a multiplier of 2. This means that if autonomous government purchases increase by $40 billion, the U.S. national output and income rise by $80 billion after one year. The multiplier for Canada is 0.5, which tells us that if U.S. autonomous expenditures rise by $40 billion, Canadian national output and income rise by $20 billion (0.5 × $40 billion) after one year.

The second part of the table shows the sensitivity of U.S. income to changes in Canadian government spending. The multiplier is only 0.2, which tells us that if autonomous government purchases increase by $40 billion in Canada, U.S. national output and income are $8 billion higher after one year. U.S. spending changes have a much larger effect on foreign income than foreign spending changes have on U.S. income.

▼   ▼   ▼   ▼   ▼   ▼   ▼   ▼   ▼   ▼   ▼
Conclusions

This chapter began the process of constructing a model of the macroeconomy and developed the aggregate expenditures or *AE* model. The *AE* model shows how planned spending works to define output and income and thus defines the number of workers required in the economy—employment. The *AE* model assumes the price level to be fixed (the *AS* curve to be horizontal) and thus focuses all attention on output and through it on employment. The next chapter introduces money and interest rates into the *AE* model. Then the discussion moves on to relax the fixed price assumption and develop the *AD* model.

▼   ▼   ▼   ▼   ▼   ▼   ▼   ▼   ▼   ▼   ▼
Summary

1. What is the difference between aggregate expenditures and aggregate demand?
Aggregate expenditures are all the purchases of domestic goods and services all sectors plan to make at various income levels when the price level is assumed to be fixed. Aggregate demand is total planned purchases when the price level is allowed to vary.
2. What is the aggregate expenditures function?
The aggregate expenditures function relates total planned purchases to national income and output.
3. What are the components of AE?
AE consists of consumption, investment, government purchases, and net exports.
4. What are the determinants of each component of spending?
In addition to income, purchases depend on real wealth, expectations, taxes and

transfer payments, the health of the economy, the health of foreign economies, the domestic price level, the price levels of foreign nations, and exchange rates.

5. What causes the AE *curve to shift?*

The *AE* function shifts whenever a determinant of spending (other than domestic income) changes.

6. What is the multiplier?

The multiplier is the factor by which a given autonomous change in expenditures is multiplied to calculate how much national income and output will change as a result of the autonomous change in expenditures. The algebraic formula for the multiplier is the reciprocal of 1 minus the slope of the *AE* function, or the reciprocal of the fraction of new income that is not passed on in additional spending.

▼
Key Terms

consumption   55
dissaving   55
marginal propensity to consume
  (*MPC*)   55
saving   59
marginal propensity to save
  (*MPS*)   59
investment   62
inventories   62

expected rate of return   64
government purchases   66
net exports   66
exports   67
imports   67
marginal propensity to import
  (*MPI*)   68
leakages   76
multiplier   77

▼
Problems and Exercises

1. Discuss the relationship, if any, between the government budget deficit (or surplus) and equilibrium income.

2. Consider the following data:

Y	Consumption (C)	Investment (I)
0	180	90
300	360	120
600	540	150
900	720	180
1,200	900	210
1,500	1,080	240

    a.   At the income level of 1,200, what is the average propensity to consume (*APC*) and save (*APS*)?

    b.   What is the value of autonomous consumption? What is the value of the marginal propensity to consume?

    c.   Write the equation that represents the consumption schedule, savings schedule, and investment schedule for this economy.

    d.   What is the value of equilibrium income?

3.   Explain the concept of *equilibrium* as used in macroeconomics. Is the economy ever in equilibrium? How can the idea of a *business cycle* be interpreted in the context of equilibrium?

4.   During 1974–1975, the U.S. economy was in a serious recession. In the last quarter of 1975, most signs indicated that the trough of the recession had been in July 1975. At this time, President Ford proposed to cut taxes and government spending by $28 billion each to aid the recovery. The Democrats countered by proposing that only taxes should be cut.

    a.   Discuss and evaluate these two proposals.

    b.   During 1980–1981 and then 1982–1983, the United States again fell into recession. During the recession, the Democrats suggested raising taxes to balance the budget. President Reagan resisted. Evaluate their positions.

5.   Suppose the economy is described by the following equations:

$$Y = C + I + G$$
$$C = 100 + 0.75\,(Y - T)$$
$$T = 100$$
$$G = 150$$
$$I = 125$$

    a.   What is the equilibrium level of income?

    b.   At the equilibrium level of income, is the government running a surplus or a deficit?

    c.   Assume the full-employment level of income is $1,500. How would you characterize this economy? Suppose you are asked to recommend policies to improve the state of the economy. What is the appropriate change in government expenditure? What will happen to the government's budget position if such a policy is enacted?

    d.   Instead of a change in government expenditures, a change in taxes could be advocated. What is the appropriate change in taxes, and what will happen to the government budget position?

    e.   Could the state of the economy be improved without incurring an increase in the government budget deficit? How?

6.   Consider the model in which both government spending and taxes are autonomous. If the present income level exceeds the equilibrium income level, will the economy automatically move to the equilibrium level? Explain.

7.   In a model with government spending and taxes (exogenous), we defined consumption spending to be a function of disposable income, or

$$C = C_0 + c_y(Y)$$

a.   Derive the corresponding saving function.

b.   Throughout this chapter, all the behavioral relationships have been drawn in diagrams with income (Y) on the horizontal axis. Why?

c.   If the saving function derived in *a* is to be plotted in a diagram with income (Y) on the horizontal axis, what will the intercept of this function equal?

8.   Suppose that a state government, say Michigan, issues bonds and borrows the savings of other U.S. citizens to fund a project. Why would it be wrong to apply the simple Keynesian multiplier (for the U.S. economy as a whole) to this state expenditure to find the effect on the *state's* economy?

9.   Which of the following actions shift the aggregate expenditure curve, and which do not shift the curve? Give reasons for your answers.

a.   A reduction in interest rates

b.   An increase in wages rates

c.   Lower oil prices

d.   An increase in inflation

e.   An increase in expected inflation

f.   A reduction in the national income

Chapter 4

Money and Aggregate Expenditure: The IS–LM Framework

What to Expect

The previous chapter discussed aggregate expenditures without discussing money. Yet we usually need money to make expenditures. Not income, but money. Money is not the same thing as income; money is simply some asset that people generally are willing to accept in exchange for goods and services. Even though money is not income, money is important. The quantity of money in an economy affects prices, interest rates, foreign exchange rates, and the level of national income and output. This chapter shows how money affects aggregate expenditures.

In the *AE* model, the level of output is determined in what is called the **commodity or output market** by finding that output level at which planned expenditures are equal to actual expenditures. Because aggregate expenditures depend on the interest rate, we can't determine the level of output unless we know the interest rate. The interest rate is determined in the **money market** by the demand for and supply of money. To define the interest rate, we must know what the demand for and supply of money are. But money demand depends on the level of income. So we can't determine the interest rate unless we know the income level. We need the interest rate to determine income or output, and we need output to determine the value of the interest rate. How do we resolve this problem? One way would be to continuously go back and forth between the two markets. For instance, we could begin with some interest rate and determine the level of aggregate expenditures. This would establish an output level that we could use to determine money demand and thus an interest rate level. This interest rate level could then be used to determine aggregate expenditures and a corresponding output level. The process would continue back and forth until we found the one interest rate and output level at which the money and commodity markets are both in equilibrium. But this process would be very cumbersome. Fortunately, there is a much easier way to account for the feedback effects. A single diagram, called the *IS–LM* diagram, allows us to explicitly consider how the money market and the commodity market affect each other.[1]

The purpose of this chapter is to develop the *IS–LM* framework. With the *IS–LM* framework, we can discuss an important way that money affects aggregate expenditures. The first section of the chapter introduces the interest rate as a determinant of aggregate expenditures. Having established the importance of the interest rate in the commodity market, the next order of business is to see how money demand and supply determine the level of interest rates. Questions considered include the following:

1. *How do the money and commodity markets interact?*

2. *What role does the interest rate play in determining aggregate expenditures?*

3. *What is the demand for money?*

4. *What effects do changes in the money supply have on aggregate expenditures?*

5. *What is the* IS *curve?*

6. *What is the* LM *curve?*

7. *What role does the foreign sector play in the* IS–LM *analysis?*

▼

The Interest Rate and the Commodity Market

Interest rates affect planned purchases, business purchases in particular. Businesses base their decisions to buy a machine or build a new plant on their ex-

1   The role of monetary variables in the Keynesian model was first pointed out by Nobel laureate John R. Hicks in 1937. Hicks developed the *IS–LM* model, a model that integrated money and interest rates into aggregate expenditures. The *IS−LM* model of the economy involves two markets: the goods market and the money market. The *IS* curve represents the commodity market (*I* stands for investment and *S* for saving) and the *LM* curve represents the money market (*L* stands for the demand for money, often called *liquidity preference*, and *M* for the supply of money).

pectation of the profitability of that particular investment project. In making an investment decision, a firm must calculate the expected rate of return from its proposed investment project. As discussed in Chapter 3, the *expected rate of return* is calculated by dividing the expected annual dollar earnings, less all expenses (except interest payments on borrowed funds), by the cost of the asset. For example, suppose a firm is contemplating the purchase of a machine expected to increase net earnings by $1,000 each year. Because the machine costs $10,000, the expected rate of return is 10 percent, or $1,000/$10,000. The expected rate of return is then compared with the expected opportunity cost for the life of the investment. The opportunity cost is the best alternative use of the money. As a first example, suppose a firm has $10,000 sitting in its cash drawer. The firm is contemplating the purchase of a machine that has a rate of return of 10 percent. The firm can make this investment decision by comparing the 10 percent return on the machine with the opportunity cost of $10,000. But what is the opportunity cost of $10,000? It is the alternative return available from a comparable use of the money, comparable in terms of time and risk. Suppose the firm could put the $10,000 in some type of money market account that was comparable to the risk of buying the machine, and thus earn 6 percent. In this case, the machine should be bought because the expected return on the investment exceeds the expected return from the money market account.

Now consider the situation in which the firm does not have the required amount of cash on hand for the investment, but instead must borrow the money at a 6 percent interest rate. Obviously, the expected rate of return must exceed the borrowing cost if the investment project is to be undertaken. Borrowing the money or using retained earnings presents the same problem to the firm — choose the alternative use of the funds that provides the greatest return.

Suppose our firm is contemplating the purchase of not just one machine for $10,000 but two or more of these machines, and suppose the rates of return from various investment alternatives are those presented in Table 4-1, where the machines are ranked in terms of expected rates of return. Let's also assume that the interest rate provides the best measure of opportunity costs for the firm. Depending on the interest rate, the firm will buy none, one, two, or three machines. If the interest rate is less than 6 percent, the firm will buy all three machines. If the interest rate is 9 percent, the firm would buy only the first machine. The higher the interest rate, the less investment the firm will undertake.

TABLE 4-1 *Investment Alternatives*	*Number of Machines*	*Total Amount of Investment*	*Expected Rate of Return on Last Machine*
	1	$10,000	10%
	2	20,000	8
	3	30,000	6

Let's specify investment to be dependent on the interest rate (r), and then let's use this investment function to determine output. The investment function is captured in the following equation:

$$I = I_0 - I_r r$$

where I_0 is the autonomous component of investment spending, and I_r measures the sensitivity of investment spending to the interest rate.

In the previous chapter, the national output level was determined by setting aggregate expenditures equal to the value of output produced. The only thing different here is the investment function.[2]

In the *AE* diagram, the components of aggregate expenditures are measured on the vertical axis and the quantity of output is measured along the horizontal axis. Because there is no explicit measurement of the interest rate on either axis, we must take the interest rate into account by including it as part of the intercept. (Any time a variable is not measured explicitly on the axis, it will affect the intercept.) In the investment equation noted earlier, $I_0 - I_r r$ is the intercept. With the interest rate as part of the intercept, the intercept changes each time the interest rate changes. Thus, to plot just one investment curve, we must choose just one interest rate. In Figure 4-1, for example, investment curve $I(r_1)$ is drawn by assuming that the interest rate is r. Then the aggregate expenditures curve is derived by vertically summing the investment, consumption, government purchases, and net exports curves. The expenditures curve $AE(r_1)$ in Figure 4-1 is drawn, given that the interest rate is r_1.

The national output level is determined by the intersection of the aggregate expenditures curve and the 45-degree line. In terms of Figure 4-1, the value Y_1 is the national output level when the interest rate is r_1. Because aggregate expenditures depend on a specific interest rate, so does the level of national output. What happens if the interest rate changes? At a lower interest rate, we expect more investment to be undertaken at each level of sales (or output and income). Graphically, the lower interest rate means the investment function shifts upward by the amount $-I_r$ times the change in the interest rate, $r_1 - r_2$, or by $-I_r(r_1 - r_2)$. The intercept at interest rate r_2 is $I_0 - I_r r_2$, which is larger than $I_0 - I_r r_1$.[3] The aggregate expenditures curve also shifts up, be-

---

2   It might be argued that the interest rate is also a determinant of consumption spending. For example, a consumer might undertake more borrowing, the lower interest rates are. From a technical point of view, it can be argued that the change in consumption spending due to an interest rate change is properly captured in the investment function. Consumption should measure current consumption. When a consumer durable is purchased, this good yields a stream of services beyond the current period. Thus, if consumption is to be measured correctly, it should include only the imputed consumption from durables. The remainder of the purchase price of a consumer durable could be considered investment. Interest rate changes, by influencing exchange rates, can also affect net exports. We assume, however, that the primary impact of interest rate changes is on investment. Changes in consumption or net exports are assumed to be zero in this chapter, although this assumption could be changed without difficulty.

3   Since r_1 is larger than r_2, the change ($r_2 - r_1$) is negative.

FIGURE 4-1 *Aggregate expenditures depend on interest rates. When the interest rate is* r_1, *the level of national output is* Y_1. *When the interest rate falls to* r_2, *the level of investment rises to* $I(r_2)$, *and the level of aggregate expenditures rises to* $AE(r_2)$. *As a result, the national output level rises, to* Y_2. *Tracing each level of output down to panel B, and connecting it with the appropriate interest rate yields combinations* a *and* b. *Connecting all combinations of interest rates and national output levels yields the IS curve.*

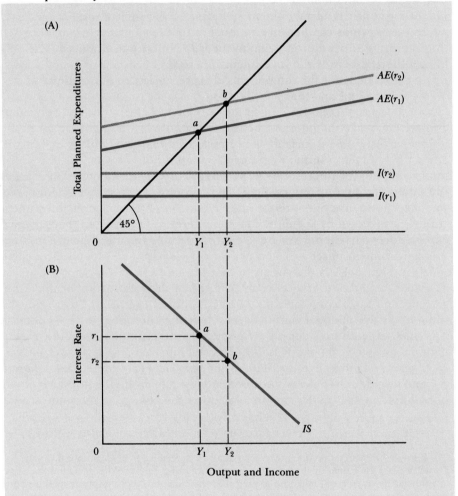

cause for each output level the quantity of aggregate expenditures is higher at the lower interest rate than it was at the higher interest rate. The new aggregate expenditures curve is identified as $AE(r_2) = C + I(r_2) + G + X$ in Figure 4-1 and the intersection between the new aggregate expenditures curve and the 45-degree line shows that the level of national output has increased to Y_2. In sum, a different interest rate results in a different level of national output.

A lower interest rate is typically associated with a higher equilibrium output level. Using the AE curves of panel A, we can trace out the various combinations of equilibrium output and interest rates in panel B. At r_1, the equilibrium output level Y_1 is plotted as point a in panel B. By assuming other interest rates, such as r_2, and then finding the corresponding output level, we can trace out in panel B a series of interest rate and output level combinations at which planned and actual aggregate expenditures are equal. The resulting locus of points is known as the **IS curve**.

The IS curve represents all combinations of interest rates and output levels at which equilibrium occurs in the commodity market. The curve slopes downward, reflecting the effect of interest rates on investment spending.

▼

Changes in the Position of the IS Curve

In deriving the IS curve, we varied the interest rate to see how equilibrium output would change. Then we plotted the interest rate and resulting output levels. Implicit in this procedure was the assumption that all other variables were held constant. What happens to the IS curve if one of the variables that was held constant now changes?

Shifts

Let us first consider an example in which autonomous spending changes. The decade of the 1990s began somewhat ominously with an economic downturn. But with a recovery, beginning in late 1991, optimism once again set in. This shift to a more bullish, or more optimistic view of the economy's performance gave rise to an autonomous investment increase—more spending on machinery and buildings to increase capacity in order to meet the public's desire for goods and services.

The IS curve can be used to represent this increase in autonomous investment. In panel A of Figure 4-2, the aggregate expenditures curve is labeled $AE(r_1)$ to indicate that this amount of aggregate expenditures occurs when the autonomous investment level is I_0 and the interest rate is r_1. The curve labelled $AE(r_2)$ represents the aggregate expenditures levels when autonomous investment is I_0 and the interest rate is r_2. The IS curve derived from these two AE curves is denoted by the autonomous investment level $IS(I_0)$. The interest rate is not included in the parentheses of the IS because the interest rate is not held constant along the IS curve.

In Chapter 3, we saw that when autonomous investment increased, the investment curve shifted up by the amount of the change in investment spending. In this chapter, note that a different investment curve exists for each possible interest rate. Hence the investment curve associated with *each interest*

FIGURE 4-2 *Effect on the IS curve of an increase in autonomous investment. The IS (I_0) curve is traced out under the assumption that autonomous investment is at its original level. The aggregate expenditures curve denoted with $I(I_0 r_1)$ indicates that total planned expenditures equal to Y_1 occur when the autonomous investment level is I_0 and the interest rate is r_1. When firms become more optimistic, the investment function shifts up and the aggregate expenditures curve (at interest rate r_1) shifts from the position denoted by AE (r_1) to the position AE' (r_1). At the new autonomous investment level and the original interest rate, national output has risen to Y_3. By plotting the combination (r_1, Y_3) in panel B, a point off the original IS curve is obtained. Now consider a lower interest rate. Another combination of interest rates and output level is obtained that is off the original IS curve. Plotting these new combinations of interest rates and output levels yields IS(I'_0).*

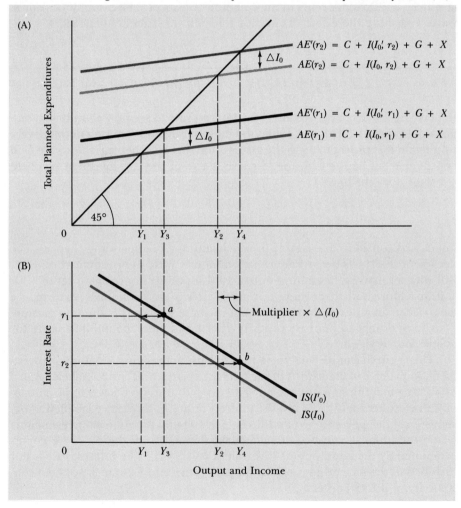

rate shifts up by the amount of the change in autonomous investment. For example, at interest rate r_1, the more bullish environment is represented by an upward shift of the investment curve that causes the aggregate expenditures curve also to shift up by the amount of the change in autonomous investment. Thus, in terms of Figure 4-2A, the aggregate expenditures curve (given interest rate r_1) shifts from the position denoted by $AE(r_1) = C + I(I_0,r_1) + G + X$ to the position $AE'(r_1) = C + I(I'_0,r_1) + G + X$. At the new autonomous investment level (I'_0) and the original interest rate (r_1), output has risen to Y_3. By plotting the combination (r_1,Y_3) in Figure 4-2B, we obtain a point that is off the original *IS* curve, point *a*.

At a lower interest rate, say r_2, the change in autonomous investment shifts both the investment curve and the aggregate expenditures curve associated with interest rate r_2 upward. Thus a new output level for the interest rate r_2 is generated. Again, plotting this new combination (r_2,Y_4), we have a point off the original *IS* curve, point *b*. By continuing to vary the interest rate and finding the corresponding equilibrium output levels, we can trace out a new *IS* curve, $IS(I'_0)$.

The Multiplier

One of the important concepts developed in Chapter 3 was the idea of a multiplier. Recall that a change in autonomous spending led to a larger or multiplied change in output. More precisely, the change in output due to a change in autonomous spending is equal to the multiplier times the change in autonomous spending. Figure 4-2 shows that at the interest rate r_1, output increases from Y_1 to Y_3 because autonomous spending increases. The horizontal distance between $IS(I_0)$ and $IS(I'_0)$, which is the change in output at each interest rate, is equal to the multiplier times the change in autonomous spending. The multiplier shows up as the horizontal distance between *IS* curves.

Slope Changes

In addition to the various autonomous variables, the marginal propensity to consume, c_y, the marginal propensity to import, X_y, and the sensitivity of investment to interest rates, I_r, were held constant in the derivation of the *IS* curve. If one of these changes, the slope of the *IS* curve changes.

Suppose that investment spending became less sensitive to interest rate changes. This change in businesses' reaction to interest rate changes is represented by a decrease in I_r. A decrease in I_r means that any given change in the interest rate causes a smaller change in investment spending and thus in aggregate expenditures after the change in I_r than before.[4] This means that the *IS* curve has become steeper.

4   A numerical example may be helpful. Suppose $I_0 = 100$ and the initial values of I_r and *r* are 50 and 0.1 respectively. If the value of I_r doubles to 100, the intercept of the investment function changes by 5 at an interest rate of 0.1. At an interest rate of 0.2, the doubling of I_r means that the investment function shifts by 10. Thus we find that the shift in the investment function due to an increase in I_r is greater at high interest rates than at low interest rates.

FIGURE 4-3   *The slope of the* AE *curve and the resulting* IS *curve. Changes in the* MPC *or the* MPI *also lead to slope changes for the* IS *curve. An increase in the* MPC *means that the* AE *curve becomes steeper, while an increase in the* MPI *means that the* AE *curve becomes flatter. A steeper* AE *curve translates into a flatter* IS *curve. You can see this with the two sets of* AE *curves, one flatter and one steeper, used to derive an* IS *curve. The flatter* AE *curves translate to a steeper* IS *curve, and vice versa.*

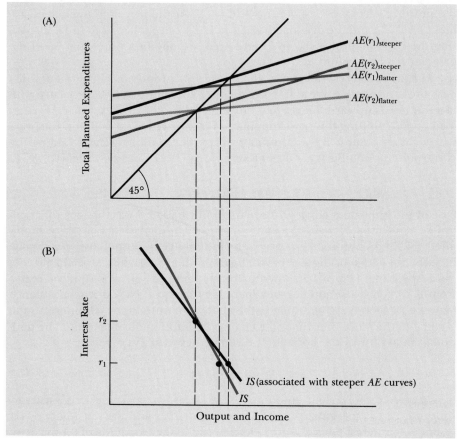

Changes in the *MPC* or the *MPI* also lead to slope changes for the *IS* curve. An increase in the *MPC* means that the *AE* curve becomes steeper, while an increase in the *MPI* means that the *AE* curve becomes flatter. A steeper *AE* curve translates into a flatter *IS* curve. You can see this in Figure 4-3, where two sets of *AE* curves, one flatter and one steeper, are used to derive an *IS* curve. The flatter *AE* curves translate to a steeper *IS* curve, and vice versa.

In summary, any change in the sensitivity of spending to interest rates or output causes a change in the slope of the *IS* curve. Any change in the autonomous variables, the *ceteris paribus* variables, causes a shift of the *IS* curve. These results are summarized in Table 4-2.

TABLE 4-2   *Changes in the IS Curve*

Variable	Change	Shift	Slope
Government spending	Increase	Outward	
	Decrease	Inward	
Taxes (lump sum)	Increase	Inward	
	Decrease	Outward	
Autonomous spending	Increase	Outward	
	Decrease	Inward	
Marginal propensity to consume (c_y)	Increase		Flatter
	Decrease		Steeper
Marginal propensity to import (X_y)	Increase		Steeper
	Decrease		Flatter
Interest sensitivity of investment (I_r)	Increase		Flatter
	Decrease		Steeper

▼

The Money Market

The *IS* curve represents all possible combinations of output and interest rate levels at which the commodity market is in equilibrium. For each interest rate, there is a unique equilibrium output level. Thus, if we want to know which output level is the equilibrium level, we must know the value of the interest rate. The interest rate is determined by the demand for and supply of money.

The term *money* is the name given to a medium of exchange; that is, an asset that people generally are willing to exchange for goods and services. The precise definition of *money* depends on what use of money is being measured. For example, in the United States one definition called *M1* is intended to be a measure of the use of money in transactions. Other definitions, such as *M2* and *M3,* are broader measures intended to include money used for purposes other than just transactions. Chapter 11 discusses the alternative measures of money in detail. For our purposes now, it is irrelevant which definition of money is used.

Demand for Money

It is important to keep in mind what is meant by the term "demand for money." When people demand money in the M1 sense, they want to hold money in the form of cash or transaction deposits. When people use money to buy goods and services, they are not holding (demanding) money. They are demanding the goods and services being purchased with the money.

Why do people hold money? The most obvious reason is that they plan to carry out transactions. If you plan to buy tickets to Saturday's concert today, you may keep enough money in your billfold to do so. Your plan to carry out a transaction causes you to demand money. Similarly, for the economy as a whole, the desire to buy goods and services is an important determinant of the demand for money. What determines the number of transactions that people plan to carry out? Primarily it is their incomes: the higher their incomes, the more transactions they will make. Thus, income is a primary determinant of the demand for money: the higher the income, the greater the quantity of money demanded.

The other primary determinant of money demand is the interest rate. The more interest you can earn on some alternative project or savings account, the less incentive you have to hold money. By holding money, you are forgoing the higher interest you could receive by using the money to purchase an alternative asset or savings account. The higher the interest rate, the lower the quantity of money demanded.

Figure 4-4 shows a money demand curve, a downward-sloping curve with the quantity of money measured on the horizontal axis and the interest rate measured on the vertical axis. The position of the demand for money curve depends on the level of output or income. If output increases from Y_1 to Y_2, the quantity of money demanded at each interest rate increases. Thus the demand for money curve shifts out, from $M^D(Y_1)$ to $M^D(Y_2)$ in Figure 4-4.

FIGURE 4-4   *The demand for money. The money demand curve* $M_2^D(Y_1)$ *drawn for output level* Y_1. *At lower interest rates, people are willing to hold more money, so the demand curve slopes downward. People demand more money at each interest rate if output increases—shifting the demand curve to* $M^D(Y_2)$.

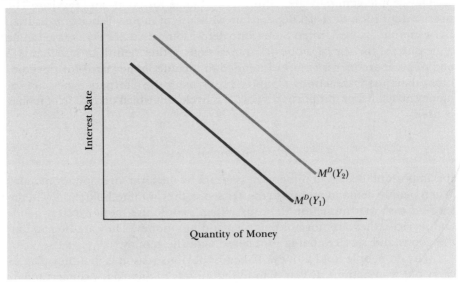

Deriving the LM Curve

To complete this introduction to the money market, we must specify the supply side. Assume for now that the central bank in the United States, the Federal Reserve (called the Fed), determines the quantity of money in the economy. The supply of money in this simplified case does not vary with the interest rate, so the money supply curve is vertical. It is written in equation form as simply the autonomous amount:

$$M^S = M_0$$

Equilibrium occurs in the money market when the quantity of money demanded is equal to the quantity supplied. In Figure 4-5A, the money supply and the money demand curves are drawn for output level Y_1. The intersection of these curves determines the market-clearing interest rate, r_1. If the interest rate is above r_1 — say, at r_2 — then the quantity of money demanded, point a, is less than the quantity supplied, point b. People want to hold less than the total

FIGURE 4-5   *The money market diagram and the LM curve. The money market is shown in panel A. The demand for money, M^D, depends on the level of national output. The higher the output level, the more money that is demanded. The money supply curve is vertical, representing a fixed money stock. The intersection between money demand and money supply yields the interest rate. Tracing the interest rate, say r_1, over to panel B and connecting it with the appropriate national output level, Y_1, yields point a, one point on the LM curve. Increasing the output level to Y_2 shifts the demand for money curve up and generates a higher interest rate, r_2. This new combination of r_2 and Y_2 is point b. Connecting points a and b yields the LM curve.*

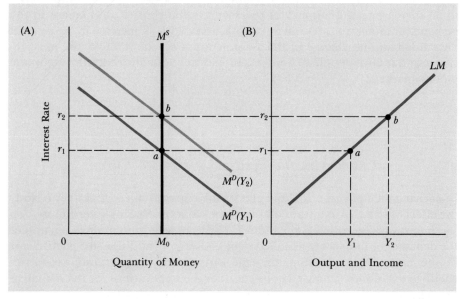

available money supply, so they try to get rid of their excess money balances — they spend the money and try to lend it to others. The result is that the interest rate begins to fall. As it does, more people are willing to hold higher money balances. The interest rate continues to fall until people are willing to hold the existing supply of money. Conversely, if the interest rate is less than r_1, the quantity of money demanded exceeds the quantity available. Again, the interest rate changes to alleviate this situation. It rises until the quantity of money demanded equals the quantity supplied.

Interest rate r_1 is an equilibrium interest rate only as long as the output level is Y_1. If the output level is greater than Y_1, then the quantity of money demanded exceeds the quantity supplied at r_1. Figure 4-5A shows that the quantity of money demanded is greater at every interest rate when the output level is the higher level, Y_2, than when the output level is Y_1.

The larger output is, the more transactions people want to make and the greater their demand for money. Because the supply of money is fixed, the interest rate must rise, so some people reduce the amount of money they want to hold. Thus, when the demand for money is $M^D(Y_2)$ the equilibrium interest rate is r_2.

By varying the income level and deriving the interest rate that will induce people to hold exactly the available quantity of money, we can obtain an entire series of equilibrium interest rate–income combinations. Plotting these points as in Figure 4-5B traces out a curve known as the **LM curve**. The *LM* curve represents all possible combinations of interest rates and output levels at which the quantities of money demanded and money supplied are equal.

The *LM* curve in Figure 4-5B slopes upward. The reason is the effects of output and interest rates on the demand for money. An increase in output leads to an increase in the number of transactions and thus to an increase in the demand for money to carry out the transactions. With an increase in the amount demanded and no change in the amount supplied, the interest rate must increase and induce people to hold less money to re-establish equilibrium in the money market.

▼
Changes in the Position of the LM *Curve*

In deriving the *LM* curve, we hold everything else constant so that we can study the effect of changes in output on the money market-clearing interest rate. Autonomous variables such as the money supply and the autonomous portion of the demand for money are assumed to be constant. In addition, the coefficients in the money demand function — the output and interest rate sensitivity coefficients — do not change. Let us consider the implications for the *LM* curve of a change in these autonomous variables or coefficients.

Shifts

Let's consider a decrease of the stock of money first. A money supply decrease acts as an autonomous change in the money market, causing the *LM* curve to shift. The nominal money supply value M_1 in Figure 4·6 represents the initial value of the quantity of money. The corresponding *LM* curve is labeled $LM(M_1)$. The new nominal money supply is labeled M_2. Note in Figure 4·6A that with the original quantity of money, the market-clearing interest rate is r_1 at output level Y_1. However, at this interest rate and with the lower money supply, the money market is characterized by an excess demand of a–b. As a result, the opportunity cost of holding money rises to r_3. The higher interest rate induces individuals to hold less money, shown as a movement from b to c. When we plot the interest rate–output level combination (r_3, Y_1) on the *LM* diagram, we obtain a point d above the original *LM* curve.

Now consider what happens at the higher national output level Y_2. With the smaller stock of money available, the interest rate r_2 no longer clears the money market. Instead, at output level Y_2, a higher interest rate r_4, is necessary to clear the market. When we plot this interest rate and output combination

FIGURE 4·6   *The effect of a decrease in the nominal money supply on the* LM *curve. A reduced stock of money leads to an upward or inward shift of the* LM *curve. The lower stock of money is shown as the move from* M_1 *to* M_2*. The interest rate is thus higher at each output level after the money stock is reduced; for example,* r_3 *instead of* r_1*. Tracing the resulting interest rate over to panel B and connecting with the appropriate output level yields a new* LM *curve. For instance, instead of interest rate* r_1 *at output level* Y_1*, the interest rate rises to* r_3 *after the money stock is reduced. The combination* r_3 *and* Y_1 *is point d. Before the money stock reduction, the combination would have been point f. Thus, the* LM *curve has shifted upward.*

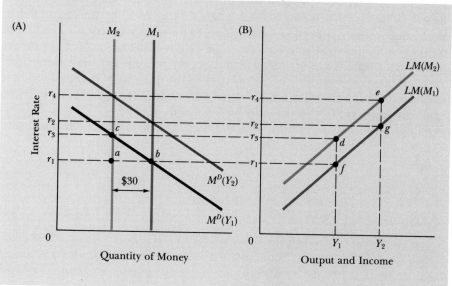

(r_4, Y_2), we discover still another point, e, off the original LM curve. If we plot other output levels and interest rate combinations, we can trace out the curve $LM(M_2)$. Thus a decrease in the money supply is represented as an upward or leftward shift of the LM curve. Conversely, an increased money supply shifts the LM curve down or to the right.

A change in an autonomous variable will cause the LM curve to shift. Now consider how a change in the slope of the demand for money affects the LM curve.

Slope Changes

The sensitivity of the demand for money to changes in the interest rate could change as a result of some event that alters people's behavior. For instance, the introduction of automatic teller machines (ATMs) allowed people to acquire money more easily and rapidly and to take more advantage of interest rate earnings. As a result, the demand for money became more sensitive to interest rate levels. How would such a change be shown with the LM curve? An increase in the interest sensitivity of money demand means that a given change in the interest rate leads to a greater change in the quantity of money demanded than previously. A greater interest rate sensitivity of money demand is represented as a flatter demand for money curve, as shown in Figure 4-7, panel A, where L_r^1 represents the initial value of the coefficient and L_r^2 denotes the new value of the coefficient.

The flatter money demand curve translates into a flatter LM curve. Consider the effect of a given change in the interest rate for different interest rate sensitivity coefficients. At the initial value of the coefficient L_r^1, a drop in the interest rate from r_1 to r_2 requires a drop in the output level from Y_3 to Y_2 if money market equilibrium is to be established. Now, consider the identical drop in the interest rate with the higher interest rate sensitivity coefficient L_r^2. The decline in the interest rate leads to a greater rise in the quantity of money demanded with L_r^2 than with L_r^1. This means that output must fall more (from Y_3 to Y_1) than was previously necessary to keep the quantity of money demanded equal to the quantity supplied. In other words, the LM curve becomes flatter when the demand for money curve becomes flatter.

Table 4-3 summarizes the effects on the LM curve that come from autonomous changes in either the demand for or supply of money.

▼

Equilibrium in the Commodity and Money Markets: IS and LM

Those combinations of interest rates and output levels that lie on the IS curve satisfy the conditions for commodity market equilibrium. Similarly, those on the LM curve satisfy the conditions for money market equilibrium. For both markets to be in equilibrium simultaneously, the same interest rate and out-

FIGURE 4-7   *The effect of a flatter demand for money curve on the* LM *curve. If the demand for money becomes more interest elastic — the demand for money curve becomes flatter — the* LM *curve also becomes flatter. In panel A, the flatter demand for money curve means that a given interest rate reduction, from* r_1 *to* r_2, *generates a larger increase in the quantity of money demanded. Only if output declines does the demand for money shift in and intersect the money supply curve at* r_2. *Clearly, the amount of the shift required for the flatter demand for money curve is larger than for the steeper curve. This means that a smaller level of output* Y_2 *combines with interest rate* r_2 *to establish equilibrium for the steeper demand for money curve than is the case for the smaller demand for money curve, where output must fall to* Y_1.

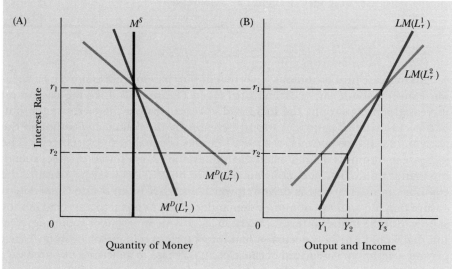

put level must occur in both the commodity and money markets. In order to determine this one interest rate and output level combination, we superimpose the *IS* and *LM* curves on one diagram, shown in Figure 4-8. The intersection of these two curves, denoted as point *a*, satisfies the condition for simultaneous equilibrium. Therefore, the equilibrium interest rate is r_1 and the corresponding output level is Y_1, *ceteris paribus*.

A shift in either the *IS* or *LM* curve causes the equilibrium interest rate and output levels to change. Suppose, for example, that the nominal money supply is increased. This change is represented by an outward shift of the *LM* curve, from LM_1 to LM_2 in Figure 4-9A. The result is that equilibrium is reestablished at a lower interest rate, r_2, and a higher output level, Y_2. The new, lower equilibrium interest rate comes about because more money is available. The public must be willing to hold or demand this additional money. And, for this to occur, the cost of holding money, as measured by the interest rate, must decrease. As the interest rate falls, investment spending increases and the increased spending generates greater aggregate expenditures and thus more output and income.

TABLE 4-3   *Changes in the* LM *Curve*

Variable	Change	Shift	Slope
Money supply	Increase	Outward	
	Decrease	Inward	
Autonomous money demand	Increase	Inward	
	Decrease	Outward	
Interest sensitivity of money demand	Increase		Flatter
	Decrease		Steeper
Income sensitivity of money demand	Increase		Steeper
	Decrease		Flatter

An increase in autonomous government purchases is represented by a rightward shift of the *IS* curve, from IS_1 to IS_2 in Figure 4-9B. Like the case of an increased money supply, the increased government purchases cause the output level to rise. In panel B, output increases by the distance *af,* although the horizontal distance between the two *IS* curves is equal to the distance *ac.* The increase in output is smaller when the money market is allowed to affect spending than it would be if the money market did not affect spending, because the equilibrium interest rate is driven upward. A higher interest rate is needed to ensure that the quantity of money demanded remains equal to the fixed money supply. But the higher interest rate reduces private investment spending, a result that would not have occurred had interest rates remained constant. When private investment is reduced because of an increase in government purchases, private spending is said to have been **crowded out**.

Alternative Shapes of the IS and LM Curves

Suppose the demand for money depended only on the output or income level, not the interest rate. A demand for money function that does not depend on the interest rate is drawn as a vertical line at a given income or output level in the money market diagram. Such a money demand function translates into a vertical *LM* curve.[5]

An increase in the money supply is reflected as a rightward shift of the vertical *LM* curve, from LM_1 to LM_2 in Figure 4-10. The shift of the *LM* curve leads to an increase in income, the magnitude of which is determined solely by the

5   When both the money demand and money supply curves are vertical, it is difficult to derive the *LM* curve graphically. However, we can reason as follows: As long as the price level is fixed, the money market may not be in equilibrium. Yet all money in existence must be held by someone. People who do not want all the money they hold try to get rid of the excess. The only way they can do so is by spending it. This drives up income, which shifts the vertical money demand curve to the right until it coincides with the vertical money supply curve. When the two curves coincide, the resulting level of income is compatible with any interest rate. Thus, the *LM* curve is vertical as well.

FIGURE 4-8   *Commodity and money market equilibrium. The* IS *curve represents all combinations of interest rates and output levels at which planned aggregate expenditures are equal to total output. The* LM *curve represents all combinations of interest rates and output levels at which money demand is equal to money supply. Only at one combination of interest rates and output levels can both markets be said to be in equilibrium. That combination is point* a, *the intersection between the* IS *and* LM *curves.*

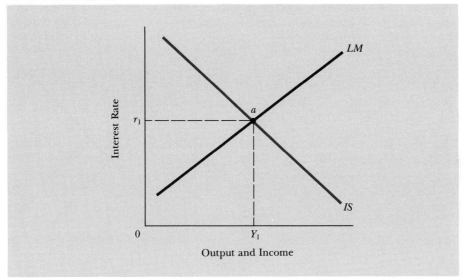

amount of the increase in the money supply. The quantities of money demanded and supplied are equalized only if income rises enough to induce people to hold the new money.

An increase in autonomous spending has no effect on income when the *LM* curve is vertical. Figure 4-11 shows that an increase in government purchases shifts the *IS* curve from IS_1 to IS_2, increasing the interest rate but leaving output unchanged. An increase in government purchases initially results in a greater output level, but this throws the money market into a state of excess demand. If the quantity of money demanded depends on the interest rate, then increases in the interest rate tend to decrease the quantity of money demanded. Without the interest rate effect on the demand for money, output must do all the work; it must fall all the way back to its original level if the demand for and supply of money are to be equal. The reason output falls is that the higher interest rate reduces investment. As investment declines, output declines. The interest rate rises until the new government purchases are offset completely by a decline in private investment. In other words, *complete crowding out* occurs.

Now let's consider the effect of a money demand function that is horizontal. The horizontal money demand function translates into a horizontal *LM*

FIGURE 4-9   *Monetary and fiscal policy in the IS–LM model. An expansionary monetary policy is illustrated as a rightward shift of the* LM *curve from* LM₁ *to* LM₂ *in panel A. The increase in money leads to a reduction in the interest rate, which in turn induces more investment and a larger level of output. An expansionary fiscal policy is represented by a rightward shift of the* IS *curve, from* IS₁ *to* IS₂ *in panel B. The higher expenditures mean a greater level of national output. The higher expenditures also mean a greater demand for money and thus a higher interest rate. The higher interest rate leads to a smaller increase in national output, distance* af, *than would have occurred if there had been no money market effects. Without the money market effects, the expansion would have been distance* ac.

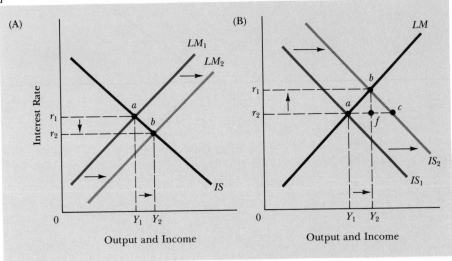

curve. Then, an increase in the money supply is simply an extension of the horizontal *LM* curve, shown as *LM*(*M₁*) to *LM*(*M₂*) in Figure 4-12. In the case of a horizontal *LM* curve, changes in the money supply have no effect on the output level. Conversely, changes in autonomous spending or shifts of the *IS* curve have a full multiplier effect on output—there is no crowding out. You can see in Figure 4-12 that output increases from *Y₁* to *Y₂*, the full multiplier effect of an increase in autonomous spending.

Monetary and Fiscal Policy

What we have been discussing in the past few paragraphs is monetary and fiscal policy. The *IS–LM* framework provides a convenient way to discuss monetary and fiscal policy. **Monetary policy** is the control of the money supply to affect output and employment; **fiscal policy** is the control of government purchases and net taxes to affect output and employment. The *IS–LM* framework puts monetary and fiscal policy in different curves. Monetary policy is illustrated with the *LM* curve. Fiscal policy is illustrated with the *IS* curve.

FIGURE 4-10   *The vertical LM curve. When the demand for money depends only on the level of output, the LM curve is vertical. An increase in the money supply, in this case, leads directly and fully to an increase in national output.*

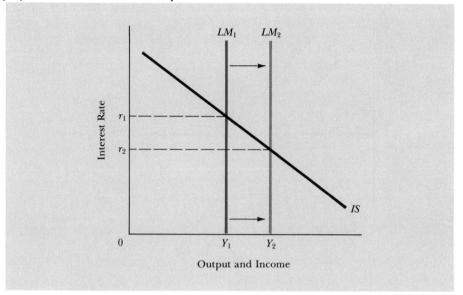

FIGURE 4-11   *An increase in government purchases with a vertical LM curve. A shift of the IS curve from IS_1 to IS_2, increases the interest rate but leaves output unchanged. Autonomous expenditure changes cannot influence the output level in this case, because the money demand does not depend on the interest rate.*

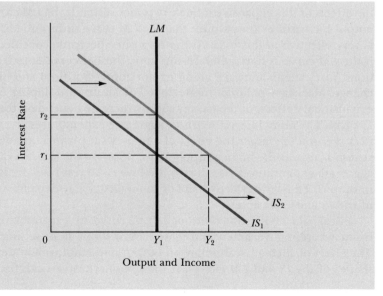

FIGURE 4-12   *The* LM *curve when the demand for money is horizontal. A horizontal demand for money curve translates into a horizontal* LM *curve. In this case, a change in the money supply has no effect on the* LM *curve. So monetary policy has no effect on the national output level.*

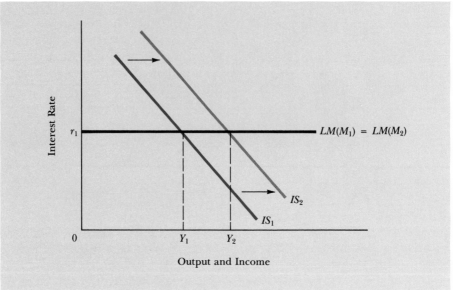

Let's consider the effects on output according to the *IS–LM* framework when monetary policy is expansive. An expansive monetary policy is represented as an increase in the money supply. An increase in the money supply means that the *LM* curve shifts out. Depending on the shapes of the *IS* and *LM* curves, the effects of this expansive monetary policy differ. If the *LM* curve is vertical, output increases by the amount that the *LM* curve shifts out. Monetary policy is very effective in this case. At the opposite spectrum, consider what occurs if the *LM* curve is horizontal. In this case, the *LM* curve doesn't change positions (just extends outward along its horizontal position) and output doesn't change. Monetary policy is ineffective. For an upward-sloping *LM* curve, the expansionary effects of the money supply increase depend on the shape of the *IS* curve. The more interest sensitive aggregate expenditures are, the flatter the *IS* curve, and the larger the effect of a money supply increase on output. The reason is that as the money supply rises, it lowers the interest rate. The more aggregate expenditures rise due to the lower interest rate, the larger the rise in output. Thus, the effectiveness of monetary policy depends on the shapes of the *IS* and *LM* curves.

Fiscal policy is illustrated through the *IS* curve. An expansionary fiscal policy is one wherein government purchases rise without an offsetting rise in taxes. The effect of such a fiscal policy on output and employment depends on the shapes of the *IS* and *LM* curves. If the *LM* curve is vertical, fiscal policy has no effect on output. The outward shift of the *IS* curve simply drives the interest rate up; the rising interest rate leads to lower investment spending. If the *LM* curve is horizontal, then there is no crowding out; fiscal policy has the full multiplier effect. Output rises by the amount that the *IS* curve shifts outward. With an upward-sloping *LM* curve, the amount by which output rises under an expansionary fiscal policy depends on the steepness of the *LM* curve. The steeper the curve, the less expansionary is the fiscal policy. The less sensitive the demand for money is to interest rates, the steeper the *LM* curve.

▼
IS, LM, *and the Foreign Sector*

As explained, net exports affect aggregate expenditures. The foreign sector may also affect the domestic economy through interest rates and the money market as well. Although this is discussed in detail in Chapter 11, a preview of the international sector's influence on the money supply and monetary policy is useful here. This section shows how the balance of payments can be introduced into the *IS–LM* framework.

The balance of payments consists of the sum of the current and capital accounts. The *BOP* must balance. When the current account is in deficit (more goods and services are being bought from foreigners than are being sold to foreigners), the capital account must be in surplus (more financial capital flows in than flows out). For instance, in 1989 the U.S. current account had a deficit of \$110 million, which meant that the capital account had a surplus of approximately \$110 million. The capital account surplus meant that bank deposits, U.S. stocks, bonds, and loans were being bought by foreigners. In short, money was flowing into the United States.

The balance of payments is specified to be

$$BOP = X(Y) + KA(r/r^f)$$

which states that the balance of payments is the sum of net exports, *X,* and the capital account, *KA.* Net exports depend on domestic income, *Y,* while the capital account depends on the value of domestic interest rates, *r,* relative to interest rates in the rest of the world, r^f.

By tracing out domestic interest rate and output level combinations at which the *BOP* will be in balance, as in Figure 4-13, we can derive a **BOP curve.** Everywhere along the *BOP* curve, the *BOP* is in balance. Points off the *BOP* curve represent interest rate and output combinations at which the *BOP* would not balance, something that cannot occur for any length of time. Let's begin at output level Y_1 and interest rate r_1 and assume the *BOP* is in balance. Now suppose output rises to Y_2. Imports will rise and the current account will be in deficit. Financial capital, or what we'll just call *money,* must flow into the domestic

FIGURE 4-13   *The* BOP *curve. On a diagram with the interest rate on the vertical axis and output on the horizontal axis, we can trace out domestic interest rate and output level combinations at which the* BOP *is in balance. The greater the domestic output level, the more imports are bought and the greater is the current account deficit. To attract foreign capital to offset this outflow of domestic spending, the domestic interest rate must rise relative to the interest rate prevailing in the rest of the world. Thus, the* BOP *curve slopes upward. However, if the interest rate differential between the domestic economy and the rest of the world is immediately offset by flows of money, then* $r_1 = r^f$. *This means that the balance of payments is in balance at the world interest rate level; the* BOP *curve is a horizontal line at the world interest rate level.*

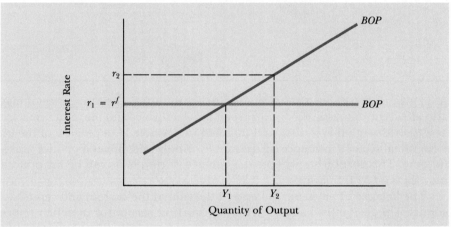

economy so that the capital account surplus offsets the current account deficit. If the domestic interest rate must rise relative to the world interest rate to attract foreign funds or capital, then the *BOP* curve requires a higher interest rate r_2 to be in balance at Y_2. In this case, the *BOP* curve slopes upward. However, if an interest rate differential between the domestic economy and the rest of the world, no matter how small the differential is, immediately attracts sufficient flows of money to offset the current account deficit, then $r = r^f$. This means that the balance of payments must be in balance at the world interest rate level and so the *BOP* curve is a horizontal line at the world interest rate level.

Now let's combine the *IS, LM,* and *BOP* curves. We'll use the upward-sloping *BOP* curve for illustration. Notice in Figure 4-14 that the *IS, LM,* and *BOP* curves all intersect at point *a.* Now suppose that an autonomous increase in spending occurs. The first effect of the spending increase is an outward shift of the *IS* curve, from *IS to IS'.* The new intersection between the *IS* and *LM* curves, at point *b,* is above the *BOP* curve. This means that the interest rate is too high for the *BOP* to be in balance. The high interest rate attracts foreign money. The result of the increase in foreign money is an increase in the domestic supply of money in the domestic economy. As a result of the money supply increase, the *LM* curve shifts out and must continue to shift until it intersects the *IS′* and *BOP* curves at point *c*.[6] You can see that when we consider the rest of the world in our *IS* and *LM* framework, we get different results from when we consider only the *IS* and *LM* curves. Instead of a change in an autonomous variable affecting output and interest rates just through the *IS* and *LM* curves, with the rest of the world considered, the autonomous change influences the money supply through the balance of payments as well. This means that the effect of an autonomous spending change when the impact of the rest of the world on the money supply is considered is different from when just the *IS* and *LM* curves are considered. In the example just discussed, output rises from

FIGURE 4-14   IS, LM, *and* BOP *curves. The* IS, LM, *and* BOP *curves all intersect at point* a. *Now suppose that an autonomous increase in spending occurs. The first effect of the spending increase is an outward shift of the* IS *curve, from* IS *to* IS′*. The new intersection between the* IS *and* LM *curves, at point* b, *is above the* BOP *curve. This means that the interest rate is too high for the* BOP *to be in balance. The high interest rate attracts foreign money. The result of the increase in foreign money is an increase in the domestic money supply. The* LM *curve shifts out to* LM(M₁) *from* LM(M₀)*. The* LM *curve must continue to shift until it intersects the* IS′ *and* BOP *curves at point* c*. Output rises from* Y₁ *to* Y₃ *due to the* BOP *curve, whereas without the* BOP *curve, the increase was from* Y₁ *to* Y₂*. This means that when the impact of the rest of the world on the money supply is considered, the effect of an autonomous spending change is different from when just the* IS *and* LM *curves are considered.*

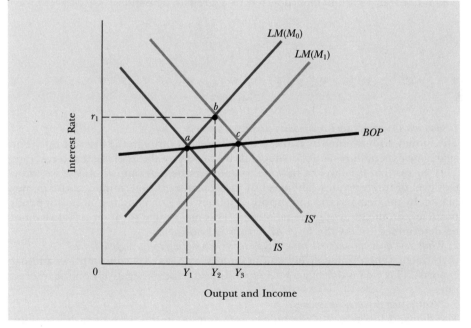

6   The assumption of fixed exchange rates is made here. The assumption is relaxed in Chapter 10 after having discussed exchange rates and exchange rate systems.

Y_1 to Y_3 due to foreign influences on the money supply, whereas it would have risen only from Y_1 to Y_2 had the *BOP* not been considered. The chapters that follow examine these rest of the world influences in much more detail.

▼   ▼   ▼   ▼   ▼   ▼   ▼   ▼   ▼   ▼   ▼
Conclusions

This chapter extends the *AE* model to include money and interest rates. A simple diagram, *IS–LM,* illustrates how the quantity of money and the demand for money influence aggregate expenditures and the determination of output and thus employment levels. The interest rate tends to reduce the size of the multiplier because when it rises, aggregate expenditures decline. The shapes of the expenditure functions and the money demand function define the shapes of the *IS* and *LM* curves. The effects of monetary policy or fiscal policy changes depend on the shapes of the *IS* and *LM* curves. The rest of the world can influence the domestic economy through the balance of payments. The next chapter relaxes the assumption of a fixed price level and derives the aggregate demand curve using the *IS–LM* framework. Because the only change is the fixed price, everything discussed regarding the *IS–LM* framework is incorporated in aggregate demand.

▼   ▼   ▼   ▼   ▼   ▼   ▼   ▼   ▼   ▼   ▼
Summary

1. How do the money and commodity markets interact?
The money and commodity markets are connected through the interest rate. The aggregate expenditures function depends negatively on the level of the interest rate. This means that the level of national output can be determined only if we know the level of interest rates. The level of interest rates is determined in the money market by the demand for and supply of money. The demand for money depends positively on the level of national output. This means that the interest rate cannot be determined unless the level of output is known.

2. What role does the interest rate play in determining aggregate expenditures?
Investment depends negatively on the interest rate (as may consumption and net exports). This means that aggregate expenditures depend negatively on the interest rate.

3. What is the demand for money?
The demand for money is the holding of money—in the form of cash, checking accounts, or some types of savings accounts. Money is demanded to carry out transactions, to be ready for emergencies, and to serve as a form in which to speculate on future prices of assets. The demand for money depends positively on the level of national output and negatively on the interest rate.

4. What effects do changes in the money supply have on aggregate expenditures?
Increases in the stock of money, *ceteris paribus,* reduce the interest rate. Lower interest rates lead to increased investment spending, so aggregate expenditures rise.
5. What is the IS *curve?*
The *IS* curve is the locus of all combinations of output and interest rates at which aggregate expenditures and national output are equal—equilibrium in the commodity market.
6. What is the LM *curve?*
The *LM* curve is the locus of all combinations of output and interest rates at which the quantity of money demanded and the quantity of money supplied are equal—equilibrium in the money market.
7. What role does the foreign sector play in the IS–LM *analysis?*
The foreign sector is shown in the aggregate expenditures (and thus the *IS* curve) with net exports. In addition, the foreign sector influences the domestic money supply through the balance of payments. The *BOP, IS,* and *LM* curves must all intersect at the equilibrium levels of output and interest rates. Otherwise, the economy will adjust until the three curves do intersect.

▼
Key Terms

commodity or output market 84	crowded out 100
money market 84	monetary policy 102
IS curve 89	fiscal policy 102
LM curve 96	*BOP* curve 105

▼
Problems and Exercises

1. Why does the point of intersection between the *IS* and *LM* curves determine the equilibrium output level and interest rate?

2. Show and explain why the multiplier is larger when just the commodity market is considered than when both commodity and money markets are considered. Use the *IS–LM* diagram.

3. A great deal of media attention has been devoted to the idea of crowding out. It is often claimed that increased government purchases may not be expansionary. Evaluate this claim.

4. Some economists argue that the money demand function is misspecified. They assert that the demand for money should be a function of disposable, or after-tax, income and the interest rate.

   a.   What are the implications for the *LM* curve of such a money demand function?

   b.   Given the revised money demand function, determine the effects of an increase in taxes on the equilibrium values of Y and r.

c. How do your results in part b of this exercise compare with the corresponding results for the case in which the money demand function does not depend on taxes?

5. The Fed recently cut back sharply on monetary growth. What does the *IS–LM* model predict will happen to the economy as a result of this policy? Using the *Economic Report of the President,* collect output, interest rate, and investment data and see if the predictions are consistent with the data.

6. Increases in the level of government purchases shift the *IS* curve to the right. Increases in the money supply shift the *LM* curve to the right. Suppose that all government purchases are paid for with money supply increases. Will the result differ from a situation in which the government purchases were paid for with taxes? Explain.

7. What could lead to a perfectly horizontal *IS* curve? What could lead to a perfectly horizontal *LM* curve? What could cause the *IS* curve to be vertical? What could cause the *LM* curve to be vertical?

8. Give a clear explanation for the sign of the slopes of the *IS* and *LM* curves.

9. Suppose each time that the interest rate rose, the Fed increased the money supply. What would occur? What would be the result of an increase in government purchases? What would this mean for the shapes of the *IS* and *LM* curves?

10. Suppose from a point of equilibrium between the *IS, LM,* and *BOP* curves, government purchases rise. What will occur?

Chapter 5

Aggregate Demand

What to Expect

The 1960s have been described as the halcyon days of the U.S. economy. The word *halcyon,* which means calm, peaceful, affluent, prosperous, does seem to describe the public's attitude toward the behavior of the economy in those days. It also adequately describes the attitude of most economists. Armed with the *IS–LM* model, economists believed they understood or controlled the economy so well that they could fine-tune it. Some economists went so far as to declare the business cycle dead.

The clearest example of this attitude was the tax cut that took place in the early 1960s. Proposed in 1962, the tax cut was finally implemented in 1964. And from 1964 to 1966 the economy boomed. Then U.S. involvement in the Vietnam War escalated, and government expenditures increased as well. U.S. inflation rose. Attempts to slow the rate of inflation led to the 1970–1971 recession. This was followed by another expansion, then another recession, another expansion, and so on, as the U.S. economy rode a roller coaster. Clearly, the business cycle was far from dead.

These experiences raised serious questions about the *IS–LM* model and its implications for the understanding and use of monetary and fiscal policy.

Economists had to be able to analyze price changes as well as output changes and thus needed a more complete framework of macroeconomic analysis than the *IS–LM* model. The tools they looked to were those used by economists to analyze many other issues: demand and supply. So macroeconomists extended the *IS–LM* model to the *AD–AS* model in the late 1970s. This chapter develops the *AD* part of the *AD–AS* model. The chapter is primarily analytical—carrying the reader through a step-by-step derivation of aggregate demand. The following questions are considered:

1. What is the relationship between aggregate expenditures and aggregate demand?

2. What is the relationship between IS–LM *and aggregate demand?*

3. What is the difference between real and nominal values?

4. What is the relationship between the slope of the IS *or* LM *curve and the slope of the* AD *curve?*

5. How do multiplier values change as we move from aggregate expenditures to IS–LM *to aggregate demand?*

▼
Real Versus Nominal Values

Once we relax the assumption of a fixed price level, we must clearly distinguish between nominal and real values of variables. Real values are the ones on which people base decisions. Simply because your income rises from $20,000 per year to $22,000 per year doesn't mean that your standard of living has risen or that you can buy more goods and services. If the general price level rose from 1.00 to 1.15 during the year, the actual amount of goods and services you can buy has decreased: your income rose 10 percent, but the price level rose 15 percent. So the purchasing power of your income fell. The **real value** of a variable is the nominal value deflated by the price level relative to some base year. The real values of the $20,000 and $22,000 income levels are $20,000/1.00 (or $20,000) and $22,000/1.15 (or $19,130), respectively.

The IS Curve

Nominal values may sometimes be important. If your sole desire in life were to be a millionaire, you could have achieved that goal more easily in 1990 than in 1982—everything else being the same—simply because the price level had risen by 31 percent between 1982 and 1990. And you might have been happier with your $1 million in 1990 than your $800,000 in 1982, even though you could have bought more goods and services with the $800,000 in 1982. For most consumers, however, it is their purchasing power, or real income, that matters, not their nominal income. We assume that the amount households plan to spend depends on their real disposable income, real wealth, and real values of other variables noted in the previous chapter.

The term *real investment* refers to the acquisition of new equipment or buildings, while *nominal investment* refers to the dollars spent in acquiring the equipment or buildings. Managers make their investment decisions in real terms. They decide to purchase a building and do not (typically) purchase only two-thirds of the building when prices rise by 33 percent. We assume that real investment spending depends on real output and the real values of the variables noted in the previous chapter, including the interest rate.

The term **real interest rate** refers to the *nominal* interest rate minus the inflation rate. The interest rate you hear quoted in news reports, listed in the newspapers and magazines, or quoted by a commercial bank for its loans, is a nominal interest rate. It rises when the inflation rate rises and falls when the inflation rate falls. For instance, on January 22, 1991, the interest rate on one-year Treasury bills was 7.47 percent. This is a nominal interest rate. If you bought a Treasury bill on January 22, 1991, for $100,000, you would receive $7,470 in interest on January 22, 1992. Would that $7,470, in addition to your original $100,000, let you buy more goods and services on January 22, 1992 than you could buy for $100,000 on January 22, 1991? If it did, then the real interest rate was positive. Inflation was running 5 percent per year as of January 22, 1991. If inflation remained at 5 percent until January 22, 1992, this means that the real interest rate was 2.47 percent: $7.47 - 5 = 2.47$. Your purchasing power increased by 2.47 percent.[1]

The sum of government purchases is interpreted in real terms. The government decides to build a bridge, a bomb, a Patriot missile, or a park with the intention of acquiring the good, not the nominal value of the good. We also specify that taxes depend on real income. This is not a totally realistic specification, for many taxes depend on the nominal value of the taxable base. Property taxes depend on the nominal value of the property, sales taxes on the nominal value of purchases, and so on. Before 1985, federal income taxes depended on nominal incomes. During the late 1970s, when inflation was running in the double digits, the public became very unhappy about paying ever higher taxes on higher nominal (but not higher real) incomes. This so-called bracket creep meant that the government was increasing taxes automatically, without a vote or without a decided policy. The public reaction caused Congress to index the federal income tax in 1985. From then on, the tax brackets

---

1   The real interest rate is defined as the difference between the nominal interest rate and the inflation rate. The inflation rate is the percentage change in the price level that occurs over some period of time. Since with *IS–LM* and *AD* we are discussing the price level, not the rate of inflation, the distinction between nominal and real interest rates is not analytically important. However, when we discuss inflation, then we are concerned with the real interest rate.

and personal exemptions have increased by the amount of the price level increase, so that people do not pay higher taxes unless their real incomes rise.

Net exports are defined in real terms. However, with net exports we are dealing with more than one price level; we are comparing price level changes in the domestic economy to price level changes in foreign economies. If domestic prices rise while foreign prices and the exchange rate remain constant, domestic goods become more expensive relative to foreign goods. Foreign households and businesses therefore buy relatively fewer domestic goods. When the price of domestic goods increases in relation to the price of foreign goods, net exports fall. When the price of domestic goods falls in relation to the price of foreign goods, net exports rise.

The *IS* curve represents combinations of real output and real interest rates at which planned aggregate expenditures equal national output. If a price level change alters the real value of autonomous spending, the *IS* curve shifts. For instance, if a price level increase reduces real wealth, then autonomous consumption decreases and the *AE* and *IS* curves shift down. Similarly, if a price level increase reduces net exports, then the *AE* and *IS* curves shift down. For each price level, there is a unique *IS* curve, as shown in Figure 5-1.

The LM *Curve*

The amount of money people hold depends on the price level. When the U.S. price level rises, the purchasing power of each unit of currency, each dollar, falls. This means that buying each quantity of goods and services requires more dollars. After a doubling of the price level, a family that once used $100 to pay for groceries now needs $200 to buy the same amount of groceries. Thus, the demand for money is defined in real terms. The family needs $100 in real money terms to buy these groceries. Recall our assumption that the Federal Reserve (Fed) determines the quantity of money supplied. It may, and most likely does, attempt to alter the money supply so as to set the real supply of money at desired levels. However, the Fed must base its decisions on the nominal supply because this is all the Fed directly controls. The real supply of money is defined as the nominal money supply divided by the price level, M^s/P, where the nominal money supply, M^s, is controlled by the Fed and the price level, P, is determined by the demand for and supply of goods and services.

Now let's consider the effect these modifications have on the *LM* curve. Consider the money market diagram in Figure 5-2A. To draw a real money demand curve, we must assume a real output level. Initially, let's assume the output level is Y_1, so that the relevant real money demand curve is $M^D(Y_1)$. Next we must draw the money supply line. But here the assumption of a varying price level complicates matters. We must assume a particular price level to draw the real money supply line. If the price level is P_1, then the real money supply is M_0/P_1. The quantities of money demanded, $M^D(Y_1)$, and supplied, M_0/P_1, are equal when the interest rate is r_1 and output is Y_1, as shown in Figure 5-2A. Other combina-

FIGURE 5-1 *The IS curve and the price level. The IS curve represents combinations of real output and real interest rates at which planned aggregate expenditures equal national output. If a price level change alters the real value of autonomous spending, the IS curve shifts. For instance, if a price level increase reduces real wealth, then autonomous consumption decreases and the AE and IS curves shift down. Similarly, if a price-level increase reduces net exports, then the AE and IS curves shift down. For each price level, there is a unique IS curve.*

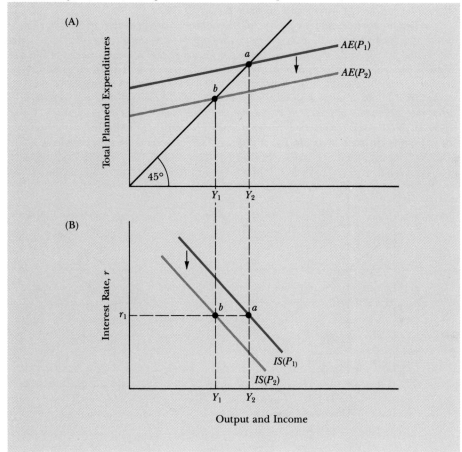

tions of interest rates and output levels at P_1 trace out the *LM* curve as explained earlier.

What happens when the price level changes? As long as the money supply is fixed at M_0, the real money supply declines from M_0/P_1 to M_0/P_2 as the price level rises from P_1 to P_2. In terms of Figure 5-2A, the real money supply curve shifts to the left. To derive the *LM* curve for this new, higher price level, assume the output level remains at Y_1. When the output level is Y_1 and the price level P_1, the money market clears at the interest rate r_1. However, at interest

FIGURE 5-2   *The LM curve and the price level. In order to draw a real money demand curve,
we must assume a real output level. Initially, let's assume that the output level is* Y_1 *so that the
relevant real money demand curve is* $M^D(Y_1)$. *Next, we must assume a particular price level in
order to draw the real money supply line. If the price level is* P_1, *then the real money supply is* M_0/P_1.
The quantities of money demanded, $M^D(Y_1)$, *and supplied,* M_0/P_2, *are equal when the interest rate
is* r_1 *and output is* Y_1, *as shown in panel A. Other combinations of interest rates and output levels
at* P_1 *trace out the LM curve shown in panel B.*

As long as the money supply is fixed at M_0, *the real money supply declines from* M_0/P_1 *to* M_0/P_2
as the price level rises from P_1 *to* P_2: *the real money supply curve shifts to the left. At the interest
rate* r_1 *and price level* P_2, *the real money supply is smaller so that the money market is in a state
of excess demand, raising the equilibrium interest rate. The money market now clears at* r_2. *When
we plot* r_2 *and* Y_1 *in panel B, we find that this combination is not a point on the original LM
curve* $LM(P_1)$. *And, if we examine other output levels and the corresponding market-clearing interest rates determined at price level* P_2, *we find that these combinations are not on the LM curve
either. In fact, the new combinations trace out a new LM curve. The LM curve for the price level*
P_2 *is presented in panel B as* $LM(P_2)$. *A different LM curve exists for each price level.*

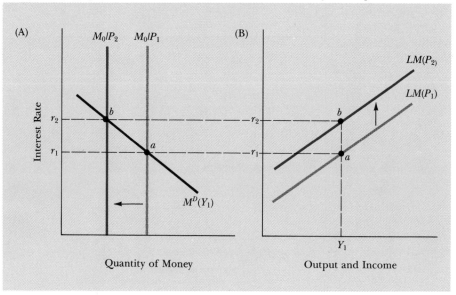

rate r_1 and price level P_2, the real money supply is smaller, so the money market is in a state of excess demand. The excess demand diminishes as the
equilibrium interest rate rises. The money market clears at r_2. When we plot
r_2 and Y_1 in Figure 5-2B, we find this combination is not a point on the original
LM curve $LM(P_1)$. And, if we examine other output levels and the corresponding market-clearing interest rate determined at price level P_2, we find that these
combinations are not on the *LM* curve either. In fact, the new combinations
trace out a new *LM* curve. The *LM* curve for the price level P_2 is presented
in Figure 5-2B as $LM(P_2)$. A different *LM* curve exists for each price level: the

LM curve shifts up or to the left with a higher price level, down or to the right with a lower price level.

The intuitive explanation of the shifting *LM* curve is perhaps more straightforward than the mechanics just described. A given quantity of money can buy fewer goods and services when the price for those goods and services rises. Therefore, as the price level rises, any given quantity of money becomes relatively more scarce. Thus, at higher price levels, a given supply of money requires a higher interest rate to bring the money market into equilibrium.

▼
The Money Market and Aggregate Demand

A move from one equilibrium to another in the *IS–LM* diagram illustrates the feedback effects between the money market and aggregate expenditures or the commodity market. Because it captures the feedback effects between commodity and money markets, the *IS–LM* diagram provides a convenient tool for deriving the *AD* curve. The price level affects the *IS* and *LM* curves through three possible channels: (1) real wealth, (2) interest rates, and (3) the domestic relative to foreign price levels. These three channels determine the shape of the *AD* curve. We'll begin with the simplest case, where the only effect of price level changes on aggregate expenditures occurs through the interest rate. In other words, we'll ignore the effect of price level changes on real wealth and the effect of price level changes on net exports for now (we'll add these later).

The Interest Rate Effect

When the U.S. price level rises, the purchasing power of each unit of currency, each dollar, falls. So buying each quantity of goods and services requires more dollars. People must sell their assets (bonds, stocks, and so on) to get that additional money. With more people trying to sell bonds, for instance, the price of bonds falls. The interest rate on a bond is equal to the fixed interest earnings, called the coupon rate, divided by the purchase price of the bond. As a result, when the price of the bond falls, the interest rate on the bond rises, because

Interest earnings/price of asset = interest rate

The higher interest rate, in turn, causes businesses and some households to forgo some interest sensitive expenditures. The **interest rate effect** is the result that higher price levels have on the rate of interest and thus on planned business and household purchases. The higher the interest rate, *ceteris paribus,* the lower the quantity of goods and services demanded.

The interest rate effect of price level changes occurs through the money market. Thus, the interest rate effect is shown by a shifting *LM* curve. The *LM* curve shifts each time the price level changes.

FIGURE 5-3   *The AD curve. The money market is drawn in panel A. Beside the money market is the IS–LM diagram in panel B. Below the IS–LM, in panel C, is the price–output diagram. As the price level rises from P_1 to P_2, the purchasing power of the money supply falls, from M_0^S/P_1 to M_0^S/P_2. Because the purchasing power of money has been reduced and yet people want to purchase the same quantity of goods and services, the quantity of money demanded exceeds the quantity supplied and the interest rate is driven up. Point b represents one interest rate–output combination at which the money market is in equilibrium at the higher price level. The new price level means that for each output level we have a higher interest rate and thus a new LM curve, $LM(P_2)$, that lies above the original curve $LM(P_1)$.*

A different LM curve exists for each price level. A new output level is determined at each intersection between an LM curve and the IS curve. Plotting combinations of P and Y in panel C yields the AD curve. At price level P_1, IS and $LM(P_1)$ determine output level Y_1. At price level P_2, IS and $LM(P_2)$ yield the output level Y_2. These combinations, when plotted in panel C, trace out an aggregate demand curve. The decrease in Y reduces the demand for money to $M^D(Y_2)$ in panel A.

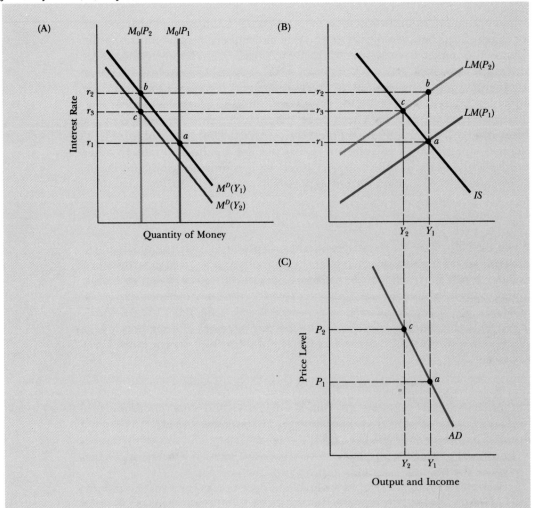

The money market is drawn in Figure 5-3A and the *IS–LM* diagram in 5-3B. Because the money market and the *IS–LM* diagram each have interest rates on the vertical axis, the two can be placed side by side and interest rates from one traced over to the other. Below the *IS–LM* diagram, in Figure 5-3C, is the price–output diagram. Both the *IS–LM* and the price–output diagrams have output measured along the horizontal axes, so the graphs can be placed one above the other.

As the price level rises from P_1 to P_2 the purchasing power of the money supply falls, from M_0^s/P_1 to M_0^s/P_2. Because income hasn't changed, people want to buy the same quantity of goods and services. Their demand for *real* money (for purchasing power) remains the same, but the quantity of real money declines, as shown in Figure 5-3A by the inward shift of the vertical M_0/P line. Because the purchasing power of money has been reduced and yet people want to buy the same quantity of goods and services, the quantity of money demanded exceeds the quantity supplied and the interest rate is driven up. Tracing the new, higher interest rate over to Figure 5-3B, we find point *b*. Point *b* represents one interest rate–output combination at which the money market is in equilibrium at the higher price level. The new price level means that for each output level we have a higher interest rate and thus a new *LM* curve, $LM(P_2)$, that lies above the original curve $LM(P_1)$.

A different *LM* curve exists for each price level. If P_1 is less than P_2, then $LM(P_1)$ will lie to the right of $LM(P_2)$. A different output level is determined at each intersection between an *LM* curve and the *IS* curve (points *a* and *c* in panel B). Plotting combinations of *P* and *Y* in Figure 5-3C yields the *AD* curve. At price level P_1, *IS* and $LM(P_1)$ determine output level Y_1. At price level P_2, *IS* and $LM(P_2)$ yield the output level Y_2. In panel A, as *Y* falls the demand for money falls so the money market is in equilibrium at point *c* with interest rate r_3. These combinations, when plotted in Figure 5-3C, trace out an aggregate demand curve.

The *AD* curve slopes downward because an increase in the price level lowers the real money supply. This drives up the interest rate, which leads to a reduction of total expenditures. The lower level of expenditures means a lower equilibrium level of output. Thus the *AD* curve is a summary of the equilibrium combinations in the money and commodity markets that occur at different price levels. Along an *AD* curve, the levels of *P*, *Y*, and *r* vary in order to keep the money market in equilibrium and $AE = Y$ in the commodity market.

Aggregate Demand from Aggregate Expenditures

The aggregate demand curve can be derived directly from the *AE* diagram as well as from the *IS–LM* framework, although it takes a little more understanding of developments that occur behind the scenes. Consider Figure 5-4, which shows the 45-degree diagram in panel A, the *IS–LM* diagram in panel B, and the *AD* diagram in panel C. Point *a* represents one equilibrium output level,

FIGURE 5-4   *From* AE *to* AD. *The 45-degree diagram is drawn in panel A, the* IS–LM *diagram in panel B, and the* AD *diagram in panel C. Point* a *represents one equilibrium output level,* Y_1. *Let us assume that* Y_1 *occurs at price level* P_1 *and interest rate* r_1. *What happens as we allow the price level to rise to* P_2? *The money market is forced out of equilibrium at interest rate* r_1: *the interest rate rises to equalize the quantities of money demanded and supplied. As the interest rate rises to* r_2, *the* AE *curve shifts down and intersects the 45-degree line at the new equilibrium output level,* Y_2. *The combination of* Y_2 *and* P_2 *plotted along with the initial combination of* Y_1 *and* P_1 *sketches out the* AD *curve.*

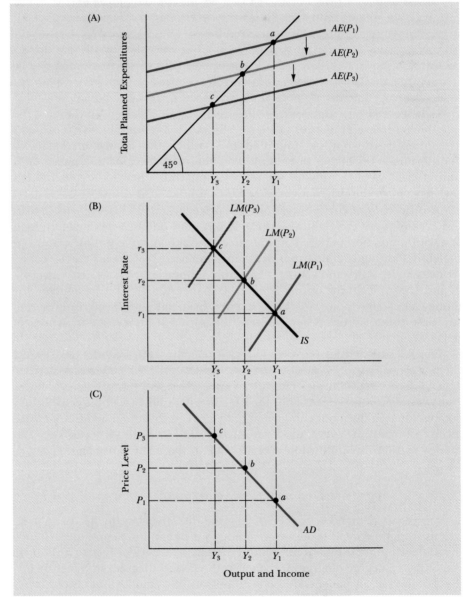

Y_1. Let's assume that Y_1 occurs at price level P_1 and interest rate r_1. What happens as we let the price level rise to P_2? The money market is forced out of equilibrium at interest rate r_1: the interest rate rises to equalize the quantities of money demanded and supplied. As the interest rate rises to r_2, the AE curve shifts down and intersects the 45-degree line at the new equilibrium output level, Y_2. The combination of Y_2 and P_2 plotted along with the initial combination of Y_1 and P_1 sketches out the AD curve. Obviously, what happens in the money market is not shown in the AE diagram. The only thing that shows up is the effect of a higher interest rate on the AE curve.

▼
The Slope of the Aggregate Demand Curve

Aggregate demand is the relation between aggregate expenditures and the price level. As shown in Figure 5-3C, the aggregate demand curve slopes down. The downward slope indicates that as the price level rises, the quantity of output demanded falls. The downward slope of the AD curve in Figure 5-3C is caused by only one thing: an increase in the interest rate that results from an increase in the price level. Economists maintain that two other effects can also make the aggregate demand curve slope downward: the wealth effect and the international trade effect. Let's consider these two effects now.

The Wealth and International Trade Effects

Individuals own money, bonds, and other assets. The real value of these assets is one determinant of expenditures. The more wealth someone has, the higher the level of his or her expenditures. When the price level falls, the purchasing power of assets increases. As a result, households spend more. When prices go up, the purchasing power of assets falls so that households spend less. This is the **wealth effect** of a price change: a change in the real value of wealth makes spending change when the price level changes.[2]

If domestic prices rise while foreign prices and the exchange rate between the two currencies stay constant, then domestic goods become more expensive in relation to foreign goods. Foreign households and businesses therefore buy relatively fewer domestic, or U.S., goods, so the total quantity of U.S. goods demanded declines. This is the **international trade effect**.

For example, suppose the United States sells automobiles to Germany. If the cars sell for $10,000 each and the rate at which the German currency, the deutsche mark (symbolized as DM), can be exchanged for dollars is 2 DM = $1, then one U.S. car costs a German buyer DM20,000. What happens if the level of prices in the United States goes up 10 percent? All prices, includ-

---

2   The wealth effect is sometimes called the *real balance effect*.

ing the price of the car, increase 10 percent so that a U.S. automobile now sells for $11,000. If the exchange rate is still DM2 = $1, then a U.S. car sells for $11,000 = DM22,000. If car prices in other countries do not change, the German buyer is going to buy cars from those other countries rather than pay the higher U.S. price.

When the price of domestic goods increases in relation to the price of foreign goods, net exports fall, reducing aggregate expenditures. When the price of domestic goods falls in relation to the price of foreign goods, net exports rise, raising aggregate expenditures. The international trade effect of a change in the domestic price level is to shift aggregate expenditures in the opposite direction.

The wealth and international trade effects occur through the *IS* curve. For instance, at price P_1, autonomous consumption is larger than if the price level rose to P_2, *ceteris paribus*, because the purchasing power of wealth decreases. Being less wealthy, people spend less. In addition, autonomous net exports decline. Foreign spending on domestic goods and services declines because domestic goods are now relatively more expensive than foreign goods. So each price level entails a different *AE* function and a different *IS* curve, as shown in Figure 5-5. The *IS* curve for price level P_1 lies above (or farther to the right) than the *IS* curve for price level P_2.

The intersection of the *IS* and *LM* curves occurs at a different output level for each price level. When plotted, these output and price level combinations trace out an *AD* curve as shown in Figure 5-5B. The difference between this derivation of *AD* (where we have the real wealth and international trade effects as well as the interest rate effect) and the derivation in Figure 5-3 (where only the interest rate effect occurs) is that now both *IS* and *LM* curves change. At P_1, $LM(P_1)$ and $IS(P_1)$ yield Y_a. At the higher price level P_2, real wealth and net exports are reduced, shifting the *IS* curve in from $IS(P_1)$ to $IS(P_2)$. In addition, the interest rate rises as the *LM* curve shifts in from $LM(P_1)$ to $LM(P_2)$. These effects together mean that the income level at which *IS* and *LM* curves intersect is lower, at Y_d, than occurred without the real wealth and international trade effects. Plotting the combinations of price and income, (P_1, Y_a) and (P_2, Y_d) yields aggregate demand curve AD_2.

Notice that AD_2 is flatter than AD_1. The slope or steepness of the *AD* curve depends on the size of the three price effects. The larger the interest rate, wealth, and international trade effects, the greater is the change in the quantity demanded that occurs from a given price change—and the flatter is the *AD* curve.

The Sum of the Price Level Effects

A lower price level in the domestic country increases expenditures on the part of households (the wealth effect), on the part of businesses (the interest rate effect), and on the part of foreigners (the international trade effect). As the

FIGURE 5-5   *The wealth and international trade effects. The wealth and international trade effects occur through the IS curve. For instance, autonomous consumption falls if the price level from price P_1 rises to P_2, causing the purchasing power of wealth to decrease. Lower real wealth induces people to spend less. In addition, autonomous net exports decline. Foreign spending on domestic goods and services declines because domestic goods are now relatively more expensive than foreign goods. Thus, for each price level there is a different AE function and a different IS curve, as in Figure 5-5. The IS curve for price level P_1 lies above (or farther to the right) than the IS curve for price level P_2. The AD curve flattens when the wealth and international trade effects are included.*

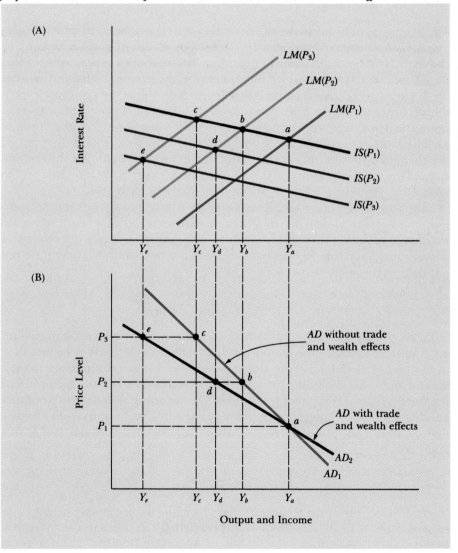

price level falls, aggregate expenditures rise. The more aggregate expenditures rise as the price level falls, the steeper the *AD* curve. The amount by which aggregate expenditures fall as the price level rises depends on the magnitude of the three price effects.

▼

Shifts of the AD Curve

The aggregate demand curve shifts whenever a determinant of expenditures (other than income and the price level) changes. A change in government purchases or taxation, autonomous investment, consumption, or net exports shifts the *AE* function. Because the *AE* function shifts, the *IS* curve shifts; and because the *IS* curve shifts, the *AD* curve shifts. Figure 5-6A shows the aggregate expenditures function. Figure 5-6B shows the *IS–LM* diagram. Figure 5-6C shows the aggregate demand curve. The diagrams are placed one above the other because each has output measured along the horizontal axis. We can directly compare the changes in output that occur in each diagram as a result of a shift in one curve. How large the shifts of the *AE*, *IS*, and *AD* curves are depends on the multiplier. However, different multipliers apply in each case.

Suppose government purchases increase from G_1 to G_2. For the *AE* function, the horizontal distance by which output increases as a result of an autonomous spending increase is given by the multiplier times the change in autonomous spending where (assuming that net taxes and investment do not depend on the level of income)

$$\text{Multiplier} = \frac{1}{(MPS + MPI)}$$

In Figure 5-6A, national output rises by *ab* as a result of the increase in government purchases. Once the money market feedback effects are accounted for in the *IS–LM* model, however, the expansion of national output is less than *ab*. The multiplier including the money market effects is still the reciprocal of the fraction of spending that leaks out of the spending stream in each round, but that fraction includes the reduction in spending that results from a higher interest rate. The formula for the multiplier associated with the *IS–LM* diagram is

$$\frac{1}{MPS + MPI + MM}$$

where *MM* represents the **feedback effects** from the money market to aggregate expenditures. (The derivation of *MM* is carried out in detail in the Appendix to this chapter, "Algebraic Presentation of Aggregate Demand.") The larger is *MM*, the smaller is the multiplier. The feedback effects from the commodity market to the money market lead to a smaller expansion of *Y*, distance *ac*, than when there are no feedback effects, distance *ab*.

FIGURE 5-6 *Comparison of multipliers. Panel A shows the aggregate expenditures function, panel B shows the IS–LM diagram, panel C shows the aggregate demand curve. The diagrams are put one above the other because each has output measured along the horizontal axis. We can directly compare the changes in output that occur in each diagram as a result of a shift of one of the curves. The size of the shifts of the AE, IS, and AD curves depends on the multiplier. However, different multipliers apply to each case. You can see this by comparing the amount by which output changes due to an autonomous change in expenditures.*

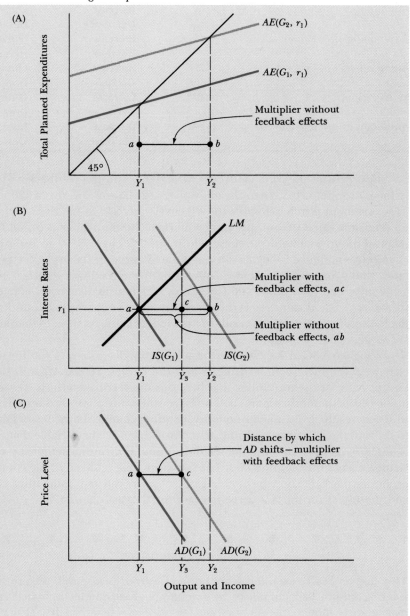

TABLE 5-1   *Effects of Changes on the Aggregate Demand Curve*

Variable	Channel	Change	Shift of AD Curve
Government purchases	IS	Increase	Outward
		Decrease	Inward
Net taxes	IS	Increase	Inward
		Decrease	Outward
Autonomous consumption	IS	Increase	Outward
		Decrease	Inward
Autonomous investment	IS	Increase	Outward
		Decrease	Inward
Autonomous net exports	IS	Increase	Outward
		Decrease	Inward
Money supply	LM	Increase	Outward
		Decrease	Inward
Autonomous money demand	LM	Increase	Inward
		Decrease	Outward

Suppose that the *MPS* is 0.1, the *MPI* is 0.1, and the feedback expression in the multiplier is 0.3. Then the multiplier is 2. This means that a $20 increase in government purchases shifts the *AD* curve only $40 to the right. If there are no feedback effects from the money market, the multiplier is 5 and the $20 increase in government purchases shifts the *AD* curve $100 to the right.

Notice in Figure 5-6B that although the *IS* curve shifts out by the same distance that *Y* increases in Figure 5-6A without the feedback effects, from *a* to *b*, the intersection of the *IS* and *LM* curves means a smaller increase in output, from *a* to *c*. The distance *cb* is the reduction in national output resulting from the higher interest rate; the result of the feedback effects from the money market to aggregate expenditures.

In Figure 5-6C, *AD* shifts horizontally by the distance *a* to *c*, reflecting the change in the intersection of the *IS* and *LM* curves. So the *AD* shift depends on the value of the multiplier that includes the feedback effects between the money and commodity markets. The larger the multiplier, the larger is the *AD* shift that results from an autonomous spending change. Those factors that lead to shifts of the *AD* curve are summarized in Table 5-1. The variable that changes is noted in the first column; the second column indicates whether the variable change occurs through the *IS* or *LM* function; that is, through the commodity or money market. The type of change that occurs is listed in the third column, and the effect on the *AD* curve is noted in the last column.

▼   ▼   ▼   ▼   ▼   ▼   ▼   ▼   ▼   ▼   ▼
Conclusions

This chapter has relaxed the assumption of a fixed price level. We are still considering only the demand side of the economy but have now incorporated aggregate expenditures, money, interest rates, and the price level in our analysis. The *AD* curve incorporates the *AE* analysis and the *IS–LM* analysis. This means that everything already discussed regarding the *AE* analysis and the *IS–LM* framework, including monetary and fiscal policy, occurs through the *AD* curve. The following chapter introduces the supply side of the economy.

▼   ▼   ▼   ▼   ▼   ▼   ▼   ▼   ▼   ▼   ▼
Summary

1. What is the relationship between aggregate expenditures and aggregate demand?
Aggregate demand is aggregate expenditures when the price level is allowed to vary. Aggregate expenditures is aggregate demand at a fixed price level.

2. What is the relationship between IS–LM *and aggregate demand?*
The *IS–LM* model incorporates the effects of the interest rate on aggregate expenditures. The model assumes a fixed price level. So aggregate demand incorporates the *IS–LM* model when the price level is allowed to vary.

3. What is the difference between real and nominal values?
A real value is the nominal value adjusted for price changes. Economic decisions are made on the basis of the real value of variables. If the price level doubles and all goods and services double in price, then all nominal values have doubled. Real values have not changed, so no economic decision has changed.

4. What is the relationship between the slope of the IS *or* LM *curve and the slope of the* AD *curve?*
Everything in the *IS–LM* model is incorporated in the aggregate demand, so the slope of the *AD* curve depends on the *IS* and *LM* curves. The slope of the *AD* curve depends on the three price effects: wealth, international trade, and interest rate. The larger these effects, the flatter is the *AD* curve, *ceteris paribus*.

5. How do multiplier values change as we move from aggregate expenditures to IS–LM *to aggregate demand?*
Each multiplier indicates the effect on output due to a change in an autonomous variable. Comparing the multipliers from each of the three models, *AE*, *IS–LM*, and *AD* indicates how each successive model incorporates more realistic elements. From the simplest model, *AE*, we find that a change in autonomous expenditures leads to a multiplied change in output. In the model where net taxes and investment do not vary with income, the multiplied change is given by the reciprocal of the sum of the *MPS* and the *MPI*. With the *IS–LM* model, we find that because the interest rate changes, the resulting change in output is reduced. The expansion of output due to an increase in autonomous expenditures is less in the *IS–LM* model than the *AE* model because as output rises, the demand for money rises, which drives up the interest rate. The higher interest rate induces a slowdown in purchases by businesses and households. Thus, output does not expand by as much as if the interest rate were constant. The *IS* curve shifts horizontally by exactly the amount that output changes in the *AE* model due to a change in autonomous expenditures. But the intersection between *IS* and *LM* is what determines output in the *IS–LM* model, not just *IS* alone. When we move to the *AD* curve, we find that the *AD* curve shifts horizontally by the amount that the intersection between the *IS* and *LM* curves changes. The *AD* curve incorporates the *IS* and *LM* curves.

▼
Key Terms

real value   112
real interest rate   113
interest rate effect   117

wealth effect   121
international trade effect   121
feedback effects   124

▼
Problems and Exercises

1. Use the *IS–LM* framework to derive the *AD* curve when
    a. There are no wealth and international trade effects.
    b. There is no wealth effect.
    c. All three effects of a price change exist (interest rate, wealth, and international trade).
2. Using your work in exercise 1, compare and contrast the shapes of the *AD* curve under each case (a, b, and c).
3. Demonstrate and explain the effect of an expansionary monetary policy on the *AD* curve.
4. Demonstrate and explain the effect of an expansionary fiscal policy on the *AD* curve.
5. Will your answers to exercises 3 and 4 differ depending on whether the *AD* curve was the one derived in exercise 1a, 1b, or 1c? How will they differ, if so?
6. Compare the multipliers resulting from an increase in autonomous spending and in the money supply in the *AE*, *IS–LM*, and *AD* analyses.

Appendix

Algebraic Presentation of Aggregate Demand

This appendix presents the algebra of aggregate demand. Deriving the *AE* function is the first step. This is followed by deriving the *IS* and *LM* functions and then the *AD* function. Let's begin with a model in which the price level is held constant at $P = 1.0$ and the interest rate plays no role. Next we'll see how the price level enters the model. Then we'll introduce interest rate and look at feedback effects between money and commodity markets.

▼ The AE *Function*

The equations of the model without net taxes or income-induced investment are:

(1) $Y = AE$ — Equilibrium condition

(2) $AE = C + I + G + X$ — Definition of aggregate expenditures

(3) $C = C_0 + c_y Y$ — Consumption function; C_0 is autonomous consumption and c_y is the *MPC*

(4) $I = I_0$ — Investment function; I_0 is autonomous investment

(5) $G = G_0$ — Government purchases function; G_0 is autonomous government purchases

(6) $EX = EX_0$ — Exports function; EX_0 is autonomous exports

(7) $IM = IM_0 + im_y Y$ — Imports function; IM_0 is autonomous imports and $im_y Y$ is the MPI

(8) $X = EX - IM$ — Net exports function

The aggregate expenditures function is derived by putting equations 2–8 into equation 1. This yields equation 9.

(9)
$$Y = C_0 + c_y Y + I_0 + G_0 + X_0 - X_y Y$$

X_0 is $EX - IM_0$ and X_y is MPI and simply rewritten from im_y in equation 7 to X_y in equation 9. The minus sign in front of MPI in equation 9 comes from the net exports function, equation 8, where imports are subtracted from exports.

We can solve equation 9 for the output level by collecting all the Y terms and taking them to the left side of the equation.

(10)
$$Y(1 - c_y + X_y) = C_0 + I_0 + G_0 + X_0$$

If we solve for Y by dividing each side by the expression $1 - c_y - X_y$, we have found the output level.

(11)
$$Y = \frac{1}{1 - c_y + X_y} \{C_0 + I_0 + G_0 + X_0\}$$

From equation 11, we can show what happens to national output in the AE model when one of the autonomous spending components changes. For instance, if government purchases change, then output changes by the following amount:

$$\Delta Y = \frac{1}{1 - c_y + X_y} \{\Delta G_0\}$$

The symbol Δ represents change; ΔY is the change in Y; ΔG_0 is the change in G_0.

The expression by which the change in autonomous government purchases is multiplied to derive the resulting change in output is the multiplier. Recall that $1 - c_y$ is the MPS and X_y is the MPI, so that the multiplier is the reciprocal of the $MPS + MPI$, as specified in Chapter 3.

$$\text{Multiplier} = \frac{1}{MPS + MPI} = \frac{1}{1 - c_y + X_y}$$

▼

Feedback Effects from the Money Market

If we add an expression for the effect of the interest rate on business spending, we then provide room for the feedback effects from the money market. Instead of equation 4, we substitute equation 4' or $I = I_0 - I_r r$. Equation 4' says that investment is part autonomous and part dependent on the interest rate. As the interest rate increases, investment spending decreases, as shown by the negative sign in front of I_r. How much investment spending changes with a change in the interest rate depends on the size of I_r. The larger is I_r, the more sensitive investment is to changes in the interest rate.

The IS *Function*

Solving for output using equation 4' instead of equation 4 yields

(11')
$$Y = \left[\frac{1}{1 - c_y + X_y} \right] \{C_0 + I_0 + G_0 + X_0 - I_r r\}$$

Expression 11' includes two *endogenous* variables: output and the interest rate. The value of an endogenous variable is determined by the model, whereas the values of the autonomous variables and coefficients are determined outside of the model. In other words, we choose values for C_0, I_0, G_0, X_0, c_y, X_y, and I_r, whereas Y and r depend on these values and are determined in the model. The implication of finding two endogenous variables in one equation is that unless we know the value of one of the variables, a unique value of the other cannot be determined. For instance, in equation 11' for each value of r we find a different value for Y.

Equation 11' is the algebraic version of the *IS* curve. The slope of the *IS* curve is given by $\Delta r / \Delta Y$ (the rise over the run) and can be found by changing r and Y and subtracting the changed expression from 11'. We then have

(12)
$$\Delta r / \Delta Y = (1 - c_y + X_y)/(-I_r)$$

The slope of the *IS* curve changes if c_y, X_y, or I_r change.

An example to illustrate the points in the preceding paragraph may be helpful. Assume that $C_0 = 200$, $c_y = 0.9$, $I_0 = 150$, $I_r = 1,000$, $G_0 = 100$, $X_0 = 50$, and $X_y = 0.1$. Equation 11' can thus be written as

(11")
$$Y = \left[\frac{1}{1 - .9 + 0.1} \right] \{200 + 150 + 100 + 50 - 1,000(r)\}$$
$$Y = 2,500 - 5,000r$$

Equation 11" points out that there is a unique output level for each interest rate. If the interest rate is 0.10, output is 2,000. If the interest rate is 0.05, the output level is 2,250, and so on.

A change in an autonomous variable shifts the *IS* curve. In our example, if autonomous investment (or any autonomous expenditures) increases by 100, the Y intercept increases from 2,500 to 3,000—the *IS* curve shifts out.

Money Market and the LM *Function*

The equations that constitute the money market are as follows:

(13)
$$M^D = L_0 - L_r r + L_y Y \qquad \text{Demand for money}$$

(14) $M^s = M_0$ Supply of money

(15) $M_s = M^D$ Equilibrium

To find equilibrium in the money market, the demand for money equation and the money supply equation are substituted into the money market equilibrium equation 15. By making these substitutions and solving for the interest rate, r, we find that

(16)
$$r = \frac{L_0 - M_0}{L_r} + \frac{L_y}{L_r} Y$$

Equation 16 points out that a unique interest rate cannot be derived in the money market unless the output level is known. In other words, there are feedback effects from the AE function to the money market.

In equation 16, notice that $(L_y/L_r)Y$ is added to the intercept to find the equilibrium interest rate. This suggests a positive relationship between the interest rate and the output level. Another approach to illustrating the direct relationship between the interest rate and output level is to find the slope of the LM equation. The slope of the LM equation (the rise over the run, $\Delta r/\Delta Y$) is L_y/L_r, which is positive.

A numerical example may be useful to illustrate the money market. Suppose that $L_0 = 200$, $M_0 = 340$, $L_y = 0.2$, and $L_r = 1,000$. Then equation 16 is written as follows:

(16′)
$$r = \frac{200 - 340}{1,000} + \frac{0.2}{1,000} (Y)$$

or

$$r = -0.14 + 0.0002Y$$

If output is 1,200, the market-clearing interest rate is 0.10; and if the output level is 2,000, the interest rate that equates money demand and supply is 0.26.

To derive the LM curve, we assumed specific values for L_0, L_r, L_y, and M_0. A change in an autonomous variable, L_0 or M_0, shifts the LM curve. Consider the effect of an increase in the money supply to 380 from 340. An increase in the money supply means that at the output levels 1,200 and 2,000 interest rates must decrease to 0.06 and 0.22, respectively, from 0.10 and 0.26.

Changes in people's sensitivity toward interest rate changes and their holding of money are reflected as changes in L_r. And changes in people's willingness to hold money as output changes are reflected in changes in L_y. Whenever L_r or L_y changes, then the LM curve becomes more or less steep. For example, if L_y increases from 0.20 to 0.25, the new equation (16″) is

(16″)
$$r = \frac{200 - 340}{1,000} + \frac{0.25}{1,000} (Y)$$

or

$$r = -0.14 + 0.00025Y$$

The slope of the *LM* curve has changed from 0.0002 to 0.00025. Thus the *LM* curve has become steeper.

The IS and LM Together

The *IS* and *LM* functions together determine the levels of output and the interest rate. By solving the *LM* function for r and substituting into the *IS* function, we can solve for Y.

$$(17) \quad Y = \frac{1}{1 - c_y + X_y + (I_r L_y)/L_r} \{C_0 + I_0 + G_0 + X_0 - [I_r/L_r](L_0 - M_0)\}$$

In equation 17 you can see that the multiplier, the first expression on the right side, is smaller than the multiplier derived in equation 11 because of the term $I_r L_y/L_r$. This is the money market feedback term we labeled *MM* in Chapter 4. It indicates that the effect of interest rates on aggregate expenditures depends on how much investment changes when the interest rate changes (I_r), and how much the demand for money depends on output and the interest rate L_y/L_r. The output level determined by the equilibrium between the *IS* and *LM* functions changes by the multiplier times the change in autonomous spending.

▼
The Aggregate Demand Function

The aggregate demand function is derived by considering the role that the price level plays. The *AD* function relates output to the price level.

The Wealth Effect

If the price level rises, consumers' real wealth declines (their purchasing power declines) and autonomous consumption declines. To make this explicit, substitute equation 3′ for equation 3.

$$(3') \qquad\qquad C = C_0/P + c_y Y$$

The International Trade Effect

Another way that the price level can enter the model is through the international trade effect. To represent the effect changing domestic price levels might have on domestic spending, we change equation 7 to 7′.

$$(7') \qquad\qquad IM = IM_0(P^F/P) + im_y Y$$

Equation 7′ tells us that a rise in the domestic price level, P, relative to the foreign price level, P^F, increases the price of domestic goods and services relative to foreign goods and services and thus reduces foreign spending on those domestic goods and services. Assuming that $P^f = 1.0$, and solving the model with equations 3′ and 7′ yields

(10′) $Y(1 - c_y + X_y) = C_0/P + I_0 + G_0 + X_0/P$

Equation (10′) is the aggregate demand function with wealth and international trade effects. Let's substitute some numerical values in the equation to see how Y and P are related. If

$$C_0 = 200$$
$$I_0 = 150$$
$$G_0 = 100$$
$$X_0 = 50$$
$$c_y = 0.9$$
$$X_y = 0.1$$

and P is 1.0, then the output level is 2,500. This is derived by substituting the values into equation 10′:

$$Y(1 - 0.9 + 0.1) = 200 + 150 + 100 + 50$$
$$Y = 5(500) = 2,500$$

Now, let's change P to 2.0. This reduces C_0/P from 200 to 100 and X_0/P from 50 to 25. Because real autonomous consumption declines by 100 and real autonomous net exports declines by 25, total real autonomous spending declines by 125 when P rises from 1.0 to 2.0. A decline in autonomous spending of 125 means a multiplied decline in output, from 2,500 to 2,500 − 625 = 1,875. Plotting the two combinations of Y and P yields an AD curve, as shown in Figure A5-1.

FIGURE A5-1   *Plotting the two combinations of* Y *and* P *yields an* AD *curve.* Y *falls to 1,875 as the price level increase reduces real autonomous net exports—which has a multiplied effect on output.*

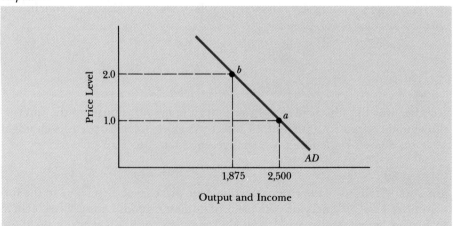

The Interest Rate Effect

The price level affects the amount of purchasing power any given stock of money has. This can be incorporated in the model of the money market by changing the money supply equation from M_0 to M_0/P. With this alteration, the money market becomes

(18) $M^D = L_0 - L_r r + L_y Y$ Demand for money

(19) $M^S = M_0/P$ Supply of money

(20) $M^S = M^D$ Equilibrium

To find equilibrium, the demand for money equation and the money supply equation must be substituted into equation 20. By making these substitutions and solving for the interest rate, r, we find that

(21) $$r = \frac{L_0 - M_0/P}{L_r} + \frac{L_y}{L_r}(Y)$$

Substituting these values substituted earlier into equation 16, into equation 21, we have

(21') $$r = \frac{200 - 340/P}{1{,}000} + \frac{0.2}{1{,}000}(Y)$$

Equation 21' states that as the price level rises, the equilibrium interest rate rises. For instance, at price level $P = 1.0$, the equilibrium interest rate at output level $Y = 2{,}000$ is 0.26. At price level $P = 2.0$ and output level $Y = 2{,}000$, the equilibrium interest rate is 0.43. Although unrealistic numbers occur in our hypothetical economy for the interest rate, the result shows that the price level and the interest rate are positively related.

The AD Function with the Interest Rate Effect

Because a price level change changes the equilibrium interest rate and feeds back into the AE function and affects output, to solve for the AD function we must incorporate the money market into the AE function. The output level determined by the AE function is

(22) $Y(1 - c_y - X_y) = C_0/P + I_0 + G_0 + X_0 - I_r r$

The expression for the interest rate from the money market is given in equation 21. Substituting equation 21 for r into equation 22 yields equation 23:

(23) $Y(1 - c_y + X_y + I_r L_y/L_r) = C_0/P + I_0 + G_0 + X_0/P - I_r[L_0 - M_0/P]/L_R$

Equation 23 is the AD equation when all the price effects are included. The wealth effect shows up as C_0/P, the international trade effect as X_0/P, and the interest rate effect as M_0/P.

Shifts in the AD curve are illustrated as a change in Y that results from a change in an autonomous variable at each price level. For instance, suppose autonomous government purchases rise. Then the *AD* curve shifts by the following amount:

(24)
$$\Delta Y = \Delta G \left\{ \frac{1}{1 - c_y + X_y + \dfrac{I_r L_y}{L_r}} \right\}$$

The expression in curved brackets { } in equation 24 is the multiplier. Compare this multiplier with that in equation 11. With $I_r L_y / L_r$ in the denominator of equation 24, the denominator is larger and thus the multiplier is smaller than is the case in equation 11. You can also see this in a numerical example. For instance, if

$$c_y = 0.9$$
$$X_y = 0.1$$
$$I_r = 1,000$$
$$L_y = 0.2$$
$$L_r = 1,000$$

then the multiplier without money feedback effects would be the reciprocal of $1 - 0.9 + 0.1 = 0.2$ or 5. With the money feedback effects, the multiplier is $1 - 0.9 + 0.1 + 1,000(0.2)/1,000 = 0.4$ or 2.5. The shift of the *AD* curve from any autonomous spending change is only 2.5 times rather than 5 times the autonomous spending change.

▼
Comparison of Multipliers

The multiplier indicates the effect on output due to a change in autonomous spending. In the *AE* function (equation 11), the multiplier is

$$\Delta Y / \Delta G = 1/(1 - c_y + X_y)$$

The *IS* function of equation 11′ yields the same multiplier of

$$\Delta Y / \Delta G = 1/(1 - c_y + X_y)$$

Because the multipliers of the *AE* function and the *IS* curve are the same, we know the *IS* curve shifts out by the distance that output expands as the *AE* function shifts.

   When the money market is introduced, the expansion of output that occurs in the *IS–LM* as a result of a spending increase is less than the shift of the *IS* curve alone. In the *IS–LM* solution, equation 17, the multiplier is

$$\frac{\Delta Y}{\Delta G} = \frac{1}{1 - c_y + X_y + (I_r L_y)/L_r}$$

And in the aggregate demand function, equation 23, the multiplier is the same as that in the *IS–LM* solution:

$$\frac{\Delta Y}{\Delta G} = \frac{1}{1 - c_y + X_y + (I_r L_y)/L_r}$$

Because the *IS–LM* solution and the *AD* function have the same multipliers, the *AD* curve shifts out by the same distance by which the equilibrium between *IS* and *LM* changes.

▼
Problems and Exercises

Consider the following model of the economy:

$C = 250/P + 0.75(Y)$
$I = 100 + 0.1Y - 30r$
$G = 200$
$X = 50/P - 0.1Y$
$Y = C + I + G + X$
$M^s = 500/P$
$M^D = 10 + 0.4Y - 50r$
$M^s = M^D$

1. Derive the *AE* function.
2. Derive the *IS* and *LM* functions.
3. Set $P = 1$ and find the values of Y and r.
4. Set $P = 2$ and compare to the answers in exercise 3.
5. a. Derive the *AD* function.
   b. Demonstrate and explain the roles of the wealth, interest rate, and international trade effects.

Chapter 6

Aggregate Supply

What to Expect

In the first quarter of 1991, the U.S. found itself in the midst of a war with Iraq. Economists at that time were predicting that the war would compound the existing recessionary problems. This is an interesting contrast to previous wars, which had stimulated the U.S. economy: World War II had pulled the economy out of the Great Depression, and the Korean and Vietnam wars had led to rapid growth and inflation. What is the difference? The answer is that the Iraq war affected the aggregate supply curve more than had previous wars.

The aggregate demand curve was derived in the previous chapter. To complete the macroeconomic model, we must derive the aggregate supply curve. Aggregate supply shows the quantities of final goods and services producers are willing and able to produce at each price level. In this chapter, we examine the aggregate supply curve and discuss the alternative shapes the curve might take. Questions considered include the following:

1. What is the relationship between the labor market and aggregate supply?

2. What is the shape of the aggregate supply curve in the short run?

3. What is the shape of the aggregate supply curve in the long run?

4. What causes the aggregate supply curve to shift?

5. What is the relationship between the aggregate supply curve and the potential output level?

▼
The Total Product Curve and the Labor Market

For an individual business, the decision of how much to produce at each price depends on the costs of doing business. The entrepreneur organizes production in the most efficient manner, combining the inputs—land, labor, capital—so as to produce output at the least cost. To know how much to produce, the entrepreneur must determine the costs of producing each level of output and the revenue generated when each quantity is sold. The firm chooses to produce the amount that maximizes the difference between revenues and costs. Because each firm operates this way, the entire economy must, too.

The Total Product Curve

The mechanism through which inputs are combined to produce output is called the **aggregate production function** and is represented graphically as the **total product curve (TP)**. The total product curve shows the quantity of output that can be produced by combining different quantities of one input with fixed quantities of all other inputs.

The total product curve in Figure 6-1 has the quantity of the labor input measured along the horizontal axis (number of hours, N) and the quantity of output measured along the vertical axis. Thus, the curve shows that as we add more labor to the fixed combinations of the other inputs—capital and land—the economy produces more output. At labor quantity N_1, Y_1 is produced; at labor quantity N_2, Y_2 is produced, and so on. Which quantity will be produced, Y_1, Y_2, or some other amount? To know how much output the economy produces, we must know the quantity of labor employed. The quantity of labor employed is determined in the labor market. So let's turn to the labor market.

The Labor Market

The **labor market** is represented by the demand and supply curves of Figure 6-2. The number of labor-hours (symbolized by N) is measured on the horizontal axis.[1] The vertical axis shows the wage rate per hour. We have measured

---

1   We can measure the wage rate in two ways: in nominal terms, W, or in real terms, W/P. The choice makes no difference for the analysis. It turns out, however, that the use of nominal wage rates on the vertical axis simplifies the discussion. Because individuals and firms care about the real wage, we must be sure the demand and supply curves are defined relative to the price level. The role of price is indicated by placing a P in parentheses next to the demand and supply curves.

FIGURE 6-1   *The total product curve. The total product curve has the quantity of the labor input measured along the horizontal axis (number of hours, N) and the quantity of output measured along the vertical axis. Thus, the curve shows that as we add more labor to the fixed combinations of the other inputs—capital and land—the economy produces more output. At labor quantity N_1, Y_1 is produced; at labor quantity N_2, Y_2 is produced, and so on.*

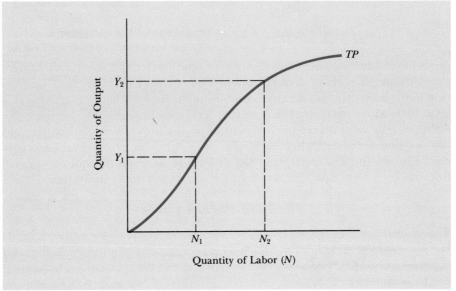

the **nominal wage** on the vertical axis even though the number of hours people are willing and able to work depends on the **real wage** they expect to earn. (The *real wage* is the nominal wage divided by the price level.) The reason is simplicity; it is easier to illustrate several events and to focus on the price level in the labor market when the nominal wage is measured on the vertical axis and the price level is shown to affect the demand and supply curves. For instance, in Figure 6-2 the labor demand and supply curves are drawn for price level P_1. For P_1, as the nominal wage increases the real wage rises. The labor supply curve slopes upward, because the greater the real wage, the more willing people are to work more hours. The greater the real wage, the greater the cost to firms of employing workers for additional hours. As the real wage rises, firms are willing and able to employ people for fewer hours. The labor demand curve slopes downward.

As the price level changes, the labor demand and supply curves shift. For instance, a higher price level, P_2, means that the real wage is lower for each nominal wage. The labor supply curve shifts in or up, indicating that people are willing and able to work fewer hours for each nominal wage because the corresponding real wage has fallen; people work the same number of hours only if they receive the same *real* wage. The labor demand curve shifts up or

FIGURE 6-2   *The labor market. The labor demand and supply curves are drawn for price level*
P_1. *For P_1, as the nominal wage increases the real wage rises. The labor supply curve slopes upward,*
because the greater the real wage, the more willing people are to work more hours. As the real wage
rises, firms are willing and able to employ people for fewer hours — the labor demand curve slopes
downward. Equilibrium in the labor market occurs where $N^D = N^S$. The equilibrium nominal wage
rate is W_1 and the equilibrium quantity is N_1 at price level P_1. Thus, the equilibrium real wage
is W_1/P_1. The supply curve shifts in, from $N^s(P_1)$ to $N^s(P_2)$, as the price level rises. Workers do
not offer to work as much because the real wage has declined. At the same time, the demand curve
shifts out, from $N^D(P_1)$ to $N^D(P_2)$. Firms are happy to pay workers for more hours of work because
the real wage declined. The new equilibrium between labor demand and labor supply, $N^D(P_2)$ and
$N^s(P_2)$, defines a new higher nominal wage, W_2. Because the equilibrium real wage was W_1/P_1,
the new higher nominal wage, W_2, must be such that $W_2/P_2 = W_1/P_1$.

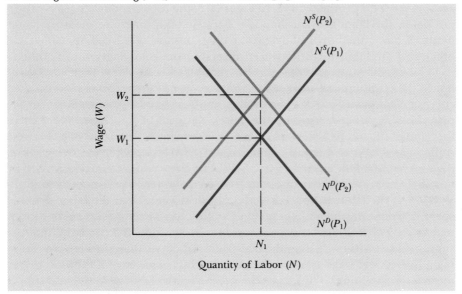

out, indicating that firms are willing to employ people for more labor-hours
at each nominal wage.

Equilibrium in the labor market occurs where $N^D = N^S$. In Figure 6-2 the
equilibrium nominal wage rate is W_1 and the equilibrium quantity is N_1 *at price*
level P_1. Thus, the equilibrium real wage is W_1/P_1. Changes in W alone or P alone
will lead to a situation of excess demand or supply. For instance, whenever the
price level changes, the demand and supply curves shift. The supply curve shifts
in, from $N^S(P_1)$ to $N^S(P_2)$, as the price level rises. Workers would not offer to
work as much if the real wage declined, which is what a higher price means.
At the same time, the demand curve shifts out, from $N^D(P_1)$ to $N^D(P_2)$. Firms
would be happy to pay workers for more hours of work if the real wage declined.
The new price level means that at the original wage of W_1, there is an excess
demand for labor. The new equilibrium between labor demand and labor sup-

ply, $N^D(P_2)$ and $N^S(P_2)$, defines a new higher nominal wage, W_2. Because the equilibrium real wage was W_1/P_1, the new higher nominal wage, W_2, must be such that $W_2/P_2 = W_1/P_1$.

If the nominal wage increases from W_1 to W_2 while the price level remains at P_1, an excess supply of labor exists. The excess supply of labor means that the nominal wage will be bid down. Wages fall until W_1 is re-established and the real wage of W_1/P_1 is re-established.

From Employment to Output

In order to derive the aggregate supply curve, we must combine the labor market and the total product curve. In Figure 6-3, the total product curve is drawn just below the labor market diagram. Because both diagrams measure labor-hours, N, along the horizontal axis, the diagrams can be placed one above the other and the labor quantity traced directly from one diagram to another.

The equilibrium quantity of labor employed is N_1. With that number of hours, the economy can produce the total output Y_1 given in the total product curve at N_1 at price level P_1. The total quantity of output produced is Y_1 at the price level P_1. What happens if the price level rises to P_2? The demand curve for labor shifts out to $N^D(P_2)$, as shown in Figure 6-3A. The labor supply curve shifts in to $N^S(P_2)$ as a result of the higher price level. After the curves shift, the new equilibrium nominal wage is W_2, but employment remains at N_1. The nominal wage rate is bid up just enough to keep the real wage unchanged: $W_2/P_2 = W_1/P_1$. If the labor supply curve did not shift as much as the labor demand curve, it would imply that workers are willing to work more hours at a lower real wage, which doesn't seem reasonable. In contrast, if we assume that the supply curve shifts more than the labor demand curve, then workers are receiving a higher real wage to work fewer hours. But firms have no reason to pay more for fewer hours. Thus, after the price rise, the labor demand and supply curves must intersect at the same quantity of labor as before the price rise.

Employment is N_1 at price level P_2. Combining N_1 with the other inputs in the total product curve again generates output level Y_1. Thus, the quantity of output supplied is the same for price levels P_1 and P_2. We have derived two combinations of output and price, (P_1, Y_1) and (P_2, Y_1). These two combinations, when plotted in Figure 6-3C, trace out a vertical aggregate supply curve.

The *aggregate supply curve* shows the quantity of output that producers are willing and able to produce at each level of prices. The vertical AS curve says that no matter the price level, the quantity of output producers are willing and able to supply is the same. The reason for the vertical curve is that the demand for and supply of labor adjust immediately and fully to any price changes so that the real wage level does not change; everyone willing and able to work has a job. The quantity of output, Y_1, generated at the labor market equilibrium, N_1, is called the **potential output level**. It is the level the economy can produce if inputs are used efficiently and fully; no one is underemployed or involuntarily unemployed.

FIGURE 6-3 *The aggregate supply curve. The equilibrium quantity of labor-hours employed is N_1. With that number of hours, the economy can produce the total output Y_1 given in the total product curve at N_1 at price level P_1. The total quantity of output is Y_1 at the price level P_1. What happens if the price level rises to P_2? The demand curve for labor shifts out to $N^D(P_2)$ and the labor supply curve shifts in to $N^S(P_2)$, as shown in Panel A. The new equilibrium nominal wage is W_2, but employment remains at N_1. The nominal wage rate is bid up just enough to keep the real wage unchanged: $W_2/P_2 = W_1/P_1$. Employment is N_1 at price level P_2. Combining N_1 with the other inputs in the total product curve again generates output level Y_1. Thus, the quantity of output supplied is the same for price levels P_1 and P_2. We have derived two combinations of output and price, (P_1, Y_1) and (P_2, Y_1). These two combinations, plotted in panel C, trace out a vertical aggregate supply curve.*

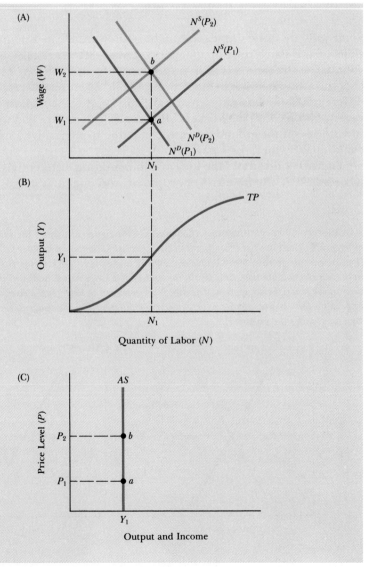

▼
Labor Market Realities

If all workers are the same to a firm (that is, if a firm doesn't care whether it hires Bob, Kate, Ray, or Allie) and if all firms and jobs are the same to workers (that is, if IBM is no different from Ted's Hot Dog Stand to individual workers), then the one demand for labor and the one supply of labor define the one equilibrium wage. But, in reality, firms are different, workers are different, and wages differ.

Compensating Wage Differentials

Some jobs are quite unpleasant because they are located in undesirable locations or are dangerous or unhealthy. In market economies, enough people voluntarily choose to work in unpleasant jobs that the jobs get filled. People choose to work in unpleasant occupations because of **compensating wage differentials** — a wage difference that makes up for the high risk or poor working conditions of a job. Workers mine coal, clean sewers, and weld steel beams fifty stories off the ground because, compared to alternative jobs for which they could qualify, these jobs pay well.

Figure 6-4 illustrates the idea of compensating differentials. There are two labor markets, one for a risky occupation and one for a less risky occupation.

FIGURE 6-4   *Compensating wage differentials. This figure illustrates the idea of compensating differentials. There are two labor markets, one for a risky occupation and one for a less risky occupation. At each wage rate, fewer people are willing and able to work in the risky occupation than in the less risky occupation. As a result, the equilibrium wage rate is higher in the risky occupation than in the less risky occupation. The difference between the wage in the risky occupation and the wage in the less risky occupation is an equilibrium differential — the compensation a worker receives for undertaking the greater risk.*

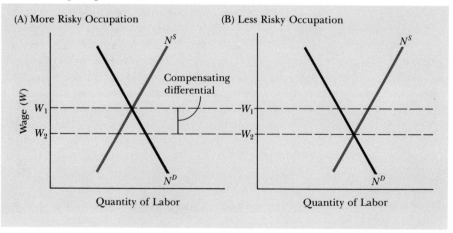

At each wage rate, fewer people are willing and able to work in the risky occupation than in the less risky occupation. As a result, the equilibrium wage rate is higher in the risky occupation than in the less risky occupation. The difference between the wage in the risky occupation and the wage in the less risky occupation is an *equilibrium differential*—the compensation a worker receives for undertaking the greater risk. If the difference were higher, workers would move from the low-risk job to the higher-risk job, driving the wage in the higher-risk occupation down and the wage in the low-risk occupation up until the differential equaled the equilibrium differential.

Any characteristic that distinguishes one job from another may result in a compensating wage differential. A job that demands more travel or time away from home, has less prestige, has worse hours or longer commutes, or some other difference, results in compensating wage differentials. Although we observe these differentials in the real world, they do not suggest that a revision is needed in our model of the labor market. When we speak of a wage increase in our simple labor market, we are referring to a comparable shift in all real-world labor markets. We are assuming no change will occur in compensating wage differentials.

Human Capital

People differ with respect to their training and abilities. The expectation of higher income induces people to acquire **human capital**—skills, training, and job experience. People go to college or vocational school or enter training programs because they expect the training to increase their future income. When people purchase human capital, they are said to be investing in human capital. Like investments in real capital (machines and equipment), investments in education and training are made in order to generate output and income in the future. Not everyone encounters the same costs and benefits of acquiring human capital. So some choose not to attend college; others earn advanced or professional degrees.

If you decide to attend college, you must then decide what field to major in. Your decision depends on the opportunity costs you face. If your opportunity costs of devoting a great deal of time to a job are high and your expected benefits from the job are low, you may choose to major in a field that is not overly time consuming. For instance, for several years after college, men and women who have studied to become medical doctors, lawyers, and accountants face long training periods and very long workdays, and they have to devote significant amounts of time each year to staying abreast of new developments in their profession. The greater the opportunity costs of any one occupation, the smaller the number of people who will select that occupation, *ceteris paribus*.

The existence of human capital differences and resulting wage differences do not mean we must necessarily alter our model of the labor market. As long as we assume that when the demand for labor rises, the demand for all types of labor rises, our labor market suggests how the economy responds. However, if the demand for skilled labor rises relative to that for unskilled, or if the demand for engineers rises more rapidly than the demand for doctors, and if these different subgroups are not perfect substitutes, then our labor market must be altered. For instance, if there is a significant period of time — say one to three years or more — before an increase in the demand for physicians or for engineers will result in more doctors or engineers, then an excess demand for doctors and engineers may exist for a period of one to three or more years. The labor market does not adjust to the increased demand instantaneously, because unskilled workers are not perfect substitutes for the skilled workers.

Efficiency Wages

Figure 6-5 shows the normal pattern of income earned over a lifetime. The colored curve is an **age–income profile**. It shows that income is low during a person's early years as human capital is acquired, rises rapidly until middle age,

FIGURE 6-5   *Age–income and age–productivity profiles. The colored curve shows the normal pattern of income earned over a lifetime, called an* age–income profile. *It shows that income is low during a person's early years as human capital is acquired, rises rapidly until middle age, and then rises more slowly until retirement. The black curve is called an* age–productivity profile. *It shows that a worker's productivity rises until about age 45 and then declines. Comparing the age productivity and age income profiles indicates that firms pay older workers more than their contributions to the firm's profits, called* marginal revenue product, *and pay younger workers less than their marginal revenue product. A firm may use wages to motivate long-time employees to stay with the firm so that any training the firm has given the employee is not lost. In addition, this pay scheme might provide an incentive for young workers to be more productive because they see the prize they can achieve in later years.*

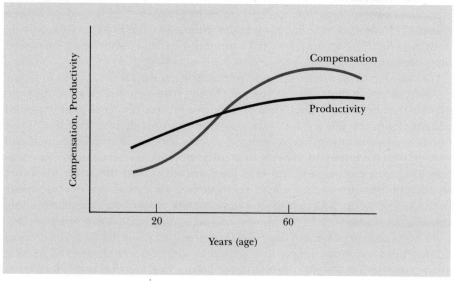

and then rises more slowly until retirement. Why does someone earn more at age 55 than at age 25? One reason might be the skills and training gained during thirty years on the job. An older worker is more productive or more valuable to the firm than a younger worker.

The black curve in Figure 6-5 is called an **age–productivity profile**. It shows that a worker's productivity rises until about age 45 and then declines. Comparing the age–productivity and age–income profiles indicates that firms pay older workers more than their contributions to the firm's profits, called *marginal revenue product,* and pay younger workers less than their marginal revenue product. If a firm pays less than marginal revenue product during the early years and more during the later years, then an employee will want to stay with the firm in order to get his or her bonus of compensation above marginal revenue product. A firm may use wages to motivate long-time employees to stay with the firm so that any training the firm has given to the employee will not be lost. In addition, this pay scheme might provide an incentive for young workers to be more productive because they see the prize they can achieve in later years. A young employee wouldn't want to lose his or her job after just a few years.

Often a firm cannot differentiate employees by their individual contributions to the firm's profits. Under *team production,* a firm can't identify whether an employee is contributing more than his or her share or whether the employee is shirking and allowing other members of the team to carry his or her share. To minimize shirking, the firm pays a wage that exceeds the equilibrium wage because it wants to retain its high-quality, highly trained workers. An employee might fear that being identified as a shirker will lead to losing a job that provides higher compensation than available elsewhere. So the employee is less likely to shirk.

These wage schemes are known as **efficiency wages**. A firm sets a wage level above the equilibrium wage to motivate workers or ensure that the firm retains workers with high on-the-job training. Because the efficiency wage is not the equilibrium wage, an excess supply of workers for that job exists. But this excess supply doesn't induce any changes. Because the efficiency wages let the firm maximize profits, the firm will not lower wages even though there is an excess supply of workers.

Long-Term Contracts

Several sectors of the economy use **long-term contracts**. About half of all U.S. workers agree to contracts that specify wages and working conditions over more than one year. Borrowers and lenders agree to multiyear contracts; suppliers and retailers agree to long-term supply contracts; and there are others. Long-term contracts are used because both parties believe they are better off with than without the contract. But such contracts inhibit adjustments. For example, if the price level increases workers who agreed to a certain wage growth over several years may find their real wages have decreased. But the workers can't do anything about the real wage decline until the contract expires.

Imperfect Information

As long as wages are perfectly flexible and individuals have complete information, wages adjust to equate quantities supplied and demanded. Other than in the case of efficiency wages, whenever there are members of the labor force who are willing and able to work and who do not have jobs, wages fall. Whenever firms want to hire workers but all are employed, wages rise to induce workers to switch jobs. However, if workers and/or firms don't have perfect information, wages and prices may not immediately respond to demand or supply changes.

If it cost nothing to get information — if it took no time to compare prices or jobs or workers — everyone who was interested would always know everything about current economic conditions. However, because there are costs of obtaining and understanding information about the economy, people make mistakes in the short run. Both managers and employees make mistakes due to lack of information. Such mistakes are not due to stupidity but to basic economics — information is costly to obtain, so it is not perfect and is not the same for everyone. Imperfect information means that wages may not respond immediately to price level changes. Once we allow for the possibility that workers and firms do not have complete and perfect information, we must also allow for periods of excess demand or supply in our labor market model.

▼

The Long- and Short-Run Aggregate Supply Curves

The aggregate supply curve is a vertical line when it is assumed that all adjustments take place immediately, that all workers and firms have complete and perfect information, and that the market is perfectly competitive. Altering these assumptions alters the shape of the aggregate supply curve.

Sticky Adjustments in the Labor Market

Let's consider what happens when wages are not adjusted immediately each time the price level changes. We'll assume that nominal wages do not adjust for at least one period after a real wage change. This delay in nominal wage adjustments can represent any of the labor market realities discussed earlier: the unwillingness of firms to alter their efficiency wage structure, the length of time it takes people to switch occupations and to acquire additional human capital, long-term contracts that exist in the economy, or imperfect information. What does the delay mean for the aggregate supply curve?

In Figure 6-6, we have drawn the total product curve below the labor market. Let's begin with point a in the labor market with the price level P_1, the

FIGURE 6-6   *Short- and long-run aggregate supply curves. At point a in the labor market, the price level is* P_1, *the wage rate is* W_1, *and the equilibrium quantity of labor is* N_1. *The resulting combination of output* Y_1 *and price level* P_1 *is plotted on the aggregate supply diagram as point a. What occurs when the price level increases if workers do not realize that the price level has changed (or for some other reason nominal wages do not change)? The labor demand curve shifts out to* $N^D(P_2)$, *driving the nominal wage rate up to* W_2 *at point b in the labor market. Workers, thinking that their real income has risen, offer to work more hours. The new quantity of labor employed is* N_2, *and a higher output level is produced,* Y_2. *The new price level,* P_2, *and the new output level,* Y_2, *provide another combination on the AS curve, point b. Connecting points a and b, we derive an upward-sloping AS curve labeled* AS^{sr}. *This aggregate supply curve is called* short-run *aggregate supply curve because it is derived under conditions where workers have not realized the true price level or for some other reason the nominal wage has not adjusted to the new price level. Once enough time has elapsed for workers to realize their mistake (or for other adjustments to occur), workers reduce the number of hours they are willing to work and demand a wage rate that re-establishes their real wage. The labor supply curve shifts to* $N^S(P_2)$ *and the wage rate rises to* W_3. *The new real wage* W_3/P_2, *is equal to the original level,* W_1/P_1, *so that the quantity of labor employed is at its initial level,* N_1, *and output falls back to* Y_1. *Connecting the original combination* (P_1, Y_1) *and the new combination* (P_2, Y_1), *yields the vertical aggregate supply curve,* AS^{lr}. *This curve is called the* long-run *aggregate supply curve because it is derived after adjustments have taken place.*

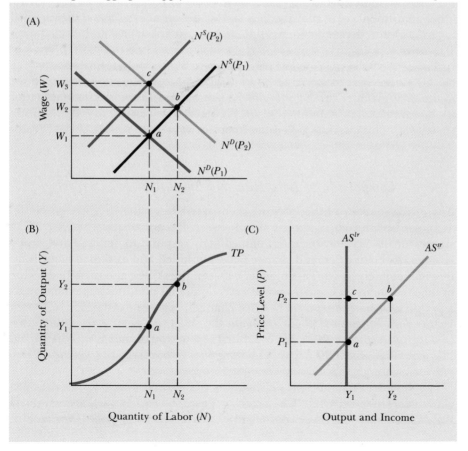

wage rate W_1, and the equilibrium quantity of labor N_1. Tracing the labor quantity N_1 down to the total product curve gives us the combination of output Y_1, and price level P_1, that is plotted on the aggregate supply diagram as point a. What occurs when the price level increases? We're assuming workers do not realize the price level has changed (or for some other reason nominal wages do not change). Firms, experiencing increasing profits, attempt to hire more labor and produce more goods and services. The labor demand curve shifts out to $N^D(P_2)$. This drives the nominal wage rate up to W_2 at point b in the labor market. Workers, thinking that their real income has risen, offer to work more hours. The new quantity of labor employed is N_2. Tracing this higher employment down to the total product curve indicates that a higher output level is produced, Y_2. The new price level, P_2, and the new output level, Y_2, provide another combination on the AS curve, point b. Connecting points a and b, we derive an upward-sloping AS curve labeled AS^{sr}. This aggregate supply curve is called the **short-run aggregate supply curve** because it is derived under conditions where workers have not realized the true price level or for some other reason the nominal wage has not adjusted to the new price level.

Once enough time has elapsed for workers to realize their mistake (or for other adjustments to occur), workers reduce the number of hours they are willing to work and demand a nominal wage rate that re-establishes their real wage. The labor supply curve shifts to $N^S(P_2)$ and the wage rate rises to W_3. The new real wage W_3/P_2, is equal to the original level, W_1/P_1, so that the quantity of labor employed is at its initial level, N_1. Tracing the employment level N_1 down to the total product curve generates Y_1. Connecting the original combination (P_1,Y_1) and the new combination (P_2,Y_1), yields the vertical aggregate supply curve, AS^{lr}. This curve is called the **long-run aggregate supply curve** because it is derived after all adjustments have taken place.

Comparison of Long-Run and Short-Run AS Curves

Any of the realities of the labor market described earlier can be represented as an upward-sloping aggregate supply curve. Paying efficiency wages, for instance, means that wages do not immediately respond to demand and supply changes. A relative demand change between skilled and unskilled labor is not met immediately by workers moving between the skilled and unskilled sectors of the labor market. Long-term contracts do not let nominal wages change for a period of time in response to price changes. All these and other real-world factors suggest that **sticky wages** cause the short-run aggregate supply curve to slope upward. The short run is defined as a period of time just short enough that not all adjustments occur. The long run, in contrast, is a period of time just long enough that all adjustments do take place.

In the long run, the slow adjustments of nominal wages do not exist—all adjustments have occurred. When contracts expire, new contracts are negotiated that take into account all price changes that have occurred. Once labor acquires its additional human capital, excess demand in one occupation doesn't exist. Once firms and workers have realized what has occurred in the economy, the equilibrium differentials and efficiency wage structures are maintained. In other words, the long-run labor market is the perfectly competitive labor market we initially described. As a result, the long-run aggregate supply curve is a vertical line at the potential output level.

Aggregate supply in the short run is different from aggregate supply in the long run. The short-run AS curve slopes upward because resource prices, especially wages, do not change in the short run. Fixed nominal wages allow the real wage to move in the opposite direction to a change in the price level. When the price level rises, the real wage falls and firms expand production by increasing employment. When the price level falls, the real wage rises and firms reduce production by decreasing employment. Over time, labor and other contracts expire and wages and other resource costs adjust to current conditions. When this occurs, the vertical AS curve is traced out.

Relationship Between Short- and Long-Run AS Curves

Assume that the economy is currently in equilibrium at point a in Figure 6-7. The price level is P_1 and the output level is the potential output level Y_1. Now suppose that some event drives the price level up and causes the economy to move to point b on the short-run aggregate supply curve AS_1^{sr}. The economy can produce Y_2, which exceeds the potential output level because of the sluggishness in which the costs of production rise in response to output price changes. Because of long-term contracts, efficiency wages, imperfect information, or lags in the acquisition of human capital, the nominal wage does not increase in proportion to the price level rise. Thus, as firms charge higher prices and realize greater profits, they produce more output by employing more workers. They may be able to hire temporary or part-time people, or may provide overtime to existing employees.

Eventually the causes of the nominal wage rigidity disappear and firms and workers adjust to a new nominal wage, one that restores the real wage to its original equilibrium level. Because the costs of doing business rise, profit declines and firms produce less—in fact, firms produce the quantity they produced before the output price rose. As employment declines and output falls, the price level remains at its new higher level. The economy moves from point b to point c in Figure 6-7.

Points a and b in Figure 6-7 reflect the rigidities in the labor market and thus trace out the short-run AS curve. As adjustments occur over time, employment decreases and real wages rise. Points a and c reflect the long-run adjustment to the economic change and so trace out the long-run AS curve. Once the economy is in equilibrium at point c, any further changes in the price level are reflected initially as movements along a short-run aggregate supply curve. As the economy moves from point b to point c, the short-run aggregate supply

FIGURE 6-7 *Sticky wages and the aggregate supply curve. Assume that the economy is currently in equilibrium at point* a. *The price level is* P₁, *and the output level is the potential output level* Y₁. *Now suppose some event drives the price level up and moves the economy to point* b *on the short-run aggregate supply curve* AS₁ˢʳ. *Because of long-term contracts, efficiency wages, imperfect information, or lags in the acquisition of human capital, the nominal wage does not increase as the price level rises. Thus, as firms charge higher prices and realize greater profits, they produce more output* (Y₂) *by employing more workers. They may be able to hire temporary or part-time people or may provide overtime to existing employees. Eventually the causes of the nominal wage rigidity disappear and firms and workers adjust to a new nominal wage, one that restores the real wage to its original equilibrium level. Because the costs of doing business rise, profit declines and firms produce less — in fact, firms produce the quantity they produced before the output price rose. As employment declines and output falls, the price level remains at its new higher level. The economy moves from point* b *to point* c.

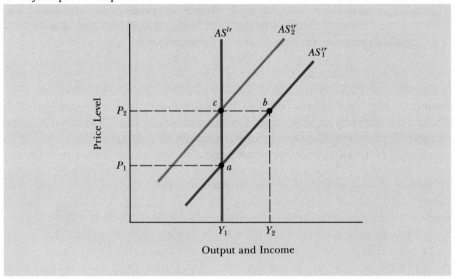

curve shifts up from AS_1^{sr} to AS_2^{sr}, indicating that firms reduce production and employment as their costs of production rise. Once having reached point c, any new economic events will bring on movements along the short-run aggregate supply curve AS_2^{sr}.

Potential Output and Economic Growth

The long-run aggregate supply curve AS^{lr} is a vertical line at the potential level of national output (Y_p). Everyone willing and able to work will be employed efficiently and fully at the potential level of output. The fact that the long-run aggregate supply curve is vertical does not mean that the economy is forever fixed at the current level of potential output. Over time, as new technologies are developed and the quantity and quality of the resources increase, potential output also increases. An increase in potential output is represented as an outward shift of the long-run aggregate supply curve. Figure 6-8 shows long-run economic growth with a series of shifts in the aggregate supply curve from AS_1^{lr} to AS_2^{lr} to AS_3^{lr}. The movement of the long-run aggregate supply curve to the right reflects the increase in potential national output from Y_{p1} to Y_{p2} to Y_{p3}.

Economic growth occurs because of technological improvements and increases in the quantity and quality of other inputs. More inputs enable more output to be produced. For instance, an increase in the quantity of capital is represented by an upward shift of the total product curve from TP_1 to TP_2 in Figure 6-9. The upward shift of the total product curve represents an increase in labor productivity—an increase in the output each worker can produce. For example, at employment level N_1, total output is Y_1 according to TP_1. The same employment level, with more machines, more equipment, and more buildings, allows more output to be produced as is shown by the output Y_2 from TP_2.

The total product curve also shifts if the quantities of other inputs change. For instance, when the price and supply of petroleum changed in 1974, due to action by OPEC (Organization of Petroleum Exporting Countries) and again in 1990 due to Iraq's invasion of Kuwait, the economy was affected through the aggregate supply curve. With a change in the quantity of the fixed inputs (oil), the total product curve shifts down. Each unit of labor produces less total output. Thus, at employment level N_1, a smaller quantity of output Y_3 can be produced. In this case, the long-run aggregate supply curve shifts to the left.

FIGURE 6-8   *Economic growth. An increase in potential output is represented as an outward shift of the long-run aggregate supply curve. Long-run economic growth is illustrated as a series of shifts of the aggregate supply curve from* AS$_1^{lr}$ *to* AS$_2^{lr}$ *to* AS$_3^{lr}$. *The movement of the long-run aggregate supply curve to the right reflects the increase in potential national output from* Y$_{p1}$ *to* Y$_{p2}$ *to* Y$_{p3}$.

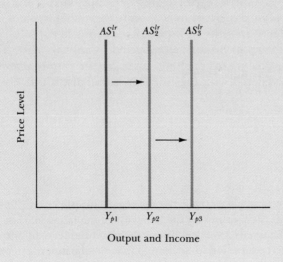

FIGURE 6-9   *Shifts in the total product curve. An increase in the quantity of nonlabor inputs shifts the TP curve upward. A decrease in the quantity of nonlabor inputs shifts the TP curve downward. The TP curve is also affected by changes in technology or the quality of labor or nonlabor inputs.*

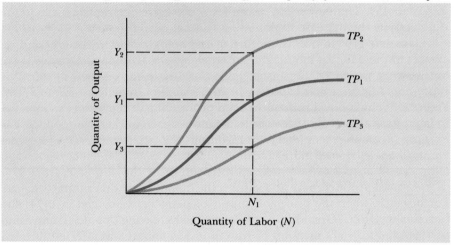

Thus, we have seen that the vertical aggregate supply curve reflects the long run, a period long enough that all adjustments to an economic event have occurred. The short-run aggregate supply curve is an upward-sloping curve that reflects the lags, restrictions, rigidities, or sluggishness that exist in the economy for short-run periods of time. The short- and long-run aggregate supply curves are related, with a series of short-run upward-sloping curves intersecting or tracing out the long-run aggregate supply curve. Shifts in the long-run aggregate supply curve occur as economic growth takes place, due to increases in technology or quantities of inputs. Reductions in supplies of inputs and increases in the costs of inputs are reflected in an inward shift of the long-run aggregate supply curve. As the long-run aggregate supply curve shifts, the short-run curves associated with the long-run curve also shift.

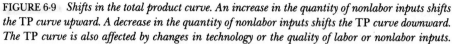

Conclusions

In this chapter we have derived the aggregate supply curve. The curve may take different shapes, depending on the behavior of the labor market. The long-run aggregate supply curve is a vertical line at the potential level of output. The long run is considered to be a period long enough that all adjustments to price changes have taken place. The short-run aggregate supply curve slopes upward, its shape depending on the rigidities or sluggishness in the labor market. The short run is a period just short enough that not all adjustments in the labor market have occurred.

▼   ▼   ▼   ▼   ▼   ▼   ▼   ▼   ▼   ▼   ▼
Summary

1. What is the relationship between the labor market and aggregate supply?
The quantity of labor hours employed and the wage rate of labor are determined in the labor market. The quantity of labor determines the quantity of output that can be produced. If the demand for and supply of labor adjust perfectly and immediately to any changes, then the equilibrium number of labor hours employed does not change as the price level changes. In this case, the aggregate supply curve is vertical. If the labor demand or supply do not change completely or immediately, then the labor hours employed varies as the price level varies. In this case, the aggregate supply curve slopes upward.

2. What is the shape of the aggregate supply curve in the short run?
The short run is any period short enough that labor demand, labor supply, or nominal wages do not adjust completely and fully to price level changes. In this case, the aggregate supply curve slopes upward.

3. What is the shape of the aggregate supply curve in the long run?
The long run is a period of time just long enough that the labor demand and labor supply and wages adjust completely to price level changes. In this case, the aggregate supply curve is vertical at the potential level of national output.

4. What causes the aggregate supply curve to shift?
Anything that alters the aggregate production function (total product curve) or the labor demand or labor supply curve will cause the aggregate supply curve to shift. Such factors are technological changes, productivity changes, changes in the prices of related resources, and changes in the quantities of other resources.

5. What is the relationship between the aggregate supply curve and the potential output level?
The potential output level is the total output level that an economy can produce, using its resources fully and efficiently. That potential output level is illustrated as the vertical or long-run aggregate supply curve.

▼
Key Terms

aggregate production function   139
total product curve (*TP*)   139
labor market   139
nominal wage   140
real wage   140
potential output level   142
compensating wage differentials   144
human capital   145

age–income profile   146
age–productivity profile   147
efficiency wages   147
long-term contracts   147
short-run aggregate supply curve   150
long-run aggregate supply curve   150
sticky wages   150

▼

Problems and Exercises

1. Derive the AS curve graphically and explain each step in the derivation, for the following two conditions:
   a. A perfectly competitive labor market.
   b. Wage rigidities.
2. What is the difference between the short-run and long-run aggregate supply curves?
3. What determines the shape of the short-run aggregate supply curve? What things might make it more or less steep?
4. What is potential output? If you recall from your first economics course what the production possibilities curve *(PPC)* is, compare potential output as defined by the *AS* curve and potential output as defined by the *PPC*. If you do not recall what the PPC is, find a book in which the topic is discussed, and refresh your memory. Are they the same? Why or why not?
5. What is meant by economic growth? How is growth illustrated with the *AS* curves?
6. How would a decrease in the quantity of oil affect the *AS* curve? What if the quantity did not change but the price did?

Chapter 7

Aggregate Demand and Supply

What to Expect

In some cases, business cycle expansions go hand in hand with rising prices. In others, recessions are marked by a rising price level. This chapter shows under what conditions each of these sets of events may occur. Previous chapters developed the aggregate demand and supply curves. This chapter puts the two curves together and shows how they can be used to illustrate economic developments. After a brief review, we'll turn to demand and supply shocks and business cycles. Some of the important questions we consider are:

1. Why does the aggregate demand curve slope downward?

2. What causes the aggregate demand curve to shift?

3. Does the aggregate supply curve slope up, or is it vertical?

4. What causes the aggregate supply curve to shift?

5. What are demand and supply shocks?

▼
Aggregate Demand

Recall that aggregate demand is the quantity of aggregate expenditures that households, businesses, government, and the international sector plan to make at each domestic price level. The aggregate demand curve slopes down, indicating that as the domestic price level rises, the quantity of output demanded falls. The downward slope of the *AD* curve is caused by three effects: the wealth effect, the interest rate effect, and the international trade effect.

The Slope of the AD Curve

Price changes alter the value of financial assets held by households, and this affects household spending. When prices go up (down), the value of financial assets falls (rises) and households and businesses spend less (more). This is the *wealth effect* of a price change: a change in the real value of wealth that causes spending to change when the level of prices change.

The *interest rate effect* is the result that higher price levels have on the rate of interest and thus on business and household spending. As the price level increases, the real supply of money falls relative to the demand, which causes interest rates to rise. The higher the interest rate, *ceteris paribus,* the lower the quantity of goods and services demanded.

The third effect of higher prices on aggregate expenditures occurs because of the change in domestic versus foreign price levels. If domestic prices rise while foreign prices remain constant, domestic goods become more expensive in relation to foreign goods. Foreign households and businesses therefore buy relatively fewer domestic (U.S.) goods, so the total quantity of U.S. goods demanded declines. This is the *international trade effect.*

These three price effects — wealth, interest rate, and international trade effects — account for the slope of the *AD* curve. The larger these effects are, the flatter the *AD* curve.

Shifts in the AD Curve

The aggregate demand curve is derived by varying the price level and the level of income, holding all other things constant. Those "other things" are anything other than the price level and quantity of output that affects aggregate expenditures. When the other things change, the aggregate demand curve shifts. Those other things — the nonprice determinants of aggregate demand — include expectations, foreign income and price levels, and government policy.

Household and business spending are affected by expectations. Households vary their spending depending on their view of future income, prices, and wealth. For example, when people expect the economy to do well in the future, they increase consumption today. In contrast, if people expect a recession in the near future, they tend to spend less and save more, to protect themselves against a greater likelihood of losing a job or a forced cutback in hours worked.

Expectations are also very important to businesses. Businesses forecast future economic or business conditions and the future returns from any projects in which they might get involved. Before undertaking a particular investment, a firm forecasts the likely revenues and costs associated with that project. When the profit outlook is good, the project is undertaken.

When foreign income increases, so does foreign spending. Some of this increased spending is for goods produced in the domestic economy. For instance, a higher income in Japan means greater expenditures by the Japanese— on U.S. goods and services as well as on Japanese goods and services. If foreign prices rise in relation to domestic prices, domestic goods become less expensive than foreign goods. This means that more domestic goods are sold and net exports increase.

In addition to changes in expectations and foreign income and price levels, government economic policy causes the aggregate demand curve to shift. Increases in government spending shift the aggregate demand curve out; increases in net taxes shift the curve in. Money supply changes also are reflected in shifts in the aggregate demand curve. Increases in the money supply shift the aggregate demand curve out, while decreases in the money supply shift the curve in.

▼
Aggregate Supply

The aggregate supply curve shows the quantity of national output or income (GNP) produced at different price levels. With aggregate supply, we are analyzing how the amount of all goods and services produced changes as the price level changes.

Slope of the AS Curve

The aggregate supply curve represents a relationship between output and the price level, everything else held fixed. If for some reason the costs of production—wages, rent, and interest—are constant or do not respond immediately to price level changes, then the aggregate supply curve slopes upward. If the level of prices rises while the costs of production remain fixed, business profits rise. As profits rise, firms are willing to produce more output. The quantity supplied increases. The result is the positively sloped aggregate supply curve, called the *short-run aggregate supply curve*.

Although production costs may not rise immediately when prices rise, eventually they do. Labor demands higher wages to compensate for the higher cost of living, and suppliers charge more for materials. When the costs of production change, then profits are reduced and firms are not willing to produce more output. The positive slope of the *AS* curve, then, is a short-run phenomenon. How short is the short run? It is the period of time over which production costs are unable to adjust fully to changes in the price level. The long run is the time when all costs can change or are variable. For the economy as a whole, the short run can be a matter of months or as long as a few years.

The slope of the aggregate supply curve depends on how rapidly the costs of business change in response to an output price change. The aggregate supply curve can be relatively flat, even horizontal at very low levels of national income. The flat shape of the *AS* curve may occur when substantial unemployment and excess capacity exist. Here output can be increased with little need for price level increases because the unemployed resources can be put to work without an increase in the costs of production. As some areas of the economy begin to approach their limits or potential output levels, the costs of production rise as output increases. This is the upward-sloping short-run *AS* curve. As long as the costs of production do not respond immediately to output price changes, the aggregate supply curve slopes upward. The concepts of *rigidities, sluggishness, restrictions,* and *sticky wages* are all used to describe why the short-run aggregate supply curve slopes upward

Fixed wages allow real wages to move in the opposite direction to a change in the price level. When the price level rises, real wages fall and firms expand production. When the price level falls, real wages rise and firms reduce production. Over time, labor and other contracts expire and wages and other input costs adjust to current conditions. When this occurs, the vertical long-run *AS* curve is traced out.

The long-run aggregate supply curve (AS^{lr}) is a vertical line at the *potential level of national output* (Y_p). In the long run there is no relationship between changes in price level and changes in output because wages and other input costs have the time to *fully adjust* to price changes. In the long run, because the costs of production adjust completely to the change in prices, neither profits nor production increase. What we find here are higher wages and other costs of production to match the higher level of prices.

Shifts of the AS Curve

If the price of output changes and the costs of production do not change immediately, then a change in profits induces a change in production. When costs eventually change in response to the change in prices, the short-run aggregate supply curve shifts. When the cost of inputs—labor, capital goods, land—falls, the short-run aggregate supply curve shifts to the right. This means firms are willing to produce more output at any given price level. When the cost of resources goes up, the short-run aggregate supply curve shifts to the left, as firms are willing to produce less output at any given price.

Remember, the aggregate supply curve is a relationship between the price level for the whole economy and national output. So only changes in resource prices that raise the production costs across the economy affect the aggregate supply curve. A change in the production costs in manufacturing may have no effect on the short-run aggregate supply curve if offset by an opposite change in production costs in the service sector. For example, oil is an important raw material. If the price of oil increases substantially, aggregate supply decreases in the short-run. In 1990, when Iraq invaded Kuwait and threatened the oil supplies of Saudi Arabia, the price of oil rose from $15 per barrel to $42. This cost increase affected the entire economy. As a result, the short-run AS curve shifted up (or inward). But when the cost of components to U.S. electronics firms rose at the same time that the cost of steel to auto manufacturers fell, little effect on aggregate supply was discernible.

Expectations and Aggregate Supply. Actual cost increases cause the short-run aggregate supply curve to shift up. Expected cost increases could do the same thing. We've seen how expectations affect aggregate demand. Expectations in the business community play an important role in aggregate supply as well. The short-run aggregate supply curve is drawn as an upward-sloping line because we assume that higher prices increase profits, creating an incentive for more production. The curve is drawn holding constant technology and resource prices, including wages. What happens if businesses anticipate future cost increases?

To understand how expectations can affect aggregate supply, consider labor contracts. Workers typically contract for a nominal wage based on what they and their employers expect the future level of prices to be. Because wages typically are set for at least a year, any unexpected increase in the price level during the year lowers real wages. Firms receive higher prices for their output, but the nominal cost of labor stays the same. So profits and production go up. For instance, suppose workers agree to wages of $10 per hour for the next three years because they expect the price level to remain stable at 1.0. But then, the price level doubles during the three years to 2.0. The real wage declines from $10 to $5 per hour and as a result, business profits rise so that business firms increase output. Such a situation is illustrated by an outward shift of the short-run AS curve.

If wages rise in anticipation of higher prices but prices do not go up, then the real cost of labor rises. Higher real wages reduce profits and the firms reduce production as a result, moving the short-run aggregate supply curve to the left. Anticipated higher prices cause the short-run aggregate supply to fall, *ceteris paribus;* anticipated lower prices cause the short-run aggregate supply to rise.

Long Run Versus Short Run. Technological innovations allow businesses to increase the productivity of their existing resources. As new technology is adopted, the amount of output that can be produced by each unit of input increases, moving the long-run aggregate supply curve to the right. Changes in the *quantity or quality* of inputs—changes in population, land (including natural resources associated with land), stock of capital, level (or stock) of education and human capital—all lead to shifts of the long-run aggregate supply curve. Changes in the *costs* (unrelated to changing input quantity or quality) of doing business lead to shifts of the short-run aggregate supply curve but not of the long-run aggregate supply curve.

▼
Equilibrium: Combining Aggregate Demand and Supply

Figure 7-1 shows the level of equilibrium in a hypothetical economy. Initially, the economy is in equilibrium at point *a*, where AD_1, AS^{sr}, and AS^{lr} intersect. At this point, the equilibrium price is P_1 and the equilibrium income is $500. At price P_1, the amount of output demanded is equal to the amount supplied. Suppose aggregate demand increases from AD_1 to AD_2. In the short run, the cost of doing business does not change in proportion to any resulting change in output prices, so the new equilibrium is at the intersection of the new aggregate demand curve, AD_2, and the same short-run aggregate supply curve, AS_1^{sr}, at point *b*. The new equilibrium price is P_2 and the new equilibrium income is $600.

The higher price without a corresponding increase in costs means that profits rise. Firms therefore produce more and employ more workers. However, once the costs of production rise in response to the higher price level, profits fall and firms produce less. The short-run aggregate supply curve shifts to AS_2^{sr}. The final or long-run equilibrium is at point *c*, where the price level is P_3 and national income is $500. Points *a* and *c* lie along the long-run aggregate supply curve, AS^{lr}. Points *a* and *b* trace out the upward-sloping short-run aggregate supply curve, AS_1^{sr}.

In the long run, there is no relationship between the level of prices and the level of output. The initial shock to or change in the economy was an increase in aggregate demand. The change in aggregate expenditures initially led to higher output and higher prices and more employment. Over time, however, output fell back to its original value as employment declined and prices continued to rise. Short-run equilibrium occurred at point *b*. Long-run equilibrium occurred initially at point *a* and ultimately at point *c*.

Short Run Versus Long Run

How long is the short run? It is a period short enough that input prices are not perfectly flexible; the costs of production do not change fully as the output price changes. How long is the long run? It is a period just long enough that

FIGURE 7-1 *Aggregate demand and aggregate supply. Initially, the economy is in equilibrium at point a, where AD_1, AS_1^{sr}, and AS^{lr} intersect. At this point, the equilibrium price is P_1 and the equilibrium income is $500. Suppose aggregate demand increases from AD_1 to AD_2. In the short run, the new equilibrium is at the intersection of the new aggregate demand curve, AD_2, and the same aggregate supply curve, AS_1^{sr} at point b. The new equilibrium price is P_2, and the new equilibrium income is $600. The higher price without a proportionate increase in costs means that profits rise. Firms therefore produce more and employ more workers. However, once the costs of production rise in proportion to the higher price level, profits fall and firms produce less. The short-run aggregate supply curve shifts to AS_2^{sr}. The final or long-run equilibrium is at point c, where the price level is P_3 and national income is $500.*

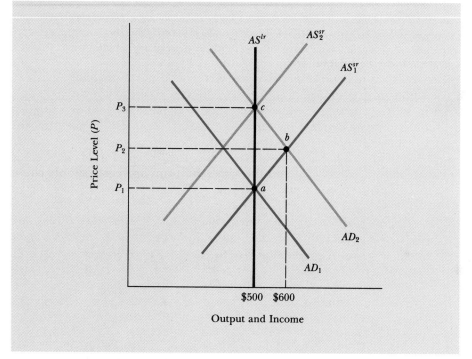

resource prices are completely flexible; the costs of production change to match output price changes. Neither the long run nor the short run is a specific calendar period, such as a month or year or decade. They are, instead, periods in which economic adjustments take place.

Perhaps it is somewhat confusing to note that the long run is not the same period as the period of economic growth. In other words, the *long-run aggregate supply curve* is a vertical line at potential output. Economic growth occurs when the potential output level rises and the long-run aggregate supply curve shifts out. Assuming a long-run aggregate supply curve being a vertical line at the potential output level is nothing more than a convenience, a simplification, that lets us analyze economic events. In reality, the economy is always moving and the potential output level is always changing.

For instance, Figure 7-2A shows the path of real GNP for the United States between 1960 and 1990. You can see that over this time period the potential

FIGURE 7-2 *Economic growth. Panel A shows the path of real GNP for the United States between 1960 and 1990. As indicated by the black trend line, over this time the potential level of GNP rose. Actual real GNP fluctuated around the trend line as it adjusted to economic changes. To represent panel A using the AD–AS model, we must show the long-run aggregate supply curve continuously shifting out, as in panel B, and the short-run aggregate supply and the aggregate demand curves shifting out and in around each long-run aggregate supply curve. This would get very messy. So we ignore the shifts of the long-run curve and focus on the shifts of the short-run aggregate supply curve and the aggregate demand curve. In other words, we focus most of our attention on the fluctuations of the economy—business cycles.*

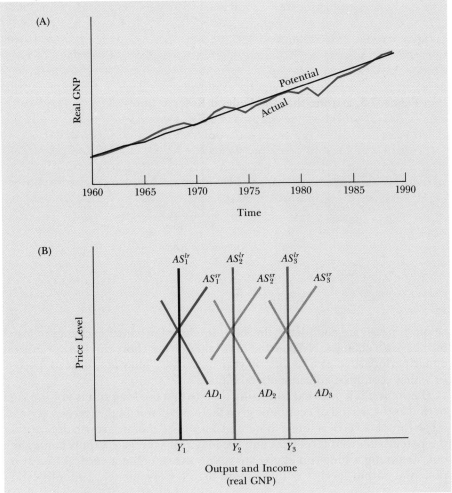

level of GNP rose; it is indicated by the black trend line. The economy fluctuated around the trend line as it adjusted to economic changes. To represent Figure 7-2A using the *AD–AS* model, we would have to show the long-run aggregate supply curve continuously shifting out, as in Figure 7-2B, and the short-run aggregate supply and the aggregate demand curves shifting out and in around each long-run aggregate supply curve. This would get very messy. So we focus on shifts of the short-run aggregate supply and aggregate demand curves. This lets us separate the topics of business cycles and economic growth. With shifts in the short-run *AS* and the *AD* curves, we are focusing on business cycles. With shifts in the long-run *AS* curve, we focus on economic growth.

Economic Shocks

We have mentioned the term *shock* several times. An **economic shock** is an unexpected change in aggregate demand and/or aggregate supply. Demand shocks may be the result of economic policy, such as money supply changes or government spending or tax changes. Demand shocks may also result from changes in expectations or events that occur in other economies. When a **demand shock** occurs, the aggregate demand curve shifts unexpectedly and the economy's equilibrium is disrupted. For instance, with the economy in equilibrium at point *a* in Figure 7-3, assume that the Federal Reserve unexpectedly increases the rate of growth of the money supply. This is a demand shock.

The aggregate demand curve shifts out from AD_1 to AD_2. With more money, individuals seek to purchase more goods and services. Realizing that inventories are declining, firms raise prices. As a result, profits rise and firms begin to increase their production. They hire more workers and use existing workers more hours. Because workers have not recognized the decline in real wages or for some other reason can't adjust their nominal wages, they agree to work more hours. With more employment, production increases. The economy moves from point *a* to point *b* along the upward-sloping short-run aggregate supply curve.

Eventually, nominal wages rise in proportion to the rise in output prices and the costs of doing business rise. Firms experience a decline in their profits and thus cut back employment and production. Employment falls, output declines, but prices rise to a higher level. The short-run aggregate supply curve shifts in from AS_1^{sr} to AS_2^{sr}. Eventually, the economy settles back to point *c*.

You can see in Figure 7-3B the result of the demand shock. It drove output, employment, and prices up for a while. Eventually, employment and output declined, but prices did not. The end result is a higher price level and the same output and employment levels. The economy boomed and then declined as a result of the demand shock. As we discuss in the next chapter, this is a business cycle; the demand shock led to a business cycle.

We call *unexpected* demand changes *demand shocks*. If the demand change had been fully anticipated, the results would have been different. Everyone would have known that the final result of the money supply increase was a price rise

FIGURE 7-3   *A demand shock. If the Federal Reserve unexpectedly increases the growth rate of the money supply, this is a demand shock. The aggregate demand curve shifts out from* AD$_1$ *to* AD$_2$. *With more money, people try to purchase more goods and services. Firms, recognizing that inventories are declining, raise prices. As a result, profits rise and firms increase their production. The economy moves from point* a *to point* b. *Eventually, nominal wages rise and the costs of doing business rise. Firms experience a decline in their profits and thus cut back employment and production. The short-run aggregate supply curve shifts in from* AS$_1^{sr}$ *to* AS$_2^{sr}$. *The economy settles back to point* c. *You can see the result of the demand shock in panel B with the dashed line. The shock drives output (shown in panel B), employment, and prices up for a while. Eventually, employment and output decline but prices do not. The end result is a higher price level and the same output and employment levels.*

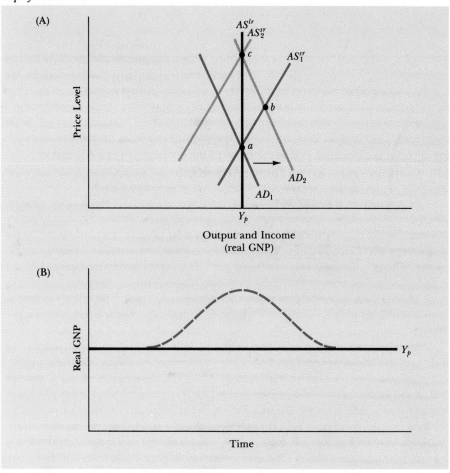

with no employment nor output changes. Firms would not have increased production, and workers would not have put in more hours. The costs of production would have risen as the output price rose. Fully anticipated demand changes cause movements along the long-run aggregate supply curve only. Anticipated demand changes are not considered shocks.

The term **supply shock** refers to an unexpected change in aggregate supply. Events that can affect supply include quantities and costs of inputs, technology, and expectations. Consider the effect of a change in the price of an essential resource, oil. In August 1990, Iraq invaded Kuwait. Oil prices more than doubled. Then, following the bombardment of Iraq by the U.N. forces in January 1991, oil prices fell back to their original level. What effects do the large changes in the price of oil have on economies?

Let's begin with the economy in equilibrium at point a in Figure 7-4. An increase in the price of an essential resource such as oil affects the entire economy. The costs of production rise, as indicated by the upward shift of the short-run aggregate supply curve AS_1^{sr} to AS_2^{sr}. As firms realize lower profits, they cut back production and lay off workers. The economy moves to point b. If the oil price hike is a one-time increase and the supply of oil is not permanently reduced, the economy adjusts to the price change and moves back to the potential output level. As oil prices return to their previous level, profits begin to rise. As profits return to their previous levels, firms recall their employees and increase production. The economy moves back to point a. In this case, the supply shock leads to a temporary decrease in employment and production and an increase in prices. Eventually employment and production rise, and prices fall. The supply shock leads to a business cycle as shown in Figure 7-4B by the dashed curve moving from Y_{p1} to Y_{p2} and back to Y_{p1}. The economy adjusts from point a to point b, then back to point a'.

If the oil price hike is a permanent relative price rise and is enforced by permanently lower supplies of oil, the supply shock takes a different form. The long-run aggregate supply curve shifts in. In this case, the initial decline in employment and production is not eventually reversed. The economy adjusts permanently to a lower potential output level—moving from point a to point b permanently in Figure 7-4A and from Y_{p1} to Y_{p2} in Figure 7-4B.

How Expectations Form

Expectations play a very important role in influencing individual behavior. Whether a business believes a demand change to be temporary or permanent determines whether that business hires additional workers, increases production, accumulates inventories, raises prices, or perhaps does nothing. Similarly, whether workers believe that inflation will increase or decrease for a short or long period of time influences their wage demands and the hours they are willing to work.

FIGURE 7-4   *A supply shock. Let's begin with the economy in equilibrium at point* a. *An increase in the price of an essential resource such as oil increases the costs of production as indicated by the upward shift of the short-run aggregate supply curve* AS_1^{sr} *to* AS_2^{sr}. *Firms realize lower profits, cut back production, and lay off workers. The economy moves to point* b. *If the oil price hike is a one-time increase and the supply of oil is not permanently reduced, the economy adjusts to the price change and moves back to point* a'. *Eventually employment and production rise and prices fall. The supply shock has led to a business cycle as shown in panel B by the dashed curve moving from* Y_{p1} *to* Y_{p2} *and back to* Y_{p1}. *If the oil price hike is permanent and is enforced by permanently lower supplies of oil, the supply shock takes a different form. The long-run aggregate supply curve shifts in. The economy adjusts permanently to a lower potential output level—moving from point* a *to point* b *permanently in Figure 7-4A and from* Y_{p1} *to* Y_{p2} *in panel B.*

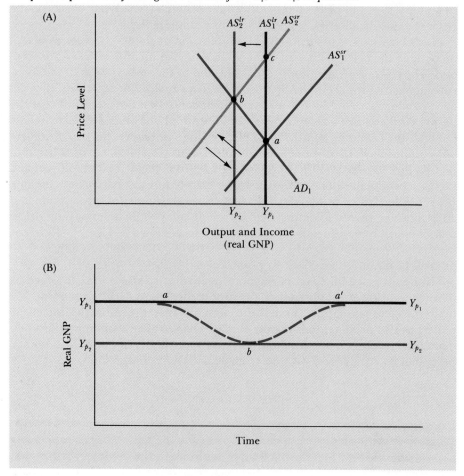

How people form expectations, what information enters their thought processes, and how quickly they forget, are very important components of the economy's behavior. If it is difficult (costly) for people to get valid information about economic variables or if it takes a long time for their expectations to adjust to reality, then it may take longer for the short-run aggregate supply curve to shift. In this case, whenever some demand shock hits the economy (that is, when *AD* unexpectedly shifts), output and employment are affected for a considerable length of time. In contrast, if information is readily available and people adjust their expectations to reality quite rapidly, then the short-run aggregate supply curve shifts rapidly after the event. Under these conditions, demand shocks have relatively small and short-lived impacts on output and employment.

Let's consider a couple of examples. Suppose the economy is described by the *AD* and *AS* curves of Figure 7-5. The economy currently is at equilibrium point *a*, so the price level is P_1 and the output level is Y_1. Now suppose the money supply is increased very rapidly. Such an increase shifts the *AD* curve out. What can we expect to happen to output and employment? The answer depends on how quickly the economy adjusts to the demand shock, the move from *a* to *c* in Figure 7-5.

At the one extreme, where individuals and firms have complete and correct information and there are no long-term contracts or other rigidities, adjustments take place immediately. The result is that the labor demand curve shifts out immediately, just as the labor supply curve shifts in leading to a higher nominal wage, the same real wage, and the same quantity of employment as before the demand shock. Thus, the economy moves immediately from point *a* to point *c* on the vertical *AS* curve. The money supply increase drives the price level up; output and employment levels do not change as labor market adjustments cause the short-run *AS* to fall.

If workers do not have the same information as firms or, as we have just seen, if workers and firms have negotiated long-term contracts that fix the nominal wage, the adjustment path is quite different. As aggregate demand increases and the price level is driven up, the labor demand curve shifts out. But the labor supply curve does not respond. As a result, employment rises, enabling firms to produce more output. At the new higher price level P_2, the quantity of output produced is Y_2 on AS^{sr} (point *b*). Eventually adjustments to the increased price level occur, and employment returns to its original level as output returns to Y_1. The important question is "How long does it take the adjustments to occur?" The answer depends on how expectations are formed.

Adaptive Expectations

One explanation of how people form expectations is known as the **adaptive expectations hypothesis (AEH)**. According to this idea, the price level that people expect to prevail in the next period is based on the behavior of prices in the recent past. More precisely, if the price level that people expect this period differs from the price level that actually occurs, people then adjust their expectations of next period's price. Individuals may, however, be reluctant to adjust their expectations fully to a one-period increase in the price level because they are not sure whether the increase is permanent. Perhaps they feel it is too risky to adjust completely to price changes or it is too costly for them to

FIGURE 7-5 *Adjustment to demand shocks. The economy currently is at equilibrium point* a. *Suppose that the money supply is increased very rapidly so the AD curve shifts out. What can we expect to happen to output and employment? At the one extreme, individuals and firms have complete and correct information, there are no long-term contracts or other rigidities, and the labor demand curve shifts out immediately just as the labor supply curve shifts in leading to a higher nominal wage, the same real wage, and the same quantity of employment as before the demand shock. Thus, we find movement from point* a *to point* c *on the vertical AS curve. The money supply increase drives the price level up; output and employment levels do not change. If workers do not have the same information as firms or if workers and firms have negotiated long-term contracts that fix the nominal wage, the adjustment path is quite different. At the new higher price level* P₂, *the quantity of output produced is* Y₂ *on* AS^sr *(point* b*). Eventually adjustments to the increased price level occur and employment returns to its original level as output returns to* Y₁.*

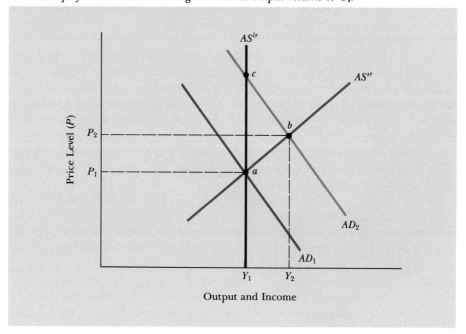

continually change their prices. Thus, if the price level yesterday was $P = 1.0$, and today is $P = 2.0$, people may have expected the price level to have been only $P = 1.0$. Realizing their mistake, they may alter their expectations for next year by adjusting to the current price level. They could revise their forecast of price level to be above $P = 1.0$ but not as high as $P = 2.0$ or they could forecast that price tomorrow is today's $P = 2.0$. In either case, it is said that the expectations are being formed adaptively.

The adaptive expectations scheme has some interesting implications for macroeconomics. In particular, the gradual adjustment of expected price levels to actual price levels means that *AD* shifts affect the levels of output and em-

FIGURE 7-6   *Adaptive expectations. Point* a *represents long-run equilibrium because the* AD *curve, the short-run* AS *curve, and the long-run* AS *curve all intersect there. The aggregate demand for goods equals the value of goods being produced at full employment, and individuals' forecasts of the price level match the actual price level. Suppose that point* a *is the output level associated with a 6 percent unemployment rate, and monetary or fiscal policy is employed to reduce the unemployment rate. The* AD *curve shifts to* AD$_2$. *The increase in aggregate demand drives the price level up to* P$_2$, *causing the labor demand curve to shift and hence the nominal wage to increase. Because under the adaptive expectations hypothesis workers do not expect the price level to increase, they believe their real wage has risen and consequently supply more labor. As a result, firms realize an increase in profits and thus produce more. The economy expands from* Y$_1$ *to* Y$_2$. *We see then that an "expansionary" economic policy does bring the unemployment rate down. However, because actual real wages and expected real wages differ, workers eventually realize their forecasting errors and correct them; and long-run equilibrium is restored at point* e.

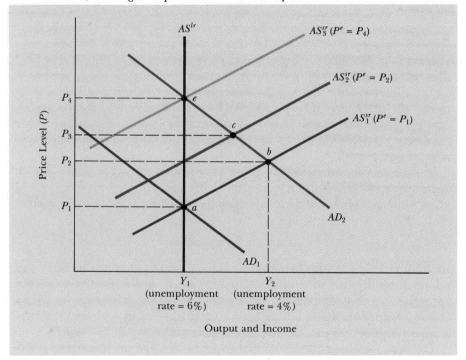

ployment. Suppose the economy is at point *a* in Figure 7-6. This point represents long-run equilibrium because the *AD* curve, the short-run *AS* curve, and the long-run *AS* curve all intersect there. Not only is the aggregate demand for goods equal to the value of goods being produced at full employment, but individuals' forecasts of the price level are identical to the actual price level. Suppose that point *a* is the output level associated with a 6 percent unemployment rate— and that is a rate policymakers find unacceptable. As a result, a change in monetary or fiscal policy is enacted to reduce the unemployment rate. This policy action is reflected in a rightward shift of the *AD* curve to AD_2. The increase in aggregate demand drives the price level up to P_2, causing the labor demand curve to shift and hence the nominal wage to increase. Because under the adaptive expectations hypothesis workers have no reason to expect the price level to increase to P_2, they believe their real wage has risen and consequently offer to supply more labor. As a result, firms are realizing an increase in profits and thus produce more. The economy expands from Y_1 to Y_2 where the unemployment rate is 4 percent. We see then that an "expansionary" economic policy does bring the unemployment rate down. However, because actual real wages and expected real wages differ, workers eventually recognize their forecasting errors and correct them.

If people adjust their price expectations fully to price level changes within one period, then the labor supply curve shifts up in the second period, because people expect the price to be P_2, the price that prevailed today. The short-run *AS* curve, denoted as $AS_1^{sr}(P^e = P_2)$ to represent the idea that the position of the curve depends on price expectations, now intersects the *AD* curve at point *c*. But the price level rises to P_3, so once again people are wrong. As a result, another adjustment occurs; people revise their expectations of inflation, thinking that the price level next period will be today's price level P_3, and the *AS* curve shifts up once again. This process continues until the economy comes to rest several periods later at point *e*, where the actual price level matches the expected price level.

In the long run, the economic policy has not altered output, but has caused the price level to rise. But the long run has been several periods—the periods during which people adjust their expectations according to the adaptive scheme.

Rational Expectations

The adaptive expectations hypothesis has been criticized as being overly rigid and much too limited to describe actual behavior. Economists who offer an alternative view suggest that people use whatever information they can get to form their expectations and do not merely adjust to reality in an adaptive way. These economists suggest the **rational expectations hypothesis (REH)**.

The general argument of rational expectations is that people acquire information and adjust expectations in a way that maximizes their satisfaction or utility. If it is costly or impossible to acquire every piece of information, then it is unlikely that people know everything and avoid all errors. If information is readily available, that information is used by people to form their expectations. In any event, people react and respond to changes; they don't simply stand by and adapt their expectations in a mechanical way time after time.

The strictest form of the REH is **perfect foresight**. According to the perfect foresight assumption, individuals always predict the future price level correctly. This allows absolutely no room for forecast errors or for *AD* changes to affect income and employment. Suppose the monetary authorities increase the money supply in an attempt to lower the unemployment rate. Such a policy change is reflected as an outward shift of the *AD* curve from AD_1 to AD_2 in Figure 7-7. The initial equilibrium at point *a* is disrupted. Under the adaptive expectations hypothesis, the economy would go from point *a* to point *b* to point *c*. Under the perfect foresight form of REH, however, individuals forecast perfectly the final effect of the change in the money supply. Because these same individuals know that an upward shift of the *AD* curve raises the price, they expect the price level to rise and their real wage to fall. They demand higher nominal wages to work the same number of hours. This leads to an inward shift of the labor supply curve and an upward shift of the short-run *AS* curve from AS_1^{sr} to AS_2^{sr}. Because workers will forecast the price effects of the monetary expansion correctly under the perfect foresight assumption, the short-run *AS* curve shifts immediately to intersect the *AD* and the *AS* curves at point *e*.

FIGURE 7-7   *Rational expectations. Suppose the monetary authorities increase the money supply in an attempt to lower the unemployment rate. The* AD *curve shifts out from* AD$_1$ *to* AD$_2$. *Under the perfect foresight form of REH, people expect the price level to rise and their real wage to fall. They demand higher nominal wages to work the same number of hours. This leads to an inward shift of the labor supply curve and an upward shift of the short-run* AS *curve from* AS$_1^{sr}$ *to* AS$_2^{sr}$. *Because workers forecast the price effects of the monetary expansion correctly under the perfect foresight assumption, the short-run* AS *curve shifts immediately to intersect the* AD *and the* AS *curves at point* e.

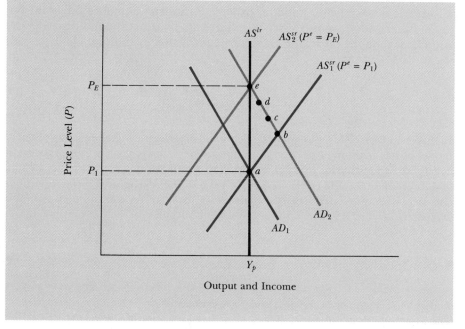

Information is neither perfectly available nor costless in the real world. The manager of a department store who wants to know the price of each item charged by a competitor must survey the competitor or spend time reading ads. Similarly, for that manager to know whether an increase in the number of customers in his or her store is an increase in the demand for his or her merchandise alone or an increase in the demand for all such merchandise, he or she must spend time visiting the other stores or pay someone to get that information. It is not rational for people to gather every bit of information; they gather information up to the point where the marginal cost of search equals the marginal benefit. It is logical, then, that individuals have different amounts of information and different qualities of information about various markets. They may know the price of their product or their wages but perhaps may not know the prices of other products or the wages of other laborers. Under these conditions, some forecasting mistakes are probably made and the economy adjusts to a demand change by moving from a to b to c rather than directly from a to c. However, the length of time it takes for the move varies according to how well informed people are, how consistently economic policy has been carried out, the state of the economy, and other factors that we consider in later chapters.

You can see now how the macro model of the economy functions. You can also imagine the possibilities for disagreements among economists over the speed with which adjustments occur and thus over whether economic policy is useful or not. Depending on the existence of long-term contracts, imperfect information, adaptive or rational expectations formation, and other institutional factors, the economy behaves differently. The next chapter discusses the schools of thought regarding the operation of this macro model.

▼   ▼   ▼   ▼   ▼   ▼   ▼   ▼   ▼   ▼   ▼
Conclusions

In this chapter, we have put aggregate demand and supply together. The complete model of the economy has been developed. The *AD* expresses the interaction of aggregate expenditures, money, and interest rates, and the interest rate, wealth, and international trade effects of price changes. The *AS* captures input quantities and prices, production, profits, the behavior of the labor market, and expectations. Together, *AD* and *AS* determine the levels of output, prices, and employment.

▼   ▼   ▼   ▼   ▼   ▼   ▼   ▼   ▼   ▼   ▼
Summary

1. Why does the aggregate demand curve slope downward?
The aggregate demand curve slopes downward because of the wealth effect, the interest rate effect, and the international trade effect.

2. What causes the aggregate demand curve to shift?
The aggregate demand curve shifts when one of the autonomous spending components changes, such as a change in expectations, exchange rates, price of foreign goods, tastes, or government policy.

3. Does the aggregate supply curve slope up, or is it vertical?
The long-run aggregate supply curve is vertical; the short-run curve may slope upward. The slope of the aggregate supply curve depends on the speed with which wages and prices adjust to economic events and the amount of knowledge consumers and firms have regarding economic events and their impacts on the economy.

4. What causes the aggregate supply curve to shift?
Shifts in the aggregate supply curve stem from technological changes, changes in the quantities of resources, and changes in the costs of production. When the costs of production (costs of inputs or resources) change, the short-run aggregate supply curve shifts. When the quantity or quality of resources or technology changes, the long-run aggregate supply curve shifts.

5. What are demand and supply shocks?
Demand and supply shocks are economic events that are not anticipated, events that can affect the position of either the aggregate demand or aggregate supply curve.

▼
Key Terms

economic shock   165
demand shock   165
supply shock   167
adaptive expectations hypothesis
  (AEH)   169

rational expectations hypothesis
  (REH)   172
perfect foresight   172

▼
Problems and Exercises

1.   Derive and explain the differences between the short-run aggregate supply and the long-run aggregate supply curves.

2.   What are efficiency wages? What effects does the existence of an efficiency wage have on the aggregate supply curves?

3.   Explain how a decline in the expected price level affects the short-run *AS* curve.

4.   Consider the following statement: "If price expectations are important, very restrictive aggregate demand policies may not restore reasonable price stability in the next five years." What does this statement mean?

5.   Suppose policymakers want to attain a lower price level and propose to do so by reducing government purchases and the money supply. Discuss this policy in terms of both the adaptive and rational expectations schemes. Explain what would be expected for output and prices.

6.   Explain the effects of a law passed by the U.S. Congress restricting oil imports by over half of current levels.

7.   Explain the effects of a law implemented in the United States that would guarantee workers a four-week vacation each year.

8.   Explain the effects on the U.S. economy if the European Economic Community (EEC) passed a law restricting imports of U.S. products.

Appendix

The Algebra of Aggregate Supply and Aggregate Demand

The aggregate demand equation is equation 23 in the appendix to Chapter 5. It is

$$Y\left(1 - c_y + X_y + I_r \times \frac{L_y}{L_r}\right) = C_0/P + I_0 + G_0 + X_0/P - I_r\left(\frac{L_0 - M_0/P}{L_r}\right)$$

Let us rewrite that in very simple form as

$$Y = aZ - bP$$

so that Z represents all the variables other than output and the price level, a, represents all the coefficients not related to output and the price level, and b represents the coefficients related to the price level — the wealth, interest rate, and international trade effects.

The aggregate supply function is written as

$$Y - Y_p = c(P - P^e).$$

This form, which is sometimes referred to as the Lucas supply curve, indicates that actual output, Y, differs from the potential output level, Y_p, if expected prices, P^e, differ from actual prices, P. For instance, the actual output level is less than the potential output level whenever the expected price level is greater

177

than the actual price level. In Figure 7-1, this is shown as the upward-sloping aggregate supply curve to the left of the long-run vertical aggregate supply curve. The actual output level exceeds the potential output level when the expected price is less than the actual price. When the actual price is the expected price, then actual output and potential output are the same.

The aggregate supply and aggregate demand functions can be solved for one output level and one price level. The result depends on how expectations are formed and the relation between actual and expected price levels. If the expected and actual price levels are the same, then the *AD* and *AS* functions result in actual output and potential output being equal and defined by the relation $Y_p = -bP + aZ$.

▼
Adaptive Expectations

Let us consider the supply and demand equations again but with a slightly different form.

$$\textit{Supply:} \qquad Y_t - Y_p = c(P_t - P_t^e) + U_t$$
$$\textit{Demand:} \qquad Y_t = aZ_t - bP_t$$

The only new variable added here is U_t, which represents a random term having an average value of zero.

In the text, we stated that an adaptively formed price expectation uses only past values of prices to forecast the future price. This can be shown by rewriting the adaptive scheme

$$P_t^e = P_{t-1}^e + L(P_{t-1} - P_{t-1}^e)$$

for period $t - 1$ rather than period t as

$$P_{t-1}^e = P_{t-2}^e + L(P_{t-2} - P_{t-2}^e)$$

and substituting the $t - 1$ expression into the t expression. Substituting for P_{t-1}^e we obtain

$$P_t^e = LP_{t-1} + (1 - L)[P_{t-2}^e + L(P_{t-2} - P_{t-2}^e)]$$

Now, writing the adaptive form for the expected price in period $t - 2$, $t - 3$, $t - 4$, and so on, and substituting, we obtain an expression that states that the expected price level today depends only on past prices:

$$P_t^e = LP_{t-1} + L(1 - L)P_{t-2} + L(1 - L)^2 P_{t-3} + \dots$$

In words, the adaptive scheme requires that expectations of prices be formed on the basis of past values of prices only. In this specification, the value of L indicates how important the more recent past is relative to the more distant past. Suppose L is three-fourths. Then the price expected for period t consists of three-fourths of last period's price plus three-sixteenths of the price two periods ago plus a diminishing portion of previous periods' past prices. (This type of expectations scheme is also referred to as **autoregressive**, which means that the forecast value, P^e, is determined by past values of P.)

▼

Rational Expectations

Under rational expectations, P_t^e is the expected price level for period t given all information in period $t - 1$, not just past prices. Setting demand equal to supply yields

(1) $$P_t = [1/(b + c)]\{cP_t^e + aZ_t - Y_p - U_t\}$$

The rational expectations forecast is the solution given in this equation where Z and U must be forecast because only their past values are known. Hence

$$P_t^e = [1/(b + c)]\{cP_t^e + aZ_t^e - Y_p^e - U_t^e\}$$

U_t^e is zero so that

(2) $$P_t^e = [1/(b + c)]\{cP_t^e + aZ_t^e - Y_p^e\}$$

Subtracting equation 2 from 1 yields

(3) $$P_t - P_t^e = [1/(b + c)]\{a(Z_t - Z_t^e) - U_t\}$$

and substituting equation 3 into the supply function yields

(4) $$Y_t - Y_{pt} = [ca/(c + b)]\{Z_t - Z_t^e) + [b/(b + c)]U_t\}$$

Equation 4 says that the deviation of output from the potential output level in period t depends only on the surprises that come from those variables Z, such as government purchases or monetary changes and on random events. If $Z^e = Z$ for any period, then the only deviations between actual and potential output are random deviations.

Part Three

Controversies and Issues of Aggregate Demand and Supply

Chapter 8

The Evolution of Economic Thought

What to Expect

Some economists argue that policies lowering the inflation rate tend to cause more unemployment. Others insist that only unexpected changes in inflation can affect the levels of national income and employment. Some assert that the government can only affect the level of output and employment if it can fool the public; others argue that government actions can always be used to reduce the violent swings of the business cycle. To understand macroeconomics today, one really has to understand how the field has evolved over time. Since its beginnings, several different views have developed on how the economy functions, and these views influence policies. A recent political cartoon captures the evolution of macroeconomics quite well. It shows two bums sitting on a park bench. One bum says to the other, "First I was a Keynesian, then a monetarist, and now I'm nothing."

Macroeconomics has evolved, changing emphases as different issues and problems were encountered. The evolution has been described as a series of schools of thought; the classical economists, followed by the Keynesian economists, the monetarists, and finally the new classical and new Keynesian economists. Are these schools of thought distinct and different? Can one be both a Keynesian and a monetarist? What do the schools imply for economic policy? Should we know from which school the chairman of the Fed comes, or to which the chair of the Council of Economic Advisers (CEA) suscribes, before they are appointed to their positions? In this chapter, we discuss how the various schools of thought view the economy and illustrate their approaches, using aggregate demand and aggregate supply. The following questions are considered:

1. Why do economists disagree?

2. What are the alternative schools of thought?

3. What do the various schools of thought imply for economic policy?

▼

Aggregate Demand and Supply and the Schools of Thought

It is easy to classify people or economists as belonging to a particular school of thought or a specific political philosophy, but easy is not always right. An economist might believe in free markets for some types of activities and in government regulation for others. Is this economist a liberal or a conservative, a classicalist, or a Keynesian? Although the schools of thought are discussed as if they were quite distinct and distinguishable, in fact most economists are eclectic, picking and choosing elements from more than one school of thought. Moreover, although the schools are described as having very clear, sharp distinctions, often they are not so distinct. In fact, the ideas of one school often merge into the ideas of another.

The distinction between the schools of thought can be represented as different shapes of the *AD* and *AS* curves. As we have seen, the aggregate supply curve can take on several shapes: it can be vertical—the long-run aggregate supply curve; it can slope upward and vary from quite flat to quite steep in the short run. The adjustment from the short run to the long run can take a little or a great deal of time. It all depends on institutional factors that exist in the economy and the degree to which individuals obtain and assimilate information. These features define the schools of macroeconomic thought.

Let's assume that the economy is currently in equilibrium at point *a* in Figure 8-1. The price level is P_1, and the output level is the potential output level Y_1. Now suppose that some event causes the *AD* curve to shift in to AD_2. Such an event might be a decrease in autonomous consumption, investment, net exports, government spending, or the money supply. The schools of thought often attribute the shifts to different causes. Whatever the cause, according to our diagram the economy could move to point *b*, the intersection of AD_2 and the short-run aggregate supply curve AS_1^{sr}, or to point *c*, the intersection of the new *AD* curve and the long-run *AS* curve, AS^{lr}.

FIGURE 8-1   *Aggregate demand, aggregate supply, and the various schools of macroeconomic thought.*
The economy is currently in equilibrium at point a. The price level is P_1 and the output level is
the potential output level Y_1. Now suppose that some event causes the AD curve to shift in to AD_2.
The schools of thought often attribute the shifts to different causes. Whatever the cause, according
to our diagram, the economy could move to point b, the intersection of AD_2 and the short-run ag-
gregate supply curve AS_1^{sr}, or to point c, the intersection of the new AD curve and the long-run
AS curve, AS^{lr}.

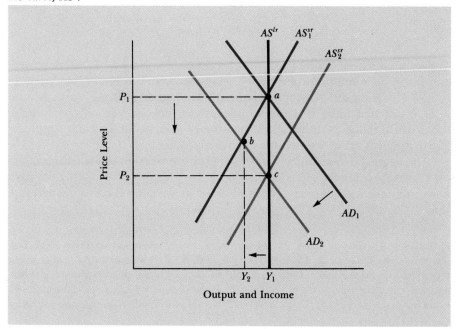

How the economy adjusts depends on whether wages and prices are flexible or sticky. If for some reason, nominal wages are fixed, then as aggregate
demand decreases, firms charge lower prices, realize lower profits, and produce less output. Eventually the costs of doing business fall, so firms produce
more—in fact, they are willing to produce the quantity they did before AD
changed. The short-run aggregate supply curve shifts down to AS_2^{sr} and the intersection between AD and AS_2^{sr} defines the new price and output levels, P_3 and
Y_1, at point c.

Points a and c reflect the long-run adjustment to the AD change and so trace
out the long-run AS curve. Points a and b reflect the rigidities in the labor market and trace out the short-run AS curve. In the short run (however long that
is) the multiplier effect is the change in output from Y_1 to Y_2. In the long run,
the only effect of the AD decrease is a price level decrease. The multiplier is zero.

Does the economy move from a to b to c, or directly from a to c? If it moves
from a to b, how long does it take for the adjustment from b to c to occur? If

the economy moves from *a* to *b* to *c*, can economic policy be used to reduce the output and employment fluctuations that result? The answers to these questions vary according to the school of thought that is providing the answer. Let's now briefly consider the schools of thought in the order in which they emerged: classical, Keynesian, monetarist, and finally, new classical and new Keynesian.

▼
Classical Economics

The classical school of thought includes most economists who wrote, practiced, and taught at some point during a period of about 160 years (roughly 1770 to 1930) and included Adam Smith, David Ricardo, Alfred Marshall, and A. C. Pigou as its most important theorists. As with most schools of thought, the classical model is an idealized framework that synthesizes and simplifies the writings of many economists over many years.

The aggregate demand and aggregate supply diagram of Figure 8-2 shows the classical economist's view of the world. The supply curve is vertical, which means that the level of output depends only on the determinants of aggregate

FIGURE 8-2   *The classical system. This aggregate demand and supply diagram shows the classical economist's view of the world. The supply curve is vertical, which means that the level of output depends only on the determinants of aggregate supply: the quality and quantity of inputs and technology. Aggregate demand plays a role only in determining the level of prices. In the classical scheme, prices and wages are perfectly flexible. As a result, there is no disequilibrium or adjustment period in which wages and prices do not change in response to demand changes.*

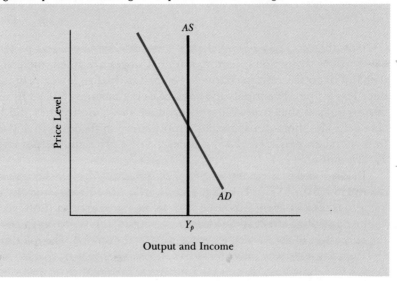

supply: the quality and quantity of inputs and technology. Aggregate demand plays a role only in determining the level of prices; it has no effect on the level of output. In the *classical scheme,* prices and wages are perfectly flexible; there are no long-term contracts, no asymmetric or imperfect information, nor any other rigidity that creates a sluggish adjustment of wages and/or prices to demand or supply shocks. As a result, there is no disequilibrium or adjustment period in which wages and prices do not change in response to demand changes.

In the classical system, there is no involuntary unemployment. Everyone willing and able to work has a job. If the demand for a particular type of job falls, then so does the wage rate, and some people voluntarily choose not to work in that job. Because there is no involuntary unemployment and no recessionary gap that can exist for any length of time, there is no reason for economic policy to do anything other than to minimize inflation.

Say's Law

The classical view of *AD* and *AS* is called **Say's law**, which simply says that supply creates its own demand. According to Say's law, the quantity of output and employment are determined by those factors that define the level of potential output or the location of the long-run aggregate supply curve—the "real" factors such as productivity and technology. The aggregate demand curve does nothing more than define the price level; it has nothing to do with determining the levels of real output and employment. Thus, supply defines output. Supply creates its own demand because the production process automatically creates income equal to the value of output while flexible prices and interest rates ensure that total spending equals total income. A belief in Say's law implies that unemployment, as a long-term proposition at least, is not possible. This is evident in the derivation of a vertical *AS* curve. The demand for and supply of labor determine the quantity of labor employed, and wages and prices adjust to ensure that the quantity of labor demanded and the quantity of labor supplied equate—that full employment occurs. According to Say's law, the economy is self-adjusting; that is, shocks or disturbances to the economy that drive the economy from its potential output level are only very temporary. With flexible interest rates, planned saving always equals planned investment, so planned expenditures always equal total production. Prolonged overproduction—which would cause firms to reduce employment—is impossible.

The Role of Money

In addition, the role of money in the classical system is limited to determining the level of prices. Using what is referred to as the *equation of exchange—MV = PY,* where M is the money supply, V is the **velocity** or number of times the money supply changes hands in a year, P is the price level, and Y is real output—the classical economists demonstrate a direct link between money, M, and the price level, P. The equation of exchange can be rewritten as $M = PY/V$. They argue that because Y is fixed at potential output, then changes in M lead to changes in P/V. Moreover, because they assume that V is constant, changes in M are translated directly to proportionate changes in P. The equation of exchange comes from a tautology or definition: $GNP = GNP$. As we saw in Chapter 2, GNP measured as output is equal to GNP measured as expenditures. Nominal output is PY. Expenditures require money and thus equal MV. Hence, $MV = PY$.

▼
Keynesian Economics

The *Keynesian model* of macroeconomics was developed during the Great Depression of the 1930s, a period when worldwide unemployment rose significantly, reaching 25 percent in the United States and Germany. Given this event, Say's law did not seem to be a very satisfying explanation of how the economy functioned. The economy did not seem to be self-correcting. J. M. Keynes provided the alternative to Say's law that most economists of the time accepted. Keynes's *General Theory of Employment, Interest, and Money,* published in 1936, took apart the classical system and built an alternative.

Wage and Price Rigidities

To argue that an economy can be mired in a recession with large-scale unemployment for long periods of time, Keynes had to tear apart the classical system: he rejected Say's law, argued that wages and prices were not flexible, and asserted that the economy was not self-correcting. In an economy hit with a demand shock, as shown in Figure 8-3, unemployment increases and output decreases as the economy moves from point a to point b. According to the Keynesian view, there is no reason for the economy to move from point b because wages and prices do not change. Keynes argued that rigidities in the economy, such as monopolies and labor unions, thwart the movement of wages and prices. Moreover, he argued that workers are under a **money illusion** because they care more about the nominal (or money) wage, W, than the real wage, W/P. As a result, workers refuse to take cuts in their nominal wages even if the real wage remains the same. This, he said, results in an economy that is not self-correcting.

According to Keynes, instead of waiting for falling wages and prices to move the economy back to its potential level, policymakers must attack unemployment by manipulating aggregate demand. Price increases that result from an increase in demand lower real wages and increase employment, given stable nominal wages. Thus, Keynes essentially reversed what the classical economists had argued: employment does not rise as a result of an automatic drop in real wages; instead, real wages fall because of increased employment resulting from an increase in aggregate demand.

FIGURE 8-3   *The Keynesian system. An economy hit with a demand shock experiences increasing unemployment and reduced output as it moves from point a to point b. According to the Keynesian view, rigidities in the economy, such as monopolies and labor unions, thwart the movement of wages and prices. Moreover, workers are under a "money illusion" because they care more about the nominal wage, W, than the real wage, W/P. As a result, workers refuse to take cuts in their nominal wages even if the real wage remains the same. This, Keynes said, resulted in an economy that is not self-correcting.*

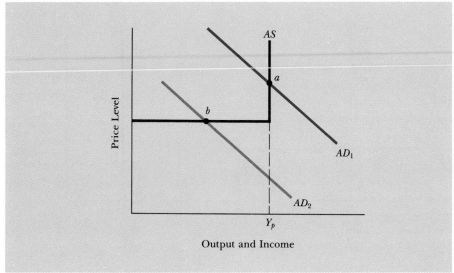

Keynes had to construct a case for a general or widespread market failure if he was to dismantle the classical system. He had to demonstrate that the economy could come to rest at an output level below the potential output level. Looking at the *AD–AS* diagram in Figure 8-4A, we can see that Keynes had to argue either that *AD* and *AS* would intersect at some point like *a*, which is below the potential output level Y_p, or that *AD* and *AS* would not even intersect, as shown in Figure 8-4B. Either of these events can occur as a result of a couple of reasons: if wages and prices are not flexible and/or if the economy is caught in a liquidity trap.

The rigidity of wages and prices could result in a short-run *AS* curve shown in Figure 8-4A. The *AS* curve may slope upward or be quite flat or even horizontal, depending on whether wages and prices adjust at all. If the economy is at point *a* where *AD* intersects the *AS* curve below the potential output level, is there any mechanism for the economy to "automatically" adjust to the potential output level? According to Keynes, the answer is no. Because Say's law does not hold, the *AD* curve must shift out if output is to rise. Keynes didn't see any reason for the *AD* curve to shift on its own accord. Instead, only through government actions—fiscal policy—would the *AD* curve shift.

FIGURE 8-4   *The Keynesian view. Keynes had to argue either that* AD *and* AS *intersect at some point like* a, *which is below the potential output level* Y_p, *or do not intersect, as shown in panel B. Rigidity of wages and prices can result in a short-run* AS *curve, as shown in panel A. The* AS *curve may slope upward or be quite flat or even horizontal, depending on whether wages and prices adjust at all. If a liquidity trap exists, then the outcome shown in panel B is possible. Again, the question becomes "Is there anything that will shift* AD *in order for an intersection with* AS *to occur at the potential output level?"*

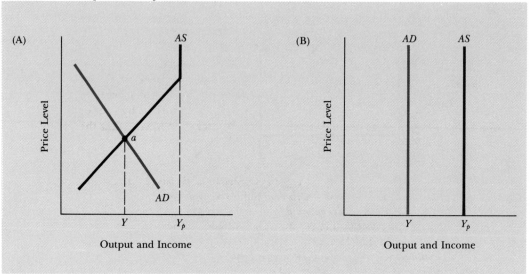

The Liquidity Trap

The **liquidity trap** was another mechanism Keynes developed for arguing that the economy would not follow Say's law. According to the classical economists and embodied in the quantity theory of money, $M = PY/V$, people only hold or demand money to carry out transactions. According to the quantity theory, the demand for money, M^D, depends on people's nominal income, PY, and the speed with which they carry out transactions, $1/V$. Keynes argued that people not only hold or demand money in order to carry out transactions, but also to speculate in the bond markets. This he called *liquidity preference*. He argued that at high interest rates people prefer to invest in bonds instead of money (the opportunity cost of holding money is too high). But as the interest rate falls, people begin to sell their bonds and hold more money. The interest rate can, in theory, fall so low that everyone believes bonds are a bad investment. As a result, everyone now wants to hold the more liquid asset—money. Then, even as the supply of money rises, people hold the money as money rather than purchase bonds. The economy is thus stuck in a liquidity trap.

What did the liquidity trap have to do with the functioning of the economy? Keynes argued that if the economy is in a liquidity trap, then monetary policy has no effect on the economy, because increases in the money supply do not lower the interest rate. Keynes believed that an increase in the money supply can affect the price level but does so by affecting the interest rate first. A larger supply of money might lead to lower interest rates and an increase in interest-sensitive spending—investment and consumption. The increased spending then leads to higher prices. But if the increased money supply cannot affect the interest rate, then it does not necessarily affect the price level through interest-sensitive spending. This means that monetary policy is ineffective in the face of depression and large-scale unemployment.

In the liquidity trap that Keynes envisioned, the demand for money curve is perfectly horizontal, which translates into a horizontal *LM* curve, as shown in Figure 8-5A. The horizontal *LM* curve has dire implications for monetary policy. An increase in the money supply is automatically absorbed by money holders without the need for a drop in the interest rate. This means that the

FIGURE 8-5   *The liquidity trap. In the liquidity trap Keynes envisioned, the money demand curve is perfectly horizontal, which translates into a horizontal* LM *curve, as shown in panel A. An increase in the money supply is automatically absorbed by money holders without the need for a drop in the interest rate. This means that the* LM *curve is simply extended horizontally rightward, as shown in panel A by noting that* LM(M₁) *equals* LM(M₂). *The change in the money supply fails to alter either the equilibrium interest rate or the income level.*

The liquidity trap translates into a vertical AD *curve. Note in panel B that when changes in P have no effect on the IS or LM curves, the AD curve is vertical. Combined with a vertical AS curve, there is a distinct possibility that no intersection between AD and AS will occur. This market failure implies that prolonged unemployment can exist.*

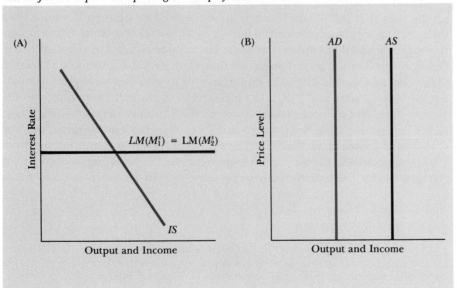

LM curve is simply extended horizontally rightward, as shown in panel A by noting that $LM(M_1^s)$ equals $LM(M_2^s)$. The change in the money supply fails to alter either the equilibrium interest rate or the income level. Monetary policy is ineffective in a liquidity trap.

What does the liquidity trap imply for the shape of the AD curve? It translates into a vertical AD curve. Note in Figure 8-5B that when changes in P have no effect on the IS or LM curves, the AD curve is vertical. This means that the AD and AS curves might not intersect—a market failure that affects the whole economy, as shown in panel B. This is the theoretical argument with which Keynes wanted to demonstrate that Say's law was invalid and that the AD curve had to be shifted by fiscal policy in order for the intersection of AD and AS to occur at the potential output level.

The Real Balance Effect

In attacking the classical system Keynes had used one of the most well-known classical economists' writings as his straw man, A. C. Pigou's *Theory of Unemployment*. Interestingly, one of Pigou's ideas, the **Pigou effect**,[1] was used to criticize the Keynesian system early on. Pigou believed that when the real value of people's money holdings increases, people will spend more. Thus, changes in real money balances, M/P, affect the AD. A lower price level increases real wealth, M/P, and thus increases consumption. With the Pigou effect, the AD curve could not be vertical, as was the case with the liquidity trap.[2] The Pigou effect could not be rendered ineffective even by the liquidity trap, because the Pigou effect did not depend on the interest rate.

Although the Pigou effect seemed to offset the liquidity trap, it did not offset the idea that the AS curve might be horizontal or upward sloping rather than vertical. And an intersection between AD and AS at a point below potential output seemed to explain the Great Depression. Thus, even though the attacks on the Keynesian system arose almost immediately on the publication of the *General Theory* in 1936, the importance of Keynes's message grew throughout the 1940s, 1950s, and 1960s. The message grew within the economics profession as well as in the policymaking corridors. Students were schooled in the Keynesian system from the first economics course they encountered; the first *Principles of Economics* textbook, written by Paul Samuelson and published in 1948, was steeped in the Keynesian approach. Thus, economists emerging from colleges in the 1950s and 1960s were often oriented toward the Keynesian

---

1   The Pigou effect is the wealth or real balance effect discussed earlier in this book.
2   In Chapter 4, we saw that the AD curve slopes down when there is a wealth effect. The Pigou effect thus means that the AD curve is not vertical, and intersects the AS curve.

theme. And, economists who became involved in policymaking for the Kennedy and Johnson administrations in the 1960s and 1970s typically argued the Keynesian side.

▼
Monetarism

The Keynesian view dominated macroeconomics during the 1950s and early 1960s. The two primary themes of Keynesian economics were that the government had to be an active participant in the economy and that its activity had to consist of fiscal policy rather than monetary policy. But even as predominant as Keynesianism was, some economists were not satisfied with its two main themes. Milton Friedman, in particular, had been arguing a monetarist approach since the 1940s. *Monetarists* criticized the Keynesian view that the government had to be an active participant in the economy and that monetary policy played no role. But monetarism was not just warmed-over classical economics. The monetarists and the classical economists may have had the same view of the economy in the long run (the stock of money determines the price level but has nothing to do with output or relative prices), but the monetarists argued, in contrast to the classical school, that the economy can diverge from potential output in the short run and that monetary policy can be an important factor in the divergence.

The Role of Money

The foremost monetarist was Milton Friedman. In the heyday of Keynesianism, Friedman published a set of essays demonstrating the importance of money. He set out a new version of the demand for money in which the demand for money was a function of many important variables, including wealth, income, and interest rates. Friedman's restatement altered two points of the earlier writers: (1) he did not argue that velocity, V, is stable or fixed but instead noted that V varies as wealth, income, and interest rates vary; and (2) he said that real wealth affects the amount of money people want to hold or demand. Friedman's work argued persuasively that money does matter, that Keynes was wrong in ignoring the role of money in the economy. Friedman refuted the idea of a liquidity trap, but also argued, in contrast to the classical school, that interest rates and income affect the demand for money.

Keynesians believed that monetary policy could affect aggregate demand only by changing the interest rate and, consequently, investment spending. Monetarists asserted a much broader role for money supply changes, arguing that an increase in the money supply pushes aggregate demand up by increasing business and household spending through interest rate changes and through the wealth effect.

The Role of Government Policy

Unlike Keynesian economists, monetarists do not believe that the economy is subject to instability and market failure that must be offset by government action. Most monetarists believe that the economy tends toward equilibrium at the level of potential national output in the long run. In fact, monetarists often argue that government policy, especially monetary policy, creates economic fluctuations rather than reduces them. To prove their point, they note that throughout history periods of relatively fast money growth have been followed by booms and inflation, while periods of relatively slow money growth have been followed by recessions. Monetarists favor little (or nonactivist) government policy because they believe that the government's attempts to make the economy better off by aiming money supply and government spending and taxation policies at low inflation and low unemployment often make things worse. They argue that there are long lags between economic policy and the the resulting effects on the economy and that these lags can lead to incorrect policy decisions. In other words, they argue that the economy will by itself eventually return to the equilibrium level at potential output. Thus, to change economic policy is to take the chance that the policy will throw the economy into a boom and inflationary period. Then, to offset the inflation, another policy will be implemented that then deepens the decline in the economy.

This monetarist view of government policy is illustrated in Figure 8-6. Assume that the economy is initially in equilibrium with full employment—at point *a*. An adverse demand shock shifts the aggregate curve to AD_2, so output and employment fall in the short run as the economy moves to point *b*. A Keynesian economist would argue for government intervention to shift aggregate demand back to AD_1 and the economy back to point *a*. A monetarist would argue that automatic adjustments in the labor market would occur before government policy changes were able to affect *AD*. Because of the long lags associated with the impact of government intervention on the economy, the short-run aggregate supply curve would move to AS_1^s before aggregate demand shifted back to AD_1. Consequently, the change in government policy would cause the economy to overshoot potential output, moving to point *d*, while creating inflationary pressures.

Much of the lag in the economy is due, according to the monetarists, to the fact that people revise and form expectations adaptively. Thus, it takes several periods for a complete reaction to economic shocks to take place. Because of these lags, which are long and variable—in other words, not the same every time—monetarists argue that policymakers should set policy according to *rules* that do not change from month to month or even from year to year. For instance, one rule they favor is to require that the money supply grow at a fixed rate over time. This would let people learn what to expect and would reduce the fluctuations associated with forecast errors and surprises.

FIGURE 8-6   *Monetarist view of government policy. The economy is initially in equilibrium with full employment — at point* a. *An adverse demand shock shifts the aggregate demand curve to* AD_2, *so output and employment fall in the short run as the economy moves to point* b. *A monetarist would argue that automatic adjustments in the labor market occur before government policy changes can affect AD. The short-run aggregate supply curve moves to* AS_2^{sr} *before government intervention can shift aggregate demand back to* AD_1. *Consequently, the change in government policy causes the economy to overshoot potential output, moving to point* d.

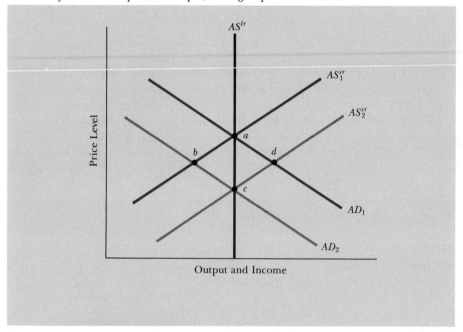

New Classical Economics

The events of the 1970s caused many to discard the Keynesian system, but they also raised a few questions about monetarism. Inflation and unemployment rates rose during the 1970s, and economic policy actually seemed to make matters worse. Economists began to question whether monetary or fiscal policy could affect real output and employment in the short run. The result of these questions was a refinement of the classical school of thought known as **new classical economics**. New classical economics updated the classical scheme and incorporated elements of the monetarist system. In particular, new classical economics does not assume that people know everything that is happening, as the old theory did, nor that prices and wages adjust immediately and fully to demand and supply shocks. According to new classical economics, people do make mistakes because their expectations of prices or some other critical variable are different from the future reality. In contrast to the monetarist school, the new classical school assumes that people form their expectations based on all available relevant information—*rational expectations*—not adaptively and because of rational expectations, forecast errors can't last very long.

The Role of Expectations

New classical economics emphasizes expectations. It is argued that changes in economic policy (*AD* shifts) can change the level of national output only if those policy changes are *unexpected*. If it is costly to acquire information, then firms and households do not have the same nor complete and perfect information at all times. For instance, firms might find that they can acquire information about prices in their industry quite readily, but cannot acquire information about economy-wide prices until some time after a change occurs. Firms make a best guess or form an expectation about what is going on by looking at their own industry and market. If the prices of the goods they are selling are rising, that is seen as an indication that their relative prices are rising. Firms produce more when their relative prices rise more than the firms expected—their expected profits rise. Each firm in the economy sees a higher price but mistakenly assumes that only it is experiencing the higher price. Conversely, firms produce less when the price is unexpectedly low. There is, therefore, a positive relationship between GNP and unexpected price rises. This relationship is called the **Lucas supply curve**.

The Lucas supply curve shown in Figure 8-7 is the upward-sloping short-run aggregate supply curve previously derived. The Lucas supply curve is based on mistaken expectations, however, not on other rigidities. When a demand shock such as an unexpected money supply increase occurs, real GNP rises and prices rise. The economy moves from point *a* to point *b*. Whether the aggregate supply curve remains at AS_1^{sr} depends on whether people's expectations of the price level change. When the expectations adjust, then the AS^{sr} curve shifts up.

The analysis changes dramatically if the money supply change is anticipated or expected. At the time of the money supply increase, the economy moves immediately to the higher price level at point *c*. There is no temporary increase in output or employment.

Unemployment in the New Classical Model

Another element of new classical economics is the belief that markets are in equilibrium. Keynesian economics argues that disequilibrium in markets or market failure demands government intervention. For instance, Keynesian economists define a recession as a disequilibrium in the labor market—a sur-

FIGURE 8-7   *The Lucas supply curve. The Lucas supply curve is the upward-sloping short-run aggregate supply curve previously derived, but based on mistaken expectations rather than on other rigidities. When aggregate demand unexpectedly increases, real GNP and prices rise. The economy moves from point a to point b. The position of the aggregate supply curve depends on people's expectations of the price level. When the expectations adjust upward, then the AS^{sr} curve shifts up.*

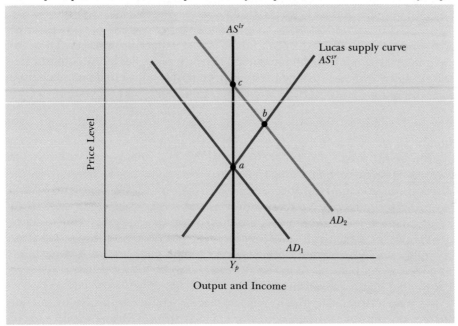

plus of labor. New classical economists believe that because real wages fall during a recession, people are more willing to substitute nonlabor activities (going back to school, early retirement, or leisure) for work. Thus, fewer people *choose* to work. As the economy recovers and real wages go up, people substitute away from nonlabor activities toward more working hours. The substitution of labor for leisure and leisure for labor, over time, suggests that much observed unemployment is *voluntary*, in the sense that those who are unemployed choose not to take a job. Because it is voluntary, there is no reason for government policies to try to resolve unemployment problems.

The lesson of new classical economics for economic policymakers is that *AD* changes can have an effect on national output only if the change is unexpected. Any anticipated changes simply affect prices. The new classical economists argue that economic policies should be aimed at maintaining a low, stable rate of inflation, not at altering national output and employment. Thus, the prescriptions of the new classical economists are not unlike those of the monetarists.

▼
New Keynesian Theory

New Keynesian theory also arose in the 1970s, partly as a response to new classical theory and partly as a refinement of the original Keynesian theory. New Keynesians believe that (1) wages and prices are not flexible in the short run, (2) the economy is not always in long-run equilibrium, and (3) it takes a considerable period of time for the economy to adjust to demand changes. These are not unlike the original Keynesian views. The difference lies in the sophisticated reasons for why output prices might only sluggishly adjust to demand changes and why input prices, particularly wages, might be sticky.

Output Price Rigidities

Whereas classical and new classical theory base their macro analysis on the microeconomic foundations of perfect competition, new Keynesians rely on *imperfect competition* and the price rigidities that might result. Price rigidity occurs in many of the imperfectly competitive market structures. For instance, an oligopolistic firm may be reluctant to lower prices because competing firms will follow the initial price decrease and the resulting price war will mean losses for everyone. A price increase, in contrast, at worst means a very temporary loss for the higher-priced firm.

Because a firm could lose its market share or could lose profits by not correctly taking into account the behavior of rivals, firms have an incentive to create a mechanism by which rivals act together to coordinate pricing and output activities. In order to preserve their status, protect against invasion of market shares by rivals, protect against retaliation, and attempt to secure monopoly profits, firms devise various means of cooperating. Cooperation may take the form of formal agreements where executives sit down at a table and agree to produce a certain amount or to set a certain price, or cooperation may be less formal, as when common industry practices lead to common behavior.

Several actions on the part of oligopolistic firms can contribute to cooperation and collusion even though the firms don't formally agree to cooperate. These are called *facilitating practices*. Pricing policies can leave the impression that firms are explicitly fixing prices when, in fact, they are merely following the same strategies. For instance, the use of **mark-up pricing** or **cost-plus pricing** tends to induce similar if not identical pricing behavior among rival firms. Suppose that the firms set prices by determining the average variable cost of an item and adding a 50 percent margin to the cost. This is variable cost plus 50 percent pricing. If all firms face the same variable cost curves, then all firms set the same prices. And, if variable costs decrease, then all firms lower prices the same amount and at virtually the same time.

Input Price Rigidities

The factors that make input prices less than perfectly flexible include efficiency wages, long-term contracts, and a dual labor market. Firms retain high wages for their remaining employees in order to maintain morale and productivity. Firms pay an efficiency wage—a wage above the equilibrium wage—because the higher wage reflects the nonmeasurable aspects of the labor market, such as morale. The higher wage keeps employees happier and thus more productive than if their wages were cut each time a business downturn occurred.

In the United States, union wage contracts last as long as three years. The contracts are staggered—they do not all expire at the same time. Nonunion workers typically have wages adjusted every six months or once a year. These adjustments are staggered over the year so that not all adjustments occur at the same time. Wages are set for long periods because collective bargaining, threats of strikes, or constant evaluations of employees makes adjusting the wage costly.

The term **dual labor market** refers to a skilled–unskilled dichotomy of the labor market. Workers face a great deal of difficulty in an attempt to move from one market to the other. Someone in the unskilled labor market would have to acquire human capital and other training to attempt to move into the skilled market. The time and cost involved in the move make that quite difficult. As a result, economic shocks tend to be reflected in excess supplies of labor in the unskilled market.

Policy Implications of the New Keynesian School

Because they believe the economy is subject to slow adjustments or points at which the long-run equilibrium will not prevail, Keynesians believe the government must take an active role in the economy. Traditional Keynesians identified the private sector as an important source of shifts in aggregate demand. For example, they argued that investment is susceptible to sudden changes. Thus, if business spending falls, as it always does at some point, then the only recourse is for the government to offset the private sector decline. In other words, government intervention is necessary to stabilize aggregate demand and avoid recession. Conversely, if private spending increases and creates inflationary pressure, then fiscal policies should restrain spending.

New Keynesian macroeconomics does not focus solely on fluctuations in aggregate demand as the primary source of the problems facing policymakers. New Keynesian economists realize that aggregate supply shocks (changes in the determinants of *AS*) can be substantial. But whatever the source of the instability—aggregate demand or aggregate supply—new Keynesians, like Keynesians, tend to look to government to solve the problem. New Keynesians look more to monetary policy as an effective method for manipulating aggregate demand than did the Keynesians, however.

▼
Comparisons of the Schools of Thought

A brief summary of the alternative schools of thought is provided in Table 8-1. The main differences among the schools are the source of problems, the behavior of prices and wages, the information assumptions, and the role for government.

The macroeconomic theories we have been talking about often are treated as though they are different in every way. Yet at times they overlap and even share conclusions. Moreover, as we mentioned at the beginning of the chapter, it is an oversimplification to categorize economists as belonging to a single school of thought. Many if not most economists do not classify themselves by the schools of thought.

Macroeconomic theories have developed over time in response to the economy's performance and the shortcomings of existing theories. Keynesian eco-

TABLE 8-1   *Comparison of the Schools of Macroeconomic Thought*

	Source of Problem	Labor and Product Market	Information Assumption	Role for Government
Classical	Random events	Equilibrium	Perfect, complete	None
Keynesian	Fixed price; instability of investment	Long-term or permanent disequilibrium	Imperfect	Active control of government spending and taxation
Monetarist	Mistaken policies and random events	Temporary disequilibrium	Adaptive expectations	Follow fixed rules for money growth and minimize government spending and taxation shocks
New classical	Mistaken expectations about government policies	Temporary disequilibrium	Rational expectations	None; government policies have an effect on output only if unexpected
New Keynesian	Rigidity of prices and wages	Long-term disequilibrium	Rational expectations	Active management of money supply and government spending and taxation

nomics, introduced in the 1930s, became popular in the 1950s and 1960s. This school of thought was a response to the classical conclusions of perfect competition that the economy would return automatically to its equilibrium at potential output. Faced with ten years of depression, Keynesians doubted the value of a system that required so long to adjust. They provided a view wherein the adjustment could be speeded up. The Keynesian influence on policy was most evident in the 1960s and early 1970s. Fiscal policy was relied on extensively in this period.

The monetarist view emerged as a reaction to the Keynesian conclusions. First, monetarists disagreed with the Keynesian argument that the money supply played virtually no role in affecting aggregate demand. Second, the monetarists argued that the economy was self-correcting, albeit slowly, and that policy measures would create worse problems than leaving the economy alone. Monetarist influence was at its peak when Paul Volcker, chairman of the Federal Reserve Board, announced a change in policy in 1979, a change that would follow what the monetarists had been advocating. The new policy led to an abrupt drop in the U.S. rate of inflation, from more than 13 percent in 1979 to less than 4 percent in 1982, as the monetarists had claimed it would. During the next few years, however, many of the monetarist contentions did not seem to hold true, so monetarism lost much of its influence.

The new classical and new Keynesian economics both emerged in the 1970s and 1980s. The new classical emphasis on expectations called for more information from economic policymakers so that private citizens would have the information they needed to make correct decisions. Its influence on economic policy was seen in the Federal Reserve Act of 1977 and the Full Employment and Balanced Growth Act of 1978, which require the monetary authorities to report to Congress semiannually on their policies in the upcoming year. But these acts also were evidence of the influence of the new Keynesians, because the acts re-established the role of government in maintaining full employment.

▼   ▼   ▼   ▼   ▼   ▼   ▼   ▼   ▼   ▼   ▼

Conclusions

Macroeconomics today does not look very different from the way it looked forty years ago. The debate among economists concerns the speed with which the economy moves back to its potential output level following a demand or supply shock and whether fiscal or monetary policy can increase the speed of the adjustment. The arguments of the new Keynesian and new classical schools are much more sophisticated than those of the Keynesian and classical schools, but the issues are very similar.

▼   ▼   ▼   ▼   ▼   ▼   ▼   ▼   ▼   ▼   ▼

Summary

1. Why do economists disagree?
Economists may disagree about normative aspects of economics: which policy is best, how to solve income distribution, discrimination, unemployment, and other issues. Economists may also disagree about the positive aspects of economics: how the economy functions. This chapter has focused on the historical disagreements regarding primarily the positive aspects. The main schools of thought that have existed since about 1776—classical, Keynesian, monetarist, new classical, and new Keynesian—express these disagreements.

2. What are the alternative schools of thought?
The classical school of thought captures the writings of economists during the 160 years from about 1770 to 1930. The approach to macroeconomics taken during these years was primarily microeconomic and was based on perfect competition, flexible wages and prices, and perfect information. In this view, the economy could only deviate from its potential level on a very temporary basis. There was no such thing as disequilibrium and involuntary unemployment. The Keynesian school of thought was a response to the inability of the classical scheme to explain the ten-year Great Depression. Keynes had to dismantle the classical system, first by discarding Say's law and then demonstrating the possible ways that the economy could become mired in recession or depression. Keynes focused on the rigidity of wages and prices and the liquidity trap as theoretical arguments for why market failure might occur. The Keynesian view dominated macroeconomics throughout the 1950s and 1960s. It was criticized, first, by those supporting the classical system for the Keynesian failure to recognize the Pigou effect and, second, by those supporting the view that monetary policy played an important role in the economy, the monetarists. The Keynesian system really fell onto hard times when it failed to explain the simultaneous rise of inflation and unemployment rates in the 1970s. From this period arose the two schools of thought that are dominating the macroeconomic scene today: the new classical and new Keynesian schools.

3. What do the various schools of thought imply for economic policy?
The classical scheme suggested no policy: let the economy alone, as it is self-correcting. The Keynesian view was that the economy was not self-correcting; government action was required and the only government action that was effective was fiscal policy. The monetarists argued that the economy was self-correcting but the correction might take a long time. However, policymakers should avoid the temptation to become active participants in the economy and to speed the self-correction process because long and variable lags might lead to worse problems than might occur if the economy were left alone. Moreover, because money is important, a monetary policy of stability or rules should be implemented. The new classical school argues that the economy is self-correcting and that implementing policy will only cause worse problems. The new Keynesians argue for active participation by government, both fiscal and monetary policy.

▼
Key Terms

Say's law   187
velocity   187
money illusion   188
liquidity trap   190
Pigou effect   192
new classical economics   195

Lucas supply curve   196
new Keynesian theory   198
mark-up pricing   198
cost-plus pricing   198
dual labor market   199

▼
Problems and Exercises

1.   Define the key terms.
2.   Compare the classical and new classical schools of thought.
3.   Compare the Keynesian and new Keynesian schools of thought.
4.   How would you describe the history of macroeconomic thought as described in this chapter? Have we made progress in understanding how the economy functions?
5.   What did monetarism add to macroeconomic thought? How do the monetarists and new classical schools of thought differ?
6.   Draw one *AD–AS* diagram to show the differences between the new classical and new Keynesian schools of thought.

Chapter 9

Inflation, Unemployment, and Business Cycles

Economies go through cycles, periods of expansion followed by periods of contraction. These cycles have a major impact on people's lives, their incomes and standards of living. When the economy is growing, the demand for goods and services tends to increase and firms hire more workers. Expansions also affect inflation. As the demand for goods and services rises, the prices of those goods and services also tend to rise. Conversely, during recessions people are thrown out of jobs and inflation tends to slow.

This chapter describes the business cycle: the ways in which the business cycle, unemployment, and inflation are related, and their effects on the participants in the economy. The *AD–AS* model can be used to describe business cycles and provide insights into the causes of business cycles. The following questions are considered:

1. What is a business cycle?

2. What occurs to inflation and unemployment over the course of a business cycle?

3. What is the relationship between unemployment and inflation?

4. What is the Phillips curve?

5. What causes business cycles?

▼
Business Cycles

Over time, most economies grow. The growth is anything but regular, however. In some periods it rises, and in others it falls. This pattern—real GNP rising and then falling—is called a *business cycle*. The pattern occurs over and over again; but as the graph of changes in U.S. real GNP since 1933 in Figure 9-1 shows, the pattern over time is anything but regular. Historically, the duration of business cycles and the rate at which real GNP rises or falls vary considerably.

FIGURE 9-1   *Business cycles and changes in real GNP. Historically, the duration of business cycles and the rate at which real GNP rises or falls vary considerably.*

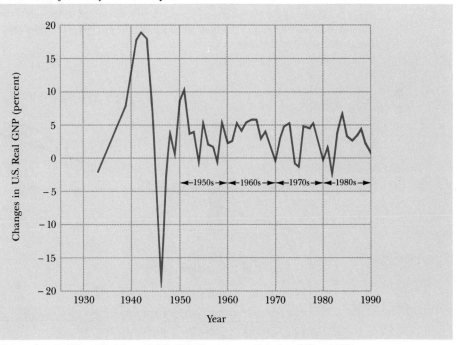

Source: Economic Report of the President (Washington, DC: U.S. Government Printing Office, 1991).

Phases of the Business Cycle

The cycles of Figure 9-1 are shown for a hypothetical economy in Figure 9-2. The vertical axis in Figure 9-2 measures the level of real GNP; the horizontal axis measures time in years. In year 1, real GNP is growing; the economy is in the *expansion* phase or *boom* period, of the business cycle. Growth continues until the *peak* is reached in year 2. Real GNP begins to fall during the *contraction* phase of the cycle. In year 4, the bottom or *trough* of the cycle is reached. Then the economy begins an expansion phase again. The full cycle runs from one peak to the next peak or one trough to the next trough as the economy cycles around its long-term trend.

It is clear from Figure 9-1 that the U.S. economy has experienced upswings and downswings since 1929. Nevertheless, real GNP has grown at an average rate of almost 3 percent per year. If an economy grows over time, and most do, why do economists worry about business cycles? To many economists, the reason is like the answer to "Why climb a mountain?"—"Because it is there." Economists are puzzled by cycles and believe that an understanding of the econ-

FIGURE 9-2   *The business cycle. The vertical axis on the graph measures the level of real GNP; the horizontal axis measures time in years. In year 1, real GNP is growing; the economy is in the* expansion *or* boom *period. Growth continues until the* peak *is reached in year 2. Real GNP begins to fall during the* contraction *phase. In year 4, the bottom or* trough *of the cycle is reached. Then the economy begins an expansion phase again. The full cycle runs from peak to peak, or from trough to trough, of the cycle.*

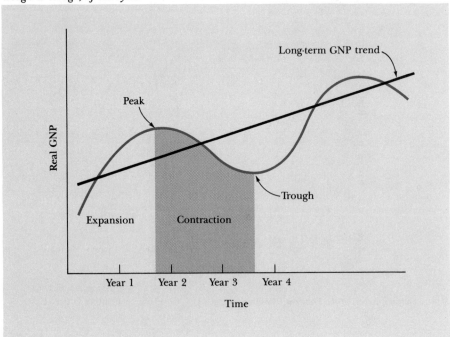

omy may be enhanced by an understanding of cycles. To some economists, the importance of understanding the causes of cycles lies in devising a means of minimizing the economic hardships that accompanied cycles.

Pattern of Cycles in the United States

The official U.S. dating of a recession or expansion is the responsibility of a private research organization, the National Bureau of Economic Research (NBER). Recessions are periods between peaks and the troughs that follow. A recession typically is defined as at least two consecutive quarters (at least 6 months) of decline in real GNP. Expansions are periods between troughs and the peaks that follow. Since 1929, there have been eleven U.S. recessions. The most severe was the Great Depression. A **depression** is a prolonged period of severe recession. U.S. recessions since World War II have been shorter (averaging about one year) and less severe than previous recessions. Peacetime expansions have had an average duration of three years.

▼

Unemployment

Recurring periods of prosperity and recession are reflected in the nation's labor markets. Unemployment rises during each recession and then falls during each expansion. Unemployment rates in the United States from 1948 to 1990 are shown in Figure 9-3; recessions are the shaded regions, while expansions

FIGURE 9-3 *Unemployment rates and the business cycle. Unemployment rates in the United States from 1948 to 1990 are shown; recessions are the shaded regions, while expansions are unshaded regions. The unemployment rate increases during those periods when the growth rate for real GNP is decreasing and declines when the growth rate for real GNP is rising.*

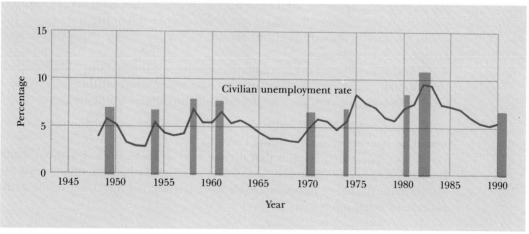

are the unshaded regions. The unemployment rate increases during those periods when the rate of growth of real GNP is decreasing and declines when the rate of growth of real GNP is rising.

As discussed in Chapter 1, the unemployment rates of all countries go through cycles. Moreover, nations are tied together — their unemployment rates tend to rise and fall together.

Types of Unemployment and Full Employment

Economists have identified four basic types of unemployment:

1. **Seasonal unemployment** is the result of regular, recurring changes in the production requirements of certain industries. For instance, when crops are harvested, farms need lots of workers; the rest of the year, they do not. When resorts are in their peak season, lots of workers are needed; during off periods, fewer workers are used. The Christmas season is a peak season for most businesses, and more workers are needed during this period.

2. **Frictional unemployment** is the result of the movement of workers between jobs and first-time job seekers. Workers quit one job and find another; students graduate and find a job. Jobs are available, but it takes time to match up employers with people seeking jobs. This kind of unemployment cannot be eliminated in a free society; in fact, it often increases during expansions because people feel better opportunities are opening up, and thus seek other jobs. Frictional unemployment is often called *search* unemployment.

3. **Structural unemployment** is the result of technological change or a change in the demand structure of the economy. Workers are displaced as products go out of favor or as new technologies are created to improve the efficiency of production in a particular industry. For instance, farm workers were replaced by tractors, harvesters, and other machinery; workers were replaced in assembly lines as industries began using robots. When workers are displaced by technology, the workers often do not have skills that let them find a comparable job paying a comparable salary elsewhere. Hence, rather than accept a lower-paying job, these unemployed people often choose to continue to search for a job. Eventually they must either retrain or readjust their expectations and accept a lower-paying job.

4. **Cyclical unemployment** is the result of business cycle fluctuations. When a recession occurs, businesses must cut production and costs, and this often means layoffs. People are thrown out of jobs and thus become unemployed.

Economists used to refer to *full employment* as the employment level that would be consistent with potential output. Today, the term *full employment* is rarely used because it implies that no one who wants to work is without a job. But that's impossible, because seasonal, frictional, and structural unemployment always exist. Rather than use *full employment*, economists now refer to the **natural rate of unemployment**.

What is the value of the U.S. natural unemployment rate? In the 1950s and 1960s, economists generally agreed on a 4 percent unemployment rate. By the 1970s, the thinking was that the rate had gone up to 5 percent, and in the early 1980s many economists placed the natural rate of unemployment between 6 and 7 percent. By the late 1980s, some had revised their thinking, placing the rate near 5 percent. The fact is, economists don't know exactly what rate of unemployment is the natural rate.

Costs of Unemployment

The cost of being unemployed is more than the obvious loss of income and status suffered by the person who is not working. Society loses when resources are unemployed. When unemployment exists, society is not producing all it could — some output is forgone because not all inputs (labor specifically) are fully and efficiently used. Economists measure this lost output in terms of the **GNP gap**:

$$\text{GNP gap} = \text{potential GNP} - \text{real GNP}$$

Potential GNP measures what society is capable of producing at the natural rate of unemployment. Real GNP is what society is actually producing. The difference between the two provides a measure of the output (and hence income) that is not produced, due to unemployment — that is, the cost to society due to unemployment.

▼
Inflation

Recurring patterns of growth and recession are also reflected in inflation rates. Inflation is a sustained rise in the average level of prices. Inflation does not entail a one-time increase in prices; instead, prices are rising over several periods of time. The inflation rate in the United States in 1990 was 5.2 percent. This means that the level of prices in January 1991 was 5.2 percent higher than in January 1990 — the price level rose throughout 1990 by 5.2 percent.

Inflation is a relatively new problem for the United States. As shown in Figure 9-4, from 1789, when the U.S. Constitution was ratified, until 1940, there was no trend in the general price level; at times prices rose and at times they fell; overall, the price level did not change. Since 1940, prices in the United States have risen markedly. The price level today is seven times what it was in 1940. Nevertheless, although the price level has continued to rise during expansions as well as recessions, the rate of inflation has varied, as shown in Figure 9-5. In general, the rate of inflation rises during expansions and falls during recessions. Also, recall from Figure 1-4 (in Chapter 1) that the rates of inflation of different countries tend to rise and fall together.

FIGURE 9-4   *Price levels throughout U.S. history. From 1789, when the U.S. Constitution was ratified, until 1940, there was no trend in the general price level; at times prices rose and at times they fell; overall, the price level did not change. Since 1940, prices in the United States have risen markedly. The price level today is seven times what it was in 1940.*

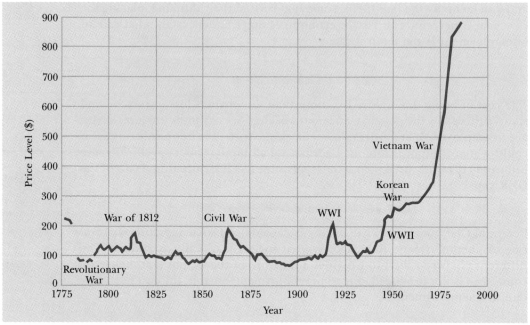

Source: U.S. Bureau of the Census, *Historical Statistics of the United States, Colonial Times to 1970,* bicentennial ed. (Washington, DC: U.S. Bureau of the Census, 1975), Series E-82; *Economic Report of the President* (Washington, DC: U.S. Government Printing Office, 1983, Table B-57, and 1991).

The term *hyperinflation* refers to an extremely high rate of inflation. Hyperinflation makes a country's currency worthless and often leads to the introduction of a new currency. The most dramatic hyperinflation occurred in Europe after World War I. The price level in Germany rose so rapidly between 1914 and 1924 that it was virtually impossible to carry out transactions. The price index of Germany is shown in Table 9-1. By 1924, German prices were more than 100 trillion times higher than they had been in 1914.

Types of Inflation

Economists often classify inflation according to the source of the inflationary pressure, associated with *AD* or with *AS*. The term **demand–pull inflation** refers to increases in spending that lead to higher prices. The term **cost–push inflation** refers to increases in production costs that cause firms to raise prices to avoid losses.

FIGURE 9-5 *Inflation rates in the United States. Although the price level has risen, the rate of inflation has varied. In general, the rate of inflation rises during expansions and falls during recessions.*

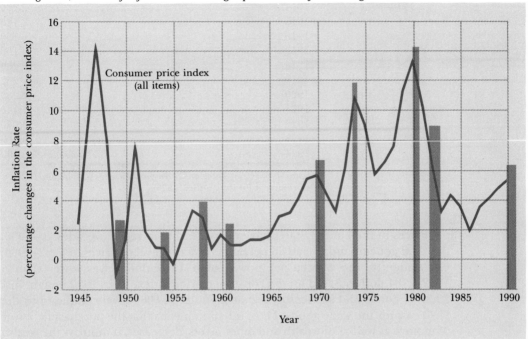

Source: Economic Report of the President (Washington, DC: U.S. Government Printing Office, 1991).

Demand–pull inflation occurs whenever the *AD* curve shifts out, causing the price level to rise. Cost–push inflation, on the contrary, arises when the *AS* curve shifts in. Those factors leading to *AD* shifts — autonomous spending changes — are causes for demand–pull inflation. Those factors leading to *AS* curve shifts — technological change, resource price changes, and changes in other costs of doing business — are causes for cost–push inflation.

Costs of Inflation

When inflation occurs, the purchasing power of the currency declines. The real value of money or its purchasing power is

Real value of $1 = $1/price level

As the price level rises, the real value of $1 falls. For instance, suppose that over the period 1982–1984 one dollar had an average worth of $1, and we are using 1982–1984 as the base or comparison period. How has the purchasing power of the dollar changed? In 1946, a dollar bought five times more than a dollar bought in the early 1980s, as shown in Table 9-2.

TABLE 9-1
*German Wholesale Prices
1914–1924*

Year	Price Index
1914	100
1915	126
1916	150
1917	156
1918	204
1919	262
1920	1,260
1921	1,440
1922	3,670
1923	278,500
1924	117,320,000,000,000

Source: J. P. Young, *European Currency and Finance* (Washington, DC: U.S. Government Printing Office, 1925).

Prices in the United States have risen steadily in recent decades. By 1990, they had gone up more than 26 percent above the level of prices in 1982–1984. Consequently, the purchasing power of a 1990 dollar was lower than a 1982–1984 dollar. Based on the consumer price index, $1 in 1990 bought just $0.79 of goods and services priced at their 1982–1984 level compared to the 1990 cost for the same goods. Thus, inflation means that the purchasing power of money, as well as of wealth and other assets, decreases. It destroys the wealth of those owning or holding assets the prices of which do not rise as rapidly as the general price level.

Inflation that is unexpected causes more distortions and thus more harm than expected inflation. When people correctly anticipate inflation, they can prepare for it and protect themselves against it. When it is unexpected, then some people gain and others lose as a result of the inflation. For instance, suppose Mary agrees to loan Dan $100 and in return Dan agrees to pay Mary $110 one year from now. When Mary and Dan agreed to the loan, they expected an inflation rate of 5 percent. This means that $105 would be required to buy the same goods and services in one year as $100 does now. The extra $5 is the reward to Mary for lending the $100; it is an increase in her purchasing power or real interest. If, however, the inflation rate is unexpectedly high — say, 10 percent — then Mary will get $110 in one year. But that is exactly the same in purchasing power as her $100 is now. Real interest is zero, and she gets nothing in return for lending (for forgoing current consumption). Dan, on the contrary, gets to use $100 for the year and repays only the equivalent of $100. Dan is better off; Mary is worse off as a result of the unexpected inflation. Unexpected inflation redistributes income. If the actual rate of inflation turns out to be higher than the expected rate, then borrowers are better off and lenders worse off. If the actual rate of inflation turns out to be lower than the expected rate, then borrowers are worse off and lenders better off.

TABLE 9-2   *Real Value of the U.S. Dollar for Selected Years Since 1946 (1982–1984 = base)*

Year	Price Level (consumer price index)	$1/Price Level
1946	0.195	1/0.195 = 5.13
1950	0.241	1/0.241 = 4.15
1955	0.268	1/0.268 = 3.73
1960	0.296	1/0.296 = 3.38
1965	0.315	1/0.315 = 3.17
1970	0.388	1/0.388 = 2.58
1975	0.538	1/0.538 = 1.86
1980	0.824	1/0.824 = 1.21
1982–1984	1.000	1/1.00 = 1.00
1985	1.076	1/1.076 = 0.93
1990	1.260	1/1.260 = 0.79

Unexpected inflation affects more than just borrowers and lenders. Any contract calling for fixed payments over a long period of time changes in value as the rate of inflation changes. For instance, a long-term wage contract that provides an employee with 5 percent raises each year for five years gives workers more purchasing power if inflation is low than if it is high. Similarly, a contract that guarantees a certain supply of an input to a manufacturer at a particular price over a long period changes in value as inflation changes. Unexpectedly high inflation redistributes real income or purchasing power away from those receiving fixed payments to those making fixed payments.

▼
The Phillips Curve

Over the course of a business cycle, unemployment and inflation move inversely to each other. This pattern is captured in a diagram known as the **Phillips curve**. In 1958 a New Zealand economist, A. W. Phillips, published a study of the relationship between the unemployment rate and the rate of change of nominal wages in England. He found that over the period from 1826 to 1957, there had been an inverse relationship between the unemployment rate and the rate of change in wages. The unemployment rate fell in years when there were relatively large increases in wages, and rose in years when wages increased relatively little. Phillips's study stimulated a search by other economists for similar relationships in other countries. In these other studies, it became common to use the rate of inflation instead of the rate of wage increase.

The Phillips curve, or inverse relationship between inflation and the unemployment rate, in the United States for the years 1951 through 1969 is shown in Figure 9-6. In 1961, 1 percent inflation occurred with 6.5 percent unemploy-

FIGURE 9-6 *The Phillips curve. Combinations of inflation and unemployment rates for the United States from 1951–1969 are plotted in the form of a Phillips curve. The slope of the curve shows an inverse relationship between the inflation rate and the unemployment rate. In 1961, 1 percent inflation occurred with 6.5 percent unemployment. By 1969 the inflation rate had risen to the relatively high figure of 5.5 percent, while the unemployment rate had declined to 3.4 percent.*

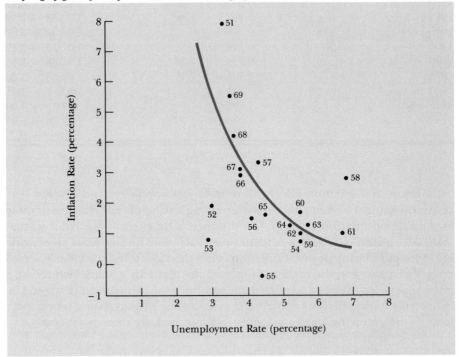

Source: Economic Report of the President (Washington, DC: U.S. Government Printing Office, 1991).

ment. By 1969 the inflation rate had risen to the relatively high figure of 5.5 percent, while the unemployment rate had declined to 3.4 percent. The Phillips curve reflects the pattern we'd expect during a business cycle. Moving up the curve, we find that inflation rises and unemployment falls—the typical expansion; as the economy dips into recession, inflation falls and unemployment rises, shown as a move down the curve.

The Phillips curve was developed at a time when Keynesian economics was at its most popular. Thus, many economists interpreted the Phillips curve as illustrating a permanent **tradeoff** between unemployment and inflation that could be exploited. A country could choose to lower the unemployment rate by accepting higher inflation or to lower the rate of inflation by accepting higher unemployment. Just where on the Phillips curve the economy operated would depend on where policymakers wanted it to operate. The policymakers would simply design government spending or taxation policies to move the economy to the desired point on the Phillips curve.

Does an Inflation–Unemployment Tradeoff Exist?

As time passed, the evidence appeared to run counter to the idea that a permanent exploitable tradeoff existed. In Figure 9-7, each yearly combination of inflation and unemployment rates are plotted for the years 1960–1990 in the United States. The points in Figure 9-7 do not lie along a downward-sloping Phillips curve like the one shown in Figure 9-6. For example, in 1960 the unemployment rate was 5.5 percent and the inflation rate was 1.7 percent. In 1974 the unemployment rate was 5.6 percent and the inflation rate was 11.0 percent. Both unemployment and inflation rates increased after 1969. By 1980, the unemployment rate was 7.1 percent and the inflation rate was 13.5 percent. The points in Figure 9-7 appear to show no evidence of a tradeoff between unemployment and inflation.

Short-Run Versus Long-Run Tradeoffs

In Figure 9-8 are a series of Phillips curves that could represent the data in Figure 9-7. For more than two decades, the tradeoff between inflation and unemployment worsened as the Phillips curves shifted up so that higher and higher inflation rates were associated with any given level of unemployment. On the 1960s curve in Figure 9-8, 5 percent unemployment is consistent with 2 percent inflation. By the early 1970s, the curve had shifted up. Here 5 percent unemployment is associated with 6 percent inflation. On the late 1970s curve, 5 percent unemployment is consistent with 10 percent inflation. Then in the 1980s, the tradeoff seemed to improve as the Phillips curve shifted down. On the late 1980s curve, 5 percent unemployment is consistent with about a 4 percent rate of inflation.

The Phillips curves in Figure 9-8 could represent the changes that took place over time in the United States. We cannot be sure of the actual shape of a Phillips curve at any particular time, but an outward shift of the curve in the 1970s and an inward shift during the 1980s are consistent with the data.

Why do the curves shift over time? Figure 9-9 uses the aggregate demand and supply curves to explain the Phillips curves. Initially, the economy is operating at point a in both panels. The aggregate demand curve, AD_1, and short-run aggregate supply curve, AS_1, intersect at price level P_1 and income level Y_p, the potential output level. This corresponds to point a on Phillips curve I, where the inflation rate is 3 percent and the unemployment rate is 5 percent. We'll assume that the natural unemployment rate (U_n) (the unemployment rate at the level of potential output) is 5 percent. When aggregate demand rises from AD_1 to AD_2, a new equilibrium at price level P_2 and income level Y_2

FIGURE 9-7   *The Phillips curve. The unemployment and inflation rates in the United States for 1960 to 1990 are shown. The points do not lie along a downward-sloping Phillips curve like the one shown in Figure 9-6. Moving through time, you can see that the inflation rate tended to increase along with the unemployment rate through the 1970s. There appears to be no evidence of a tradeoff between unemployment and inflation.*

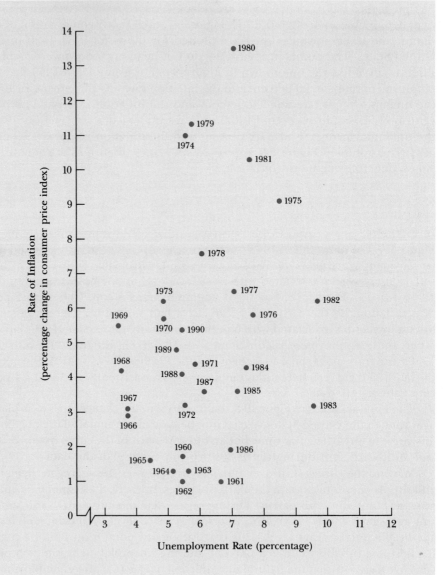

Source: *Economic Report of the President* (Washington, DC: U.S. Government Printing Office, 1991).

FIGURE 9-8   *A series of Phillips curves. This series of Phillips curves could represent the U.S. economy since 1960. For more than two decades, the tradeoff between inflation and unemployment worsened as the Phillips curves shifted up so that higher and higher inflation rates were associated with any given level of unemployment. Then, in the 1980s, the tradeoff seemed to improve as the Phillips curve shifted down.*

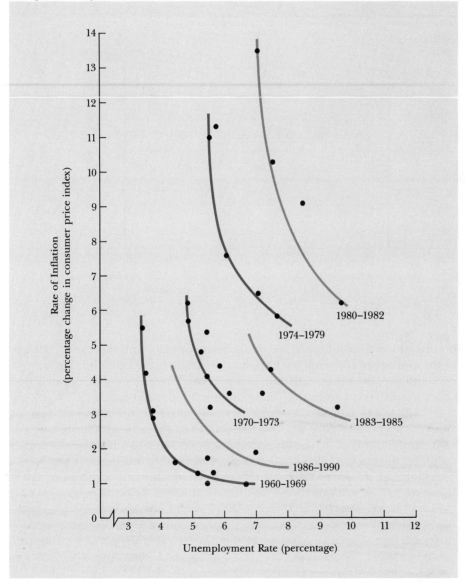

Source: Economic Report of the President (Washington, DC: U.S. Government Printing Office, 1991).

FIGURE 9-9 AD–AS *and the Phillips curve. Initially, the economy is operating at point* a *in both panels. The aggregate demand curve,* AD₁, *and short-run aggregate supply curve,* AS₁ˢʳ, *intersect at price level* P₁ *and income level* Yₚ, *the potential output level. This corresponds to point* a *on Phillips curve I, where the inflation rate is 3 percent and the unemployment rate is 5 percent. When aggregate demand rises from* AD₁ *to* AD₂, *a new equilibrium at price level* P₂ *and income level* Y₂ *occurs. Along the Phillips curve, the increase in price and income is reflected in the movement from point* a *to point* b. *The increase in expenditures raises the inflation rate and lowers the unemployment rate.*

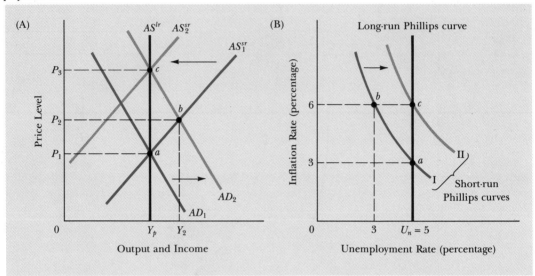

occurs. Along the Phillips curve, the increase in price and income is reflected in the movement from point *a* to point *b*. At point *b*, the inflation rate is 6 percent and the unemployment rate is 3 percent. The increase in expenditures raises the inflation rate and lowers the unemployment rate.

There appears to be a tradeoff between inflation and unemployment on Phillips curve I in Figure 9-9. The increase in spending increases output and stimulates employment, so that the unemployment rate falls. And the higher spending pushes the rate of inflation up. But this tradeoff is only temporary. The short-run *AS* curve shifts over time as production costs rise in response to higher prices. With the curve shifting from AS_1^{sr} to AS_2^{sr}, the price level rises to P_3 and income returns to the potential level Y_p. The shift in AS^{sr} lowers the income level, which means that unemployment goes up. The decrease in short-run aggregate supply is reflected in the movement from point *b* on Phillips curve I to point *c* on Phillips curve II. As national income returns to its potential level, unemployment returns to the natural rate, U_n.

In the long run, there is no relationship between the price level and the level of output. This is shown by the vertical or long-run aggregate supply curve. It is also shown by a vertical Phillips curve.

Causes of Shifts of the Phillips Curve

What causes the short-run Phillips curve to shift over time? The same factors that lead to a shift of the short-run *AS* curve — expectations, long-term contracts, lack of information — lead to shifts of the Phillips curve. Consider, for instance, the effect of inflation expectations on the Phillips curve.

In Figure 9-10 are two Phillips curves, one drawn for a 3 percent expected inflation rate and one for a 6 percent expected inflation rate. If people expect that inflation will be 3 percent, then they behave according to Phillips curve I. If the actual rate of inflation is 3 percent, the economy is operating at point *a*, with an unemployment rate of 5 percent. If the inflation rate unexpectedly increases to 6 percent, the economy moves from point *a* to point *b* along Phillips curve I. Over time, as expectations catch up with reality, the economy moves from point *b* to point *c*.

If *AD* increases unexpectedly, then prices, output, employment, and wages go up. An unexpected increase in inflation means that prices are higher than

FIGURE 9-10 *The shifting Phillips curve. Two Phillips curves, one drawn for a 3 percent expected inflation rate and one for a 6 percent expected inflation rate, are shown. If people expect that inflation will be 3 percent, then they behave according to Phillips curve I. If the actual rate of inflation is 3 percent, the economy is operating at point a, with an unemployment rate of 5 percent. If the inflation rate unexpectedly increases to 6 percent, the economy moves from point a to point b along Phillips curve I. Over time, as expectations catch up with reality, the economy moves from point b to point c.*

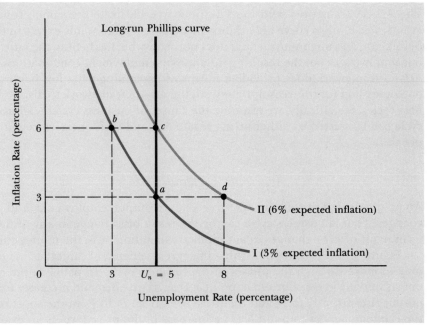

anticipated, as are nominal income and wages. People and firms experience an increase in their own wages or prices but don't realize this is a general price rise. Unemployed workers find it easier to obtain a satisfactory wage offer during a period when wages are rising faster than the workers expected. This means that more unemployed workers find jobs, and that they find those jobs quicker than they do in a period when the rate of inflation is expected. So the unemployment rate falls during a period of unexpectedly high inflation.

Businesses hold inventories based on what they expect their sales to be. When aggregate demand is greater than expected, inventories fall below targeted levels. To restore inventories to the levels wanted, employment is increased so that production can rise. If *AD* is lower than expected, inventories rise above targeted levels. To reduce inventories, production is cut back and workers are laid off. In Figure 9-10, for example, if expected inflation is 6 percent but actual inflation is 3 percent, the economy is operating at point *d* and actual unemployment exceeds the natural unemployment rate.

The effect of incorrect expectations is reflected in a movement along a Phillips curve, such as the move from point *a* to point *b* in Figure 9-10. Once people realize that the expectations were wrong, adjustments occur and the Phillips curve shifts, such as in the move from point *b* to point *c*.

▼
AD–AS *and Business Cycles*

The *AD–AS* framework and the Phillips curve illustrate the same economic events. The Phillips curve only shows the outcome of economic events in terms of inflation and unemployment. It does not show what lies behind the outcomes but simply traces out the resulting inflation–unemployment combinations. The *AD–AS* framework does provide a means of explaining what lies behind the outcomes, and for this reason we rely on the *AD–AS* framework to discuss business cycles. Specifically, we examine the causes of business cycles—a business cycle can be started by either an aggregate demand shift or an aggregate supply shift.

Aggregate Demand Changes

An unanticipated shift of the *AD* curve leads to output, employment, and price changes. Thus, a business cycle can be the result of a change in any of the determinants of *AD*—changes in autonomous spending or in the money supply.

Figure 9-11 illustrates how shifts in aggregate demand can cause the economy to move through the phases of the business cycle. In panel A, the economy is initially in equilibrium at point *a*. If aggregate demand increases to AD_2, output rises from Y_1 to Y_2 and the price level from P_1 to P_2 in the short run—the economy moves to point *b*. (The increase in the price level is an example

FIGURE 9-11 *AD–AS and the business cycle. In panel A is an AD–AS diagram indicating that output is at Y_1 and the price level at P_1. Suppose that the AD curve shifts out to AD_2 from AD_1. The result is a temporary increase in output to Y_2, with an eventual move back to output level Y_1. The speed at which the adjustments occur and the path of the adjustment describes the movement of output, prices, and employment over time. Panel B shows a diagram with time measured on the horizontal axis and output on the vertical axis. Beginning from Y_1, the economy expands to Y_2 and then smoothly moves back to Y_1 over time. Panels C and D show another combination of AD–AS and time–output diagrams where the adjustment occurs in cycles rather than just smoothly from one output level to another. Here you can see that the demand shock caused not just one cycle, but a series of smaller and smaller cycles.*

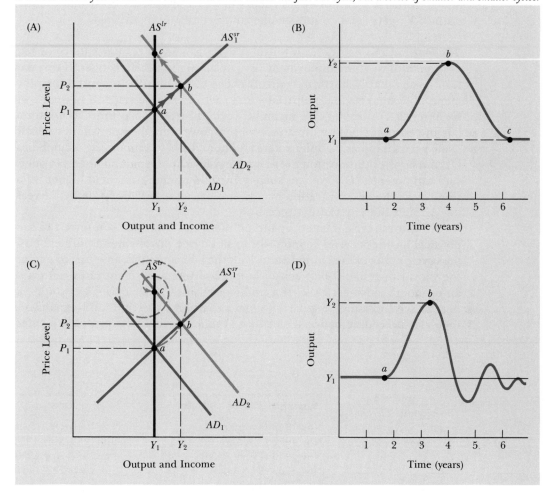

of demand–pull inflation.) In the long run, adjustments in the labor market shift output back to potential output, Y_1 — the economy adjusts to point c. If there is a smooth adjustment from point a to point b and then to point c, then the economy will move along a time path similar to that in panel B. The economy moves smoothly from output level Y_1 to Y_2 and back to Y_1.

Panels C and D show an economy whose adjustment to an unexpected change in aggregate demand occurs in cycles rather than smoothly. The increase in aggregate demand initially moves the economy from point *a* to point *b* in panel C. Eventually, the economy adjusts back to the potential output level, Y_1, but along the path indicated by the dashed arrow. In panel D, the time path shows the economy initially moving from Y_1 to Y_2. In the eventual adjustment back to Y_1, the economy moves below Y_1, then above Y_1, then again below Y_1, and so forth. A series of cycles occurs in which the deviation from potential output, Y_1, gets smaller and smaller and eventually disappears.

The Political Business Cycle. A business cycle is a fairly regular pattern of real GNP growth rate, unemployment rate, and inflation rate changes. If this pattern means that a short-run tradeoff exists between inflation and unemployment, policymakers and politicians may seek to use that tradeoff in their own self-interest. For instance, an incumbent administration may think it can stimulate the economy just before an election to lower the unemployment rate and make voters happier; happier voters are more likely to support the incumbents. Of course, after the election the adjustment back to the natural unemployment rate and potential GNP means some growth in unemployment at higher inflation rates. The administration may try to lower the inflation rate by decreasing *AD* and thereby cause a recession.

A business cycle created by the political election cycle is referred to as a **political business cycle**. Economists do not agree on whether a political business cycle exists in the United States, but they do agree that an effort to exploit the short-run tradeoff between inflation and unemployment rates can cause an economic business cycle. If a political business cycle exists, we would expect to see recessions regularly following national elections and expansions regularly preceding national elections. Table 9-3 shows the presidential elec-

TABLE 9-3 *Presidential Elections and U.S. Recessions, 1948–1988*	Presidential Election (Winner)	Next Recession
	Nov 1948 (Truman)	Nov 1948–Oct 1949
	Nov 1952 (Eisenhower)	Jun 1953–May 1954
	Nov 1956 (Eisenhower)	Jun 1957–Apr 1958
	Nov 1960 (Kennedy)	Apr 1960–Feb 1961
	Nov 1964 (Johnson)	
	Nov 1968 (Nixon)	Oct 1969–Nov 1970
	Nov 1972 (Nixon)	Dec 1973–Mar 1975
	Nov 1976 (Carter)	Jan 1980–Jul 1980
	Nov 1980 (Reagan)	May 1981–Nov 1982
	Nov 1984 (Reagan)	
	Nov 1988 (Bush)	Oct 1990–[a]

[a] Formal ending date not defined as of July 1991.

tions since 1948, along with the recessions that followed them. In five cases, a recession occurred the year after an election. A recession began before Kennedy's election, and there was no recession during the Johnson and the second Reagan administrations. Of course, this evidence is not irrefutable. Many other things occur in an economy, and these may offset the efforts of politicians to create a business cycle.

Money Supply Effects. Unexpected changes in money supply growth can affect the economy and lead to business cycles. Why do unexpected money supply changes occur? One reason for changes in money supply growth might be termed the "benevolent dictator rationale." Suppose that the central bank of a nation (the Federal Reserve in the United States) believes that there is a permanent tradeoff between inflation and unemployment or at least a short-run tradeoff that can be exploited to minimize cycles. Based on this belief, money supply growth rates are changed in what these officials believe to be the public's best interest. Although the officials might guess right quite often, they can't always be right. As a result, their policy changes may lead to fluctuations in business activities.

Another explanation of money supply growth changes stems from the self-interest of the members of the central bank. In the United States, Federal Reserve Board members, even though appointed to fourteen-year terms, are subject to pressure from the politicians; they receive media attention; their future income and influence might be affected by their behavior. Political pressure from the administration and from Congress forces the Federal Reserve Board to increase the money supply or decrease it even when the Board does not think the change will be particularly beneficial to the economy. The Federal Reserve Board also receives pressure from the behavior of the U.S. economy relative to other economies. If U.S. producers are losing business to foreign producers, there is pressure to increase the money supply in order to stimulate the economy. Or government spending may affect the rates at which the currencies of different countries are exchanged and thereby detrimentally affect U.S. producers. This too may elicit a response from the Federal Reserve Board. In some other nations, the central bank members face the same pressures as do members of the board in the United States. In other nations, the central bank is part of the executive office rather than an independent agency. In these cases, money supply changes are directly controlled by the political leaders.

Nonpolicy Changes. In addition to the policy-induced changes, changes in autonomous investment, net exports, and consumption can cause the *AD* curve to shift and lead to a business cycle. The early Keynesians focused on investment as the principal culprit, claiming that its inherent instability led to *AD* changes. According to Keynes, investment is determined by "the animal spirits" of business — profit expectations and speculation. These can change at the whim of business and for no apparent reason. As investment spending changes, aggregate demand changes by the size of the multiplier. More recently, economists have looked at the effects of the savings and loan crisis and banking problems as affecting the economy through business and consumer spending. Fears of recession cause business and consumers to retrench and decrease spending.

Aggregate Supply Changes

In recent years, economists have paid increasing attention to unexpected changes in the economic structure as a source of business cycles. These unexpected aggregate supply changes are called *real shocks*, and the resulting business cycles are called **real business cycles**. A real business cycle is generated by technological change, labor strikes, weather, input supply changes, or other real changes. Interest in the real business cycle was stimulated by oil price shocks in the early 1970s and by the following deep recession of 1973–1975. At that time, many economists had been focusing on the role of unexpected changes in government policy in generating business cycles. They argued that changes in the money supply were responsible for the shifts in aggregate demand that led to expansions and contractions but they were troubled because they did not find money supply changes large enough to justify the business cycles. However, when OPEC raised oil prices it caused a major shift in aggregate supply and a resulting series of economic fluctuations. Higher oil prices in 1973 and 1974, and in 1979 and 1980, reduced aggregate supply and pushed the level of national income down. Lower oil prices in 1986 then raised aggregate supply and national income. And again, with the 1990 invasion of Kuwait by Iraq, oil prices increased and national income fell only to be followed by a reduction in oil prices at the end of the Iraq War. To many economists, these shocks seemed much more significant than the unexpected money shocks or other aggregate demand shocks.

An economy-wide shock, like a substantial change in the price of oil, can affect output and employment across all sectors of the economy. But even an industry-specific shock can generate a recession or expansion in the entire economy if the industry produces a substantial amount of the nation's output. For example, a labor strike in the steel industry can have major recessionary implications for the economy as a whole. If the output of steel falls, the price of steel can be bid up by all the industries that use steel as an input. This shifts the short-run aggregate supply curve in and lowers income, as in panel A of Figure 9-12. (The increase in the price level is an example of cost–push inflation.) Eventually, the economy adjusts back to potential output at point *a*.

Real shocks can also have expansionary effects on the economy. For example, a major oil discovery in the United States would lower the price of oil, the short-run and long-run aggregate supply curves would shift out and national income would rise. For example, in panel B of Figure 9-12, the economy adjusts from point *a* to point *b*.

FIGURE 9-12   AD–AS *and real shocks. In panel A, a labor strike in the steel industry shifts the short-run aggregate supply curve to* AS_2^{sr}. *As the economy moves from point* a *to point* b, *output drops below potential and the price level rises. Eventually, the economy will adjust back to potential output at point* a. *In panel B, a major oil discovery increases both short-run aggregate supply and long-run aggregate supply. As the economy moves from point* a *to point* b, *output rises and the price level falls.*

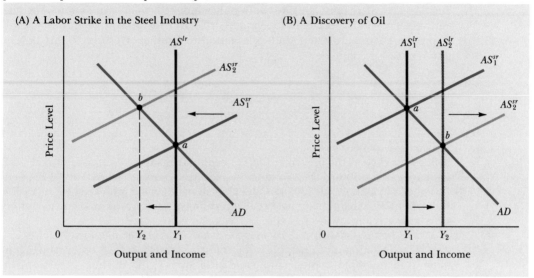

(A) A Labor Strike in the Steel Industry   (B) A Discovery of Oil

Conclusions

The idea that business cycles are the result of real shocks is called the *real business cycle theory*. The real business cycle theory is the latest installment of the "old" classical view of economic fluctuations. The business cycle is, according to this theory, the natural and efficient response of the economy to changes in the available production technology. Thus, unemployment occurs because of this natural response not, as suggested by Keynesians, because of a disequilibrium in the labor or output markets.

In the early 1960s, many economists proclaimed that the business cycle was dead. Armed with the Keynesian view of how business cycles occur and the Phillips curve idea of a permanent and exploitable tradeoff, many economists believed they could use government policies to offset fluctuations in output, inflation, and unemployment. Today, business cycles lie at the heart of macroeconomic research. The 1970s proved that the Phillips curve was not a permanent tradeoff and showed that aggregate supply plays a role at least equal to that played by aggregate demand in causing business cycles.

There are two issues of primary importance in the debate over business cycles: what causes them and what keeps them going. The answers provided so far are only partially satisfactory. No research to date has shown one theory or approach to always be better than another. Hence, the continuing debate between Keynesian and classical economists has taken on a new, spirited flavor. To fully understand business cycles, we must consider both policy-induced changes in national income and real shocks that occur independently of government actions and how these changes are communicated from one nation to another. We turn to this task in the next set of chapters.

▼   ▼   ▼   ▼   ▼   ▼   ▼   ▼   ▼   ▼   ▼

Summary

1. What is a business cycle?
A business cycle is the movement of the economy measured in terms of real GNP from a peak downward to a trough and back up to another peak. The NBER definition of a business cycle includes an expansionary period followed by a recession followed by an expansionary period. A recession typically is two consecutive quarters of negative real growth of GNP.

2. What occurs to inflation and unemployment over the course of a business cycle?
Typically, inflation and unemployment move inversely to each other. During an expansion, unemployment is falling and inflation is rising; during a recession, unemployment is rising and inflation is falling. In several historical periods, however, inflation and unemployment have risen at the same time or fallen at the same time.

3. What is the relationship between unemployment and inflation?
There is considerable debate over whether inflation and unemployment are related. The debate centers around the Phillips curve and whether there is a tradeoff between inflation and unemployment. The earliest Keynesians believed in a fixed tradeoff that could be exploited by economic policy. In the past two decades, economists have come to believe not so much in a fixed tradeoff but an inverse relationship between inflation and unemployment that may or may not be exploited in the short run but definitely cannot be exploited in the long run.

4. What is the Phillips curve?
The Phillips curve originally showed a relationship between unemployment rates and rates of wage change in Britain. The idea was extended to relate rates of unemployment and inflation. Today, the Phillips curve is considered to be a diagram relating unemployment rates and inflation rates.

5. What causes business cycles?
Business cycles may be the result of policy-induced shocks or external shocks; they may be the result of an accumulation of small events or the result of one large event.

▼

Key Terms

depression 207
seasonal unemployment 208
frictional unemployment 208

structural unemployment 208
cyclical unemployment 208
natural rate of unemployment 208

GNP gap   209
demand–pull inflation   210
cost–push inflation   210
Phillips curve   213

tradeoff   214
political business cycle   222
real business cycles   224

▼
Problems and Exercises

1.   What is the difference between a long-run Phillips curve and a short-run Phillips curve?

2.   What reasons might be presented for the existence of a short-run tradeoff between unexpected inflation and the unemployment rate?

3.   Using a graph of the Phillips curve and the *AD–AS* diagram, illustrate the effect of unexpected increases in the money supply, unexpected decreases in the money supply, and an unexpected increase in the supplies of some vital resource such as oil.

4.   Suppose an economy has experienced a 10 percent rate of growth of its money supply and prices over recent years. How do you think the public will respond to an announced plan to grow the money supply at only 4 percent per year? Using the Phillips curve and *AD–AS* diagrams, illustrate the effect of such an anticipated policy change. If the policy change were implemented unexpectedly, how would that differ from the anticipated change?

5.   Explain what is meant by a political business cycle.
    a.   Using actual data for the United States, see if you can discover evidence of a political business cycle.
    b.   How might a political business cycle differ between a government with fixed terms of office, as in the United States where presidential elections occur every four years, and a government with variable terms, such as a parliamentary system where a vote can be called by the prime minister at any time within a six-year period?

6.   What is a real business cycle? What factors might lead to a real business cycle? How would you differentiate the real business cycle from a policy-induced business cycle?

7.   Inflation is often measured using the rate of change in a price index. Suppose the price index relies on listed prices but people rarely purchase at listed prices, paying less than listed prices for items during recessionary times and more than listed prices during expansionary times. What difference would this make for the Phillips curve?

8.   Suppose it has been shown that the frictional, structural, and seasonal unemployment rates rise during high inflation periods and fall during low inflation periods. Does this have any implications for the Phillips curve and economic policy?

Part Four

Business Cycles and Economic Policy

Chapter 10

Links Among Nations

What to Expect

Previous chapters have noted how economies of different countries appear to be linked—output growth, unemployment, and inflation rates move in concert. This chapter discusses how national economies are tied together. The discussion applies to **open economies**, economies that trade goods and financial assets with the rest of the world. A *closed economy* is isolated economically from the rest of the world; it does not trade with other nations. Although no economy is absolutely closed, there are different degrees of openness. Table 10-1 lists several countries and the value of their international trade as a fraction of GNP. Nations with a large domestic market in relation to the value of international trade, such as Japan and the United States, are considered relatively closed, even though their laws and the behavior of their citizens and firms may be more open than other nations. Nations where the value of international trade is large in relation to the size of the domestic market, such as Malaysia and Jamaica, are considered to be relatively open. The definition of "open" is based on the ratio of exports plus imports to GNP or GDP. The more open the economy, the more sensitive are prices and interest rates in the country to changes in international economic conditions.

TABLE 10-1   *A Sample of National Economies Ranked in Order of Openness*

Country	(Exports + Imports) /GNP	Country	(Exports + Imports) /GNP
Malaysia	1.33	Germany	0.63
Jamaica	1.23	Philippines	0.51
Israel	0.90	United Kingdom	0.50
Korea	0.74	Egypt	0.37
Thailand	0.72	Australia	0.36
Austria	0.71	Pakistan	0.30
Sweden	0.65	Japan	0.27
Sri Lanka	0.64	United States	0.20

Source: International Monetary Fund, *International Financial Statistics* (Washington, DC: International Monetary Fund, 1990).

Countries are linked through their trade in goods, services, and financial assets. These links have implications for economic policy and for the behavior of economies. This chapter discusses how countries are linked. The following questions are considered:

1. What are exchange rates?

2. What is appreciation and depreciation?

3. What is arbitrage?

4. What is purchasing power parity?

5. What is interest rate parity?

6. How are exchange rates determined?

7. What exchange rate systems exist and are used today?

▼

The Sources of Links Among Nations

The economic ties among nations are not unlike the ties among any markets in different locations. People buy goods and services where they are priced low and sell them where they are priced high.

Arbitrage

For example, liquor is much less expensive in New Hampshire than in Massachusetts. As a result, people in Massachusetts often drive to New Hampshire to stock up on liquor. Some buy enough to sell to friends and acquaintances back in Massachusetts. Similarly, Native Americans living on reservations are able to buy cigarettes much less expensively than other Americans. So Native Americans often set up shops on the edge of the reservations where they sell the cigarettes to citizens not living on the reservations. And when the Miata sports car was first introduced in the United States, it was so popular that dealers were marking very high prices on it—significantly higher than the manufacturer had suggested. In California, where the demand was particularly high, the car was selling for nearly $10,000 above the price in Michigan. As a result, several people bought cars in Michigan and drove them to California for resale.

In each of these cases—liquor, cigarettes, the Miata car—buying a product in a low-price area and reselling in a high-price area tends to drive the low price up and the high price down. This strategy of buying in one market and selling in another is referred to as **arbitrage**. Arbitrageurs equalize prices of identical goods in different markets. When they buy in the low-price market, prices there go up. When they sell in the high-price market, prices there fall. Arbitrage can be expected to equate prices on identical products in different markets and in different countries.

Purchasing Power Parity

An exchange rate is the price of one currency in terms of another. Table 10-2 shows the names and symbols of currency in several countries. In addition, exchange rates on June 7, 1991 are listed. An exchange rate between U.S. dollars and Japanese yen is shown as $/¥; the exchange rate between U.S. dollars and French francs is shown as $/FF.

An exchange rate doesn't enter into the purchase and sale of a product across state lines in the United States because each state uses the U.S. dollar. Because prices are quoted in terms of a single currency within one country, all we need to know is the price in the domestic currency of an item in two different locations. If John's in Los Angeles charges $40 for a shirt and Carter's in Los Angeles charges $80 for the same shirt, the purchasing power of our money is twice as great at John's as at Carter's. But for goods and services traded across national borders, the exchange rate is an important part of the total price.

International comparisons of prices must be made using exchange rates because different countries use different currencies. If John's clothing store in Los Angeles charges $40 for a shirt and Illese's shop in Paris charges FF80, we can't compare the prices unless we know the exchange rate between dollars and francs. If we find that goods sell in Paris for the same price as in Los Angeles, then our money has the same purchasing power in those two markets, which means that we have **purchasing power parity (PPP)**. PPP reflects a relationship among the domestic price level, the exchange rate, and the foreign price level:

$$P = EP^F$$

where P = domestic price, E = the exchange rate (units of domestic currency per unit of foreign currency), and P^F = the foreign price.

TABLE 10-2   *Selected Currency Symbols and Exchange Rates*

Country	Currency	Symbol	Exchange Rate[a]
Australia	dollar	A$	.7650
Austria	schilling	Sch	.07934
Belgium	franc	BF	.02711
Canada	dollar	Can $	.8760
Denmark	krone	DKr	.1448
Finland	markka	FM	.23455
France	franc	FF	.16419
Germany	deutsche mark	DM	.5583
Greece	drachma	Dr	.005089
India	rupee	Rs	.04728
Italy	lira	Lit	.007499
Japan	yen	¥	.007239
Mexico	peso	Ps	.0003314
Netherlands	guilder	FL	.4956
Norway	krone	NKr	.1428
Saudi Arabia	riyal	SR	.2663
Singapore	dollar	S$	.5602
South Africa	rand	R	.3478
Spain	peseta	PTs	.008870
Sweden	kronar	SKr	.1542
Switzerland	franc	SF	.6517
United Kingdom	pound	£	1.6355
United States	dollar	$	1.000

[a]$/currency is as of June 20, 1991, *Wall Street Journal,* June 21, 1991.

If the dollar–franc exchange rate is 0.50 ($0.50 = FF1), then a shirt priced at FF80 in Illese's in Paris costs the same as a shirt priced at $40 in John's of Los Angeles:

$$P = EP^F$$
$$= \$0.50 \times 80$$
$$= \$40$$

The domestic currency price (assuming the dollar to be the domestic currency) equals the exchange rate times the foreign price. Because the domestic currency price of the shirt in Paris is $40 and the price at home is $40, PPP holds.

The *Economist* magazine carries out an annual survey of the U.S. dollar price of Big Macs around the world. It seems the price of a Big Mac varies considerably. In 1989 a Big Mac cost $6.25 in Moscow, while in Hong Kong it was only $0.98. And Big Macs aren't the only products that differ in price. In fact, *no* goods sell for the same price in different nations. Why don't similar goods sell for the same price everywhere?

Actually, we shouldn't be too surprised at the difference because goods often don't even sell for the same price within a country. Does a Big Mac cost

the same in Tuscaloosa, Alabama, and San José, California? If the same product is priced differently at different stores in one country, it is unrealistic to
expect the price of the good to be identical worldwide. Prices differ for several
reasons. Often goods are not identical. Two shirts are similar but not identical, or one clothing store offers better service than another, so the price differs.
In many cases, people do not know about price differentials and hence can't
buy low and sell high. Often shipping costs affect prices. Prices of oranges grown
in Florida are higher in South Dakota than in Florida. Tariffs and legal restrictions on trade also affect prices. If these factors did not occur, we would expect that any time a price was lower in one market than another, arbitrageurs
would buy in the low-price market and simultaneously sell in the high-price
market, driving the prices to equality.

PPP and Inflation Rates. Even though PPP does not hold exactly for most goods,
it is a useful concept. It points out an important link between national economies. Price changes are reflected in exchange rates; exchange rates adjust to
offset price differences in different countries. Consider a shirt selling for $40
in Los Angeles and FF80 in Paris. When the exchange rate is $0.50 = FF1, FF80
equals $40, so PPP holds. Now suppose that France experiences a doubling of
prices while in the United States the price level remains constant. The shirt
now sells for FF160 in Paris while in Los Angeles the shirt remains at $40. What
happens to the exchange rate between dollars and francs? People will want to
convert their francs to dollars so they can buy the shirt in Los Angeles. As people do this, the value of francs declines and the value of dollars rises. The exchange rate will change until PPP holds.

Previously we defined purchasing power parity as $P = EP^F$, where P is the
domestic price level, P^F is the foreign price level (francs, in this example), and
E is the exchange rate of dollars to foreign currency. Rewriting PPP as $E = P/P^F$, we see that the exchange rate consistent with PPP is the ratio of the domestic price level to the foreign price level. If the shirt sells for $40 in Los Angeles
and FF160 in Paris, then the PPP exchange rate of U.S. dollars to French francs
is 0.25 (40/160). Because the price level in France doubled relative to the price
level in the United States, the dollar price of the franc was cut in half.

Absolute and Relative PPP. There are two forms of the purchasing power parity, the absolute and the relative versions. As we have just seen, the *absolute version* in equation form is

$$P = EP^F$$

where P^F represents the foreign currency price, P the domestic price, and E
the exchange rate of domestic to foreign currencies. This is also called the **law
of one price**, indicating that goods sell for the same price worldwide when defined in one currency.

Unfortunately, the world is more complicated than this equation implies.
The real world is characterized by many slightly and many greatly different

products and all sorts of impediments to the equalization of prices worldwide. Some goods, such as gold, are very similar worldwide, and the law of one price holds quite well for these goods. Most goods differ in terms of quality, size, color, and other attributes, so equalization of price does not make as much sense. In addition, international trade usually involves transportation charges and tariffs. These costs mean that PPP is not likely to hold for any particular good. Relative price changes reflect additional product differentiation or changing transportation or tariff charges, and thus keep PPP from occurring.

An alternative form of purchasing power parity, known as the **relative version of purchasing power parity** has been proposed to account for these relative price effects. This version states that the percentage change of the exchange rate equals the difference between the percentage changes of the foreign and home price levels. In equation form,

$$\%\Delta E = \%\Delta P - \%\Delta P^F$$

where $\%\Delta$ represents the percentage change. Another way of stating the relative version of PPP is that the percentage change in the exchange rate is equal to the inflation differential between the domestic and foreign countries.

Even the relative version of PPP does not hold exactly for all countries and all time periods. PPP holds better for high-inflation countries than for low-inflation countries. The reason for this is that when inflation is high, the general inflation rate swamps any relative price effects that might be occurring.

PPP also holds better for longer periods than for shorter periods. The reason is that relative price changes can have an important effect on exchange rates in the short run, but over time these relative price changes become unimportant compared to the movement of the overall price level.

A number of explanations have been offered to deal with the fact that even the relative version of PPP does not hold exactly. Explanations for deviations from PPP include factors that suggest permanent deviations (shipping costs and tariffs). Intervention by governments that do not allow the exchange rates to adjust to relative inflation differences means that PPP does not hold during the intervention period. This explanation also notes that price indexes in different countries measure different baskets of goods and therefore are not comparable among countries. A second explanation suggests that exchange rates change more rapidly than price levels — that is, financial asset prices adjust more rapidly than goods prices. A third explanation notes that international trade involves lags between orders and deliveries. Prices are often set by contract today for goods to be delivered several months later. If we compare goods prices and exchange rates today to evaluate PPP, we are using the exchange rate applicable to goods delivered today with prices that were set some time in the past. Ideally, we should compare contract prices in each country at the time contracts are signed with the exchange rate that is expected to prevail in the future period when goods are actually delivered and payment is made.

Overvalued and Undervalued Currencies. Although PPP may not hold exactly nor all the time, PPP does provide a target toward which prices will move over time. Thus, if, over time, P^F rises faster than P, we can expect E to fall. If E does not fall by the amount suggested by the lower P/P^F, then we can say that the domestic currency is *undervalued* or (the same thing) the foreign currency is overvalued.

In the early 1980s, there was a great deal of discussion about the overvalued dollar. The foreign exchange value of the dollar seemed too high relative to the inflation differentials between the United States and the other developed countries. The adjective *overvalued* implies that the exchange rate is not where it should be and that over time the exchange rate will fall back in line with the inflation differential.

In the early 1980s, for example, the percentage change in the exchange rate for the U.S. dollar versus the Japanese yen was higher than the inflation differential, which means that the yen price of the dollar grew at a faster rate than did the inflation differential between the United States and Japan. It appears that for more than four years, the dollar overvaluation developed. Then the percentage change in the exchange rate fell below the inflation differential line, which means that the exchange rate began to return to a level consistent with PPP.

Because PPP does not hold well for any pair of countries in the short run that are experiencing only moderate inflation, there always will be currencies that seem overvalued or undervalued in a PPP sense. The issue becomes important only if the deviation persists for some time or has significant macroeconomic policy consequences. For instance, the overvalued dollar was a major political issue in the United States in the early 1980s. The export-oriented industries were suffering from decreased sales and put enormous pressure on U.S. policymakers to alter the value of the dollar.

Interest Rates

Arbitrage occurs whenever a profitable opportunity exists for buying something in one market and simultaneously selling it in another market. It occurs with goods and services, and it occurs with financial assets. If U.S. stocks offer a 10 percent return while U.S. bonds offer an 8 percent return, and stocks and bonds are considered to be similar assets, people will buy stocks, driving the price of stocks up and the rates of return on stocks down, while selling the bonds and driving the price down and rates of return up.

There is an additional complication when we talk about financial assets in different countries, however. A U.S. bond is denominated in dollars while a British bond is denominated in British pounds. If the U.S. bond pays 10 percent interest, that interest is paid in dollars. Similarly, if the British bond pays 5 percent interest, it pays in pounds. As a U.S. citizen, you ultimately want dollars and thus want to compare the returns on the two bonds in terms of dollars. If you buy the U.K. bond, you exchange dollars for pounds at the time you purchase the bond. When the bond matures, you receive the principal and interest in pounds and must exchange them for dollars. If the exchange rate remains the same, then the return on the U.K. bond is 5 percent. If, however, the exchange rate changes between the time you buy the bond and the time it matures, your return may be more or less than 5 percent.

Suppose the exchange rate is $2 = £1 when the bond is purchased and the bond sells for £1. The U.S. resident needs U.S.$2 to buy the bond. A year later the bond matures. The bondholder receives the principal of £1 plus 5 percent interest for a total of £1.05. At the exchange rate of $2/£1, the £1.05 is converted into $2.10. Having paid $2 for the bond initially, the interest return in dollars is 5 percent. However, suppose the exchange rate has gone up from $2 = £1 to $2.10 = £1 during the period you held the bond. Then the £1.05 proceeds from the bond are changed into $2.205 (£1.05 × $2.10/£1 = $2.205). You are better off than you would have been if the exchange rate had not changed. You paid $2 for the bond initially and received $0.205 in interest or slightly more than 10 percent. The percentage return from the U.K. bond is the percentage difference between the dollar proceeds received after one year, and the initial dollar amount invested, approximately 10 percent:

$$\text{Dollar return} = (\$2.205 - \$2)/\$2 = \$0.205/\$2 = 0.10$$

The dollar return from the U.K. bond is the U.K. interest rate plus the percentage change in the exchange rate, not simply the U.K. interest rate. The percentage change in the exchange rate is 5 percent:

$$\text{Percentage change in exchange rate} = (\$2.10 - \$2)/\$2$$
$$= \$0.10/\$2$$
$$= 0.05$$

Thus, the dollar return from the U.K. bond equals the 5 percent interest paid in British pounds plus the 5 percent change in the exchange rate, or 10 percent.

When the pound increases in value, or appreciates, foreign residents holding pound-denominated bonds earn a higher return on those bonds than the pound interest rate. When the pound depreciates, the pounds received at maturity are worth less than the pounds originally purchased, and the dollar return from the U.K. bond is lower than the interest rate on the bond. For instance, in our example, if the pound had depreciated 5 percent, the dollar return would have been zero.

If the U.K. bond is returning a greater amount in dollar terms than the U.S. bond, then U.S. residents will purchase U.K. bonds. This drives up the price of U.K. bonds relative to U.S. bonds and lowers the return on U.K. bonds relative to U.S. bonds. Once again, arbitrage tends to force the rates of return toward equality. When the return, or effective interest rate, tends to be the same on similar bonds (when returns are measured in terms of the domestic currency), we have **interest rate parity (IRP)**. Purchasing power parity exists when similar goods sell for the same price (quoted in a single currency) in different countries. Interest rate parity is the financial asset version of purchasing power parity. Similar financial assets have the same percentage return when that return is computed in terms of one currency.

Deviations from Interest Rate Parity. Interest rate parity does not hold for all financial assets. Like PPP, which applies only to similar (identical goods), IRP applies only for similar assets. For instance, we don't expect the interest rate on a ninety-day U.S. Treasury bill to equal the dollar return on a one-year U.S. Treasury bond, because the maturity dates are different, ninety days versus a year. Financial assets with different terms to maturity typically pay different interest rates. We also don't expect different kinds of assets to offer the same return. A ninety-day bank deposit should not offer the same dollar return as a ninety-day U.S. Treasury bill. The bank deposit and the Treasury bill are different assets. If we don't expect these assets to have identical returns in one country, then we shouldn't expect them to have identical returns in different countries.

If perfect capital mobility exists, then interest rate parity holds all the time for identical assets. The term **perfect capital mobility** refers to the situation where any interest rate differential, however slight, causes funds to flow from the rest of the world to the nation with the higher interest rate, thereby lowering interest rates in the nation into which funds are flowing.

However, even with assets that seem similar we can find deviations from interest rate parity. For instance, a ninety-day peso certificate of deposit in a Mexico City bank does not offer a U.S. resident the same dollar return as a ninety-day certificate of deposit denominated in U.S. dollars in a New York City bank. Why? Government restrictions, political or national risk, and taxes can all affect rates of return on assets in different countries.

Governments often erect barriers to the free flow of money between countries. These barriers take the form of quotas on the amount of foreign exchange that can be bought or sold or restrictions on who can own what assets. These barriers are called **capital controls**. When capital controls are imposed, arbitrage cannot occur freely, and thus IRP does not hold.

It can be risky to hold assets in countries that are experiencing political instability. Many nations have imposed controls on the amount of money that can be taken out of the country or have simply confiscated assets and bank deposits. If U.S. residents believe that a foreign government is going to impose restrictions that reduce the return on assets issued in that country, those foreign issue assets must offer a higher return than is offered on similar U.S. assets. That extra return is called a **risk premium**. If political risk exists, then IRP does not hold because the return on the foreign asset includes a risk premium.

Tax rates affect the *after-tax return* on investments. If the U.K. bond we discussed earlier returns 5 percent before tax but only 2.5 percent after tax, the total return in dollar terms does not equal the 10 percent return on U.S. bonds. So IRP does not hold.

Interest Rate Parity and Inflation. Different rates of inflation in different countries are reflected in different nominal rates of interest. The **nominal interest rate**, i, is the rate actually observed in the market; it is the 7 or 10 percent you see quoted in the newspaper or on television. The real interest rate, r, adjusts the nominal interest rate for expected inflation, π^e, that occurred over the period of the loan. If you loan someone money and charge that person 5 percent interest on the loan, the purchasing power of your return—your real return—is the 5 percent less any increase in inflation. If the rate of inflation is 10 percent, then the debtor is repaying you with dollars that are worth less in that they can buy fewer goods and services today than they could when the loan was first given. As the creditor, you want to ensure that your return is greater than the purchasing power change. The nominal interest rate must incorporate the expected inflation rate. If the target real return is 3 percent and expected inflation is 10 percent, then the contracted nominal interest rate is 13 percent. If the target real return is 3 percent and the expected inflation rate is 4 percent, the contracted nominal interest rate is 7 percent. This relationship between nominal and real interest rates is illustrated in what is called the **Fisher effect** (after the economist Irving Fisher):

Nominal interest rate = real interest rate + expected inflation rate

$$i = r + \pi^e$$

If we combine the Fisher effect and interest rate parity, we can see how interest rates, inflation, and exchange rates are linked. First, consider the Fisher effect for the United States and the United Kingdom:

$$i_\$ = r_\$ + \pi^e_\$ \quad i_£ = r_£ + \pi^e_£$$

If the real interest rate is the same internationally, then $r_\$ = r_£$. In this case, the nominal interest rates, $i_\$$ and $i_£$, differ only by expected inflation, so we can write

$$i_\$ - i_£ = \pi^e_\$ - \pi^e_£$$

And if the percentage change in the exchange rate is equal to the inflation differential, then the interest rate differential will also equal the percentage change in the exchange rate.

▼
Exchange Rate Determination

We've discussed exchange rates, over- and undervalued currencies, and PPP and IRP without mentioning explicitly how the exchange rate is determined. Now let's consider exchange rate determination.

The Foreign Exchange Market

The determination of exchange rates occurs in the foreign exchange market and depends on the demand for and supply of a currency. If Micron in Boise, Idaho, sells $1 million worth of microchips to a manufacturer in Beijing, China, the exchange of the chips requires an exchange of currencies. The manufacturer in Beijing must offer the equivalent of U.S.$1 million in Chinese yuan. A banker in Beijing, or perhaps Hong Kong, might arrange for the exchange with a banker in San Francisco, offering to buy U.S.$1 million for some amount of Chinese yuan. This exchange of currencies occurs in the foreign exchange market. The relative amounts of dollars and yuan offered in the foreign exchange market determines the exchange rate between the two currencies.

Figure 10-1 shows the foreign exchange market for U.S. dollars and yuan. The price measured on the vertical axis is the exchange rate, E = U.S. dollars/yuan, or $/Y, the quantity measured along the horizontal axis is the quantity of yuan. The demand for yuan represents the U.S. demand for Chinese goods, services, and financial assets. To purchase these Chinese items, yuan are needed. U.S. residents must buy yuan. The higher the price—that is, the higher is $/Y, the lower is the quantity of yuan demanded. The quantity of yuan demanded falls because the higher exchange rate increases the price of Chi-

FIGURE 10-1   *The foreign exchange market. The price measured on the vertical axis is the exchange rate between the U.S. dollar and the Chinese yuan, E = $/Y. The demand for yuan represents the U.S. demand for Chinese goods, services, and financial assets. The higher the price—that is, the higher is $/Y—the lower is the quantity of yuan demanded. The supply of yuan represents the Chinese demand for U.S. goods, services, and financial assets. The supply curve is drawn with the typically assumed upward slope, indicating that the higher the price—that is, the higher $/Y—the higher the quantity of yuan offered.*

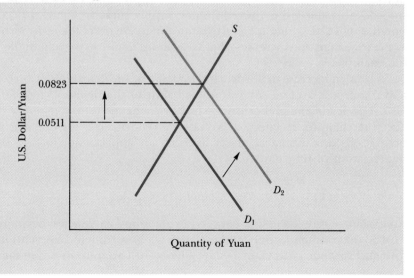

nese goods and services to U.S. residents, *ceteris paribus*. For example, an item priced at 100 yuan costs a U.S. resident $100 if the exchange rate is $1 = 1 yuan but costs the U.S. resident $200 if the exchange rate rises to $2 = 1 yuan. Consequently, if the exchange rate rises U.S. residents purchase fewer Chinese goods and services, and the quantity of yuan demanded falls.

The supply of yuan represents the Chinese demand for U.S. goods, services, and financial assets. To buy these U.S. items, Chinese buyers must offer yuan in exchange for dollars. The supply of foreign exchange is typically drawn as an upward-sloping curve: the higher the price — that is, the higher the $/Y — the higher the quantity of yuan offered.

Actually, the slope of the supply curve depends on how responsive Chinese demand for U.S. goods and services is to changes in the prices to Chinese residents. Consider a U.S. item priced at $100. If the exchange rate is $1 = 1 yuan, this item costs a Chinese resident 100 yuan. If the exchange rate rises to $2 = 1 yuan, *ceteris paribus*, the price to a Chinese resident falls to 50 yuan. The falling yuan prices increase the quantity of U.S. goods and services demanded by Chinese residents. Note that the exchange rate has doubled, or increased by 100 percent. If the quantity of U.S. items demanded by the Chinese increases less than proportionately to the exchange rate increase, the quantity of yuan supplied to this foreign exchange market drops. For example, assume that Chinese residents originally purchase 1,000 units of the U.S. good priced at $100, and after the exchange rate doubles, Chinese residents increase purchases by 50 percent, to 1,500 units. The quantity of yuan supplied as a result of these transactions falls from 100,000 yuan (1,000 units × 100 yuan) to 75,000 yuan (1,500 units × 50 yuan). Further note that if Chinese purchases of our $100 item only double to 2,000 units (that is, proportionate to the exchange rate increase), the quantity of yuan supplied remains unchanged (2,000 units × 50 yuan = 100,000 yuan), and the supply curve for yuan is horizontal. In order to achieve the upward-sloping supply curve in Figure 10-1, Chinese purchases of U.S. goods and services must increase more than proportionately to the exchange rate increase — that is, by more than 100 percent in the preceding example.

A sudden increase in the demand for yuan or the demand for Chinese goods and financial assets means an outward shift of the demand curve in Figure 10-1. This leads to a higher price — higher exchange rate. The dollar depreciates (the yuan appreciates). Conversely, a reduction in the demand for Chinese goods and financial assets leads to an appreciation of the dollar (a depreciation of the yuan).

Exchange Rate Systems

An exchange rate is the link between two nations' currencies. Exchange rates may be determined in free markets, through government intervention in the foreign exchange market, or by law. Figure 10-1 represents a free market, or

flexible exchange rate system, where the demand for and supply of a currency determines the exchange rate. If the government at times intervenes to cause the demand curve or the supply curve to shift, but normally allows the market to move freely, then the exchange rate system is called a **dirty float**, or **managed floating system**. If the exchange rate is set by law independent of demand and supply, then the exchange rate is called a **fixed exchange rate system**. Now let's consider a few of the exchange rate systems that have been used in recent history.

The Gold Standard. The first monies were commodities—the first government-issued monies were coins made from gold and silver. When governments began to issue paper money, the money was usually convertible into a fixed amount of gold. Ensuring the convertibility of paper money into gold was a way to maintain confidence in the currency's value, at home and abroad. If a unit of currency was worth a fixed amount of gold, its value could be stated in terms of its gold value. The countries that maintained a constant gold value of their currencies were said to be on a **gold standard**.

Between 1880 and 1914, currencies had fixed values in terms of gold. For instance, the U.S. dollar's value was fixed at $20.67 per ounce of gold. Any other currency that was fixed in terms of gold would have an exchange rate with the dollar. For instance, the U.K. pound was set at 4.86 pounds per ounce of gold. This meant that the exchange rate between dollars and pounds was 20.67/4.86 = 4.25. The gold standard also determined the money supply in each country. For example, if the United States owned 4 million ounces of gold, the U.S. currency supply could only be $82.68 million at a rate of $20.67/ounce. In addition, the money supply would increase only as the stock of gold rose.

The gold standard ended with the outbreak of World War I because the gold standard did not permit the rapid increase in the money supply necessary to pay for military expenditures. At the end of World War I, there was an attempt to return to fixed exchange rates and convertibility of the pound and dollar into gold. But errors in defining equilibrium rates led to rapid decreases in the money supply in the United Kingdom and other nations and contributed to the onset of the Great Depression. Not until the end of World War II was there widespread political support for an exchange rate system linking all currencies in much the same way as the gold standard had. In 1944, delegates from forty-four nations met in Bretton Woods, New Hampshire, to discuss such a system.

The Gold Exchange Standard. The exchange rate arrangement that emerged from the Bretton Woods conference was a **gold exchange standard**. Each country was to fix the value of its currency in terms of gold, just as each had under the gold standard. The U.S. dollar price of gold for instance, was $35 an ounce. There were fundamental differences between this system and the old gold standard. The U.S. dollar, rather than gold, served as the focal point of the system.

Instead of buying and selling gold, countries bought and sold U.S. dollars to maintain a fixed exchange rate with the dollar. The U.S. dollar was the *reserve currency* of the system. In effect, after World War II the world was on a U.S. dollar standard.

The Bretton Woods system of fixed exchange rates required countries to actively buy and sell U.S. dollars to maintain fixed exchange rates when the free market equilibrium in the foreign exchange market differed from the fixed rate. The effectiveness of such intervention was limited to situations in which free market pressure to deviate from the fixed exchange rate was temporary. For instance, suppose a country earns less foreign exchange than usual, due to a natural disaster. That natural disaster is a one-time event, so reduced earnings are only temporary. During the period of reduced exports, the government would have to intervene to avoid a depreciation of its currency. The government would have to buy its currency and sell other currencies.

Floating Exchange Rates. During the late 1960s and early 1970s, countries were trying to maintain exchange rates that were permanently different from the equilibrium rates, but intervention could not offset the permanent changes in foreign exchange earnings. The fixed exchange rate system had to be abandoned in March 1973. All nations did not move to freely floating exchange rates. Some kept fixed exchange rates with respect to a major currency, while others moved to an exchange rate system somewhere in between fixed and floating.

Table 10-3 lists the exchange rate arrangements of several countries. The major industrial countries maintain managed floating exchange rates. For instance, the central banks of the United States and Japan intervene from time to time to prevent undesirably wide fluctuations in exchange rates. Some countries, such as Belize and Chad, maintain a fixed value (called a *peg*) relative to a major currency such as the U.S. dollar or French franc. Still other countries, like Finland and Hungary, peg to a composite of currencies; the value of their currency is pegged to an average of several foreign currencies. Some countries, such as Libya, peg their currencies to the SDR. The SDR, or **special drawing right**, is an artificial unit of account issued by the International Monetary Fund. Its value is determined by combining the values of the U.S. dollar, German mark, Japanese yen, French franc, and British pound. Several countries belong to cooperative arrangements such as the European Monetary System, or EMS. These countries maintain fixed exchange rates against each other but allow their currencies to float jointly against the rest of the world.

Exchange Rate Systems and Policy

We have now seen how countries are linked through arbitrage and thus with PPP and IRP. This link means that what occurs in one country's economy can have profound effects on other countries. The actual effect depends on whether

TABLE 10-3 *Exchange Rate Arrangements*

	Fixed Currency pegged to		
U.S. Dollar	*French Franc*	*SDR*	*Other Composite*
Afghanistan	Benin	Burundi	Algeria
Angola	Burkina Faso	Iran, Islamic Rep. of	Austria
Antigua and	Cameroon	Libya	Bangladesh
Barbuda	Cen. African	Myanmar	Botswana
Bahamas, The	Republic	Rwanda	Cape Verde
Barbados	Chad	Seychelles	Cyprus
Belize	Comoros	Zambia	Fiji
Djibouti	Congo		Finland
Dominica	Côte d'Ivoire		Hungary
El Salvador	Equatorial Guinea		Iceland
Ethiopia	Gabon		Israel
Grenada	Mali		Jordan
Guatemala	Niger		Kenya
Guyana	Senegal		Kuwait
Haiti	Togo		Malawi
Honduras			Malaysia
Iraq			Malta
Liberia			Mauritius
Nicaragua			Nepal
Oman			Norway
Panama			Papua New Guinea
Peru			Poland
St. Kitts and Nevis			Romania
St. Lucia			São Tomé and
St. Vincent			Principe
Sierra Leone			Solomon Islands
Sudan			Somalia
Suriname			Sweden
Syrian Arab			Tanzania
Republic			Thailand
Trinidad and			Vanuatu
Tobago			Western Samoa
Uganda			Zimbabwe
Vietnam			
Yemen, Arab			
Rep. of			
Yemen, People's			
Dem. Rep. of			

(continued on next page)

TABLE 10-3   *Exchange Rate Arrangements   (continued)*

	Floating Currency pegged to	
Cooperative Arrangement	*Other Managed Floating*	*Independently Floating*
Belgium	Argentina	Australia
Denmark	China, People's Rep.	Bolivia
France	Costa Rica	Canada
Germany	Domincan Rep.	Gambia, The
Ireland	Ecuador	Ghana
Italy	Egypt	Japan
Luxembourg	Greece	Lebanon
Netherlands	Guinea	Maldives
Spain	Guinea-Bissau	New Zealand
	India	Nigeria
	Indonesia	Paraguay
	Jamaica	Philippines
	Korea	South Africa
	Lao, People's Dem. Rep. of	United Kingdom
	Mauritania	United States
	Mexico	Uruguay
	Morocco	Venezuela
	Mozambique	Zaire
	Pakistan	
	Singapore	
	Sri Lanka	
	Tunisia	
	Turkey	
	Yugoslavia	

exchange rates are flexible or fixed and on the speed with which IRP and PPP are established.

As we shall discover in later chapters, there are substantial differences (1) within a single open economy and (2) regarding the international effects of events in one country, between fixed and flexible exchange rate systems. Before we can discuss these differences fully, we need to examine monetary and fiscal policy in a domestic economy and their ramifications on the domestic and foreign economies. We can introduce the issues at this stage, however.

We can illustrate how the exchange rate systems work by examining a simple foreign exchange market such as in Figure 10-2 involving the U.S. dollar and French franc. The downward-sloping demand curve indicates that the higher the dollar price of French francs, the fewer francs are demanded. The upward-sloping supply curve indicates that the higher the dollar price of French francs, the more francs are supplied. The initial equilibrium at the intersec-

FIGURE 10-2 *The foreign exchange market and a change in equilibrium. The initial intersection of the demand and supply curves indicates that 1 franc costs $0.15 and the quantity of francs exchanged is Q_1. If U.S. residents increase their demand for French products, the demand curve shifts from D_1 to D_2 in panel A. The franc appreciates relative to the dollar to 0.18, and quantity Q_2 of francs is bought and sold. If U.S. demand for French goods falls, the demand curve shifts in from D_1 to D_3, the franc depreciates to 0.12, and quantity Q_3 of francs is exchanged.*

An increase in the French demand for U.S. goods causes the supply curve to shift out from S_1 to S_2 in panel B. The greater supply of francs causes the franc to depreciate relative to the dollar, and the exchange rate to fall from 0.15 to 0.12.

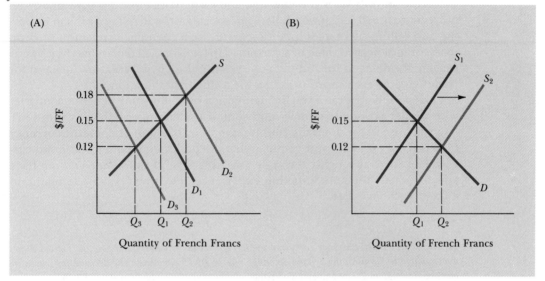

tion of the demand and supply curves indicates that 1 franc costs $0.15 and the quantity of francs bought and sold is Q_1. If U.S. residents increase their demand for French products, the demand curve shifts from D_1 to D_2 in Figure 10-2A. The franc appreciates relative to the dollar to 0.18, and more francs are bought and sold, Q_2. If the U.S. demand for French goods falls, the demand curve shifts in from D_1 to D_3, the franc depreciates to 0.12, and the quantity of francs sold and bought declines to Q_3.

The supply of francs to the foreign exchange market comes from French residents who buy goods, services, and financial assets from the rest of the world. As French residents' demand for foreign goods and services changes, the supply of francs to the foreign exchange market changes. An increase in the French demand for U.S. goods causes the supply curve to shift out from S_1 to S_2 in Figure 10-2B. The greater supply of francs causes the franc to depreciate relative to the dollar, and the exchange rate to fall from 0.15 to 0.12. If the French demand for U.S. goods falls, the supply curve shifts in and the franc appreciates.

Suppose the United States is committed to maintaining a fixed exchange rate of $0.15 per franc. The demand for francs increases, from D_1 to D_2 in Figure 10-3, and causes a shortage of francs at the exchange rate of $0.15. According to the new demand curve D_2, the quantity of francs demanded at $0.15 is Q_3. The quantity supplied Q_1 is less than Q_3. The only way to maintain the exchange rate of 0.15 is for the U.S. government to supply francs to meet the shortage of $Q_3 - Q_1$.

If the increased demand for francs is temporary, the intervention may succeed. If, however, the demand change is permanent, the intervention cannot succeed. Not only does the new demand–supply relationship continually require more francs and fewer dollars but speculators add to the problem by buying and selling currencies in anticipation of an eventual *devaluation*, or drop in the official pegged value of a currency. Speculators sell dollars and buy francs, causing the demand for francs to be even higher. The speculators' demand for francs creates even more pressure for a dollar devaluation.

Fixed exchange rates can be maintained over time only between countries with similar economic policies and similar underlying economic conditions. As prices rise in the domestic country, the value of a unit of domestic currency falls. A fixed exchange rate requires that the purchasing power of the two currencies change at roughly the same rate over time. If two nations do not have approximately the same inflation experience, they won't be able to maintain a fixed exchange rate.

FIGURE 10-3 *Fixed exchange rates and the foreign exchange market. Suppose the United States is committed to maintaining a fixed exchange rate of $0.15 per franc. The demand for francs increases, from D_1 to D_2 and causes a shortage of francs at the exchange rate of $0.15. According to the new demand curve D_2, the quantity of francs demanded at $0.15 is Q_3. The quantity supplied Q_1 is less than Q_3. To maintain the exchange rate of 0.15, the U.S. government must supply francs to meet the shortage of $Q_3 - Q_1$.*

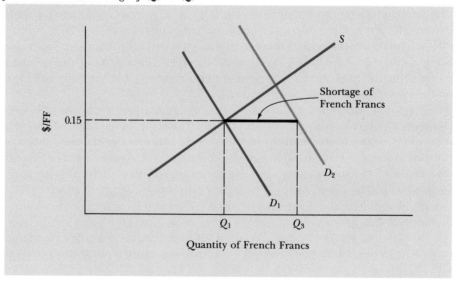

One major problem in the Bretton Woods era of fixed exchange rates was that countries were pursuing different policies. In the late 1960s, the U.S. government was trying to carry on expansionary domestic policies and fight the Vietnam War, and thus experienced inflation rates considerably higher than those experienced by other industrial nations. Between 1965 and 1970, price levels rose by 23 percent in the United States but only 13 percent in West Germany. The fixed exchange rate could not be maintained. The dollar had to be devalued.

Under fixed exchange rates, the only way that the currency values can be maintained is for the central banks of each country to buy and sell currencies on the foreign exchange market. For instance, as the United States pursued expansionary policies that led to higher inflation than experienced in West Germany, the United States sought to maintain the fixed exchange rate between dollars and deutsche marks by buying dollars and selling West German deutsche marks. This caused the U.S money supply to decline and to flow to West Germany. Thus, West Germany was accumulating large numbers of dollars and foreign exchange, which caused its money supply to rise. The United States was *exporting* its inflation problems to West Germany.

With flexible exchange rates, the story is different. Consider again the case where the United States is pursuing an expansionary monetary policy, while West Germany is not. In the United States, prices rise and the dollar falls in value relative to the German mark. The result is a depreciating dollar. The exchange rate changes to maintain purchasing power parity. The money supplies do not increase or decrease. Thus, the United States and West Germany do not export or import the other country's economic problems.

The Choice of an Exchange Rate System

As stated, in today's international financial system, different countries choose different exchange rate systems. The choice seems to be related to a country's size, its openness, and the diversity of its trade.

Size and Openness. Large countries tend to be relatively unwilling to forgo domestic policy goals to maintain a fixed exchange rate. Because large countries have large domestic markets, international issues are less crucial to everyday business than they are in a small country. In most large countries, international trade is a relatively small part of GNP. Conversely, for most small countries, trade constitutes a large portion of the GNP. The more important international trade is for an economy, the greater the impact of variations in the exchange rate on the domestic economy and thus, the greater the tendency to establish fixed exchange rates.

Trade Diversification. Countries that trade primarily with one or two other countries tend to peg their currencies to those other countries. Many countries peg to the U.S. dollar because the United States accounts for such a large part of their trade.

▼   ▼   ▼   ▼   ▼   ▼   ▼   ▼   ▼   ▼   ▼
Conclusions

Nations are linked economically. They are linked through the process of arbitrage, in which products are purchased in low-priced areas and sold in high-priced areas. Arbitrage occurs for goods and services resulting in purchasing power parity and for financial assets, resulting in interest rate parity. Exchange rates are the rates at which two currencies are exchanged. Exchange rates are determined by the demands for and supplies of the currencies in the foreign exchange market. The demand for a country's currency depends on the demand for the country's goods, services, and financial assets, while the supply of a country's currency depends on its demands for the goods, services, and financial assets of other nations. In coming chapters, we'll see how the international links among countries influence the business cycles within the countries.

▼   ▼   ▼   ▼   ▼   ▼   ▼   ▼   ▼   ▼   ▼
Summary

1. What are exchange rates?
Exchange rates are the rates at which different currencies exchange for each other.
2. What is appreciation and depreciation?
Under floating exchange rates, a currency appreciates when its value rises relative to other currencies and depreciates when its value falls relative to other currencies.
3. What is arbitrage?
Arbitrage is the practice of buying and selling an identical good or asset by buying in a low-priced area and selling in a high-priced area.
4. What is purchasing power parity?
Purchasing power parity (PPP) in absolute form is called the *law of one price*; it indicates that identical goods sell for the same price throughout the world after adjusting for currency differences. The relative version indicates that the percentage change in exchange rates equals the inflation differential between countries.
5. What is interest rate parity?
Interest rate parity indicates that the differences between interest rates on identical assets in different countries vary by the inflation differential between the countries.
6. How are exchange rates determined?
Exchange rates are determined by the demand for and supply of currencies. This occurs in the foreign exchange market.
7. What exchange rate systems exist and are used today?
Today there are fixed exchange rates, flexible exchange rates, and variations on these two exchange rate systems. In most instances, rather than pure flexible or floating exchange rates, governments manage or intervene in a flexible system. This is called a "dirty float" or "managed floating system."

▼
Key Terms

open economies   231
arbitrage   233
purchasing power parity (PPP)   233
law of one price   235
relative version of purchasing power
  parity   236
interest rate parity (IRP)   239
perfect capital mobility   239
capital controls   239
risk premium   239

nominal interest rate   240
Fisher effect   240
flexible exchange rate system   243
dirty float   243
managed floating system   243
fixed exchange rate system   243
gold standard   243
gold exchange standard   243
special drawing right   244

▼
Problems and Exercises

1. What is the price of one U.S. dollar in terms of the other currency given the
following exchange rates?
    a. One Japanese yen = $0.005
    b. One Chinese yuan = $0.33
    c. One Kuwaiti dinar = $4.20
    d. One German mark = $0.25
2. A VCR sells for $300 in the United States. Using this past Wednesday's exchange
rates (get from a newspaper), what is the price in each of the following countries?
    a. Argentina
    b. Canada
    c. Japan
    d. Korea
    e. Mexico
3. The U.S. dollar price of a Swiss franc changes from $1.40 to $1.60.
    a. Has the dollar appreciated or depreciated against the Swiss franc?
    b. Has the Swiss franc appreciated or depreciated against the dollar?
4. Explain the following statements:
    a. Purchasing power parity holds better in the long run than in the short run.
    b. Purchasing power parity is not a theory of how the exchange rate is
    determined.
    c. Interest rate parity holds perfectly if there is perfect capital mobility.
5. For what type of goods does the law of one price hold very well?
6. Why does PPP hold better for high-inflation than low-inflation countries?
7. Why does PPP hold better over long periods of time than over short periods
of time?
8. Explain the various forms of exchange rate systems. Why might one country
choose one over the other?
9. Explain the channels through which countries are linked economically.

Chapter 11

Money, Banking, and Monetary Policy

What to Expect

In previous chapters, the discussion assumed a money supply totally and easily controlled by the central bank. The supply of money is actually determined within a complex and ever changing system of financial institutions and regulations. This chapter examines the money supply process—how money is created and how the central bank seeks to control the quantity in the context of a global economy. The chapter begins with a definition of money and then looks at how the quantity of money is determined. Finally, the chapter discusses monetary policy, the central bank's attempt to control the quantity of money to influence levels of output, prices, and employment. The following questions are considered:

1. How is money defined?

2. What are international reserves?

3. How is monetary policy executed?

4. What are the objectives of monetary policy?

5. What are the limitations of monetary policy?

6. How do the alternative exchange rate systems influence monetary policy?

7. What are intervention and sterilization?

▼

The Money Supply

To understand how money is created and its supply controlled, we need to know just what money is. Many assets could be used as money, from currency to checks to stock market accounts to commodities. Which really are used and accepted as money? In the United States, there are three generally accepted definitions of money or *monetary aggregates—M1*, *M2*, and *M3*—ranging from the least inclusive, *M1*, to the most inclusive, *M3*.

The M1 *Monetary Aggregate*

M1 is a measure of financial assets that are immediately available for spending. This definition emphasizes the use of money as a medium of exchange. The *M1* **monetary aggregate** consists of currency in circulation, travelers' checks, demand deposits, and other checkable deposits. Demand and other checkable deposits are *transactions accounts;* they can be used directly to purchase goods and services. These transactions accounts are held in *depository institutions:* commercial banks, savings and loans, credit unions, and mutual savings banks.

Currency. Currency in circulation includes coins and paper money held by the nonbank public. In 1991, currency represented about 30 percent of the *M1* money supply. A common misconception about currency today is that it is backed by gold or silver. This is not true. Nothing is backing the U.S. dollar except public confidence in the government. This kind of monetary system is called a *fiduciary* monetary system. The word *fiduciary* means "trust." As long as we believe the money is an acceptable form of payment for goods and services, the system works. U.S. coins are *token money:* their exchange value exceeds the value of metal in the coins.

Travelers' Checks. Outstanding U.S. dollar-denominated travelers' checks issued by *nonbank* institutions such as American Express are counted as part of *M1*. When a bank issues its own travelers' checks, it deposits the amount paid by the purchaser in a special account that is used to redeem the checks. Because this account is counted as a part of demand deposits, it is not counted again as part of outstanding travelers' checks. Travelers' checks accounted for just 1 percent of *M1* in 1991.

Demand Deposits. **Demand deposits** are checking account deposits at a commercial bank that pay no interest. They are called *demand deposits* because the bank must pay the amount of the check immediately on the demand of the depositor. Demand deposits accounted for about 33 percent of the *M1* money supply in 1991.

Other Checkable Deposits. Until 1978, demand deposits at commercial banks were the only kind of checking account. Today there are many different kinds of checking accounts, known as **other checkable deposits (OCDs)**. OCDs represented about 36 percent of the *M1* money supply in 1991. Among the OCDs included in the *M1* money supply are the following:

1. *Negotiable orders of withdrawal (NOW)* and *automatic transfer service (ATS)* accounts. NOW accounts are interest-bearing checking accounts. ATS accounts combine an interest-earning savings account with a checking account that does not earn interest. The depositor keeps a small balance in the checking account; any time the checking account balance is overdrawn, funds automatically are transferred from the savings account.
2. *Credit union share draft accounts.* Credit unions offer their members interest-bearing checking accounts called *share drafts.*
3. *Demand deposits at thrift institutions.* Thrift institutions include savings and loan associations, credit unions, and mutual savings banks.

The M2 *Monetary Aggregate*

The *M2* **monetary aggregate** is a broader definition of the U.S. money supply, which includes *M1* plus overnight repurchase agreements, overnight Eurodollar deposits, savings deposits, small-denomination time deposits. lances in individual money market mutual funds, and money market deposit accounts.

1. An *overnight repurchase agreement (RP)* is an agreement between a bank and a customer under which the customer buys U.S. government securities from the bank one day and sells them back to the bank the next day at a price that includes the interest earned overnight. Overnight RPs are used by firms that have excess cash one day that may be needed the next.
2. *Overnight Eurodollar deposits* are deposits of U.S. residents denominated in dollars but held outside the U.S. domestic bank market. They mature the day after they are deposited.
3. *Savings deposits* are accounts at banks and thrifts that earn interest but offer no check-writing privileges.
4. *Small-denomination time deposits* often are called *certificates of deposit*, or *CDs*. Funds in these accounts must be deposited for a specified period of time. ("Small" means less than $100,000.)
5. *Individual money market mutual fund balances* combine the deposits of many individuals and invest them in U.S. Treasury bills and other short-term securities. Many money market mutual funds grant check-writing privileges but limit the size and number of checks.

6. *Money market deposit accounts* are accounts that provide services similar to money market mutual funds, but are offered by commercial banks and savings and loan institutions. They require a minimum balance and place limits on the number of withdrawals allowed per month.

The M3 *Monetary Aggregate*

The *M3* **monetary aggregate** equals the *M2* money supply plus large time deposits ($100,000 or larger), term RPs, term Eurodollar deposits, and institution-only money market mutual fund balances.

Why So Many Definitions?

Why are there so many definitions of money? The definitions are attempts to measure different uses of money. The narrow definition, *M1*, is intended to include the assets used primarily for transactions. The broader definitions seek to include assets used for precautionary or speculative purposes—money used for purposes other than transactions. The central bank needs these distinctions to help it carry out monetary policy. If the central bank wants to affect aggregate demand by manipulating the money supply, it wants to know which assets are used as money in making transactions. Controlling the quantity of assets not used to make transactions has little effect at best on aggregate demand.

Do the *M1*, *M2*, and *M3* definitions measure what they are intended to measure? In 1986 the Federal Reserve carried out a survey to determine how U.S. families pay for their goods and services. It found that 39 percent of all transactions were paid for with the family's main checking account; 34 percent were cash transactions; and in general that fully 82 percent of family transactions were made using those assets included in the *M1* definition of money. Clearly, *M1* measures the transactions use of money. By controlling *M1*, the Federal Reserve controls a major portion of the source of transactions carried out by U.S. families.

International Reserves

One nation's money supply can spill over and affect the supply of money in another nation. In most cases, this occurs through official reserve settlements.

International Reserve Currencies. Governments hold other nations' currencies until they are needed to settle international debts. Before World War II, gold was the primary *international reserve asset,* an asset used to settle debts between governments. After World War II, a few national currencies increasingly replaced gold as the international reserve assets. The currencies held for this purpose are called *international reserve currencies.* In some cases one nation's currency dominates another nation's currency and, in essence, becomes the currency of the second nation as well. This has occurred in some Latin American nations vis-à-vis the U.S. dollar.

Composite Currencies. In addition to national currencies, some composite currencies are used to settle international debts. There are two main composite currencies, the ECU and the SDR. Composite currencies are accounting or book-keeping entries more than real currencies. For instance, in March 1979 the industrial nations of Western Europe introduced the European currency unit (ECU) because they were trying to integrate their economies more closely. These nations use ECUs to settle debts between them. The value of the ECU is an average of the values of the different national currencies.

The SDR, or special drawing right, was created by the International Monetary Fund (IMF) in 1944 to more closely integrate all member country economies and provide a way to influence the behavior of individual economies. The IMF is an international organization that oversees the monetary relationships among countries. SDRs, like ECUs, are an international reserve asset; they are used to settle international debts by transferring governments' accounts held at the IMF.

In the mid-1970s, the U.S. dollar comprised almost 80 percent of international reserve holdings. By 1986, its share had fallen to less than 57 percent. The deutsche mark, yen, and ECU have picked up the slack, as shown in Table 11-1.

International reserves can become part of the money supply of a single nation. For instance, when a nation receives an amount of international reserves in payment for debt (to balance its BOP), those reserves are usually deposited in a commercial bank and become part of the country's money supply.

▼

Fractional Reserve Banking

Now that we know what money is, let's consider how much money exists in a nation and how that quantity comes into being. We'll begin with a very simple closed economy in which there is a central bank, called the Fed; a system of commercial banks; a government; and the general public. The government issues bonds to the Fed in exchange for paper money that the government may then spend—thus placing the money in the hands of the public. The commercial banking system provides a place to deposit funds. Initially, let's assume that a commercial bank may issue deposits, dollar for dollar, only in exchange for paper money and that all deposits must be transferred to the Fed or retained as vault cash. Suppose the government has run a deficit of $1,000, so that $1,000 of money has been issued to the public. The money supply, therefore, is $1,000. If the public deposits $600 in commercial banks, the banks must place the $600 in their vaults or in a Fed deposit. The money supply thus consists of $1,000, of which $400 is currency in circulation and $600 is deposits.

TABLE 11-1   *International Reserve Currencies*
(Percentage Shares of National Currencies in Total Official Holdings of Foreign Exchange)

Year	U.S. Dollar	Pound Sterling	Deutsche Mark	French Franc	Japanese Yen	Swiss Franc	Netherlands Guilder	ECUs	Unspecified Currencies
1976	78.8	1.0	8.7	1.5	1.9	2.1	0.8	0.0	5.2
1978	76.1	1.5	10.8	1.2	2.8	1.7	0.8	0.0	5.1
1980	56.6	2.5	12.8	1.5	3.7	2.8	1.1	16.4	2.7
1982	59.7	2.2	11.1	1.1	4.2	2.5	1.0	13.7	4.5
1984	60.5	2.7	11.3	1.0	5.2	1.9	0.7	11.4	5.3
1986	56.5	2.5	13.6	1.1	7.0	1.8	1.0	12.3	4.1

Source: International Monetary Fund, *International Financial Statistics, Supplement on International Liquidity* (Washington, DC: International Monetary Fund, 1987), p. 172.

Now suppose banks are allowed to make loans based on their deposits and keep only a portion of all deposits on reserve at the Fed or in their vaults. This is called a **fractional reserve banking system**. If the Fed sets the fraction—the **reserve requirement**—at 20 percent, banks can loan out 80 percent of deposits. The $600 of deposits now consists of $120 in required reserves and $480 in free or **excess reserves**, which can be loaned out.

If the banks lend all they are allowed to lend, they will create loans worth $480. That $480 is spent by the people taking out the loans and may be redeposited by those receiving the $480 of expenditures. If the whole $480 is redeposited, the banks have an additional $480 in deposits, of which 20 percent must be deposited at the Fed or in their vaults and 80 percent can be loaned out. The money supply at this stage consists of $400 in currency in circulation, $600 in deposits (the initial amount deposited and still on the books) and another $480 in deposits for a total of $1,480. Of the new deposits of $480, 80 percent can be loaned out. If this money is loaned out, spent, and then redeposited, the money supply increases once again. This process of deposits, loans, expenditures, and deposits continues indefinitely, with a smaller amount loaned and redeposited each time and the money supply expanding with each new round.

Under a fractional reserve banking system, the money supply process looks like a spiral with a very wide top and a small base; from a base of $400 in currency in circulation and the initial $600 on deposit at the Fed or in bank vaults, the money supply increased with each round of deposits. The sum of currency in circulation and reserves (vault cash plus deposits at the Fed) is called the **monetary base** or **high-powered money**. In our example, the monetary base was $1,000. Once the loan-to-deposit process is completed, the money supply (*M1*) is many times larger than the monetary base. In other words, the ultimate money supply that can be created from a given base is a multiple of that base. The value of that multiple is known as the **money multiplier**. For instance, if the money supply is *M1*, high-powered money *H*, and the money multiplier *m*, then $M1 = mH$. In the example just discussed, $H = \$1,000$ and $m = 5$, so $M1 = \$5,000$.

High-Powered Money and the International Sector

In a closed economy, the monetary base, H, is determined by the actions of the central bank. In an open economy, the base is determined by the central bank and by the balance of payments. To clarify, let's look at a central bank's balance sheet. A simplified balance sheet of a hypothetical central bank is shown in Table 11-2.

On the liabilities side of the balance sheet is the definition of high-powered money we used above: currency in the hands of the non bank public, C, plus depository institution reserves, R (vault cash plus deposits at the central bank). On the asset side is the composition of that currency and deposits; international reserves, F, and domestic securities holdings, DS. As the asset side rises, so does the liability side. For instance, if the government sells a bond to the central bank, the bank receives domestic securities as an asset and issues a deposit to the government. Similarly, if a commercial bank receives foreign exchange and deposits it in the central bank, both the assets and the liabilities of the central bank rise. International reserves increase and depository institution reserve deposits increase. In both cases, the monetary base rises.

Now, H is equal to the sum of international reserves (foreign exchange and gold), F, and domestic securities held by the central bank, DS. And H is also equal to currency in circulation, C, plus reserves, R.

$$H = F + DS$$
$$H = C + R$$

Changes in high-powered money can occur from changes in either the foreign component, F, or the domestic component, DS. We can represent that in a simple equation:

$$\Delta H = \Delta F + \Delta DS$$

where ΔH represents the change in the monetary base, ΔF the change in foreign exchange or gold, and ΔDS the change in the Fed's holdings of domestic securities. When ΔH rises due to an increase in ΔF or ΔDS, then currency in circulation plus reserves must rise, $\Delta H = \Delta C + \Delta R$.

TABLE 11-2 *Central Bank's Simplified Balance Sheet*

Assets (in billions)		Liabilities (in billions)	
International Reserves	$200	Currency	$350
		Cash in vaults	30
		Currency in the hands of the non bank public	320
Domestic Securities	240	Depository institution deposits at the central bank	90
Monetary Base	$440	Monetary Base	$440

The central bank has control of its domestic security holdings, ΔDS; it can issue more or less credit as it pleases. The central bank does not have the same element of control over the foreign component, ΔF. The foreign component of high-powered money depends on the transactions between the domestic nation and other nations; that is, on the economy's balance of payments. The balance of payments position and the resulting flow of international reserves depend on relative income levels in the nations, on relative interest rate levels, on relative price levels, and on individual tastes and preferences of the citizens of the nations. The central bank has little influence on these factors.

Fractional Reserve Banking and the Money Multiplier

Now consider the money multiplier, m. Let's define the money supply as $M1$ so that it equals currency in circulation plus checking deposits or, in symbols, $M1 = C + D$. The monetary base or high-powered money stock is currency in circulation plus reserves (vault cash and Fed deposits) or, in symbols, $H = C + R$. The $M1$ money multiplier (m) is then defined as the ratio of the $M1$ money supply to the stock of high-powered money, because $M1 = mH$ or $m = M1/H$. Because $M1 = C + D$ and $H = C + R$, then $M1/H = (C + D)/(C + R)$. Dividing both denominator and numerator by D, we have the $M1$ money multiplier defined as

$$m = \frac{(C/D + 1)}{(C/D + R/S)}$$

This formulation of the money multiplier shows that it too is not perfectly controllable by the central bank. The *currency-to-deposit ratio,* or C/D, depends on what the public chooses to do. The *reserve-to-deposit ratio,* or R/D, depends both on what regulations the Fed imposes for required reserves and on the amount of excess reserves that depository institutions decide to hold. In addition, the ratios depend on public demand for loans.

*The Reserve-to-Deposit Ratio (*R/D*).* Reserves can be either required or excess. Because the Fed specifies required reserves but not excess reserves, the reserve-to-deposit ratio is determined by both the Fed and private depository institutions. The excess R/D ratio of excess reserves to deposits depends on the desires of financial institutions. Institutions lose potential revenue by holding excess reserves (because they earn no interest) but avoid the potential costs of having insufficient reserves.

*The Currency-to-Deposit Ratio (*C/D*).* The U.S. currency-to-deposit ratio has increased since 1970. Currency in circulation has risen at more than an 8 percent rate while checkable deposits included in $M1$ have grown just over 6 percent per year. Part of the reason these checkable deposits have not kept pace with currency growth is that people have switched from using $M1$ deposits to other types of accounts, such as money market deposit accounts, that have the advantages of a checking account but also earn a higher rate of interest. In addition, people have increased their use of credit cards. Some economists suspect that the increased *C/D* ratio also reflects the growth of crime and of the underground economy. Criminals and individuals seeking to avoid income taxation have an incentive to use only cash to avoid records of illegal or taxable transactions. All these developments have led to an increase in the *C/D* ratio.

The Fed usually attempts to control *M1* by controlling *H*. If *m* is stable or its value known, then the link between *H* and *M1* is clear. If *m* is not constant or not known, then the link between *H* and *M1* is less clear. To understand how the value of *m* is determined, we must understand the banking system and the role it plays in the money supply process.

▼

U.S. Depository Institutions

Depository institutions are intermediaries between savers and borrowers. They accept deposits from individuals and firms and use those deposits to make loans. Depositors typically prefer short-term deposits; they don't want to tie their money up for a long time. Borrowers usually want a long repayment period. So depository institutions earn their revenue by packaging short-term deposits into longer-term loans and charging more for the loans than they pay on the deposits.

Depository institutions include *commercial banks* and *thrift institutions*. Before the 1980s, there was a clear distinction between commercial banks and thrifts. Today, commercial banks and thrift institutions are little different; they offer most of the same services and compete against each other.

Bank Failures and the FDIC

In the mid-1980s, low oil prices resulted in an enormous number of loan defaults in states that have large oil industries, such as Texas, Oklahoma, and Colorado. At the same time, the agricultural states of Kansas, Nebraska, Iowa, and others were hurt by falling land prices and declining agricultural prices, and their banks could not collect many outstanding loans. Table 11-3 shows how many banks failed in the United States between 1985 and 1988. You can see that the states heavily dependent on the oil industry and farming had significantly more bank failures than did other states.

What does a bank failure mean for the economy? At one time, a failure by one bank could lead to a banking system collapse because the public, fearing that it would lose its deposits in other banks if they too failed, withdrew funds from these other banks. Massive withdrawals caused banks without sufficient reserves to close. Each closure meant a small reduction in the money supply. If extensive enough, the closures could reduce the money supply enough

TABLE 11-3   *Failed U.S. Banks by State, 1985–1988*

State	Number of Failed Banks	State	Number of Failed Banks
Alabama	4	Mississippi	1
Alaska	4	Missouri	24
Arizona	1	Montana	5
Arkansas	1	Nebraska	26
California	26	New Mexico	5
Colorado	36	New York	4
Delaware	1	North Dakota	3
Florida	11	Ohio	2
Idaho	1	Oklahoma	83
Illinois	6	Oregon	4
Indiana	6	Pennsylvania	1
Iowa	33	South Dakota	4
Kansas	41	Tennessee	7
Kentucky	3	Texas	201
Louisiana	33	Utah	9
Massachusetts	2	Wisconsin	2
Michigan	1	Wyoming	17
Minnesota	28		

Source: Federal Deposit Insurance Corporation, *Annual Report, 1988* (Washington, DC: Federal Deposit Insurance Corporation, 1989).

to pull the economy into a recession. In 1933, the *Federal Deposit Insurance Corporation (FDIC)* was created to eradicate these domino effects. The FDIC insures deposits in commercial banks so that depositors do not fear the loss of funds when a bank fails. The FDIC system worked well from 1933 to 1991. But, as bank failures increased during 1990 and 1991, the FDIC system looked increasingly more perilous; it did not have enough funds to pay off all funds it insured. The perilous position of the FDIC elicited several proposals for major overhauls of the system. The system that emerges from the 1991 and 1992 Congresses is likely to be very different from the system that existed between 1933 and 1991.

International Banking

Large banks today are multinational enterprises, operating in many different countries. The international deposit and loan market often is called the **Eurocurrency market** or **offshore banking**. Today the term *offshore banking* is somewhat misleading in the United States. At one time, U.S. banks had to process international deposits and loans through offshore branches. Many branches in such places as the Cayman Islands, Virgin Islands, and the Bahamas were little more than "shells," small offices with a telephone. Yet having these branches allowed U.S. banks to avoid the reserve requirements and interest rate regulations imposed on domestic banking.

In December 1981, the Federal Reserve Board legalized **international banking facilities (IBFs)**, allowing domestic banks to do international banking on U.S. soil. IBFs are not physical entities; they are bookkeeping systems set up in existing bank offices to record international banking transactions. IBFs can receive deposits from and make loans to nonresidents of the United States or other IBFs.

Countries that allow offshore banking have two sets of banking rules: restrictive regulations for banking in the domestic market, and little or no regulation of offshore banking activities. Domestic banks must hold reserves against deposits and carry deposit insurance; and they often face government-mandated credit or interest rate restrictions. The Eurocurrency market operates with few restrictions, and international banks generally pay lower taxes than do domestic banks. Because offshore banks operate with lower costs, they can offer better terms to their customers than can domestic banks. They are also considered more risky for depositors, because they are not insured by the FDIC.

International banking today is dominated by Japanese and U.S. banks, which control almost 50 percent of total international banking assets. The Eurocurrency market exists for all the major international currencies, but the value of activity in Eurodollars accounts for about two-thirds of deposit and loan activity in the Eurocurrency market; the U.S. dollar plays a major role in global finance. Even deposits and loans that do not involve a U.S. lender or borrower often are denominated in U.S. dollars.

▼
The Federal Reserve System

The Federal Reserve System (the Fed) is the central bank of the United States. A central bank performs several functions: accepting deposits from and making loans to depository institutions, acting as a banker for the federal government, and controlling the money supply.

Structure of the Fed

Congress created the Federal Reserve System in 1913. The Federal Reserve System divides the nation into twelve districts, each with its own Federal Reserve Bank.

Board of Governors. Monetary policy is largely set by the Fed's Board of Governors in Washington, DC. The Board consists of seven members, who are appointed by the president of the United States and confirmed by the U.S. Senate. The most visible and powerful member of the Board is the chair. This individual serves as a leader and spokesperson for the Board. The chair is appointed by the president to a four-year term, although in recent years most chairs have been reappointed (see Table 11-4). The other governors serve fourteen-year terms staggered so that every two years a new position comes up for appointment. This system allows policymaking continuity and is intended to provide a sense of independence to the Board. Monetary policy is supposed to be formulated independently of Congress and the president.

District Banks. Each of the Fed's twelve district banks is formally directed by a nine-person board of directors. The primary function of the directors is to choose the president of the district bank, who is in charge of operations and participates in monetary policymaking with the Board of Governors.

Routine operations of the district banks include clearing checks among the depository institutions, issuing new currency (U.S. paper money consists of Federal Reserve Notes), collecting data on local business conditions, and researching topics related to the conduct of monetary policy. In addition, the district banks actively participate in monetary policy in three ways: (1) they recommend discount rates for their districts—the rates must be approved by the Board of Governors, (2) they decide which depository institutions can borrow reserves from the Fed, and (3) five district bank presidents serve on the Federal Open Market Committee.

The Federal Open Market Committee (FOMC). The **Federal Open Market Committee (FOMC)** is the policymaking body of the Federal Reserve System. The committee is made up of the seven members of the Board of Governors, plus five of the twelve district bank presidents. The New York bank president is always on the FOMC because the New York Fed actually executes monetary policy. The remaining district bank presidents take turns serving on the FOMC. When economists refer to the "Fed," they are in fact referring to the FOMC, because that committee implements monetary policy.

Functions of the Fed

The Fed provides several banking services to the banking community: it supplies currency to banks, holds their reserves, and clears checks. The Fed also supervises the nation's banks, ensuring that they operate soundly and prudently;

TABLE 11-4   *Recent Chairs of the Federal Reserve Board*

Name	Age at Appointment	Term Begins	Term Ends	Years of Tenure
William McChesney Martin	44	4/2/51	1/31/70	18.8
Arthur Burns	65	1/31/70	2/1/78	8.0
G. William Miller	52	3/8/78	8/6/79	1.4
Paul Volcker	51	8/6/79	8/5/87	8.0
Alan Greenspan	61	8/11/87		[a]

[a]In July 1991, President Bush reappointed Alan Greenspan to another four-year term.

it acts as the banker for the U.S. government, selling U.S. securities when the Treasury wants to borrow money to finance government spending.

The most important function of the Federal Reserve is controlling the nation's money supply. Before the Fed was created, the money supply did not change to meet fluctuations in demand. Even during the Christmas season, when a great deal more money is needed, the supply of money did not vary. As a result, the interest rate rose during the Christmas season and declined after, causing fluctuations in economic activity. That has changed with the creation of the Fed. Now seasonal fluctuations and other longer-term fluctuations are watched carefully by the Fed, and actions are taken to adjust the money supply accordingly.

▼
Implementing Monetary Policy

Monetary and fiscal policy are the primary approaches governments take to influence their economies. The two are alike in that the ultimate objective is to provide economic growth with stable prices. As discussed in the next chapter, with fiscal policy the policymakers seek to directly control spending and aggregate demand. With monetary policy, policymakers must work indirectly, changing the money supply without knowing whether the changes in the money supply will translate into spending and *AD* changes.

Intermediate Targets

The Fed does not control gross national product or the price level directly. Instead, it controls the monetary base and the money supply, which in turn affect GNP and the price level. The money supply or the growth of the money supply is an **intermediate target**. Using the growth of the money supply as an intermediate target assumes a fairly stable relationship between changes in money and changes in income and prices. The *equation of exchange* and the *quantity theory of money* are the foundations for this assumption.

Equation of Exchange. As discussed in earlier chapters, the equation of exchange relates the quantity of money to nominal GNP:

$$MV = PY$$

where M = the quantity of money

V = the velocity of money; the average number of times each dollar is spent on final goods and services during a year

P = the price level

Y = real GNP

According to the equation of exchange, nominal GNP can be defined as the average price level multiplied by the total amount of goods produced (or sold), or as the quantity of money multiplied by the number of times that money must change hands in order to purchase the goods produced during the year. Velocity is PY/M; if the price level is 2 and real GNP is $500 billion, then PY is $1,000 billion. With a money supply of $200 billion, then $V = \$1,000/\$200 = 5$. Thus each dollar must be spent an average of five times during the year.

Quantity Theory. The equation of exchange is a definition of nominal GNP that can be used to describe the relationship between money supply changes and changes in nominal GNP. When used in this manner, it is called the *quantity theory of money*. The quantity theory of money says that if the money supply (M^s) increases and velocity (V) is constant, then nominal GNP (PY) must increase. If the economy is operating at the potential level of output, then only P rises. If the economy is operating somewhere below the potential output level and substantial unemployment exists, then an increase in M^s may cause Y to rise or cause both P and Y to rise.

$$M^s\uparrow \; \rightarrow \; PY/V\uparrow \; \rightarrow \; P\uparrow \text{ or } Y\uparrow, \text{ or } P\uparrow \text{ and } Y\uparrow$$

Thus, by altering M^s the Fed can change PY/V. And if V is predictable the Fed can use M^s to control PY. The Fed's goal is to set money growth targets that are consistent with rising output and low inflation. This goal is the basis of monetary policy.

Defining Target Rates. The FOMC defines upper and lower bounds for its intermediate targets. For instance, Figure 11-1 shows the target range and actual growth of the $M2$ money supply in 1989 and 1990. The target range in both years was between 3 and 7 percent. Beginning in December 1988, the FOMC set its goal as a growth rate of between 3 percent, the lower colored line, and 7 percent, the upper colored line. These growth rates define a money supply range that widens over the year depending on the growth rates of the range. As a graph, the target range looks like a cone whose width depends on the range of growth rates between upper and lower limits. Beginning from the December 1988 $M2$ money supply of about $3.07 billion, a 3 percent increase would have yielded a December 1989 money supply of about $3.16 billion; while a 7 percent increase would have generated a money supply of about $3.3 billion in December 1989. $M2$ actually fell below the lower range of the target for part of the year—as indicated by the black line in Figure 11-1. Overall, it grew 4.6 percent. In December 1989, the money growth rates were set for 1990; the actual $M2$ growth for the year was again low, 3.7 percent.

The targeting is not an exact science. As discussed previously, the money multiplier varies, depending on the behavior of the public and commercial depository institutions. Once a quantity of money has been determined, the

FIGURE 11-1   *The money supply target. The target range and actual growth of the M2 money supply in 1989 and 1990 are shown. The target range was between 3 and 7 percent in both years. These growth rates define a money supply range that widens over the year, depending on the growth rates of the range. As a graph, the target range looks like a cone whose width depends on the range of growth rates between upper and lower limits. The actual growth of M2 is illustrated by the black line.*

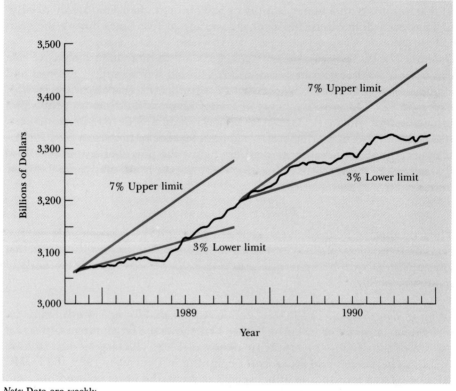

Note: Data are weekly.
Source: Board of Governors of the Federal Reserve System, *Economic Report of the President 1991* (Washington, DC: U.S. Government Printing Office, 1991), p. 42.

effect on nominal GNP is not certain. The link between changes in money supply and changes in nominal GNP depends on *V*, because $M^s = PY/V$.

$$\Delta H \rightarrow \Delta M^s \rightarrow \Delta GNP$$
$$\text{\textbackslash varies as } V \text{ changes}$$
$$\text{\textbackslash varies as } m \text{ changes}$$

From the late 1950s to the mid-1970s, the velocity of *M1* grew at a steady pace, from 3.5 in 1959 to 5.6 in 1975. Knowing that *V* was growing at a steady rate, the Fed set a target growth rate for the *M1* money supply, confident that it would produce a fairly predictable growth in nominal GNP. But when velocity is not predictable problems can arise with using money growth rates as an intermediate target. This is exactly what happened in the late 1970s and early 1980s. You can see from Figure 11-2 that the velocity of *M1* fluctuated wildly, while velocities of *M2* and *M3* were quite steady. As the relationship broke down between the *M1* money supply and GNP, the Fed shifted its emphasis from the *M1* money supply to *M2* and *M3*.

Economists are still debating why the *M1* velocity changed. Some argue that new types of deposits and other innovations in banking led to fluctuations in the money held in traditional demand deposits. These changes would affect the *M1* supply, because its definition is narrow. They would not affect *M2* and *M3*, because of their more inclusive definitions.

The uncertainty of relying solely on money growth as its intermediate target has led the Fed to watch over or monitor other key variables. These include prices, interest rates, and foreign exchange rates. Only the money data are targeted, but these other economic variables are watched closely.

FIGURE 11-2   *Velocities of* M1, M2, *and* M3, *1959–1991. The velocity of* M1 *fluctuated wildly while velocities of* M2 *and* M3 *were quite steady. With the breakdown of the relationship between the* M1 *money supply and GNP, the Fed shifted its emphasis from the* M1 *money supply to* M2 *and* M3.

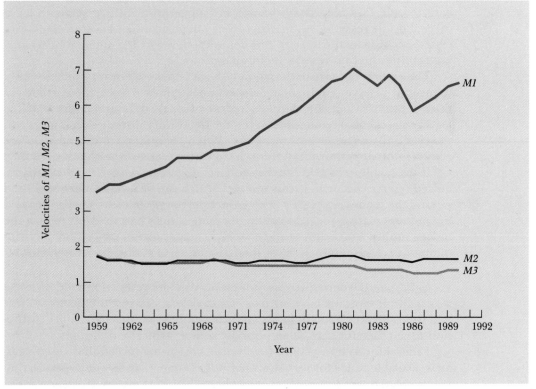

Procedures of Policy

The FOMC sets monetary targets and then implements them through the Federal Reserve Bank of New York. The mechanism for translating policy into action is the **FOMC directive**. Each directive outlines the conduct of monetary policy over the six- to eight-week period until the FOMC meets again to adjust monetary targets.

Tools of Policy. The FOMC controls the money supply by changing depository institution excess reserves. The Fed can use three tools to change reserves: the reserve requirement, the discount rate, and open-market operations.

Reserve Requirements. The Fed requires depository institutions to hold a fraction of their deposits on reserve. This fraction is the reserve requirement. The requirements are different for different types and sizes of deposits. For instance, large banks hold a greater percentage of deposits in reserve than do small banks (for 1991, the reserve requirement increased from 3 to 12 percent for transaction deposits in excess of $41.1 million). The level of transaction deposits against which the 3 percent reserve requirement applies is adjusted accordingly. There are no reserve requirements for long-term deposits because it is unlikely that banks would face surprising changes in long-term deposits that would leave them short of reserves. And Eurocurrency deposits often have smaller or no reserve requirements—in 1991 time deposits offered by U.S. international banking facilities had no reserve requirement.

   The *required reserves* are the amount that a depository institution must hold to meet its reserve requirement. The sum of vault cash (coin and currency in the institution's vault) and deposits in the Fed is called its **legal reserves**. When legal reserves equal required reserves, the depository institution has no excess reserves and can make no new loans. When legal reserves exceed required reserves, the depository institution has excess reserves available for lending.

   If the Fed lowers the reserve requirement, part of what was previously required reserves becomes excess reserves, which can be used to make loans and expand the money supply. By raising the reserve requirement, the Fed reduces the money-creating potential of the banking system and tends to reduce the money supply. And by lowering the reserve requirement, the Fed can increase the money-creating potential of the banking system and the money supply.

Discount Rate. If a depository institution needs more reserves in order to make new loans, it typically borrows from other depository institutions in the federal funds market. **Federal funds** are loans made from one depository institution to another for very short periods of time, typically overnight.

   Federal funds transactions involve the borrowing (or lending) of immediately available funds for very short periods of time. Usually one depository institution borrows the excess reserves of another, thus effectively reducing the

R/D ratio and increasing the money multiplier. However, short-term transactions often take the form of *repurchase agreements*. For example, a corporation that has $25 million in its checking account may purchase a U.S. Treasury bill from a commercial bank, which agrees to buy it back a day or two later. This transaction provides funds for the bank while allowing the corporation to earn interest. The interest rate paid for such loans is known as the **federal funds rate**.

At times depository institutions borrow directly from the Fed, although the Fed restricts access to such funds. The **discount rate** is the rate of interest the Fed charges depository institutions. (In other countries, the rate of interest the central bank charges commercial banks often is called the *bank rate*.) Another way the Fed controls the level of reserves and the money supply is by changing the discount rate. When the Fed raises the discount rate, it raises the cost of borrowing reserves and thus might reduce the amount of reserves borrowed. Lower levels of reserves limit bank lending and the expansion of the money supply. When the Fed lowers the discount rate, it lowers the cost of borrowing reserves, possibly increasing the amount of borrowing from the Fed. As reserves increase, so do loans and the money supply.

Discount rate policy can be used to signal the Fed's intentions concerning monetary policy. For example, if the Fed decides to counteract a recession by letting interest rates fall, it can "announce" this decision to the public by lowering the discount rate.

Unfortunately, this announcement effect is subject to misinterpretation. If market interest rates rise relative to the discount rate, the depository institutions tend to borrow reserves from the Fed at the discount rate in order to make loans at the higher market rate of interest. The volume of borrowed reserves tends to rise. In order to keep the amount of borrowed reserves from getting excessive, the Fed may raise the discount rate so it is more in line with market interest rates. The public may interpret this increase in the discount rate as a signal that the Fed is moving to a contractionary monetary policy — which may not be the case.

The discount rate is not often used as a policy tool. Although other interest rates can fluctuate daily, the discount rate usually remains fixed for months at a time. Table 11-5 shows the discount rate over recent years. At most the rate has changed seven times in a year.

Open-Market Operations. The primary tool the FOMC has for carrying out monetary policy is **open-market operations**, the buying and selling of previously issued U.S. government bonds. The FOMC sells bonds in order to decrease the money supply and buys bonds to increase the money supply. If the FOMC wants to increase the money supply, the committee directs the bond-trading desk at the Federal Reserve Bank of New York to buy bonds. The bonds are purchased from private bond dealers. The dealers are paid with checks drawn on the Federal Reserve, which then are deposited in the dealers' accounts at commercial banks. As bank deposits and reserves increase, banks can make new loans, mak-

TABLE 11·5   *Federal Reserve Discount Rates, January 1978–April 1991*

Date	Discount Rate (percent)	Date	Discount Rate (percent)
Jan 9, 1978	6.50	Jul 20, 1982	11.50
May 11, 1978	7.00	Aug 2, 1982	11.50
Jul 3, 1978	7.25	Aug 16, 1982	10.50
Aug 21, 1978	7.75	Aug 27, 1982	10.00
Sep 22, 1978	8.00	Oct 12, 1982	9.50
Oct 16, 1978	8.50	Nov 22, 1982	9.00
Nov 1, 1978	9.50	Dec 15, 1982	8.50
Jul 20, 1979	10.00	Apr 9, 1984	9.00
Aug 17, 1979	10.50	Nov 21, 1984	8.50
Sep 19, 1979	11.00	Dec 24, 1984	8.00
Oct 8, 1979	12.00	May 20, 1985	7.50
Feb 15, 1980	13.00	Mar 7, 1986	7.00
May 30, 1980	12.00	Apr 21, 1986	6.50
Jun 13, 1980	11.00	Jul 11, 1986	6.00
Jul 28, 1980	10.00	Aug 21, 1986	5.50
Sep 26, 1980	11.00	Sep 4, 1987	6.00
Nov 17, 1980	12.00	Aug 9, 1988	6.50
Dec 5, 1980	13.00	Feb 24, 1989	7.00
May 5, 1981	14.00	Jan 4, 1991	6.50
Nov 2, 1981	13.00	Feb 1, 1991	6.00
Dec 4, 1981	12.00	Apr 30, 1991	5.50

Source: Federal Reserve Bulletin (Washington, DC, January 1991), p. 6; and Federal Reserve announcements.

ing new loans expands the money supply through the money multiplier process. If the Fed wants to decrease the money supply, it sells bonds. Private bond dealers pay for the bonds with checks drawn on commercial banks. Commercial bank deposits and reserves drop, and the money supply decreases.

From FOMC Directives to GNP

When it sets monetary policy, the FOMC begins with its ultimate goal: economic growth at stable prices. It defines that goal in terms of nominal GNP. Then it works backward to identify its intermediate target, the rate at which the money supply must grow to achieve the wanted growth in nominal GNP. The FOMC must decide how to achieve its intermediate target; should it buy or sell bonds? The answer depends on whether the money supply is growing faster or slower than desired. The committee relies on a **short-run operating target** for this information. These operating targets should be easy for the Fed to control and have a consistent, predictable relationship to the money supply. The quantity of excess reserves in the banking system, the quantity of reserves that are not borrowed (nonborrowed reserves), and the federal funds rate can serve as short-run operating targets.

Desired nominal GNP → desired M^s → policy change → short-run operating target
(intermediate
target)

Targeting the Federal Funds Rate. The FOMC carries out its policies through directives to the bond-trading desk at the Federal Reserve Bank of New York. The directives specify a short-run operating target that the trading desk must use in its day-to-day operations. When the FOMC first began setting intermediate monetary targets in 1970, it tried to prescribe very specific target ranges for the federal funds rate. The committee chose the federal funds rate as the short-run target because it believed the rate was the best indicator of the status of reserves. The Fed believed that if the federal funds rate rose above the FOMC's target, the rise would indicate that there were not enough reserves in the banking system, that the money supply was not growing fast enough. If the federal funds rate fell, the Fed believed there were too many reserves in the banking system, that the money supply was growing too fast.

But the federal funds rate did not work well as a short-run target. When people were spending rapidly and so borrowing increasing amounts of money, the banking system's reserves fell and the federal funds rate rose. The rising rate signaled the trading desk to buy bonds and increase reserves. These reserves were lent, and the money supply grew more quickly. As long as the federal funds rate continued to rise, new reserves were being pumped into the banking system and the money supply grew faster and faster. Conversely, when people were not spending and excess reserves accumulated, the trading desk sold bonds, the money supply fell and continued to fall as long as the federal funds rate was below the target range. Thus, targeting the federal funds rate led to changes in the money supply that were *procyclical*—that augmented the fluctuations in spending.

Targeting Nonborrowed Reserves. By fall 1979, it had become very clear that the reliance on the federal funds rate was a mistake; the FOMC decided it needed a better indicator of money supply growth for its short-run operating target. The committee chose depository institution reserves, specifically **nonborrowed reserves**. With nonborrowed reserves, the Fed has an indicator of how tightly loaned up the banking system is. The greater the quantity of nonborrowed reserves, the greater the liquidity banks have and the less need to increase the money supply. If nonborrowed reserves are growing, then the FOMC concludes that the money supply is growing more rapidly than needed—banks have more than enough reserves.

▼
Foreign Exchange Market Intervention

Until the late 1970s, the FOMC virtually ignored conditions in the foreign exchange markets. But by the late 1970s it had become clear that the foreign exchange market could have large effects on monetary policy and the economy. In addition, having turned to a flexible exchange rate system for major currencies in 1973, countries were worrying about fluctuations in exchange rates and changes in the value of the dollar. As a result, the Federal Reserve not only monitored conditions in the foreign exchange market, but took an active role in trying to move the exchange rate up or down. To understand why the Fed is concerned with the exchange rate, we need to consider the differences in monetary policy under the fixed and under the flexible exchange rate systems. Let's turn to that issue now.

Exchange Rate Systems and Monetary Policy

Under fixed exchange rates, the central bank is committed to buying or selling foreign currencies on demand, to prevent the exchange rate from moving. So the central bank's holdings of international reserves are influenced by the international transactions of domestic and foreign residents. Therefore, unless direct restrictions are imposed on the foreign trade and finance activities of domestic residents, the central bank can control only the domestic component of the monetary base, central bank holdings of domestic securities, not the overall monetary base.

With a flexible exchange rate system, the exchange rate changes, not the quantity of foreign exchange. This means the Fed can control both domestic and foreign components of the monetary base. A country does not experience an inflow or outflow of foreign exchange whenever domestic residents buy amounts of goods, services, and financial assets from abroad that do not match the amounts foreigners buy from domestic residents, as occurs under a fixed exchange rate system.

IS, LM, *and* BOP. Some useful insights into the interaction of economies under the different exchange rate systems can be achieved with the *IS–LM* model. Figure 11-3 adds the *BOP* curve to two *IS–LM* diagrams. The *BOP* curve typically slopes upward, illustrating the idea that rises in domestic income increase imports, while rises in domestic interest rates increase capital inflows. The two flows must offset one another for the balance of payments to be in equilibrium.

Let's use the *IS–LM–BOP* diagram to discuss the effects of monetary policy shocks on the economy under a fixed exchange rate system. If the *IS* and *LM* schedules intersect in panel A at point *a* above the *BOP* curve, the economy experiences a net surplus of the capital plus current accounts and foreign exchange flows in. This increases the monetary base and thus the quantity of

FIGURE 11-3   *Adjustments to a money supply increase under a fixed exchange rate system. In panel A, the IS and LM curves intersect at point a above the BOP curve. So the economy experiences a net surplus of the capital plus current accounts, and foreign exchange flows in. When foreign exchange flows into the country, the quantity of money in the economy rises. So the LM curve shifts to the right. The shift of the LM curve continues until all three curves intersect at point b.*

In panel B, we begin with the economy at point a. The LM curve then shifts out, due to Federal Reserve policies. This creates an intersection between the IS and LM curves at point b, which is below the BOP curve. So foreign exchange flows out of the United States, causing the domestic money supply to decrease. The LM curve shifts back to its original position at point a. Under fixed exchange rates, domestic authorities have no control over monetary policy.

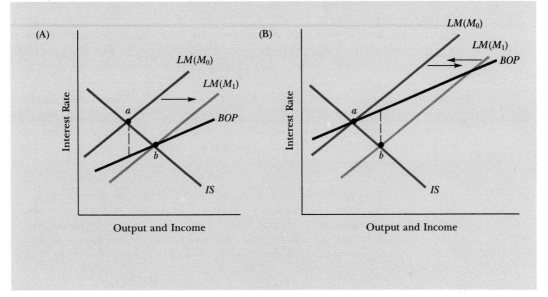

money. So the *LM* curve shifts to the right until all three curves intersect at point *b*.

Suppose domestic policymakers seek to use monetary policy to drive up output and employment. In panel B, we begin with the economy at point *a*. The *LM* curve then shifts out, due to Fed policies. This creates an intersection between the *IS* and *LM* curves at point *b*, which is below the *BOP* curve. So foreign exchange flows out of the United States, reducing the domestic money supply. The *LM* curve shifts back to its original position at point *a*. *Under fixed exchange rates, domestic authorities have no control over monetary policy.*

Flexible Exchange Rates. If the exchange rate system is flexible rather than fixed, monetary policy *can* be controlled by the domestic authorities. Under the flexible exchange rate system, the United States does not experience an inflow or outflow of foreign exchange but instead experiences an appreciation or depreciation of the dollar.

If the economy is at the initial point a in Figure 11-4, then an increase in the domestic money supply shifts the LM curve outward, driving output up and interest rates down. Imports increase in relation to exports, and the value of the dollar falls. The lower exchange rate means that the BOP and the IS curves shift out, as shown in Figure 11-4. The domestic money supply is not affected.

In summary, whereas the LM curve is at the mercy of the balance of payments under fixed exchange rates, the IS and BOP curves shift under the flexible exchange rate system. With flexible rates, the domestic money supply does not automatically change; instead, the exchange rate changes to maintain purchasing power parity.

Under a flexible exchange rate regime, the central bank has no obligation to buy or sell foreign exchange reserves and so has control of the monetary base. Indeed, in the absence of central bank intervention in foreign exchange markets, changes in central bank holdings of domestic securities directly correspond to changes in the monetary base. This autonomy of the domestic money supply from the vagaries of international transactions and the balance of payments is a basic characteristic of a flexible exchange rate regime, differentiating it from a fixed exchange rate system, and is one reason why the fixed exchange rate system was discarded in 1973.

FIGURE 11-4   *Adjustments to a money supply increase under a flexible exchange rate system. If the economy is at the initial point* a, *then an increase in the domestic money supply causes the* LM *curve to shift outward, driving output up and interest rates down. Imports increase in relation to exports, and the value of the dollar falls. The lower exchange rate means that the* BOP *curve shifts out and the* IS *curve shifts out. The domestic money supply is not affected.*

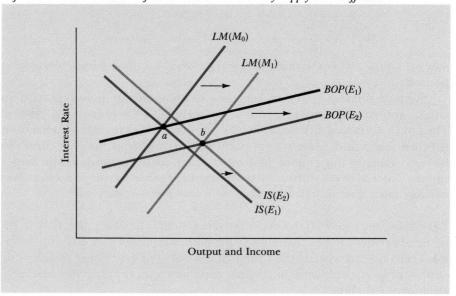

Mechanics of Intervention

Under the flexible exchange rate system, the Fed closely watches the movement of exchange rates and seeks to minimize any shocks to the economy resulting from events in the rest of the world. **Foreign exchange market intervention** is the buying and selling of foreign exchange by a central bank. The central bank's objective is to move exchange rates up or down or to keep exchange rates from moving in response to changing conditions in the foreign exchange market. For instance, suppose that over time U.S. residents have been buying more from Japan than Japanese residents have been purchasing from the United States. This puts pressure on exchange rates to change; specifically, for the dollar to depreciate. Rather than allow exchange rates to change, as they would under a flexible exchange rate system, the Fed may intervene to maintain a fixed exchange rate between the dollar and the yen.

Suppose the Fed sets a target range for the dollar at a minimum exchange rate of ¥150 = $1. If the exchange rate falls below the minimum, the Fed must intervene in the foreign exchange market to increase the value of the dollar. The Fed intervenes in the foreign exchange market by using its holdings of Japanese yen to purchase dollars and to keep the exchange rate at ¥150 = $1. This kind of intervention can be only temporary because the Fed has a limited supply of yen. Under another intervention plan, the Bank of Japan could support the ¥150 = $1 exchange rate by using yen to buy dollars. The Bank of Japan could carry on this kind of policy indefinitely because it can create yen. A third alternative is coordinated intervention, in which both the Fed and the Bank of Japan sell yen in exchange for dollars to support the minimum yen–dollar exchange rate.

An example of coordinated intervention occurred in September 1985. In the face of mounting concern over the size of the U.S. trade deficit, the "Group of 5" or G-5 countries (the United States, France, Japan, the United Kingdom, and West Germany) issued a joint policy statement aimed at reducing the foreign exchange value of the dollar. Even before official sales of the dollar began, the dollar started to depreciate as participants in the foreign exchange market reacted to the announcement. In other words, the free-market supply of dollars increased and the free-market demand for dollars decreased because traders did not want to be holding dollars when the central banks started selling.

Sterilization

Intervention not only influences the exchange rate, but foreign exchange market intervention affects the domestic money supply. The intervention to increase the dollar price of the Japanese yen also increases the central bank's holdings of foreign exchange. So the monetary base rises. To avoid the results (such as higher inflation) of the money supply increase, the Fed must offset the intervention effects on the domestic money supply. The expansionary effect of the intervention can be offset by a domestic open-market operation, in a process called **sterilization**. If the Fed creates dollars to buy yen, it increases the money supply. To reduce the money supply, the Fed can direct an open-market bond sale. The bond sale "sterilizes" the effect of the intervention on the domestic money supply. Thus, the Fed creates dollars and uses them to purchase yen. It then sells bonds to reduce the number of dollars.

Clearly, even under a flexible exchange rate system, the central bank must take into account the effects of its actions in the foreign exchange market on the domestic money supply or of its actions domestically on the foreign exchange market.

▼   ▼   ▼   ▼   ▼   ▼   ▼   ▼   ▼   ▼   ▼
Conclusions

The money supply plays a crucial role in every economy. The money supply may consist of several different assets used for different purposes. The definitions used in the United States for money are *M1*, *M2*, and *M3*. The interaction of the money supplies of different economies also affects money supply. The control of the money supply is not nearly as simple and straightforward as assumed in previous chapters. The process of monetary policy—defining the target, determining a target range, providing directives, and running day-to-day open-market operations—is complicated. In addition, the impact of the rest of the world on money supplies must be considered. That impact varies depending on whether a country operates under a fixed or a flexible exchange rate system. Most nations moved to the flexible rate system in the early 1970s, to get more control over their own money supplies. Under the fixed exchange rate system, the money supply was at the mercy of international conditions.

In the following chapter, we discuss fiscal policy and then put monetary and fiscal policy together to discuss policy in the context of a global economy.

▼   ▼   ▼   ▼   ▼   ▼   ▼   ▼   ▼   ▼   ▼
Summary

1. How is money defined?
In the United States, money is defined as *M1*, *M2*, or *M3*. *M1* is the narrowest definition, *M3* is the most general or inclusive definition.
2. What are international reserves?
International reserves are assets used to settle debts between governments. These reserves include a few national currencies such as the dollar, deutsche mark, and yen, as well as SDRs, ECUs, and gold.
3. How is monetary policy executed?
Monetary policy in the United States is the sole responsibility of the Federal Reserve System. The process of executing monetary policy is a complicated one, be-

ginning with the Fed's goals with respect to nominal GNP and inflation, moving to intermediate targets, and the monetary base. The process includes or takes into account the money multiplier and the velocity of money as well as the role of foreign exchange.

4. What are the objectives of monetary policy?

The objective of monetary policy is to provide for maximum economic growth at stable prices.

5. What are the limitations of monetary policy?

The Fed can control only certain aspects of the money determination process; as a result, it can't know with certainty whether its policies will have the desired effects. Specifically, the Fed can control a portion of the monetary base (depending on the exchange rate system) and can influence aspects of the behavior of private individuals and banks. The Fed cannot control with certainty whether banks will make loans, whether individuals will deposit funds or ask for loans, and whether money will be used to carry out transactions.

6. How do the alternative exchange rate systems influence monetary policy?

Depending on the exchange rate system, the Fed has more or less control over the money supply. Under the flexible system, the Fed has the greatest degree of control but still may want to intervene to alter the movement of exchange rates. In addition, the Fed must consider the impact of exchange rate changes on domestic purchases, employment, and inflation.

7. What are intervention and sterilization?

The Fed intervenes in the foreign exchange market by buying and selling foreign exchange to control the exchange rate. When the Fed makes such an intervention, it increases or decreases the domestic money supply. To offset the effects of intervention on the domestic money supply, the Fed may carry out an open-market operation; this is called *sterilization.*

▼

Key Terms

M_1 monetary aggregate   253
demand deposits   253
other checkable deposits
  (OCDs)   254
M_2 monetary aggregate   254
M_3 monetary aggregate   255
fractional reserve banking
  system   257
reserve requirement   257
excess reserves   257
monetary base   257
high-powered money   257
money multiplier   257
depository institutions   260
Eurocurrency market   261
offshore banking   261

international banking facilities
  (IBFs)   262
Federal Open Market Committee
  (FOMC)   263
intermediate target   264
FOMC directive   268
legal reserves   268
federal funds   268
federal funds rate   269
discount rate   269
open-market operations   269
short-run operating target   270
nonborrowed reserves   271
foreign exchange market
  intervention   275
sterilization   276

▼
Problems and Exercises

1. What role does foreign exchange play in determining the domestic money supply?

2. Explain the different implications for monetary policy of the fixed and flexible exchange rate systems.

3. If capital were perfectly mobile, how would monetary policy under fixed and under flexible exchange rate systems differ?

4. Using the *IS–LM–BOP* diagram, explain the impact of an open-market purchase under flexible and under fixed exchange rate systems.

5. Define ECUs and SDRs. What role does each play in determining money supply?

6. The money multiplier measures the maximum possible expansion of the money supply in the banking system. What could cause the expansion to be different from that given by the money multiplier?

7. What, if any, is the relation between the money multiplier and velocity? What accounted for the changing velocity of money defined as *M1* during the early 1980s?

8. Suppose you are a member of the FOMC. Write a directive to the New York Fed about the conduct of monetary policy over the next two months. Your directive should address targets for the rate of growth of the *M2* and *M3* money supplies, the federal funds rate, the rate of inflation, and the foreign exchange value of the dollar versus the Japanese yen and German mark. You may refer to the *Federal Reserve Bulletin* for examples.

9. Suppose the Fed has a target range for the yen–dollar exchange rate. How could the Fed keep the exchange rate within the target range if the demand for U.S. dollars pushes the exchange rate out of this range?

Chapter 12

Fiscal Policy

What to Expect

The idea that government is responsible for the economic health of the nation became official U.S. policy with passage of the Employment Act of 1946. The act states,

It is the continuing policy and responsibility of the Federal Government to use all practical means consistent with its needs and obligations and other essential considerations of national policy to coordinate and utilize all its plans, functions, and resources for the purpose of creating and maintaining, in a manner calculated to foster and promote free competitive enterprise and the general welfare conditions under which there will be afforded useful employment opportunities, including self-employment for those able, willing, and seeking to work, and to promote maximum employment, production and purchasing power.

The act gave the U.S. national government responsibility for creating and maintaining low inflation and unemployment. The government tries to fulfill that responsibility by setting fiscal and monetary policy. This chapter examines the role of government spending and taxation in determining the level of income, employment, and inflation. These interventions are called *fiscal policy*.

The following questions are considered:

1. *What is fiscal policy?*

2. *What is the impact on the economy of changes in government purchases (and taxation)?*

3. *Do increased government purchases lead to increased output and employment?*

4. *What impacts do budget deficits and debt have on the economy?*

5. *How is fiscal policy determined?*

6. *What is the twin deficits problem?*

7. *How do other countries carry out fiscal policy?*

▼

The Theory of Fiscal Policy

Fiscal policy is the government's use of spending and taxation to influence the levels of output, employment, and prices. Fiscal policy works primarily through aggregate demand, shifting the *AD* curve out or in as conditions warrant. What the government spends on goods and services directly affects the level of aggregate expenditures. Taxes and transfer payments, on the contrary, affect aggregate expenditures indirectly, by changing the disposable income of households, which alters consumption, or the profit rate of businesses, which affects investment.

Government Purchases and the AD Curve

Changes in government purchases and net taxes shift the aggregate demand curve. In Figure 12-1, a **recessionary gap** of $Y_p - Y_1$ is eliminated by an increase in government purchases. The increase in spending shifts the *AD* curve from AD_1 to AD_2 and thus drives the economy to the potential income level. Theoretically, the only problem the government faces is how much to increase purchases.

If the *AS* curve is horizontal, then how much to increase government purchases is shown by the multiplier derived from the *IS–LM* framework. Simply increase government purchases enough that when multiplied by the multiplier it equals the amount by which Y_1 falls below Y_p. The *AD* curve shifts from point *a* to point *b*. If the *AS* curve slopes upward, then the *AD* curve must be made to shift out by more than the recessionary gap. In Figure 12-1, because the price level rises, to increase the equilibrium level of national income from Y_1 to Y_p, aggregate demand must shift from point *a* to point *c*. The desired result re-

FIGURE 12-1   *The recessionary gap. A recessionary gap of* Y$_p$ − Y$_1$ *is eliminated by an increase in government purchases. The increase in spending causes the* AD *curve to shift from* AD$_1$ *to* AD$_2$ *and thus drives the economy up to the potential income level.*

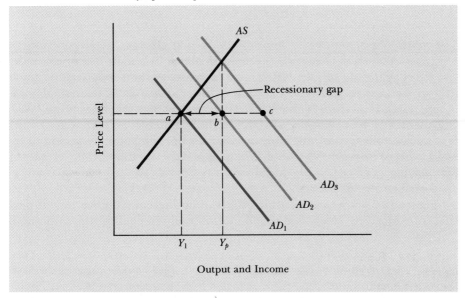

quires that we know the size of the multiplier, the size of the recessionary gap, and the magnitude of any price effects.

Taxes and Aggregate Demand

The issue is not quite as straightforward as implied in the previous paragraphs. Government purchases must be financed by some combination of taxing, borrowing, or creating additional money, and the method of finance can affect the economy. Suppose, for instance, that government purchases rise by $100 billion and that this expenditure is financed by a tax increase of $100 billion. The spending increase affects aggregate expenditures directly and thus shifts the *AD* curve out by the $100 billion multiplied by the multiplier (from the *IS–LM* framework). The tax increase reduces spendable income to households (and perhaps to businesses, depending on the type of tax). Households must then consume and save out of a smaller after-tax income level. As a result, a portion of the $100 billion tax is financed from reduced saving and a portion from reduced consumption (the portions given by the *MPC* and *MPS*). Because taxes affect aggregate expenditures through reduced consumption, the *AD* curve shifts in, not by the amount of the tax increase ($100 billion) multiplied by the multiplier, but instead by the initial consumption decrease (*MPC* × $100 billion) multiplied by the multiplier. As shown in Figure 12-2, the *AD* curve does not shift all the way back to the original position.

Taxes and Aggregate Supply

The multiplier assumes that the only thing that changes when government spending or taxation changes is aggregate demand. In fact, an increase in taxes can affect aggregate supply. When taxes increase, workers have less incentive to work because their after-tax income is lower. The cost of taking a day off or extending a vacation for a few extra days is less than when taxes are lower and after-tax income is higher. In addition, the second income earner in a family may decide that to continue working isn't worthwhile and may decide to remain at home or return to school. When taxes increase, the quantity of output that producers offer for sale at different price levels can fall, shown as an inward shift of the *AS* curve.

Figure 12-3 shows the possible effects of an increase in government purchases financed by taxes. The economy is initially in equilibrium at point *a*,

FIGURE 12-2   *Tax-financed spending. Government purchases rise by $100 billion, financed by a tax increase of $100 billion. The increase in purchases affects aggregate expenditures directly, shifting the* AD *curve out by the $100 billion multiplied by the multiplier (from the* IS–LM *framework). The tax increase reduces spendable income to households (and perhaps to businesses, depending on the type of tax). Households must then consume and save out of a smaller after-tax income level. Because taxes affect aggregate expenditures through reduced consumption, the* AD *curve shifts in by the initial consumption decrease (*MPC × *$100 billion) multiplied by the multiplier. The* AD *curve does not shift all the way back to the original position.*

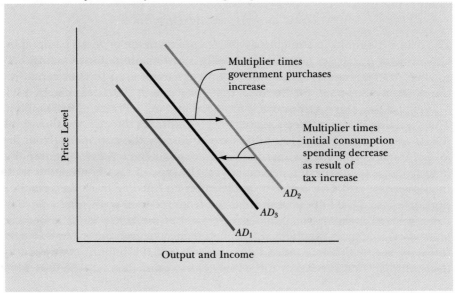

FIGURE 12-3 *Taxes and aggregate supply. The possible effects of an increase in government purchases financed by taxes are shown. The economy is initially in equilibrium at point a. An increase in government purchases shifts the aggregate demand curve from* AD₁ *to* AD₂. *If this is the only change, the economy is in equilibrium at point b. But if the increase in taxes reduces output, the aggregate supply curve moves back from* AS₁ *to* AS₂ *and output does not expand all the way to* Yₚ. *The decrease in aggregate supply creates a new equilibrium at point c, where income is at* Y₂ *and the price level is* P₃.

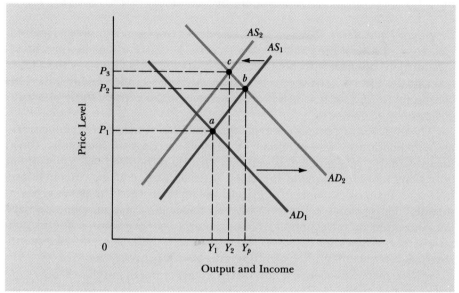

with prices at P_1 and output at Y_1. The increase in government purchases shifts the aggregate demand curve from AD_1 to AD_2. If this were the only change, the economy would be in equilibrium at point b. But if the increase in taxes reduces output, the aggregate supply curve moves back from AS_1 to AS_2, and output does not expand all the way to Y_p. The decrease in aggregate supply creates a new equilibrium at point c, where income is at Y_2 and the price level is P_3.

If tax changes do affect aggregate supply, the expansionary effects of government purchases financed by tax increases are smaller than if AS were not affected. You can even imagine a case where the economy declines as a result of equal increases in government purchases and taxation. Although economists do not agree about the effects of a tax-financed fiscal expansion, most agree the evidence in the United States indicates tax increases have a fairly small effect on aggregate supply.

Borrowing

Taxation may offset at least part of the expansionary effect of higher government purchases. Government purchases financed by borrowing also can modify the effect. A government borrows funds by selling government bonds to the public. These bonds represent a government debt that must be repaid in the future. Instead of increasing current taxes to pay for the higher spending, the government borrows the savings of households and businesses. Of course, when the debt matures it must be repaid. This may mean that taxes must be higher in the future, to provide government with the funds. In addition, by borrowing additional funds, the government may force the interest rate up.

Ricardian Equivalence. Current government borrowing may imply higher future taxes. If households and businesses consider these future taxes to be future burdens, they may decide to save more today so they can pay the higher taxes in the future. As saving today increases, consumption today falls. This consumption decline may offset at least some of the expansionary effects of government purchases.

The idea that current government borrowing can reduce current nongovernment expenditures was originally suggested by English economist David Ricardo, in the early nineteenth century. Ricardo recognized that government borrowing could function like increased current taxes, reducing current household and business expenditures. **Ricardian equivalence** is the name given to the idea that taxation and borrowing to finance government spending have the same effect on the economy. If Ricardian equivalence holds, it doesn't matter whether the government raises taxes or borrows to finance increased spending. The effect is the same: spending falls in the private sector.

If Ricardian equivalence holds, increased government purchases moves the aggregate demand curve out to AD_2 in Figure 12-4. But this increase in aggregate demand is offset in part by a reduction in private spending as saving increases in anticipation of future tax increases. The reduction in household and business spending shifts the aggregate demand curve back to the left. Just how much private spending drops, and how far to the left the AD curve shifts, depend on the degree to which current saving increases in response to expected higher taxes. The less people respond to the future tax liabilities arising from current government debt, the smaller the reduction in private spending.

There is a great deal of controversy over Ricardian equivalence. Several rationales have been suggested as to why Ricardian equivalence does not occur. One rationale focuses on imperfect capital markets, where there are some misallocation problems, or where equilibrium does not occur all the time, or where current resources are not allocated to individuals on the basis of expected future income. It is argued that in such cases the government may be able to act as an agent to raise the necessary amount of resources at a lower cost than individuals can. It is also argued that the government may provide some economies of scale or other efficiency reasons for acting as the middleman or agent in allocating resources. If so, Ricardian equivalence does not hold; it is more efficient for the government to carry out the actions than for each individual to carry out the actions, so the government "gets more bang for the buck" than

FIGURE 12-4 *Ricardian equivalence. If Ricardian equivalence holds, the increase in government purchases moves the aggregate demand curve out to* AD_2. *But this increase in aggregate demand is offset in part by a reduction in private spending as saving increases in anticipation of future tax increases. The reduction in household and business spending shifts the aggregate demand curve back to the left. The less people respond to the future tax liabilities arising from current government debt, the smaller the reduction in private spending.*

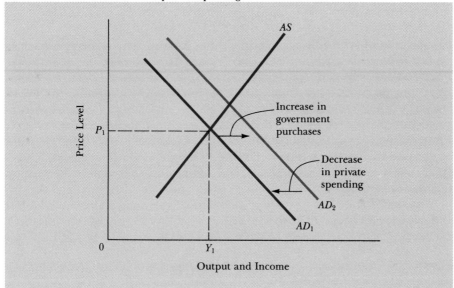

does the private sector. Another rationale argues that the public does not base current spending on future tax liabilities, so that the basis of the Ricardian equivalence does not hold up. Whatever the rationale, most economists agree that Ricardian equivalence does not occur.

Crowding Out. Ricardian equivalence theory argues that public sector spending replaces private sector spending. Another such effect is called *crowding out.* Expansionary fiscal policy can crowd out private sector spending; that is, an increase in government spending can reduce consumption and investment. Increases in government spending raise interest rates, and as interest rates go up investment and consumption fall. Crowding out works through the bond markets. The U.S. government borrows by selling Treasury bonds. Because the government is not a profit-making institution, it is not sensitive to the interest rate it must pay on its borrowed funds. It just wants the money now, irrespective of the cost. But a profit-making corporation does have to worry about the return on the bonds it sells. When interest rates rise, fewer corporations borrow and investment expenditures decline. So an increase in government spending and borrowing can reduce private-sector spending and borrowing.

Crowding out is important in principle, but economists have not demon-strated conclusively that its effects can substantially alter private sector spend-ing. Most economists claim that the increased income and expenditures far exceed the negative effects of higher interest rates.

Monetization

The government must finance its spending. It does so by raising taxes or by issuing securities — government bonds. The Federal Reserve may react to the government's financing strategy by buying the newly issued securities, thus preventing the interest rate from rising and eliminating any crowding out. When the Federal Reserve carries out an open-market operation to buy the govern-ment's bonds, the deficit is said to have been *monetized*. **Monetization** is actually a monetary policy action, an action that increases the supply of money. But because the monetization is undertaken in response to the government's spend-ing action, the effects of monetization are often compared to those of taxation and bond financing.

Figure 12-5 shows an increase in government spending as the outward shift of the aggregate demand curve, from AD_1 to AD_2. As a result of the shift, both

FIGURE 12-5   *Monetization. An increase in government spending is shown as the outward shift of the aggregate demand curve, from* AD$_1$ *to* AD$_2$. *However, the resulting deficit must be financed. If the deficit is financed through the Fed to keep the interest rate from rising, the accompanying increase in the money supply gives rise to a further shift in the* AD *curve, to* AD$_3$.

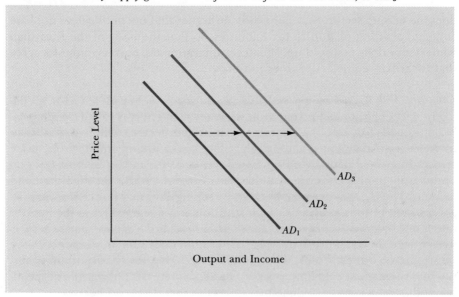

the price and output levels increase if the *AS* curve slopes upward. However, the resulting deficit must be financed. If the deficit is financed through the Fed to keep the interest rate from rising, the accompanying increase in the money supply gives rise to a further shift in the *AD* curve, to AD_3. If the increased spending is paid for with taxation, the *AD* curve shifts back toward AD_1; if the increased spending is paid for with new securities that are not monetized, the *AD* curve shifts back toward AD_1 according to the degree of Ricardian equivalence or crowding out. Even if Ricardian equivalence holds in the case of the monetization, the money supply increase leads to a more expansionary effect than does either taxation or bond financing alone.

The effect of monetization should be an increase in the money supply and consequent increases in the price level. Without monetization, the interest rate rises as the government debt is issued, and this reduces private investment and consumption. These results suggest that the way a budget deficit is financed is important. Monetization leads to more inflation and its associated costs. Non-monetization produces different effects. Bond financing yields higher interest rates and less investment, which means a smaller capital stock and productive capacity than would otherwise have been the case.

Fiscal Policy and Exchange Rate Systems

The impact of fiscal policy also depends on the exchange rate system under which an open economy operates. In contrast to monetary policy, a fiscal policy is more effective under a fixed exchange rate regime than under a flexible exchange rate regime. Let's use the *IS–LM–BOP* diagram to illustrate this result.

In Figure 12-6A, we begin at point *a*. The government increases purchases, from G_0 to G_1, which causes the *IS* curve to shift outward. The new intersection between the *IS* and *LM* curves is above the *BOP* curve at point *b*. This means there is a net surplus in the capital and current accounts (income is too low for the interest rate r_1 to offset exports). An inflow of foreign reserves occurs, increasing the money supply from M_0 to M_1. The *LM* curve shifts outward until the intersection between all three curves occurs at point *c*. Note that domestic authorities lack total control over the money supply. The demand shock simply sets off forces that automatically drive up the domestic money supply. The expansion of output is much larger than would have been the case in the closed economy, going from *a* to *c* rather than *a* to *b;* the multiplier is larger in the open economy under fixed exchange rates.

Under a flexible exchange rate system, the government purchases increase also shifts the *IS* curve outward. However, the exchange rate adjusts to maintain the BOP equilibrium rather than the money supply. As shown in Figure 12-6B it is the *IS* and *BOP* curves that shift, not the *LM* curve, under flexible exchange rates. These two curves shift because the new exchange rate increases the relative price of domestic goods relative to foreign goods. Under flexible

FIGURE 12-6 *Government spending and exchange rate regimes. In panel A, we begin at point* a. *The government increases purchases from* G_0 *to* G_1, *which causes the IS curve to shift outward. The new intersection between the IS and LM curves is above the BOP curve at point* b, *meaning there is net surplus in the capital and current accounts. An inflow of foreign reserves occurs, causing the money supply to increase from* M_0 *to* M_1. *The LM curve shifts outward until the intersection between all three curves occurs at point* c. *The expansion of output is much larger than would have been the case in the closed economy, going from* a *to* c *rather than* a *to* b.*

Under a flexible exchange rate system, it is the exchange rate that adjusts to maintain BOP equilibrium rather than the money supply. As shown in panel B, the IS and BOP curves shift, not the LM curve, under flexible exchange rates. The curves shift because the new exchange rate causes the price of domestic goods relative to foreign goods to rise. In the case of flexible exchange rates, the expansion of output due to a government purchases increase is from a *to* c, *which is less than the* a *to* b *that would have occurred in the closed economy.*

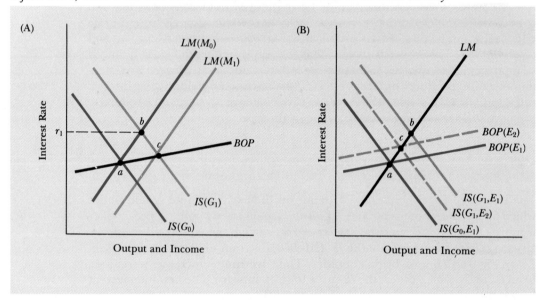

exchange rates, a government purchases increase causes output to expand from *a* to *c,* which is less than the *a* to *b* that would have occurred in the closed economy.

Whether the fiscal policy is one of increased government purchases without a net tax increase or one of decreased net taxes without a government purchases decrease, the relative effects of the policy under fixed and flexible exchange rates are the same. Fiscal policy is more effective, *ceteris paribus,* under the fixed exchange rate system.

In sum, the effects of changes in government purchases depend on (1) how the purchases are financed, (2) the exchange regime in which the economy operates, and (3) Ricardian equivalence.

▼
The Fiscal Policy Process

Economic policy is formulated and executed in the presence of politics. It emerges from a process in which politicians look at alternative policies more for their effect on constituents and thus on chances of election or re-election than for the policy impacts on the economy. A basic tenet of economics is that individuals act in their own self-interest. A congressional representative wants to get re-elected; a president wants to be re-elected or to see his or her party remain in power; an economic adviser wants to see his or her advisees continue to hold office. Economic policies are implemented because politicians believe these policies are what their constituents want. So economic policies are seldom implemented in the forms originally proposed or in the manner that the theory just discussed says is best. (Chapter 18 discusses these issues in more detail.)

The Acts

Significant changes in the U.S. economic policymaking process occurred with the passage of the Full Employment and Balanced Growth Act of 1978. This act, also known as the Humphrey-Hawkins Bill, requires that economic policy be designed to achieve specific short- and long-term numerical goals for economic performance. In addition, the act set up a framework for policy formulation involving the president, the U.S. Congress, and the Federal Reserve Board. Furthermore, it included an economic policy time schedule, presented in Table 12-1. To that schedule, the Gramm-Rudman Act of 1985 added a requirement that the government's budget must not exceed certain deficit levels or else automatic across-the-board spending cuts would be implemented. Fiscal policy takes place in the context of these acts.

Deficits and Surpluses

U.S. federal government spending and revenue have increased steadily since the 1900s, as you can see in Figure 12-7A. Figure 12-7B places the growth of government in perspective by plotting U.S. government spending as a percentage of GNP over time. Before the Great Depression, federal spending was approximately 3 percent of GNP; by 1940, it had risen to almost 10 percent. It reached a peak during World War II but then fell and has remained near 23 percent.

Before the 1960s, U.S. federal budget deficits occurred only in wartime — the 1940–1945 and the 1952–1954 periods. Since the 1960s, the budget has been in deficit virtually every year, as shown in Figure 12-8A. Figure 12-8B shows the deficit as a percentage of GNP. The deficit was at its largest percentage of GNP during World War II; that percentage fell dramatically after the war

TABLE 12-1   *Economic Policy Timetable*

January	The *President* issues his economic report containing numerical goals for employment, unemployment, production, real income, productivity, and prices during each of the next five years. Report due within the first twenty days of the new Congressional session.
February	The *Joint Economic Committee* holds hearings on the president's economic report, including review of the short- and medium-term numerical goals.
	The *Federal Reserve Board* issues a report by the twentieth to the Banking Committees of the Congress on its monetary policy plans for the calendar year and their relationship to the short-term goals of the president.
	The *Banking Committees* hold hearings on the Federal Reserve's monetary policy report.
March	The *Joint Economic Committee* issues its report on the president's economic report, including its views and recommendations with respect to the short- and medium-term numerical goals, to the Budget Committees by the fifteenth of the month.
	The *Banking Committees* issue a report to their respective bodies on the Federal Reserve's intended monetary policies, including their views and recommendations.
April	The *Budget Committees* report the first concurrent resolution on the Budget for the fiscal year beginning on October 1. The resolution may include short- and medium-term economic goals.
May	The *House* and *Senate* debate the first budget resolution, limited to four hours on economic goals, policies, and possible changes in the short- and medium-term goals. Action to be completed by the fifteenth.
July	The *Federal Reserve Board* issues a report by the twentieth to the Banking Committees on its monetary policy plans for the remainder of the year and for the next year and their relationship to the numerical economic goals of the president.
August	The *Banking Committees* issue a report on the monetary policy plan of the Federal Reserve, including views and recommendations.
September	By the first, the *Budget Committees* report the second concurrent resolution on the budget.
	By the fifteenth, the *House* and *Senate* complete action on the budget resolution.
October	Fiscal year begins.

Source: Steven M. Roberts, "Economic Policymaking in the United States," *Journal of Economic Dynamics and Control* (August 1979).

FIGURE 12-7   *U.S. government spending. Federal government spending has increased steadily since the 1900s (panel A). Panel B places the growth of government in perspective by plotting U.S. government spending as a percentage of GNP over time. Before the Great Depression, federal spending was approximately 3 percent of GNP; by the end of the Depression, it had risen to almost 10 percent. It reached a peak during World War II but then fell and has remained near 23 percent.*

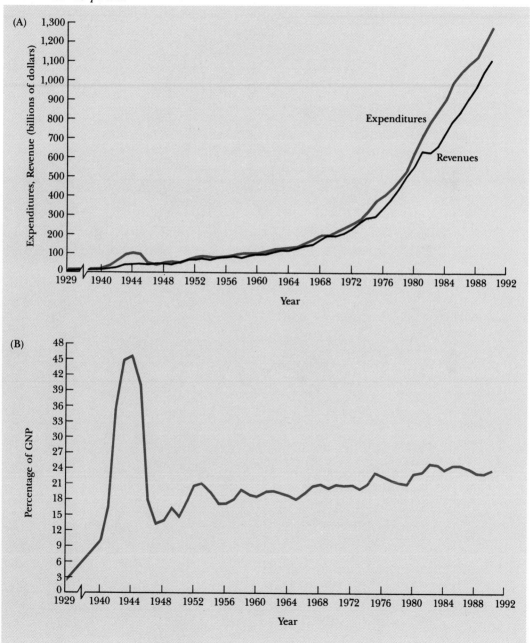

Source: Economic Report of the President, 1991 (Washington, DC: U.S. Government Printing Office, 1991).

FIGURE 12-8   *Deficits as a percentage of GNP. Since the 1960s, the budget has been in deficit virtually every year, as shown in panel A. Panel B shows the deficit as a percentage of GNP. The deficit was at its largest percentage of GNP during World War II; that percentage fell dramatically after the war and has grown slightly since the mid-1960s. The United States is not alone in having experienced growing deficits. As you can see in Panel C, the deficit as a percentage of GNP has risen for most of the industrial nations.*

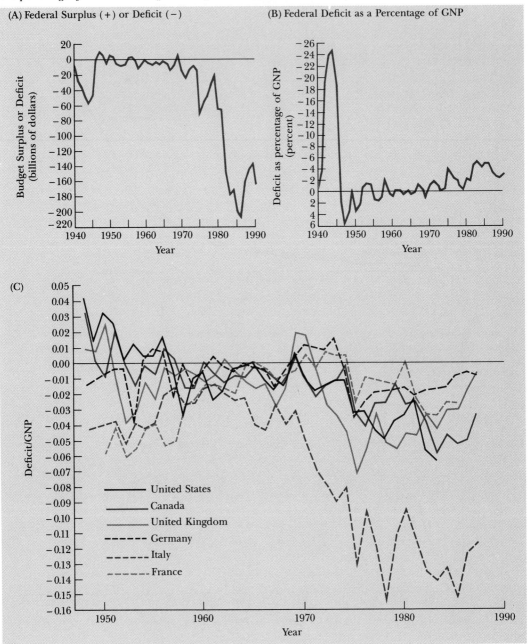

Source: Panels A and B, *Economic Report of the President, 1991* (Washington, DC: U.S. Government Printing Office, 1991). Panel C, *International Finance Statistics* (International Monetary Fund), various issues.

and has grown slightly since the mid-1960s. The United States is not the only country that has growing deficits. As you can see in Figure 12-8C, the deficit as a percentage of GNP has risen for most of the industrial nations in the past two decades.

Deficits and Debt

The rapid increase in the U.S. federal budget deficit in recent years has led many observers to wonder whether a government deficit can harm the economy. One major implication of a large deficit is the resulting increase in national debt, the total stock of government bonds outstanding. Table 12-2 lists data on the debt of the United States. Notice that the total debt doubled between 1981 ($1,003.9 billion) and 1986 ($2,130 billion) and tripled from 1981 to 1990 ($3,206 billion). Column 3 shows debt as a percentage of fiscal-year GNP. In the 1950s and early 1960s, the debt was about 50 percent of GNP. This is about the ratio today. During World War II, the debt was actually larger than GNP.

Deficits and Interest Rates

Because the government borrows in order to finance its deficits, interest rates are probably affected by government deficits. If increased government borrowing raises interest rates, investment can be depressed. A decrease in investment today means fewer capital goods are acquired than would have been the case without the government's spending. Having fewer capital goods means a lower economic growth rate and thus a smaller potential output level than would have been the case without the government spending. In other words, if government crowding out occurs, the effects may not show up for several years; when they do, they show up in the form of a lower potential GNP.

Interest Payments

The **national debt** is the stock of government bonds that are outstanding. It is the result of past and current budget deficits. As the size of the debt increases, the interest that must be paid on the debt tends to rise. Column 4 of Table 12-2 lists the amount of interest paid on the debt; column 5 lists the interest as a percentage of government expenditures. The numbers in both columns have risen steadily over time. The federal government has been paying a higher dollar amount of interest each year; interest payments have been rising faster than total government spending.

The increase in the interest cost of the national debt worries many people. However, to the extent that U.S. citizens hold government bonds, the debt is owed to ourselves. The tax liability of funding the interest payments is offset by the interest income that bondholders earn. In this case, there is no net change in national wealth when the national debt changes.

TABLE 12-2 *Debt of the U.S. Government (in billions of dollars, per fiscal year)*

(1) Fiscal Year	(2) Total Debt	(3) Debt/GNP (percentage)	(4) Net Interest	(5) Interest/Government Spending (percentage)
1958	$276.3	62.0%	$5.6	6.8%
1959	$284.7	60.9	$5.8	6.3
1960	$286.3	57.7	$6.9	7.5
1961	$289.0	56.1	$6.7	6.9
1962	$298.2	54.9	$6.9	6.5
1963	$305.9	52.8	$7.7	6.9
1964	$311.7	50.7	$8.2	6.9
1965	$317.3	47.9	$8.6	7.3
1966	$329.5	45.5	$9.4	7.0
1967	$341.3	43.9	$10.3	6.5
1968	$369.8	44.5	$11.1	6.2
1969	$367.1	40.3	$12.7	6.9
1970	$382.6	39.5	$14.4	7.4
1971	$409.5	39.7	$14.8	7.0
1972	$437.3	38.7	$15.5	6.7
1973	$468.4	37.4	$17.3	7.0
1974	$486.2	35.3	$21.4	8.0
1975	$544.1	36.8	$23.2	7.2
1976	$631.9	38.3	$26.7	7.3
1977	$709.1	38.1	$29.9	7.5
1978	$780.4	37.3	$35.4	7.9
1979	$833.8	35.4	$42.6	8.7
1980	$914.3	35.5	$52.5	9.1
1981	$1,003.9	34.9	$68.7	10.5
1982	$1,147.0	37.5	$85.0	11.6
1983	$1,381.9	42.8	$89.8	11.2
1984	$1,576.7	44.0	$111.1	13.2
1985	$1,827.0	47.7	$129.1	13.6
1986	$2,130.0	50.8	$136.0	13.7
1987	$2,335.2	53.4	$138.6	13.8
1988	$2,600.7	53.3	$151.7	14.3
1989	$2,866.2	54.8	$169.1	14.8
1990	$3,206.3	58.7	$182.1	16.6

Source: Data are from *Economic Report of the President, 1989, 1990, 1991* (Washington, DC: U.S. Government Printing Office, 1989, 1990, 1991).

We do not owe the national debt just to ourselves, however. Foreign capital has flowed into the United States to purchase government securities. Foreign holdings of the U.S. national debt amounted to more than 14 percent of the outstanding debt in 1990. Because the tax liability for paying the interest on the debt falls on U.S. taxpayers, the greater the payments made to foreigners, the lower the wealth of U.S. residents, everything else being the same. Lower wealth means less spending.

What would the economy have been like had the debt not been sold to foreigners? Clearly, foreign savings enabled the United States to increase its investment and its productive capacity beyond what would have occurred otherwise. Interest rates were lower than they would have been, so investment spending was higher than it would have been. Thus, the presence of foreign funds may have increased the living standards of U.S. residents. Foreign savings may have offset some of the crowding out of private investment by the government. It is also possible that the government deficits have decreased the international competitiveness of U.S. firms by causing the dollar to appreciate as foreigners demand more dollars in order to purchase U.S. government bonds. The higher dollar means less foreign spending on U.S. goods and thus fewer sales by export-related U.S. industries.

Deficits and Trade: The Twin Deficits

If government deficits raise real interest rates, they may affect international trade. A higher relative return on U.S. securities makes those securities more attractive to foreign investors. As the foreign demand for U.S. securities increases, so does the demand for U.S. dollars in exchange for Japanese yen, British pounds, and other foreign currencies. As the demand for dollars increases, the dollar appreciates in value. This means that the dollar becomes more expensive to foreigners, while foreign currency becomes cheaper to U.S. residents. This kind of change in the exchange rate encourages U.S. residents to buy more foreign goods and foreign residents to buy fewer U.S. goods. Ultimately, then, as government budget deficits and government debt increase U.S. net exports fall.

Many economists believe that the growing fiscal deficits of the 1980s were responsible for the record decline in U.S. net exports and the resulting trade deficits during that period. This problem is referred to as the **twin deficits** problem. The government deficit drives interest rates up, which attracts foreign financial capital. As long as foreign capital flows in, interest rates do not rise as much as otherwise would be the case. However, the increased inflow of foreign capital causes the dollar to appreciate, leading to decreases in net exports and a deficit in the current account.

We can use the national income and balance of payments accounts to show the relationship between the federal budget and current account deficits. Aggregate expenditures are

$$Y = C + I + G + X$$

This means that net exports are

$$X = Y - C - I - G$$

Because X is the current account of the balance of payments, CA, we have

$$CA = Y - C - I - G$$

Now, from this equation, add and subtract net taxes, T:

$$CA = (Y - T - C - I) + (T - G)$$

Then, because $S = Y - C - T$,

$$CA = (S - I) + (T - G)$$

The current account balance can be associated with the gaps between (1) domestic savings and investment and (2) domestic net taxes and government purchases. If G exceeds T, then either domestic saving must exceed investment or the current account must be in deficit. The interpretation of this result is that the government sector is borrowing abroad to finance an excess of its expenditures over its income. This foreign borrowing is the counterpart of the current account deficit.

Figure 12-9 shows the U.S. current account deficit–surplus. Until about 1983, the current account was in surplus and, as seen in panel A of Figure 12-8, the budget deficit was relatively small. Since 1983 the budget deficit has been very large, and the current account deficit has expanded to record size.

▼

Budgetary Facts

The budget combines discretionary and nondiscretionary fiscal policy. The **discretionary fiscal policy** concerns changes in government spending and taxation aimed at achieving a policy goal — such as closing a recessionary gap. The **nondiscretionary fiscal policy** concerns spending and taxing changes that occur as a result of economic conditions, not specific planned actions on the part of policymakers. Discretionary policy seems to show up most as anticyclical actions. For instance, during recessions we should expect to see government deficits rising and during expansions see the deficits falling. In Figure 12-8A, you can see that until the 1980s the deficit did seem to follow what we expect from discretionary policy. The figure points out that the rapid growth of the deficit in the 1980s involved more than the recessions in 1980 and 1982. The economy grew rapidly after the 1982 recession ended, but so did the budget deficit. Much of this deficit was the result of the nondiscretionary part of fiscal policy. Much was also the result of a rapid increase in government spending to fund new programs and enlarge existing programs while not increasing taxes.

Revenues

The major sources of federal budget receipts in the United States, listed in Table 12-3, are individual income taxes, corporate profits taxes, and social insur-

FIGURE 12-9   *The twin deficits. Until about 1983, the U.S. current account was in surplus and the budget deficit was relatively small. Since 1983, the budget deficit has been very large and the current account deficit has expanded to a record size.*

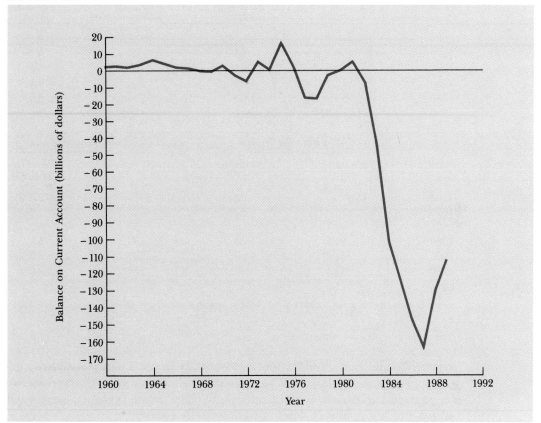

ance taxes (that is, payroll taxes). As a percentage of GNP, tax receipts have increased moderately since 1965. Because corporate profits taxes have fallen as a fraction of GNP and the ratio of income taxes to GNP has been practically constant, the increase in tax revenues as a percentage of GNP must result from the growth of the social insurance tax. Revenue from this tax has increased more than fourfold since 1975.

Expenditures

Table 12-4 presents the major types of federal expenditures. Domestic transfer payments have risen the most rapidly since the mid-1960s. Domestic transfer payments are the sum of healthcare benefits, income security, social security,

TABLE 12-3   *Sources of Receipts (in billions of dollars)*

| Fiscal Year | Total Receipts | | Individual Income Tax | |
	Receipts	Percentage of GNP[a]	Receipts	Percentage of GNP[a]
1965	$ 116.8	17.4%	$ 48.7	7.2%
1970	192.8	19.5	90.4	9.1
1975	279.1	18.3	122.4	8.0
1980	517.7	19.4	244.1	9.1
1985	734.1	18.6	334.5	8.5
1990	1,031.3	19.1	466.9	8.6

| Fiscal Year | Corporate Profits Tax | | Social Insurance Tax | |
	Receipts	Percentage of GNP[a]	Receipts	Percentage of GNP[a]
1965	$25.5	3.8	$ 17.3	2.6%
1970	32.9	3.3	45.3	4.6
1975	42.1	2.8	86.4	5.7
1980	20.2	0.8	157.8	5.9
1985	61.3	1.6	265.2	6.7
1990	93.5	1.7	380.0	7.0

[a]GNP is for fiscal year.
Source: Economic Report of the President, 1991 (Washington, DC: U.S. Government Printing Office, 1991).

veterans' benefits, and education and training. In 1965 national defense expenditures accounted for 41.9 percent of expenditures while domestic transfer payments accounted for 29.9 percent. By 1990 transfer payments exceeded 40 percent and national defense was about 27 percent.

The interest on the debt has moved into third place in total outlays. Transfer payments for income security and health care come in first, and national defense is second. Transfer payment outlays are not considered part of discretionary fiscal policy. They are instead *entitlements* that are immune to discretionary fiscal policy changes. Most of these programs are indexed so that payment increases automatically as inflation rises. Anyone who meets the qualifications of each program automatically receives payment. For example, if someone is needy and elderly, blind, or disabled, that person automatically receives Supplementary Security Income (SSI) payments.

Off-Budget Programs. A great deal of government spending is not measured in the deficit. This is called **off-budget spending**. The U.S. Railway Association, the Pension Guaranty Corporation, the Federal Financing Bank, and the Postal Service are off-budget institutions. Social Security again provides the most out-

TABLE 12-4   *Types of Outlays (in billions of dollars)*

Fiscal Year	Total Outlays		National Defense	
	Expenditure	Percentage of GNP[a]	Expenditure	Percentage of GNP[a]
1965	$ 118.2	17.6%	$ 49.6	7.4%
1970	195.6	19.8	79.3	8.0
1975	332.3	21.8	85.6	5.6
1980	590.9	22.1	135.9	5.1
1985	946.3	23.9	252.7	6.4
1990	1,251.7	23.2	299.3	5.5

Fiscal Year	Domestic Transfer Payments		Interest	
	Expenditure	Percentage of GNP[a]	Expenditure	Percentage of GNP[a]
1965	$ 35.4	5.3	$ 10.3	1.5%
1970	65.7	6.6	18.3	1.8
1975	172.5	11.3	31.0	2.0
1980	310.3	11.6	52.5	2.0
1985	366.7	9.3	129.4	3.3
1990	496.6	9.2	184.2	3.4

[a]GNP is for fiscal year.

Source: Economic Report of the President, 1991 (Washington, DC: U.S. Government Printing Office, 1991).

standing example of off-budget spending. As a result of the Balanced Budget and Emergency Deficit Control Act of 1985 (the Gramm-Rudman Act) the receipts and outlays of the old age and survivors' insurance and the disability insurance (social security) trust funds are now off budget and are exempt from any general budget limitation imposed by statute. Total federal government outlays for off-budget programs have grown significantly over the years, although the off-budget percentage of total outlays seems to have stayed at about 18.5 percent over the last decade, as shown in Table 12-5.

Loan Guarantees. Government guarantees of credit have also grown tremendously in recent years. The provision of guaranteed credit has a history dating back to the Great Depression and the establishment of agencies such as the Federal Housing Administration (FHA). The loan guarantee was originally designed to aid home buyers. The programs were placed on an actuarially sound basis, which meant that the present value of revenues met or exceeded the present value of outlays. In the 1960s, however, these guarantees were extended through subsidies to borrowers such as students and low-income families. Guarantees have been directed to relatively large organizations that faced poten-

TABLE 12-5   *Budget and Off-Budget Outlays (in billions of dollars)*

| Fiscal Year[a] | Federal Government Outlays | | | |
	On Budget	Off Budget	Total	Off Budget As Percentage of Total
1970	$ 168.0	$ 27.6	$ 195.6	14.1%
1971	177.3	32.8	210.2	15.6
1972	193.8	36.9	230.7	15.9
1973	200.1	45.6	245.7	18.5
1974	217.3	52.1	269.4	19.3
1975	271.9	60.4	332.3	18.2
1976	302.2	69.6	371.8	18.7
1977	328.5	80.7	409.2	19.7
1978	369.1	89.7	458.7	19.5
1979	403.5	100.0	503.5	19.8
1980	476.6	114.3	590.9	19.3
1981	543.0	135.2	678.2	20.0
1982	594.3	151.4	745.7	20.0
1983	661.2	147.1	808.3	18.2
1984	686.0	165.8	851.8	19.5
1985	769.5	176.8	946.3	18.6
1986	806.8	183.5	989.8	18.5
1987	810.0	193.8	1,003.8	19.3
1988	861.4	202.7	1,064.1	19.0
1989	933.2	210.9	1,144.1	18.4
1990	1,026.6	225.1	1,251.7	18.0

[a]Ending June 30 for 1970–1976 and September 30 thereafter.
Source: Economic Report of the President 1991 (Washington, DC: U.S. Government Printing Office, 1991).

tial bankruptcies, such as Lockheed, New York City, and Chrysler. In addition, deposits in the savings and loan industry are guaranteed by the Federal Savings and Loan Insurance Corporation (FSLIC), and the banking industry deposits are guaranteed by the Federal Deposit Insurance Corporation (FDIC). Both industries have faltered in recent years (particularly the S&Ls); it has been estimated that between $500 billion and $1 trillion of federal government spending is needed to pay off the S&L guarantees. The loan guarantees, when exercised, are typically off-budget items.

▼
Fiscal Policy in Different Countries

Each country's fiscal policy reflects its philosophy toward government spending and taxation. You can see in Table 12-6 that the growth of government and of the relative shares of government to GNP varies considerably across nations.

TABLE 12-6   *Share of Government Spending in GNP or GDP in Selected Industrial Countries,*
1880, 1929, 1960, and 1985 (percentages)

Year	France	Germany	Japan	Sweden	United Kingdom	United States
1880	15%	10%[a]	11%[b]	6%	10%	8%
1929	19	31	19	8	24	10
1960	35	32	18	31	32	28
1985	52	47	33	65	48	37

Note: For 1880 and 1929, data are the share of GNP; for 1960 and 1985, the share of GDP.
[a]1881.
[b]1885.
Source: World Bank, *World Development Report, 1988* (New York: Oxford University Press, 1988),
p. 44.

Government Spending

Government has played an increasingly larger role in the major industrial countries over time. Table 12-6 shows how government spending, as a percentage
of output in six industrial nations, has risen. In every case, government spending in 1985 accounted for a larger percentage of output than it did 100 years
earlier. For instance, in 1880 government spending was only 10 percent of the
GNP in the United Kingdom. By 1929, it had risen to 24 percent; by 1960, to
32 percent; and by 1985, to 48 percent.

Until the 1960s, the growth of government spending in industrial countries had been matched by growth in revenues. Since the 1960s, government
spending has grown faster than revenues, creating increasingly large debtor
nations.

Developing countries have not shown the uniform growth in government
spending found in industrial countries. In fact, in some developing countries
(Burma, Chile, Peru, and Yugoslavia, for example), government spending was
a smaller percentage of GNP in 1985 than it had been in 1972.

One important difference between the typical developed country and the
typical developing country is that government plays a larger role in investment
spending in the developing country. Table 12-7 shows government investment
as a percentage of total investment in twelve developing countries. In these
countries, government investment made up 43 percent of all investment. In
thirteen industrial countries, government represented just 30 percent of all investment. One reason for this difference is that state-owned enterprises account
for a larger percentage of economic activity in developing countries than they
do in developed countries. Also developing countries usually rely more on
government than on the private sector to build their infrastructure—schools,
roads, hospitals—than do developed countries.

The industrial countries spend, on average, 52 percent of their budgets on
social programs. Middle-income developing countries spend 36 percent of their

TABLE 12-7

Public Sector Investment as a Percentage of Total Investment for Selected Developing Countries, Averages for 1980 to 1985

Turkey	68
Egypt	65
Côte d'Ivoire	61
Argentina	58
Botswana	45
Colombia	40
Korea	35
Thailand	33
Mexico	31
Peru	29
Philippines	26
Dominican Republic	24
Average (unweighted)	
Twelve developing countries	43
Thirteen industrial countries	30

Source: World Bank, *World Development Report, 1988* (New York: Oxford University Press, 1988), p. 47.

budgets on social programs. Low-income countries spend only 20 percent of their budgets on such programs.

Taxation

Significant tax differences appear between the industrial nations and the developing nations. Personal income taxes are much more important in industrial countries, constituting about 12 percent of tax revenue in industrial nations and only 9 percent in developing nations. Personal taxes are very costly to collect in agricultural nations where a large percentage of household production is used for personal consumption. Taxes on businesses are easier to collect, and are more important in developing countries.

Industrial nations are better able to afford social programs. As a result, social security taxes are much higher than in the developing countries—about 31 percent of tax revenue in industrial nations and only 1 percent in developing nations. With so many workers living near the subsistence level in the poorest countries, their governments simply cannot tax workers for retirement and health security programs.

Taxes on international trade are very important in developing countries. Because goods arriving or leaving a country must pass through customs inspection, export and import taxes are relatively easy to collect. So developing countries depend more heavily on these indirect taxes on goods and services than do developed countries.

▼   ▼   ▼   ▼   ▼   ▼   ▼   ▼   ▼   ▼   ▼

Conclusions

Fiscal policy is the government's taxing and spending to affect the levels of output, prices, and employment. The theory of fiscal policy has varied considerably since the early 1900s. Initially, during the reign of the classical school of economic thought, there was no such thing as fiscal policy. Keynes introduced fiscal policy as the remedy for the market failures he believed occurred in the economy. Government spending was to be offset by taxation over the course of a business cycle. During the recessionary phase, the government would run a deficit; during the expansionary phase, the government would run a surplus. Whether that type of policy can be effective has been questioned in recent years. The idea that taxes may affect aggregate supply, that Ricardian equivalence may hold, and that crowding out may occur, all throw a wrench into the Keynesian view of how fiscal policy functions.

In reality, government influence has been increasing in virtually all economies, particularly the industrial ones. In addition to increased spending as a percentage of GNP, deficits have tended to increase. Governments have financed their spending with debt. This is particularly true for the United States. Debt as a percentage of GNP in the United States has risen. Consequently, interest payments today are the third largest category of U.S. government expenditures.

Although tax revenue has not kept pace with government spending, tax revenues have risen as a percentage of GNP in most countries over the past thirty or so years. The types of taxes governments impose depend on how developed the countries are. The industrial countries tend to rely on personal taxes and social security taxes, while the less developed nations rely on excise or indirect taxes.

In the next chapter, we put monetary and fiscal policy together and consider policymaking in the context of a global economy. Although this chapter moves us much closer to understanding the realities of economic policy, there remains the task of discovering just why certain policy decisions are made. Chapter 18 completes that task by looking at the interaction of politics and economic policy.

▼   ▼   ▼   ▼   ▼   ▼   ▼   ▼   ▼   ▼   ▼

Summary

1. What is fiscal policy?
Fiscal policy is the use of government spending and taxation to alter output, employment, and price levels.
2. What is the impact on the economy of changes in government purchases (and taxation)?
The impact of changes in government purchases (and taxation) depends on the exchange rate under which an open economy operates. In a closed economy, government purchases and taxation can both be used to close a recessionary gap. In the open economy, fiscal policy is much more effective under fixed exchange rates than under flexible exchange rates.

3. Do increased government purchases lead to increased output and employment?
The answer to this question is not straightforward. For instance, if Ricardian equivalence exists, then fiscal policy becomes totally ineffective in stimulating economic growth. Also, under flexible exchange rates, the exchange rate changes that result from implementing fiscal policy can work to offset the fiscal policy itself.

4. What impacts do budget deficits and debt have on the economy?
This question also involves some controversy. Some argue that budget deficits affect interest rates, crowding out private purchases. Others argue that budget deficits lead to trade deficits, affecting exchange rates and private purchases of foreign and domestic goods and services. Some point out that government debt means increased interest payments and thus a flow of funds out of the country if the debt is owned by foreigners. Still others claim that the national debt is just money we owe to ourselves and thus has no effect on the economy.

5. How is fiscal policy determined?
Fiscal policy is the responsibility of the executive and legislative branches of the U.S. government. The process is wrapped up in the budget, which involves an annual determination of programs and items that the government pays for, and the financing of those expenditures.

6. What is the twin deficits problem?
The twin deficits are the government budget deficit and the trade deficit. Both grew rapidly during the 1980s in the United States. Many people argued that the two were inextricably linked, that the budget deficit caused the trade deficit.

7. How do other countries carry out fiscal policy?
Fiscal policy varies from country to country depending on the type of economy and level of development of the country. The industrial or developed economies have tended to experience increased government sectors in the last four or five decades, but the growth has been very small compared to the influence of the government sector in the less developed countries. Government accounts for a much larger proportion of total investment in developing countries than in the industrial countries. The types of taxes countries use to finance their expenditures also vary according to development level. Industrial nations tend to rely more on income and social security taxes while the less developed countries rely more on tariffs and on export and import taxes.

▼
Key Terms

recessionary gap   280

Ricardian equivalence   284

monetization   286

national debt   293

twin deficits   295

discretionary fiscal policy   296

nondiscretionary fiscal policy   296

off-budget spending   298

▼
Problems and Exercises

1.   In 1776 Adam Smith said, "What is prudence in the conduct of every private family can scarce be folly in that of a great kingdom." Does this quotation apply to the U.S. government budget?

2.   The Fed is not required by law to monetize the deficit. If the Fed buys outstanding debt rather than newly issued debt of the Treasury, is the debt still monetized?

3.   Comment on this statement: "All deficits are not alike even when they are the same size because it makes a big difference how each deficit is financed."

4.   In an article in the *Wall Street Journal* dated July 21, 1981, David Meiselman stated, "The conventional wisdom holds that budget deficits are a major cause of inflation. . . . Contrary to these widely and deeply held beliefs, the evidence is that there is little, if any, direct historical connection between deficits and inflation." Can Meiselman's claim be explained in terms of the *AD–AS* model? How about in terms of the *IS–LM–BOP* model under fixed exchange rates? Under flexible exchange rates?

5.   Between 1941 and 1951, there was a more or less automatic association between the Federal Reserve System open-market purchase and Treasury borrowing. The agreement between the Fed and the Treasury was made so that the interest rate on government bonds would remain constant. Analyze the macroeconomic implication of this agreement today.

6.   Is the government debt a burden?

7.   Discuss the crowding-out issue using the *IS–LM–BOP* model (under fixed and flexible exchange rate systems) and the *AD–AS* model.

8.   Using the *IS–LM–BOP* model and the *AD–AS* model, explain what Ricardian equivalence means.

Chapter 13

Macroeconomic Policy in an Open Economy

What to Expect

During the last half of 1990, the U.S. economy was teetering near the brink of recession. The value of the dollar was falling, domestic interest rates were rising, Congress had hammered out a government budget that increased taxes and reduced the budget deficit, the trade deficit remained near record high levels, and the flow of foreign capital into the United States had declined. In August 1990, Saddam Hussein's Iraqi forces invaded Kuwait and perched on the borders of Saudi Arabia. The United States sent 500,000 soldiers to the U.N. campaign against Iraq. Oil prices jumped from $27 per barrel to $42 per barrel. The U.S. economy fell into recession. What should U.S. policymakers have done? In such situations, should they worry about the exchange rate, the recession, or future inflation? If they try to support the value of the dollar, what will happen to the domestic economy? Will other countries be affected by U.S. policies, and will they act to offset the U.S. policies?

This chapter considers macroeconomic policy in the context of an open economy and discusses recent events and their impacts on the economy. The following questions are considered:

1. How does a nation's exchange rate regime affect its AD curve?

306

2. How effective are fiscal and monetary policies under fixed versus flexible exchange rates?

3. How do open economies adjust to demand and supply shocks?

4. Should macroeconomic policies be coordinated among nations?

▼
Aggregate Demand

Let's begin by reviewing some aspects of the theory of economic policy in a global context. We'll then look at some realities of policymaking. The economy behaves differently depending on whether it is a closed or open economy. If open, it behaves differently depending on whether it has a fixed or floating exchange rate system. With a closed economy, monetary and fiscal policy are effective in shifting the aggregate demand curve (unless stymied by a liquidity trap or offset by Ricardian equivalence). In an open economy, the effects of monetary and fiscal policy changes differ according to whether the exchange rate system is fixed or flexible.

The Slope of the AD Curve

Recall that the slope or steepness of the aggregate demand curve depends on the size of the wealth, international trade, and interest rate effects. Suppose we lower the price of domestic goods, P, say from P_0 to P_1. What are the effects on aggregate spending? First, a reduction in the price of domestic goods increases real wealth so consumption rises. This is the wealth effect. Second, the increase in real money balances, M/P, causes a decrease in interest rates so investment rises. This is the interest rate effect. And third, at a given level of the exchange rate, a reduction in domestic prices raises the relative price of foreign goods in terms of domestic goods, enhancing the price competitiveness of domestic goods relative to foreign goods in international markets and switching demand toward domestic goods. This is the international trade effect. These three effects trace out the *AD* curve AD_1 in Figure 13-1 as the movement from *a* to *b*.

The international trade effect behaves differently under fixed exchange rates from the way it behaves under flexible exchange rates. In a fixed exchange rate system, a fall in the price of domestic goods tends to reduce demand for foreign goods and services and to raise quantity demanded of domestic goods and services. Like a devaluation, this effect operates by affecting the price of foreign goods relative to domestic goods. Under flexible exchange rates, point *b* in Figure 13-1 cannot be an equilibrium. Before the economy ever reaches that point, other changes occur. As domestic real money balances increase, a reduction in domestic interest rates relative to world interest rates immediately

FIGURE 13-1   *The AD curve. The slope or steepness of the aggregate demand curve depends on the size of the wealth, international trade, and interest rate effects. First, a fall in the price of domestic goods from P_0 to P_1 increases real wealth so consumption rises. Second, the rise in real money balances reduces interest rates so investment rises. And third, at a given level of the exchange rate, a fall in domestic prices enhances the price competitiveness of domestic goods relative to foreign goods in international markets and switches demand toward domestic goods. These three effects trace out the AD curve AD_1 as the move from a to b. Under flexible exchange rates, the drop in domestic interest rates leads to a depreciation of the domestic currency and hence to a further switch of demand toward domestic goods. The resulting AD curve, AD_2, goes through points a and c.*

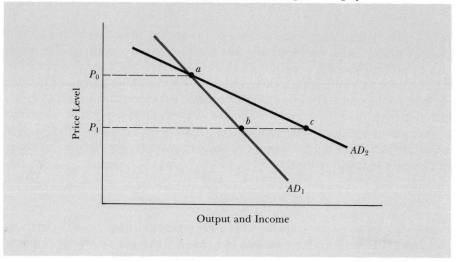

generates capital outflows that cause a domestic currency depreciation. The exchange rate increase (depreciation means more domestic currency per unit of foreign currency, or an increase in the exchange rate) makes domestic goods less expensive relative to foreign goods and increases aggregate expenditures until point *c* is reached. At that point, the domestic interest rate equals the world interest rate, and consequently no further capital flight and no subsequent changes in the exchange rate ensue. The adjustment in spending from point *a* to point *c* takes into account both (1) the direct effects of the decrease in the price of domestic goods on domestic spending and (2) the effects of the associated depreciation of the domestic currency. The effect on spending of a domestic price change is thus greater under flexible than under fixed exchange rates.

The *AD* curve is flatter under flexible exchange rates than it is under fixed exchange rates. You can see in Figure 13-2 that a flatter *AD* curve means smaller output and price changes due to a shift in the *AD* curve. Compare the equal horizontal shifts of size *a–b* of curves AD_f and AD_s (subscripts stand for *flat* and *steep*). With AD_f, the new output and price levels are given by point *c*. With AD_s, they are given by point *d*. Clearly, point *d* shows greater changes in both quantity and price than point *c*. So any given demand shock has greater price

FIGURE 13-2   *The* AD *curve and exchange rate regimes. The* AD *curve is flatter under flexible exchange rates than it is under fixed exchange rates. A flatter* AD *curve means smaller output and price changes when the* AD *curve shifts. Compare the equal horizontal shifts of size a–b of curve* AD_f *(flat) and* AD_s *(steep). With* AD_f *the new output and price levels are given by point* c. *With* AD_s, *they are given by point* d. *Clearly, point* d *shows greater changes in quantity and price than point* c. *This means that any given demand shock has greater price effects in the fixed exchange rate regime than in the flexible exchange rate regime.*

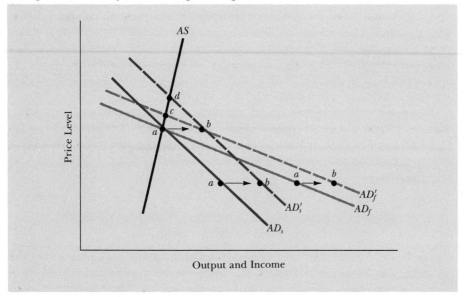

effects in the fixed exchange rate regime than in the flexible exchange rate regime.

Technically, the difference between the two *AD* curves results from what is held constant along the curve. Under fixed exchange rates, the central bank lets the domestic nominal money supply vary, to clear the foreign exchange market while maintaining a given exchange rate. Hence, the *AD* curve assumes a constant exchange rate. Under flexible exchange rates, the exchange rate varies to clear the foreign exchange market. Hence, the *AD* curve assumes a constant domestic nominal money supply.

Monetary Policy and Autonomous Spending Changes Under Fixed Exchange Rates

The aggregate demand curve is derived on the basis of given levels of the money supply, the exchange rate, and fiscal policy parameters. Changes in any of these shifts the aggregate demand curve. The size of the shifts depends on the exchange rate system and the degree of capital mobility.

Consider first the fixed exchange rate system. Suppose that the domestic nominal money supply increases. This increase can arise mainly from two sources: through an open-market purchase of bonds by the central bank or through a net surplus of the current plus capital accounts of the balance of payments. Let's consider an open-market operation. The rise in the nominal money supply increases real money balances, at a given domestic price level. As domestic interest rates decline, investment increases. If there are no international capital flows, the *AD* curve shifts out to the right. However, if capital is very mobile, then when the domestic interest rate falls relative to the rate prevailing in the rest of the world, capital flows out of the country and offsets the money supply change. As a result, the *AD* curve does not shift. As we saw in Chapter 11 with the *IS–LM–BOP* diagram, monetary policy is ineffective under fixed exchange rates with capital mobility.

Changes in autonomous spending, such as an expansionary fiscal policy, shift the *AD* curve. As government spending rises, the BOP position causes foreign exchange to flow in and the domestic money supply to rise. This larger money supply keeps increased government spending from crowding out private spending.

Monetary Policy and Autonomous Spending Changes Under Flexible Exchange Rates

Under flexible exchange rates, changes in the domestic nominal money supply induce shifts of the *AD* curve. For instance, an open-market purchase of bonds by the central bank increases the money supply. The resulting increase in real money balances then pushes down domestic interest rates, inducing capital to flow out of the economy. The domestic currency depreciates as a result. So spending switches out of foreign and into domestic goods, with a resulting increase in spending on domestic goods. In other words, at a given price level desired aggregate spending on domestic goods increases. This corresponds graphically to a shift of the *AD* curve to the right. When the domestic money supply decreases, exactly the opposite occurs: if real balances decline, aggregate demand for domestic goods contracts at any given price of domestic goods. The *AD* curve shifts to the left.

In contrast to monetary disturbances, changes in autonomous spending, such as may arise from fiscal policy changes or an exogenous change in demand for domestic exports, do not induce any shifts in the *AD* curve under the flexible exchange rate system. The increased spending at the same time raises money demand and pushes up domestic interest rates. This is then associated with capital inflows and an appreciation of domestic currency. With the appreciation, both the price competitiveness of domestic products and the trade balance deteriorate. The declining net exports then offset the increased autonomous expenditures, leaving planned aggregate spending on domestic goods unchanged. Under perfect capital mobility, these changes occur instantaneously; the increased autonomous spending does not shift the *AD* curve, it only changes the composition of spending among domestic expenditures and net exports.

▼
Aggregate Demand and Aggregate Supply

Having reviewed the *AD* curve in an open economy, we can now discuss the behavior of the economy in terms of *AD* and *AS*. We'll examine how the economy responds to both demand and supply shocks.

Adjustments to Demand Shocks

The economy's long-run equilibrium occurs when the *AD* curve intersects the short-run and long-run *AS* curves at the same point. In other words, long-run equilibrium occurs when the economy is at its potential output level. The economy is in short-run equilibrium when the quantity demanded of domestic goods is equal to the short-run quantity supplied. This occurs at a point where the aggregate demand curve intersects the short-run aggregate supply curve. The economy's short-run equilibrium level of output can differ from its potential output level if for some reason wages and/or prices don't adjust immediately to *AD* changes.

Let's assume the economy has slipped into a situation where less than potential output is produced and unemployment has risen above the natural rate, represented by point *a* in Figure 13-3. In the presence of unemployment, nominal wage rates tend to decline relative to the price level over time. As labor contracts come up for revision, or as expectations adjust to match reality, or as people learn about the resulting unemployment situation, production costs begin to fall. Lower production costs induce producers to raise output and to pass on some price cuts to consumers. The short-run aggregate supply curve shifts right, from AS_1^{sr} to AS_2^{sr}. The economy moves from *a* to *b*, where the *AD* curve intersects the long-run *AS* curve.

The unemployment at the short-run equilibrium results from real wages that are too high for the potential output level to be attained. The effect of the high real wage is to make domestic real labor costs high, compared with foreign firms, thereby generating domestic production at prices that are not competitive in world markets. The resulting slack demand for domestic goods is then associated with the shortfall of domestic output and employment below the potential level.

As real wages decline over time, real labor costs also decline. Firms cut prices, which raises the international competitiveness of domestic goods. The economy moves to its potential output level at point *b*. The output boom represented by the move from *a* to *b* is led by rising net exports.

FIGURE 13-3   *The adjustment to recession. Assume the economy is producing less than potential output and unemployment is above the natural rate, as represented by point* a. *In the presence of unemployment, real wage rates tend to fall over time, as labor contracts come up for revision, or as expectations adjust to match reality, or as people learn of the unemployment situation. The resulting lower production costs induce producers to raise output and to pass on some price cuts to consumers. The short-run AS curve shifts right, from* AS_1^{sr} *to* AS_2^{sr}. *The economy moves from* a *to* b *where the AD curve intersects the long-run AS curve.*

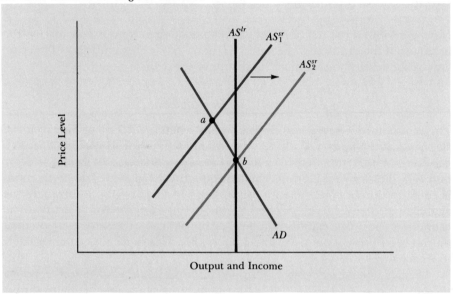

If policymakers are unhappy with the speed of adjustment or with the high levels of unemployment associated with point *a*, they may implement an *AD* policy change. For an aggregate demand policy to have effects on domestic output, it must be able to influence aggregate demand positively. As noted earlier, however, disturbances in the form of changes in autonomous spending, such as fiscal policy disturbances, tend not to be effective in altering aggregate demand under flexible exchange rates and perfect capital mobility. Any positive effects of the increased autonomous spending on aggregate demand are seriously hampered by the negative impact of the spending increase on net exports. With no net effect on domestic spending, real disturbances are powerless to shift aggregate demand, and consequently to increase domestic output, whether in the short run or in the long run.

Monetary disturbances, in contrast, tend to be more successful in altering the aggregate demand curve under flexible exchange rates. Consider the case of an expansionary monetary policy in the form of an open-market purchase of bonds by the central bank. The sudden injection of money into the banking system pushes down domestic interest rates, causing capital to flow out and domestic currency to depreciate. So expenditures switch toward domestic goods, shown by an outward shift of the *AD* curve. The economy moves from its initial equilibrium at point *a* to the equilibrium at point *b* in Figure 13-4.

The short-run output boom induced by the increased money supply is closely linked to declining costs of doing business. With sticky nominal wages during the short run, the inflationary spurt of the monetary expansion reduces real wages. These reduced real labor costs and the resulting stimulus to domestic production are accompanied by greater competitiveness of domestic goods in international markets. This occurs in spite of the rising prices of domestic goods, which by themselves tend to reduce international competitiveness of domestic products. The exchange rate depreciation of the monetary expansion more than offsets the effects of the domestic price hike. The depreciation of domestic currency improves the autonomous trade balance by switching demand away from foreign and toward domestic goods. In conclusion, the short-run expansionary impact of the monetary disturbance is closely linked to falling real wages, which elicits an increase in net exports.

FIGURE 13-4   *Reaction to a monetary disturbance. Monetary disturbances tend to be more successful in altering the aggregate demand curve under flexible exchange rates. The sudden injection of money into the banking system, for example, pushes down domestic interest rates, causing capital to flow out and domestic currency to depreciate. Expenditures switch toward domestic goods, shown by an outward shift of the* AD *curve. The economy moves from its initial equilibrium at point* a *to the equilibrium of point* b.

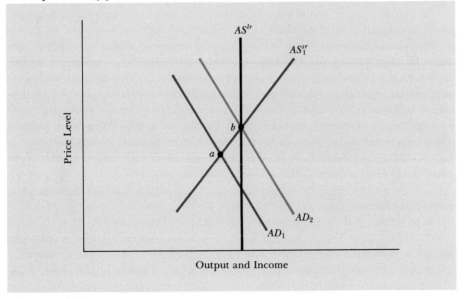

If the *AD* policy is imposed on an economy already at its potential output level, then domestic output and employment rise temporarily but at the cost of domestic inflation. The fall in real wages associated with output above potential output is reversed in the long run. As real wages rise, firms face higher labor costs. At least part of these costs are passed on to consumers as higher prices of domestic goods. This reduces net exports and pushes domestic output back toward its natural unemployment level. The long-run effect of an expansionary monetary policy is inflation.

Adjustment to Supply Shocks

A wide range of disturbances can destabilize an economy, leading to stagnation, unemployment, inflation, or to all these problems combined. When oil prices spiraled upward in 1973–1974, in 1979, and again in 1990, most industrial economies were dramatically affected. In 1973, the price of oil increased from $1.90 per barrel to $9.76 per barrel. In 1979, it rose to nearly $20 per barrel. And in 1990 it reached $42 per barrel. All these price hikes made big dents in the industrial economies.

The immediate impact of the 1973–1974 and 1979 oil price shocks was recession associated with rising inflation rates. The U.S. inflation rate jumped from 5.7 percent in 1973 to 9.3 percent by 1975 and from 8.6 percent in 1979 to 9.4 percent in 1981. The term *stagflation* has been used to characterize these periods, a combination of recession (*stag*nation) and in*flation*. The oil price shock in 1990 again led to more inflation and more unemployment.

In Figure 13-5 the initial equilibrium of the economy at point *a* corresponds to the intersection of the *AD* curve and the short-run and long-run *AS* curves at the potential output level. With a sudden increase in the real cost of raw materials, everything else remaining constant, the short-run aggregate supply curve shifts in. Producers face higher production costs and thus are willing to supply each quantity of domestic goods only if they receive higher prices. The rise in price of imported raw materials increases the prices of domestic goods and reduces domestic output, as shown by the move from point *a* to point *b*. The reduction in domestic output may result from a deterioration in the price competitiveness of domestic goods if domestic prices increase more than the prices in other countries. The output reduction also results from the interest rate and wealth effects. The supply shock reduces output and increases the price level—**stagflation**.

The leftward shift of the aggregate supply curve is associated with rising prices of imported raw materials. Short-run nominal wage rigidity leads to the output and employment effects. The short-run equilibrium of the economy at point *b* is not sustained over time. Given a pool of unemployed workers, as time passes labor contracts are renegotiated and expectations adjusted so that

FIGURE 13-5   *Stagflation. The initial equilibrium of the economy at point* a *corresponds to the potential output level. A sudden increase in the real cost of raw materials (everything else remaining constant) shifts in the short-run AS curve. The higher price of imported raw materials thus raises the prices of domestic goods and reduces domestic output, as shown by the move from point* a *to point* b*. The supply shock reduces output and raises the price level—stagflation. With monetary accommodation, expansionary monetary policy shifts the AD curve to* AD₂.

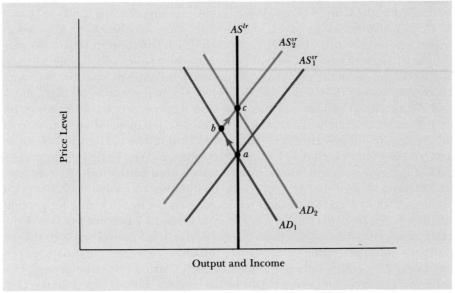

Output and Income

Source: *Economic Report of the President, 1991* (Washington, DC: U.S. Government Printing Office, 1991).

the real wage declines. As production costs decline, some of the increased profits are passed on to consumers as lower prices. The economy automatically begins to return to its potential output level.

Accommodation and Alternative Policies

Suppose the authorities decide to minimize the output and employment effects of the oil price rise. Given the general impotence of autonomous fiscal policy actions followed independently by any single country under flexible exchange rates and in the presence of a high degree of capital mobility, one possibility is to engage in an expansionary monetary policy. An expansion of the domestic money supply shifts the *AD* curve outward. By increasing the money supply, policymakers could move the economy to the potential output level, as shown by the move from *AD₁* to *AD₂* in Figure 13-5. The expansionary monetary policy in reaction to negative supply shocks is called **monetary accommo-**

dation. Monetary accommodation increases domestic inflation while it decreases unemployment. For policymakers committed to controlling inflation, accommodation is undesirable.

Clearly, depending on the specific policies followed by specific countries, different inflation rates surface in the aftermath of a supply shock. Situations may thus arise where inflation declines after the shock. That seems to be what happened to the United States, Japan, and Germany after the 1973–1974 and 1979 oil price shocks. In Japan, the quantity of money had been growing at higher and higher rates from 1971 to early 1973. Inflation in Japan was running at 7.6 percent per year. At that point, monetary policy was sharply reversed so that the growth of the money supply declined. Inflation in Japan, even though increasing during 1974, fell dramatically in 1975. In the second oil price shock of 1979, monetary growth was curtailed from 12.3 percent in the first quarter of 1979 to 8.4 percent by the third quarter of 1980. Japanese inflation rose from 3.7 percent to 7.8 percent from 1979 to 1980 but fell in 1981 and 1982. From 1982 to 1989, it averaged only 1.6 percent per year. In West Germany, the growth rate of the money supply was approximately halved between the first quarter of 1973 and mid-1974. The West German inflation rate equaled 7.8 percent in both 1973 and 1974, but then fell to 6.0 percent in 1975 and 4.2 percent in 1976. Between 1976 and 1979, inflation averaged 3.7 percent per year. Contractionary monetary policy during the 1979 to 1980 period was also drastic and associated with stable West German inflation. West German inflation averaged only 2.2 percent between 1982 and 1989. During this same period, U.S. inflation averaged 4.0 percent. The inflation rates of the United States, Germany, and Japan during the past two decades are shown in Figure 13-6.

The value of the dollar fell relative to the yen and the mark during the 1970s, as is shown in Table 13-1. The dollar depreciated against the yen by 5 percent per year between 1970 and 1979 and by 7 percent per year against the mark. It is widely believed that the increased U.S. oil imports resulting from the oil shocks caused U.S. current account balance deficits and declines in the value of the U.S. dollar. Indeed, an increase in the bill paid on oil imports tends (everything else being constant) to make the importing country's current account deteriorate and its currency depreciate. However, not everything else was held constant. For instance, because the oil price shock was recessionary, domestic income and imports of final goods both shrank. This improved rather than worsened the current account. The U.S. current account had a large surplus in 1975. In addition, even if the current account balance deteriorated significantly as a result of an oil shock, this would not imply any definitive connection with short-run currency depreciation. Over the short run, the exchange rate adjusts to eliminate balance of payments disequilibria, not current account disequilibria. Thus, we must consider how the capital account reacts to a supply shock. There is no clear-cut answer as to how the capital account of any specific oil-importing country is affected because that depends on how the oil

FIGURE 13-6   *Inflation rates during the 1970s and 1980s. The inflation rates of the United States, West Germany, and Japan during the past two decades are shown. During the 1980s, inflation in the United States exceeded that in Germany and Japan.*

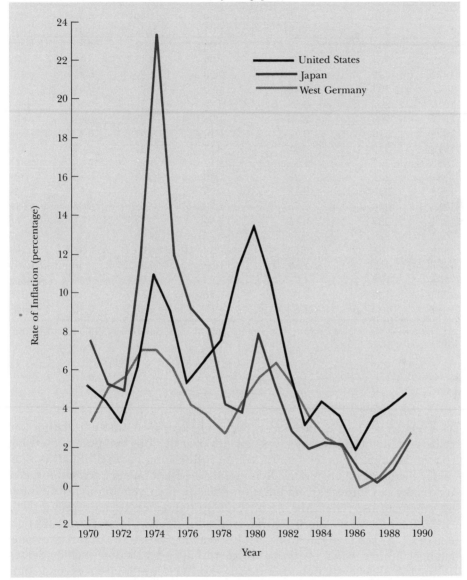

exporters (OPEC) invest their trade surpluses. If OPEC investments in dollars are large enough, the consequent U.S. capital account improvement tends to induce an exchange rate appreciation of the dollar rather than a depreciation.

TABLE 13-1 *Exchange Rates of Selected Countries (currency units per U.S. dollar)*

Year	Japanese Yen	West German Mark	Canadian Dollar	French Franc	British Pound	Italian Lira
1970	358	3.65	1.04	5.53	0.42	627
1971	348	3.48	1.01	5.51	0.41	618
1972	303	3.19	0.99	5.04	0.40	584
1973	271	2.67	1.00	4.45	0.41	582
1974	292	2.59	0.98	4.81	0.41	651
1975	297	2.46	1.02	4.29	0.45	653
1976	297	2.52	0.99	4.78	0.55	834
1977	269	2.32	1.06	4.92	0.57	883
1978	210	2.01	1.14	4.51	0.52	849
1979	219	1.83	1.17	4.26	0.47	831
1980	227	1.82	1.17	4.23	0.43	856
1981	221	2.26	1.20	5.44	0.49	1,139
1982	249	2.43	1.23	6.58	0.57	1,354
1983	238	2.55	1.23	7.62	0.66	1,519
1984	237	2.85	1.30	8.74	0.75	1,756
1985	238	2.94	1.37	8.98	0.77	1,909
1986	168	2.17	1.39	6.93	0.68	1,491
1987	145	1.80	1.33	6.01	0.61	1,297
1988	128	1.76	1.23	5.96	0.56	1,302
1989	138	1.88	1.18	6.38	0.61	1,372
1990	145	1.62	1.17	5.45	0.56	1,198

Source: Economic Report of the President, 1991 (Washington, DC: U.S. Government Printing Office, 1991).

▼

Policy Coordination Issues

The relatively close connection between changes in domestic inflation and changes in domestic money supply growth over the long run points to the key role of national monetary authorities in influencing national inflation rates under flexible exchange rates. By stepping on the monetary accelerator, central banks can impose rising inflation rates on their economies. In the same way, they can also reduce the inflation rate by tightening money supply growth. Given the relative ability of central banks to influence domestic inflation under flexible exchange rates, one can expect wide variability of inflation rates among countries when countries are operating under flexible exchange rates.

In Table 13-2, inflation rates during the 1980s are listed for several countries, along with their monetary growth rates. You can see the connection between the monetary growth rate and the inflation rate. Exchange rate flexibility allows persistent divergences of national inflation rates. Inflation differentials can be sustained because exchange rate changes can offset the changes in international competitiveness implied by such differentials. For example, if domestic inflation exceeds world inflation, a depreciation of domestic currency restores domestic competitiveness in international markets by reducing the foreign currency price of domestic goods. Similarly, if domestic inflation is below world inflation, domestic currency appreciation offsets the relative gain in domestic competitiveness that such a differential implies, avoiding a long-run systematic deterioration of foreign competitiveness. Under floating exchange rates, currencies of countries with relatively high inflation tend to depreciate and currencies of low-inflation countries tend to appreciate.

Vicious Circles

The relative autonomy of monetary policy under flexible exchange rates has prompted the frequent argument that flexible exchange rates eliminate monetary discipline and consequently are more inflationary than fixed exchange rates. Notice the difference between the 1965–1980 period and the 1980–1988 period in Table 13-2. For most countries, the money supply growth and inflation rates are higher in the latter period, a period characterized by flexible exchange rates.

Consider the case when sudden pressure for higher nominal wages in the labor market raises real labor costs and pushes prices up and employment down. With a completely accommodating monetary policy, the central bank will increase the money supply to offset any negative effects of rising prices on real money balances and hence on output. The monetary expansion validates the price increase, however, and is associated with an exchange rate depreciation that sustains domestic competitiveness in international markets and thus employment and output. But rising prices may induce workers to bargain for further nominal wage increases, to sustain their new rise in living standards. Wages and prices continue to rise and the currency depreciates as workers continue to demand nominal wage hikes and monetary authorities validate them through money supply increases. This is called a **vicious circle**.

This vicious circle hypothesis is based on the relative control over the money supply that domestic monetary authorities have under exchange rate flexibility and on the fact that currency depreciation keeps rising prices from destroying domestic competitiveness in international markets. The vicious circle can be sustained only if the monetary authorities create more money to finance the initial increase in nominal wages and prices.

Beggar-Thy-Neighbor Policies

A domestic currency depreciation vis-à-vis a foreign currency represents an appreciation of that foreign currency. Therefore, whatever the impact of domestic currency depreciation on the domestic economy, the foreign currency appreciation might be expected to have the opposite effect on the foreign country concerned. For instance, a domestic monetary expansion leading to increases

TABLE 13-2   *Money Growth and Inflation in Selected Countries*

	Money		Prices	
	Average Annual Nominal Growth Rate (percentage)		Average Annual Rate of Inflation (percentage)	
	1965–1980	*1980–1988*	*1965–1980*	*1980–1988*
Low-Income Economies			8.8%	8.9%
Ethiopia	12.7%	11.9%	3.4	2.1
Tanzania	19.7	21.5	9.9	25.7
Malawi	15.4	17.7	7.2	12.6
Somalia	20.4	42.4	10.3	38.4
Zaire	28.2	59.4	24.5	56.1
Nepal	17.9	19.3	7.8	8.7
Madagascar	12.2	16.3	7.7	17.3
Mali	14.4	12.3	9.3	3.7
Uganda	23.1	77.8	21.2	100.7
Nigeria	28.5	11.9	13.7	11.6
Zambia	12.7	28.9	6.4	33.5
Niger	18.3	6.1	7.5	3.6
China	N.A.	25.9	0.1	4.9
India	15.3	17.0	7.5	7.4
Pakistan	14.7	14.4	10.3	6.5
Kenya	18.6	14.9	7.3	9.6
Central African Rep.	12.7	6.3	8.5	6.7
Haiti	20.3	8.1	7.3	7.9
Ghana	25.9	45.0	22.8	46.1
Sri Lanka	15.4	16.0	9.4	11.0
Indonesia	54.4	23.8	34.2	8.5
Sudan	21.6	28.1	11.5	33.5
Middle-Income Economies			20.4	66.7
Lower-Middle Income			21.7	80.8
Bolivia	24.3	589.2	15.7	482.8
Philippines	17.7	16.1	11.7	15.6
Senegal	15.6	7.6	6.5	8.1
Egypt, Arab Rep.	17.7	22.2	7.3	10.6
Morocco	15.7	14.5	6.0	7.7
Honduras	14.8	11.7	5.6	4.7
Guatemala	16.3	14.7	7.1	13.3
Congo, People's Rep.	14.2	8.6	6.7	0.8
El Salvador	14.3	17.1	7.0	16.8
Thailand	17.9	18.0	6.3	3.1
Cameroon	19.1	10.8	8.9	7.0
Jamaica	17.2	25.9	12.8	18.7
Ecuador	22.6	31.8	10.9	31.2
Paraguay	21.3	20.0	9.4	22.1

(continued)

TABLE 13-2   *Money Growth and Inflation in Selected Countries   (continued)*

	Money		Prices	
	Average Annual Nominal Growth Rate (percentage)		Average Annual Rate of Inflation (percentage)	
	1965–1980	*1980–1988*	*1965–1980*	*1980–1988*
Turkey	27.5	50.3	20.7	39.3
Peru	25.9	100.8	20.5	119.1
Syrian Arab Rep.	21.9	19.8	8.3	12.9
Costa Rica	24.6	26.7	11.3	26.9
Mexico	21.9	62.6	13.0	73.8
Malaysia	21.5	13.0	4.9	1.3
Upper-Middle Income			18.9	45.0
South Africa	14.0	15.8	10.1	13.9
Algeria	22.3	17.5	10.5	4.4
Uruguay	65.8	57.1	57.8	57.0
Argentina	86.0	284.0	78.2	290.5
Yugoslavia	25.7	67.0	15.3	66.9
Venezuela	22.3	16.4	10.4	13.0
Korea, Rep. of	35.5	19.5	18.7	5.0
Portugal	19.5	21.4	11.7	20.1
Greece	21.4	25.1	10.5	18.9
Libya	29.2	2.1	15.4	0.1
High-Income Economies			7.9	4.9
Saudi Arabia	32.1	9.4	17.2	− 4.2
Spain	19.7	9.7	12.3	10.1
Ireland	16.1	6.0	12.0	8.0
Israel	52.7	137.9	25.2	136.6
Singapore	17.6	12.1	4.9	1.2
Australia	13.1	12.7	9.3	7.8
United Kingdom	13.8	13.2	11.1	5.7
Italy	18.0	12.2	11.4	11.0
Kuwait	17.8	5.3	16.4	− 3.9
Netherlands	14.7	5.8	7.5	2.0
Austria	13.3	7.3	6.0	4.0
France	15.0	9.9	8.4	7.1
Canada	15.3	7.8	7.1	4.6
Denmark	11.5	15.6	9.3	6.3
Germany, Fed. Rep.	10.1	5.7	5.2	2.8
Sweden	10.7	10.7	8.0	7.5
United States	9.2	9.3	6.5	4.0
Japan	17.2	8.8	7.7	1.3
Switzerland	7.1	8.0	5.3	3.8

Source: World Bank, *World Development Report 1990* (New York: Oxford University Press, 1990), Tables 1, 13, pp. 178–179, 202–203.

in nominal and real exchange rates raises aggregate demand by improving the trade balance. At the same time, this policy implies that the foreign countries whose currencies appreciate face deteriorating net exports and a contraction of aggregate demand. So expansionary domestic monetary policy can be seen as a **beggar-thy-neighbor policy**: it raises domestic real income, even if only temporarily, at the expense of reducing real income abroad. International policy conflicts arise from currency-depreciating policies under flexible exchange rates, just as such conflicts emerge from devaluation under fixed exchange rates.

In a world of unemployment and recession, countries may undertake domestic money supply expansions intended to raise domestic output by exporting the unemployment abroad. Similarly, in a world of inflationary pressures, countries that tighten the growth rates of their money supplies may be able to reduce their inflation rate by transmitting it to other countries. A domestic monetary contraction, for example, lowers domestic prices but, at the same time, tends to appreciate domestic currency, implying foreign currency depreciation. Even though such depreciation may be associated with a short-run improvement in net exports and output abroad, it may also raise foreign prices.

The drastic appreciation of the U.S. dollar vis-à-vis major European currencies in the early 1980s (see Table 13-1) shows the acute interdependence of countries under floating exchange rates. Even though the dollar appreciation led to increased U.S. imports from Europe, its impact on European inflation seems to have been significant. French finance ministry officials, for example, have estimated that the appreciation of the dollar added approximately 1 percent to French retail prices during 1983.

Bubbles and an Overvalued Dollar

Exchange rate changes can dramatically affect economies. If those changes don't reflect fundamental differences in inflation rates and interest rates among countries, then the exchange rate change can act much like a demand shock. A situation in which a given economic variable progressively or cumulatively deviates from the path consistent with its fundamental long-run equilibrium, or PPP value, is called a **bubble**. In the foreign exchange market, a bubble may cause a currency to remain overvalued or undervalued; that is, to remain above or below its fundamental long-run value for extended periods of time. Many people ascribe the U.S. dollar appreciation of 1980–1985 to an exchange rate bubble. This bubble increased aggregate demand in countries other than the United States and, as noted earlier, led to more inflation in these other countries.

The most frequent explanation of exchange rate bubbles is an imperfect or costly information argument similar to the rationale for sticky real wage rates or prices. For example, unfounded rumors may generate a belief that the dollar will soon change drastically in value. As these rumors spread among investors in the foreign exchange market, much as fads and fashions spread, they strongly influence exchange rate expectations and, as a result, the behavior of the exchange rate. In the same way fashions change and misperceptions are corrected, eventually the bubble bursts and the exchange rate returns to its fundamental value—but it might take a long time to eliminate the speculative effects.

A second explanation of bubbles assumes that people form rational expectations about the future (basing their anticipations on all the information currently available about the fundamental determinants of future exchange rates and about the structure of the foreign exchange market). The bubble is explained in the following terms. When a disturbance, such as a contractionary monetary policy, changes the exchange rate in a given direction (say a currency appreciation), people must decide whether the movement will continue or not. As new investors enter the market expecting that the original exchange rate movement will continue, the movement becomes self-sustained, leading to a persistent exchange rate deviation from its fundamental long-run, or PPP, value. For example, if increasing numbers of investors and speculators jump on the bandwagon of an expected dollar appreciation, the sustained capital inflows maintain the exchange rate appreciation. In this explanation, the bubble is known as a **rational bubble**. Participants in the market are not relying on rumors in predicting that the original disturbance will provoke an exchange rate movement. They just don't know how much movement there will be.

The presence of bubbles underlies the fact that the exchange rate does not always move toward its long-run value; instead, it often deviates and remains away from the long-run value for long periods of time. Why should we be concerned about such deviations? The reason is that given the path of policy variables, an exchange rate bubble has real effects on competitiveness, inflation, and employment. The bubble can represent a macroeconomic shock.

Policy Coordination and Strategic Behavior

Vicious circles, beggar-thy-neighbor policies, and exchange rate bubbles have focused a great deal of attention on the need for governments to implement economic **policy coordination**. The 1980–1985 appreciation of the U.S. dollar greatly concerned the United States and other nations. After 1981, while U.S. fiscal policy had become expansionary, that in Germany and Japan had become contractionary. The U.S. current account widened while the value of the dollar rose strongly, as shown in Figure 13-7 with the yen–dollar exchange rate. Because U.S. inflation was running over 4 percent per year while Japan's was less than 2 percent per year, the dollar rose nearly 50 percent in real terms relative to the yen. In 1984, interest rate differentials between the United States and other countries narrowed, yet still the dollar rose.

Other countries, while complaining to the United States about the inflationary consequences for them of the dollar's rise, were nevertheless quite happy to accept the favorable effects on their export industries. However, as the conviction grew that the dollar was too high, policymakers became interested in

FIGURE 13-7 *The value of the U.S. dollar. The dollar kept on falling in the mid-1980s. Squabbling among the Plaza partners grew louder. The United States blamed Japan and West Germany for the continuing drop: their economies were growing too slowly to absorb the increased U.S. exports needed to shrink the U.S. trade gap and hence to ease pressure on the dollar. Unless they did more, the United States threatened to let the dollar crash. Japan and Germany blamed U.S. fiscal policy and its large budget deficits. Attempts at coordination continued with more meetings and pacts among the G7 countries. The era of coordination died with the stock market crashes of October 1987.*

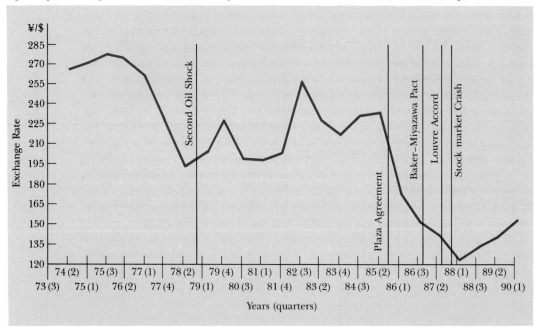

an orderly decline of the dollar. They wanted to avoid a free-falling dollar that would chase the other economies into recession.

Calls for coordination grew, but coordination is not a simple matter. Macroeconomic policymaking in the world economy can be thought of in much the same way that the market structure of oligopoly is analyzed. In an oligopoly, each firm is affected by what its competitors do; each firm must take into account the responses of its competitors to any action. This is called **strategic behavior**. Strategic behavior characterizes oligopoly and may characterize the behavior of policymakers in a world economy. Policy actions undertaken by Germany have different consequences depending on how the United States, Japan, and the United Kingdom respond.

Each country takes into account and reacts to what its rivals are doing. Anything can occur; rivalry may be very intense, or means may be devised to "live and let live." Because of the great variety of behavior possible under oligopoly, no single explanation of behavior is always appropriate. In an attempt to better understand strategic behavior, economists and mathematicians have relied on the theory of games. The name *game theory* describes a behavioral model that requires participants to assess potential gains and losses from all possible strategies by all participants in some activity, to ascertain the most likely combinations of choices and outcomes.

There are many different types of games. The two most commonly discussed types of games are cooperative and noncooperative. A simple game known as the *prisoners' dilemma* can illustrate how the theory of games works. Two people have been arrested for a crime but the evidence against them is weak. Unless they confess, the criminals will be cleared of all but a minor charge and will serve only two days in jail. If either of them confesses, however, conviction of a felony is guaranteed and a sentence of no less than ten years will result. The options are shown in Figure 13-8.

The police keep the prisoners separated and offer each a special deal. The deal says that if one prisoner confesses, that prisoner can go free as long as only he or she confesses, and the other prisoner will get ten or more years in prison. The police say that if both prisoners confess, each will receive a reduced sentence of two years in jail. What will the prisoners do?

Let's say you are prisoner B. You can (1) confess and either go free or serve two years or (2) not confess and serve either two days or ten years. Because you don't know what prisoner A will do, you must think in terms of a strategy.

FIGURE 13-8   *The prisoners' dilemma. The police keep the prisoners separated and offer each a special deal. If one prisoner confesses, that prisoner can go free as long as only he or she confesses; the other prisoner gets ten or more years in prison. If both prisoners confess, each receives a reduced sentence of two years in jail.*

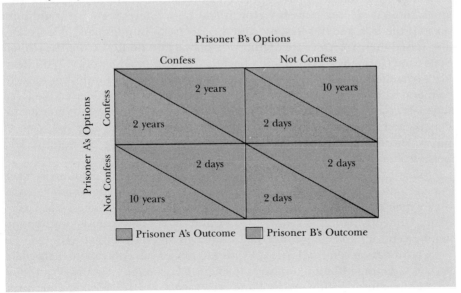

If you confess, A's best choice is to confess as well. If you don't confess, A's best choice is to confess. Thus, A will surely confess, and so you must confess as well.

Both prisoners confess, and both serve two-year sentences. If the prisoners had been loyal to each other, each would have received a much smaller penalty. Because both chose to confess, each is worse off than would have been the case if each had known what the other was doing.

The prisoners' dilemma is an example of what is called a **noncooperative game**. It could represent the case where the United States and Japan want to implement certain macroeconomic policies that might be detrimental to the other. The parties all lose, compared to what they would have achieved had they cooperated. A **cooperative game** is the case where the countries form their policies jointly, in consultation with each other. Such would be the case if the prisoners could meet and agree to a policy — not to confess. Each would be better off as a result of the cooperation.

Policy coordination issues arose in conjunction with the debates over fixed and flexible exchange rates. As we have seen, there are advantages and disadvantages to flexible exchange rates. On the one hand, the flexibility of the exchange rate allows the central bank more independence to use monetary policy to stabilize prices and output when the economy is shocked out of long-run equilibrium. Because the structures of different economies vary, the appropriate response of the central banks to shocks may differ. On the other hand, large swings in the exchange rates, due either to demand disturbances or to speculative activity in the financial markets, can destabilize exports and thus increase both internal and external volatility.

Coordinated economic policies under fixed exchange rates seem almost to be a given. If the Bank of Japan faced an inflation rate it thought excessive and wanted to decrease money growth and raise interest rates, it could only do so if the U.S. Federal Reserve and the Deutsche Bundesbank of Germany also raised their interest rates. Otherwise, money would flow from the United States and Germany to Japan and offset the Bank of Japan's policy. With flexible exchange rates, it was believed that the governments would not have to cooperate; they could pursue their policies independently. However, the large fluctuations in exchange rates and net exports of the 1980s showed interdependencies among nations even under flexible exchange rates, and the issue of policy coordination arose as a principal concern among economists and policymakers.

Since 1975, officials of the Group of Seven (G7) industrial countries have met periodically to examine world macroeconomic developments and to coordinate their policies. The group of seven includes the United States, Japan, Germany, United Kingdom, France, Canada, and Italy. The greatest coordination among central banks has concerned exchange market intervention.

Coordination can take several forms. Countries can coordinate their goals, such as targeting inflation or unemployment, for example. They also can coordinate their information, exchanging forecasts of key macroeconomic variables based on their economic plans. Finally, they can coordinate the policymaking and implementing processes. The potential gains of coordination are a product of the form that the coordination takes.

Setting joint goals can induce policy changes that make those goals attainable. For example, let's say that all countries set a goal of reducing the unemployment rate. To meet that goal, the countries must set expansionary monetary policies. Even if the countries don't explicitly discuss their future policies, the goals they set guide those policies. Of course, this assumes that policymakers target the agreed-on goals when they formulate their domestic economic policy.

Information on the current state of the economy and forecasts of future changes can be coordinated both informally and through formal meetings of key policymakers. Central bank and treasury staff members may regularly talk to compare notes on the world economy.

Coordination of the policymaking process offers the hope of making every country better off. For instance, in the mid-1980s the United States had a large international trade deficit, while Japan and West Germany had trade surpluses. At several international conferences, leading policymakers proposed that the United States reduce its federal budget deficit to reduce domestic spending and improve its international balance of trade. Simultaneously, Japan and West Germany were urged to increase their federal budget deficits and to stimulate spending, to increase their imports from the United States. Similarly, if U.S. expansionary policies could be coordinated with expansionary policies in other large countries, so that incomes rise in all the countries simultaneously, the balance of trade might not change, even though all the countries are increasing their national income. This is a potential benefit of international cooperation: by acting together, nations can achieve better outcomes than if they act individually.

It would seem that international coordination of macroeconomic policy makes a great deal of sense, that countries can only gain from coordination. In reality, this conclusion is not so obvious. In practice, several problems stand in the way of designing and implementing economic policy across countries and may make coordination worse than noncooperation. First, countries may not agree on goals. Some countries may try to exploit the short-run tradeoff between inflation and the unemployment rate, while other countries follow passive policies, refusing to manipulate aggregate demand.

Second, the national leaders may not agree on current economic conditions. Policymakers cannot always be sure whether the economy is expanding or contracting, so they may disagree on an appropriate course of action simply because they don't agree on current economic conditions. For instance, in mid-1991, U.S. policymakers weren't sure whether the economy was still contracting or was beginning to come out of its recession. Had the United States led the major developed countries in a coordinated effort to expand aggregate demand, international policy would have turned out to be almost the opposite of what was needed. The economies would have been expanding by the time the policy initiatives took effect, and thus the additional stimulation may have brought on rapid inflation.

Since 1985 there has been some *de facto* coordination of monetary policy. Japan, for example, raised interest rates, and large-scale interventions were not entirely sterilized in their effect on domestic monetary conditions in 1985–1986. After about a year of a falling dollar, the consensus that the dollar should go lower gave out. In the Plaza agreement, Japan and the United States agreed that the dollar had fallen far enough and that the two governments would start to concern themselves more with currency stability than with driving the dollar down.

As shown in Figure 13-7, the dollar kept on falling. Public squabbling among the Plaza partners grew louder. The United States, willing to agree that the dollar had fallen far enough, blamed Japan and West Germany for the continuing drop: their economies were growing too slowly to absorb the rise in U.S. exports needed to shrink the trade gap and hence to ease the pressure on the dollar. Unless they did more, the United States threatened to let the dollar crash. Japan and West Germany blamed U.S. fiscal policy and its large budget deficits. This clearly was a noncooperative game.

The quarrels continued until February 1987 when a spirit of cooperation was revived with the Louvre accord. The G7 affirmed that the dollar's value was about right. In 1987, the G7 countries intervened on a large scale, spending roughly $100 billion to prop up the dollar. In June 1987, the G7 met in Venice and affirmed the Louvre agreement. They asked the IMF to monitor country-by-country developments in several economic measures, presumably to provide an early warning of incompatibilities.

In October 1987, stock market crashes in most industrial nations removed the aura of coordination. Since then, little coordination has occurred. Although economic summits continue, the gap between the promises made by ministers at international gatherings and the ministers' ability to follow through makes coordination unlikely. For instance, the promises of the U.S. finance minister (the secretary of the U.S. Treasury) mean little to nothing. The secretary has almost no control of either fiscal or monetary policy. The other finance ministers know this and therefore don't expect the United States to carry out the secretary's promises.

Although policy coordination may be worthwhile, the gains may not be large relative to the gains that can be made by designing policies in a noncooperative framework with improved information exchanges. Policymakers may prefer not to cooperate if they feel that other countries won't stick to their part of the bargain, or if they think potential errors in the information or external shocks would invalidate their calculations, or if they think they may have miscalculated the priorities of other policymakers. However, the prisoner's dilemma need not occur if information flows relatively quickly from one economy to another.

▼   ▼   ▼   ▼   ▼   ▼   ▼   ▼   ▼   ▼   ▼
Conclusions

The theory of economic policy is difficult enough when considering just a closed economy. The control over the money supply and the use of spending and taxing authority are neither straightforward nor easily carried out. In an open economy, several other issues further confound the problem. The flow of foreign exchange alters the theoretical effectiveness of monetary and fiscal policy, depending on whether countries are operating under fixed or flexible exchange rate systems. In addition, coordination (or lack thereof) of countries in formulating and implementing policies requires that the nations consider how other nations behave and react to policy initiatives. Attempts at coordination have not proven entirely successful. Much as we would predict from studying cartels, there are incentives to cheat on any coordination agreement and so coordination agreements tend to collapse. Economists have described global policymaking as a game.

Although in this and the previous two chapters we have made considerable progress in describing and understanding policymaking in the real world, considerable work remains. We must discover why policymakers make the decisions they do. In addition, there are refinements to the theory such as more complicated consumption or investment behavior, that need to be examined. The remaining chapters are devoted to these issues

▼   ▼   ▼   ▼   ▼   ▼   ▼   ▼   ▼   ▼   ▼
Summary

1. How does a nation's exchange rate regime affect its AD curve?
The *AD* curve is steeper under fixed exchange rates than under flexible exchange rates. With flexible exchange rates, the real domestic money supply varies with changes in the domestic price level. This leads to changes in domestic interest rates and therefore in the exchange rate — generating changes in expenditures that don't occur under fixed exchange rates.
2. How effective are fiscal and monetary policies under fixed versus flexible exchange rates?
Under fixed exchange rates, monetary policy tends to be ineffective as international capital flows offset the money supply change. Fiscal policy tends to be more effective. Under flexible exchange rates, monetary policy tends to be effective because the central bank controls the money supply. Fiscal policy, however, tends to be ineffective, as increased spending leads to higher domestic interest rates and therefore appreciation of the domestic currency — which results in lower net exports.
3. How do open economies adjust to demand and supply shocks?
The impact of demand and supply shocks depends on the exchange rate system the country operates with as well as on the structure of the economy — which determines the speeds at which wages and prices adjust.
4. Should macroeconomic policies be coordinated among nations?
Policy coordination is complicated; even if coordination would prove beneficial

theoretically, practically speaking each country puts its own welfare first. Because coordination means putting each country's individual welfare *below* that of the world as a whole, it is unrealistic to expect countries to coordinate their economic policies.

▼
Key Terms

stagflation 314
monetary accommodation 315
vicious circle 319
beggar-thy-neighbor policy 322
bubble 322

rational bubble 323
policy coordination 323
strategic behavior 324
noncooperative game 326
cooperative game 326

▼
Problems and Exercises

1. Describe how the *AD* curve is affected by a money supply increase and then by a government spending increase under fixed and flexible exchange rates.
2. Derive the *AD* curve from the *IS–LM–BOP* diagram, using first fixed and then flexible exchange rates.
3. What are the wealth, interest rate, and international trade effects?
4. Assume you are minister of finance of a small open economy facing the ever-growing trade deficits of the United States. How would you protect your economy from the negative effects resulting from the U.S. deficits?
5. Describe the conditions under which policy coordination does and doesn't make sense for a small open economy and for a large open economy.

Part Five

Cycles and Growth

Chapter 14

Economic Growth

What to Expect

Although much of macroeconomics is aimed at understanding business cycles, remember that most economies grow over time. Moreover, different rates of growth can lead to vastly different living standards. Over the decade of the 1980s, the industrial countries had an average annual growth rate of 3 percent. Over the same time period, the average annual growth rate for developing countries was 4.3 percent. This difference might seem quite insignificant, but it isn't. It takes 24 years for GNP to double at a 3 percent annual rate but only 16.7 years to double at a 4.3 percent rate.[1] More dramatically, during the 1970s Japan grew at a 6.5 percent rate while the United States grew at only 2.4 percent; had these rates continued, Japan's economy would have doubled in 11 years while it would have taken the U.S. economy 30 years to double.

What accounts for the differences in growth rates? Are the workers in industrial nations less motivated and productive than in the developing nations? Do the developing nations have more resources than the industrial nations?

---

1   This is called the law of 72. Dividing the growth rate into 72 yields the number of years it takes for the base to double.

Are Japanese workers more diligent or more highly motivated than U.S. workers? Do Japanese students study more than U.S. students? Are Japanese firms
more concerned with developing new products and new production techniques
than U.S. firms? Are Japanese monetary and fiscal policies more conducive to
growth than U.S. policies? Are the developing nations' policies more conducive
to growth than those of the industrial nations?

This chapter discusses economic growth, examines the determinants of
growth, and looks at factors that differ from one country to another. The
following questions are considered:

1. *What is economic growth?*

2. *What factors contribute to economic growth?*

3. *What policies affect economic growth?*

▼
What Is Economic Growth?

Economic growth is an increase in real income, measured as the year-to-year
percentage change in real GNP or real GDP. In the *AD–AS* diagram, economic
growth is shown as a series of outward shifts of the AS^{lr} curve, while business
cycles are shown as shifts of *AD* and AS^{sr} about the potential output level, AS^{lr}.
These are shown as panels A and B of Figure 14-1. Panel C shows the dynamic
illustration of panels A and B. The cycles are shown as the deviations or movements about the long-term trend line; the growth is shown as the upward slope
of the trend line.

Growth and Per Capita Income

Table 14-1 shows GDP growth rates for several countries during the period
1965–1988. The countries listed have rates of growth that range from a low
for West Germany of 2.6 percent to a high of 9.7 percent for South Korea. A
country can have a positive growth in real GNP or GDP and yet generate less
output per person because the population is growing faster than output. If economic growth is defined as a rising per capita real GNP or per capita real GDP,
then growth only occurs when a nation's output of goods and services increases
more than its population. The second column of Table 14-1 shows per capita
growth rates.

During the 1980s, per capita real GDP grew at an average annual rate of
2.3 percent in developing countries and 2.5 percent in industrial countries.
Population growth rates are considerably higher in developing countries than

FIGURE 14-1   *Economic growth. Economic growth means that the potential output of the economy rises, as illustrated by a series of outward shifts of the long-run aggregate supply curve.*

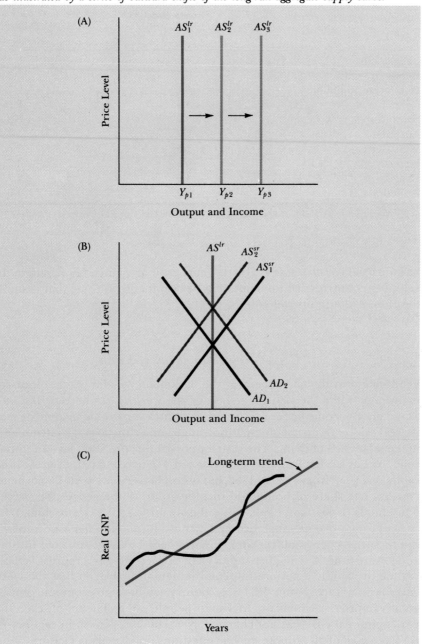

TABLE 14-1   *GDP Growth Rates*

Country	Average Annual Growth Rate (1965–1988)	Average Annual Per Capita Growth Rate (1965–1988)
Bangladesh	3.1%	0.4%
India	4.4	1.8
Dominican Republic	5.1	2.7
Colombia	4.6	2.4
South Korea	9.7	6.8
Australia	3.7	1.7
West Germany	2.6	2.5
Japan	5.3	4.3
Canada	4.2	2.7
United States	3.0	1.6

Source: World Bank, *World Development Report 1990* (New York: Oxford University Press, 1990), pp. 179–181.

in industrial countries, so real GDP must grow at a much faster rate in the developing countries just to maintain a per capita growth rate that is similar to the rate in the industrial countries.

Growth and Standards of Living

Economic growth can proceed at the national level and yet the poor can remain poor while the rich get richer, or the wealthy can become less wealthy as the poor become better off. An increase in real national income or per capita real national income doesn't indicate whether the average citizen enjoys a higher standard of living. The distribution of income also plays an important role. Sri Lanka, for instance, experienced a 3 percent rate of growth of per capita real GDP from 1970 to 1980, but not all households in Sri Lanka benefited equally. The share of household income going to the poorest 80 percent of households in Sri Lanka fell, while the wealthiest 20 percent gained.

Per capita real national income says nothing about other aspects of quality of life, such as personal freedom, environmental quality, spiritual fulfillment, and leisure time. A rising per capita GDP can accompany a repressive political regime or rapidly deteriorating environmental quality, so that the country's citizens do not feel better off. Or, a country can have no economic growth but greatly improve its quality of life, so its people can feel better off even though per capita real GDP has not changed. Nevertheless, growth in real per capita GNP is a goal of all economies. The questions policymakers face are "What determines growth?" and "What policies can be used to ensure maximum economic growth?"

▼
Determinants of Growth and Supply-Side Policies

The long-run aggregate supply curve is a vertical line at the potential level of national output, Y_p. Economic growth means that the potential output of the economy rises, as illustrated by a series of outward shifts of the long-run AS curve in Figure 14-1A.

The AS curve is derived, you may recall, from the total product curve of panel A and the labor market of panel B in Figure 14-2. The TP curve is drawn by fixing all resources but labor, and then varying the quantity of labor. A change in the quantity or quality of the fixed resources then shifts the total product curve, as shown by the move from TP_1 to TP_2 in panel A. As a result, the AS^{lr} curve shifts out, as shown in panel C. The greater the growth rate, the farther the AS curve shifts to the right. Thus, the determinants of economic growth also shift the long-run AS curve. These factors include the growth of the quantity and quality of resources and technology.

Labor

Economic growth depends on changes in the size and quality of the labor force. The size of the labor force depends on (1) the size of the working-age population and (2) the fraction of the working-age population that participates in the labor force. The labor force typically grows more rapidly in developing countries than in industrial countries because birthrates are higher in the developing countries. Figure 14-3 shows actual and predicted population growth rates for several countries as well as average growth rates for all low-income, all middle-income, and all industrial countries. The World Bank defines low-income countries as those with a 1988 GNP per capita of $545 or less. Middle-income countries had a 1988 GNP per capita of more than $545 but less than $6,000. Both low- and middle-income countries are often referred to as *developing countries*. Industrial countries had a 1988 GNP per capita of at least $6,000, but not all countries at that income level are considered industrial. Over the 1980s, the average annual growth rate of the population was 2 percent in low-income countries, 2.2 percent in middle-income countries, and 0.6 percent in industrial countries. The World Bank forecasts that population growth will be 1.9 percent per year for the low-income countries, 1.9 percent for the middle-income countries, and 0.5 percent for the industrial countries until the year 2000.

Considering only population growth, it would seem that developing countries could grow faster than the industrial countries. Population growth means that the labor supply curve and thus the AS^{lr} curve shift out, as shown in panels B and C of Figure 14-4. But labor force quantity is not the only factor that affects production of goods and services; the productivity of that labor force is

FIGURE 14-2 *The TP curve and growth. The aggregate supply curve is derived from the total product curve of panel A and the labor market of panel B. The TP curve is drawn by fixing all resources but labor, and then varying the quantity of labor. A change in the quantity or quality of the fixed resources or in technology then causes the TP curve to shift, as shown by the move from* TP_1 *to* TP_2 *in panel A. As a result of the shift, the* AS^{lr} *curve shifts out, as shown in panel C. The greater the growth rate, the farther the long-run AS curve shifts to the right.*

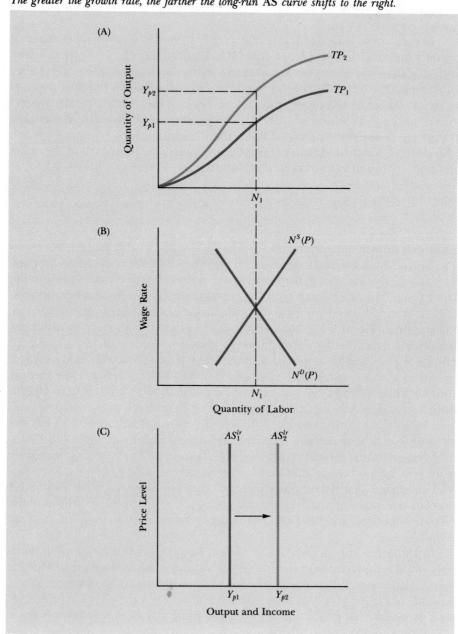

FIGURE 14-3 *Growth rates. Actual and predicted population growth rates for several countries as well as average growth rates for all low-income, all middle-income, and all industrial countries are shown. According to the World Bank, all low-income and middle-income countries are developing countries. Over the 1980s, the average annual growth rate of the population was 2 percent in low-income countries, 2.2 percent in middle-income countries, and 0.6 percent in industrial countries. The World Bank forecasts that population growth will be 1.9 percent per year for the low-income countries, 1.9 percent for the middle-income countries, and 0.5 percent for the industrial countries until the year 2000.*

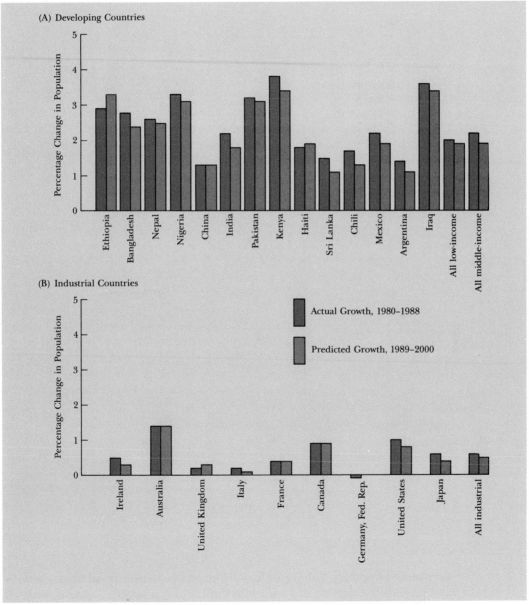

Source: World Bank, *World Development Report 1990* (New York: Oxford University Press, 1990).

FIGURE 14-4 *Population growth. Given population growth alone, it would seem that developing countries could grow faster than the industrial countries. Population growth means that the labor supply curve and thus the AS^{lr} curve shift out, as shown in panels B and C.*

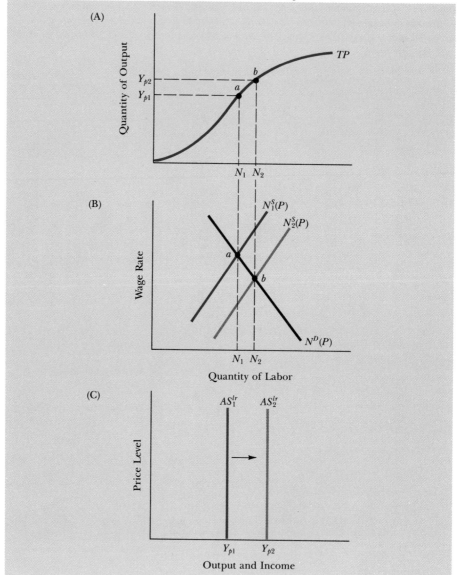

even more important. Labor productivity depends on the capital stock—human and physical capital, on the availability of natural resources, and on the level of technology.

Capital

Labor is combined with other inputs or resources to produce goods and services. If a country has many workers but few machines, then the typical worker is not very productive. As the capital stock increases, productivity rises. Capital is key to economic growth.

The ability of a country to acquire capital goods is tied to its ability to save. In some less developed countries, farming continues to be done by hand, but farming is quite mechanized in most nations. No doubt it has occurred to the farmers in the less developed countries, just as it occurred at some point in history to farmers in the now developed nations, that more can be produced if the farmers have some capital—for instance, a plow and a horse. The problem in switching from labor to a more mechanized farming operation is that the capital can be obtained only by sacrificing current consumption. Getting a plow requires that the farmer take time from the planting, care, or harvesting of the crops to build the plow or to sell some crops to buy a plow. Similarly, a horse can only be obtained by selling enough crops to buy the horse, and the care and feeding of the horse, once acquired, take some of each year's crops. In other words, the farmer must forgo some current consumption of crops to get capital, and this sacrifice can be very hard if the farmer's family depends on the crops for sustenance. Nevertheless, when the benefits of additional production from plows and horses seem greater than the sacrificed consumption, the plow and horse are acquired.

Sacrificing current consumption to accumulate capital (plows, horses) to produce more and thus increase future consumption, is called **roundabout production**. With roundabout production, not everything produced today is consumed today. Some output is used to create more production in the future. If we raze the forests and use every bit of timber today, or if we dump all our garbage and wastes in the oceans, living standards might be higher today but will be considerably lower in the future. Forgoing some current consumption lets us get capital resources that we can use to increase future production and consumption. This is called *saving*. Saving is, simply, not consuming. Any economy that grows—produces increasing amounts of goods and services—must use roundabout production and thus must save; and those savings must be used for accumulating significant amounts of capital.

Two primary factors influence the size of a country's capital stock: how much saving occurs and the allocation of savings. The amount of saving affects the amount of capital accumulation. How those savings are used affects the rate of capital formation and economic growth; savings used for a nation's infrastructure, such as roads and bridges, may contribute more to economic growth than do savings used for national defense. Savings used to increase human capital (education and training) may contribute more to economic growth than savings used to construct buildings.

Determinants of Saving. Saving depends on factors that influence consumption: income, expectations, age, demographics, and wealth. Imbedded in these five factors are such things as the security of retirement (whether the government provides retirement benefits, whether benefits are privately financed, or whether there are no such benefits), cultural influences (religious implications for consumption or saving and the attitudes toward providing for elders), and the time rate of discount (whether the population lives for today or plans for tomorrow).

Allocation of Savings. The allocation of savings depends on the expected rates of return different assets provide. Households own resources. They are the labor; they own land; they own firms (they are sole proprietors, or they own shares of stock) and because they own firms or they loan firms money by buying corporate bonds, they own capital. Households can use their incomes to buy any of these resources. In fact, they can choose whether to buy additional education and training, shares of stock, acres of land, or natural resources; to begin a new business; to buy rare coins, art, foreign currencies; or simply to buy savings accounts. Which of these items households decide to purchase depends on which is expected to yield the greatest rate of return.

In the long run, rates of return on alternative assets of similar risk should be equalized. As more people purchase assets with the highest rates of return and sell assets with the lower rates of return, prices of the more heavily purchased assets rise and prices of other assets fall. For instance, if stocks are expected to yield a 10 percent rate of return while all other resources and assets are yielding a 9 percent rate of return, and they all have the same risk, households buy more stocks. This action drives up the price of stocks and lowers the rate of return on stocks. A stock selling for $100 that generates a return of $10 per year, has only a 9 percent rate of return if the stock price rises to $111. As households sell assets offering lower rates of return and buy those with higher rates of return, the purchase prices of the assets change, so that the rates of return are equalized. As long as households are free to allocate their savings among alternative assets, we can expect the rates of return on the alternative assets of similar risk to be about the same in the long run.

Government Policies and Saving. Government policies can influence both the amount of saving and the use of savings. The government influences the total amount of private saving by altering the relative prices of consumption and saving—say by levying a consumption tax or by decreasing the tax rate on saving. The government itself can save by accumulating budget surpluses or dissave by accumulating budget deficits. Government policies can also influence the allocation of savings. The rates of return that households compare are their after-tax rates of return. If tax rates differ on the income generated from owning different resources, then those tax rates can influence the allocation of savings. Indeed, within one type of asset, different tax treatments can influence the allocation of savings. For instance, a tax rate that is lower on assets held more than three years than on assets held less than three years (called a *capital gains tax*) tends to increase the flow of savings into assets that can be held more than three years. Accelerated depreciation or other tax benefits on buildings tends to draw savings into the ownership of buildings. Policies that lead to higher real interest rates on government securities draw savings into government securities and out of other assets. (This is another view of the crowding-out effect.)

National Saving Rates. The national saving rate has been much lower in the United States than in other industrial economies in recent years, as shown in Figure 14-5. Although substantial difficulties arise in measuring the rate of saving, by any measure the U.S. saving rate is the lowest of these countries. The gross national saving rate (national saving as a percent of GNP) varied around 16 percent during the post-World War II period until the early 1980s, when it fell. Although the rate has increased in recent years, it remains below the previous three decades.

The private saving rate in the United States has declined only slightly, with household saving falling by about 1 percent and business saving increasing nearly 1 percent. (Businesses save by retaining earnings to use in investment or in the business rather than allocating the earnings as dividends.) Government saving has fallen considerably; the rate of government borrowing or dissaving has risen by more than 2 percentage points between the 1950–1979 period and the 1980s. The government saving behavior seems to be the primary difference between the saving rates of the United States and other industrial countries. Although the governments of most other industrial nations ran budget deficits during the 1980s, few ran deficits as large as did the U.S. government, relative to their GNPs or GDPs.

Land

Land surface, water, forests, minerals, and other natural resources that may be combined with labor and capital can contribute to economic growth, but an abundance of natural resources alone does not create growth. Several developing countries are relatively rich in natural resources but have not been very successful in exploiting these resources to produce goods and services. Japan, in contrast, is relatively poor in natural resources, yet has experienced dramatic economic growth in recent decades. What accounts for the differences?

Government Policies Toward Natural Resources. Government policies can influence the use of natural resources. A policy that raises a country's interest rate might attract foreign funds and increase saving. It also tends to induce people to extract natural resources and sell them to get the funds with which the higher interest can be obtained. The rate of conservation or use of natural resources is a function of the interest rate; the higher the interest rate, the more rapidly resources are extracted and sold. So producers today have more resources and a lower price for those resources than will be true in the future.

FIGURE 14-5   *National saving rates. The national saving rate has been much lower in the United States than in other industrial economies. Although substantial difficulties arise in measuring the rate of saving, by any measure the U.S. saving rate is the lowest of these countries. In addition, the U.S. saving rate has fallen since the early 1970s, as shown in panel B. A major portion of the reason for this decline is the government's increasingly large dissaving.*

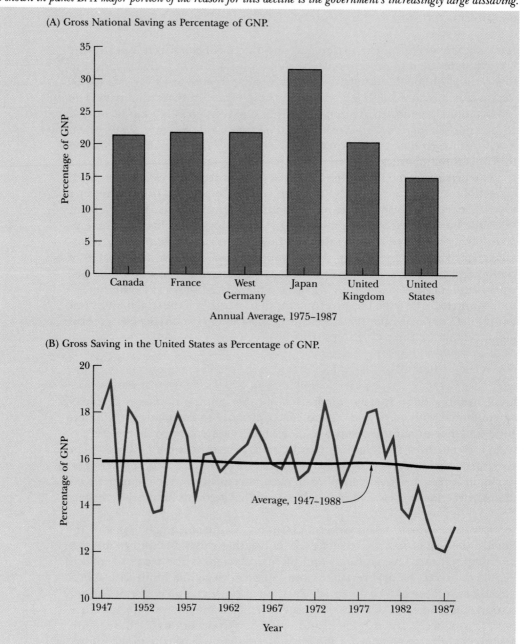

Source: Economic Report of the President, 1990 (Washington, DC: U.S. Government Printing Office, 1990), p. 128.

This tends to increase today's growth rate at the cost of a lower future growth rate. Similarly, a policy of withholding resources from the market tends to raise current prices and lower future prices, reducing growth today in return for more growth in the future.

There is a tradeoff between saving and conservation. As interest rates rise to induce increased saving, the rate of extraction and use of natural resources rises. Whether the increased saving contributes more to growth than the increased resource use depends on how savings are allocated and how important the resources are to production.

Technology

A key determinant of economic growth is technology. The term *technology* refers to ways of combining resources to produce goods and services. Innovations, such as new management techniques or scientific discoveries, improve technology. Technological advance results in the production of more output from a given amount of resources. For any given rate of growth in the labor force and the capital stock, technological progress accelerates the rate of economic growth. The influence of technology on the economy is shown through the total product curve or aggregate production function. A technological change implies that more output per worker can be produced; the *TP* curve shifts upward. With the same quantity of labor, the higher technological ability enables more output to be generated per worker. The higher output means that the long-run *AS* curve is further out along the horizontal axis; that is, the potential output level is larger.

Sources of Technological Change. Technological change depends on the scientific community. The more educational opportunities a population has, the greater the potential for technological advances. The difference in educational opportunities gives industrial countries a substantial advantage over developing countries in developing and implementing innovations. The more funding for research and development, the more likely are technological advances. Developing countries can't afford to spend nearly as much on research and development as do industrial countries. The richest industrial countries have traditionally spent 2 to 3 percent of their GNP on research and development. This amount is more than the entire GNP of some developing countries.

Low levels of education and little or no spending on research and development ensures that developing countries lag behind industrial countries in developing and implementing new technology. So, developing countries usually must follow the lead of the industrial world, adopting the technology developed in the industrial world when it is affordable and feasible given the labor and capital resources available.

Government Policies Toward Technological Change. Government policies can influence the rate of technological change. Policies that increase the after-tax rate of return on human capital acquisition increase the level of education in society. These policies include the public provision of education as well as tax benefits associated with acquiring education and training. Government policies directed toward subsidizing research and development or increasing the after-tax rate of return on research and development expenditures increases the flow of funds allocated to research and development. Patents, protection against foreign competitors, and other government policies can be used to speed the rate of technological change. A policy that raises the interest rate to increase saving may tend to reduce the rate of technological progress, however, because households and firms prefer to allocate their funds to sources that yield the higher interest rather than to human capital acquisition or to research and development.

▼
The Facts of Growth

As just noted, economic growth depends on the growth of both the quantity and quality of resources and technological progress. Advances in technology let resources be more productive. If the quantity of resources is growing and each resource is becoming more productive, then output grows even faster than the rate at which the quantity of resources is growing. Economic growth can be measured as the sum of the growth rate of productivity and the growth rate of resources:

Economic growth = growth rate of productivity + growth rate of resources

Growth and Productivity

Productivity is measured as the ratio of the amount of output produced to the amount of input used to produce that output. We can measure the productivity of a single resource such as capital or labor, or the overall productivity of all resources. Economists use the term **total factor productivity (TFP)** to describe the overall productivity of an economy. Total factor productivity is the quantity of output produced divided by the quantity of labor and capital. (Natural resources are assumed to remain constant and so are not calculated into total factor productivity, because the endowments are unlikely to change significantly. Any productivity increases due to natural resource changes are attributed to capital and to labor productivity increases.)

The amount output grows because of labor growth depends on how much labor contributes to the production of output. Similarly, the amount output grows because of capital growth depends on how much capital contributes to production. This is shown by the aggregate production function,

$$Y = f(K,N)$$

which symbolizes that capital and labor are combined to generate output. A commonly used form of an aggregate production function is the **Cobb-Douglas function**:

$$Y = AK^bN^{1-b}$$

where K = the capital stock

N = the labor supply

Y = output

The *TP* curve is obtained from the production function by fixing the capital stock, K, at some amount and varying the quantity of labor, N. For growth, both the capital stock and the quantity of labor must be allowed to change. To convert the production function to a growth equation, we rewrite the production function in terms of percentage changes. To do this, we must calculate $\Delta \log Y/\Delta t$, the percentage change in output over time; $\Delta \log Y$ is $\Delta Y/Y$ or the change in Y divided by Y, which is the percentage change of output. Similarly, $\Delta \log K$ and $\Delta \log N$ are percentage changes of capital and labor respectively. First convert the Cobb-Douglas production function to logarithms:

$$\log Y = \log A + b \log K + (1 - b) \log N$$

We then take changes in each logarithmic variable over time:

$$\Delta \log Y/\Delta t = \Delta \log A/\Delta t + b(\Delta \log K/\Delta t) + (1 - b)(\Delta \log N/\Delta t)$$

Rewriting for simplicity as

$$y = a + bk + (1 - b)n$$

simply tells us that the percentage change in output, y, equals the percentage change in total factor productivity, a, plus the percentage change in capital, k, multiplied by capital's contribution to total output, b, plus the percentage change in labor, n, multiplied by labor's contribution to total output, $(1 - b)$.

Thus, to relate the growth of labor and capital to output growth, the labor and capital growth must be multiplied by the relative contributions of each resource in producing output. In a world of perfect competition, each resource's share of national output is equal to each resource's payment or share of national income. In the United States, labor has received about 70 percent of national income and capital has received about 30 percent. If we use these ratios as labor's and capital's contributions to production, we can divide economic growth into three parts:

$$y = a + 0.3k + 0.7n$$

According to this **fundamental growth equation**, economic growth, y, thus depends on productivity changes, a, and changes in resources, k and n.

Nearly every country has experienced an increase in the labor force. Labor force growth has run about 1.5 percent per year for the industrial countries and about 3 percent per year for the developing countries. Growth in the capital stock has been steadier in the industrial countries than in the developing countries. The capital stock has grown by about 4 percent per year in the industrial countries and varied tremendously in the developing countries. Thus, even with no growth in productivity ($a = 0$) we should expect a growth rate of

$$y = 0.3(0.04) + 0.7(0.015) = 2.25 \text{ percent per year}$$

for the industrial countries. In general, as noted, the average growth rate in the industrial nations has been about 3 percent per year. This means that 0.75 percent per year of growth cannot be explained by resource growth. The remainder or residual must be the growth of total factor productivity.

What factors determine TFP changes? The experience of the United States during the past twenty years is very instructive for understanding TFP changes. Let's look at that experience.

The U.S. Productivity Slowdown

From 1948 to 1965, total factor productivity in the United States grew at an annual average rate of 2.02 percent. From 1965 to 1973, the growth slowed to an average of 1.04 percent, and between 1973 and 1987, the growth rate was only 0.21 percent. If the pre-1965 rate of productivity growth had been maintained, U.S. output would have been about 39 percent higher today than it actually is.

Many ideas have been advanced to explain the drop in U.S. productivity growth. These include a drop in the quality of the U.S. labor force, changing attitudes toward work and education, a change in the composition of the labor force, higher energy prices, a trend away from manufacturing toward service industries, and a decrease in technological innovations. Let's consider these explanations.

Labor Quality. Labor productivity is measured as output per hour of labor. Figure 14-6 shows the growth of labor productivity in the United States. You can see that although it fluctuates considerably, it has slid downward during the past forty years. Changes in the productivity of labor may be due to technological innovation, changes in the stock of capital, or changes in the quality of labor. Changes in labor quality may be due to changes in the level and quality of education, demographic changes, or changes in attitudes toward work.

Quantity and Quality of Education. Median school years completed by U.S. citizens increased from 8.6 years in 1940 to nearly 13 in 1990. The percentage of adults having at least a high school education rose from 24.5 percent to 75 percent and the percentage having a college education rose from 4.6 percent to almost 20 percent. Although the quantity of education has risen, many people claim that the quality has declined. Some suggest that college entrance exam scores

FIGURE 14-6 *Labor productivity. Labor productivity is measured as output per hour of labor. The productivity of labor in the United States is shown. You can see that although it fluctuates considerably, it has slid downward during the past forty years.*

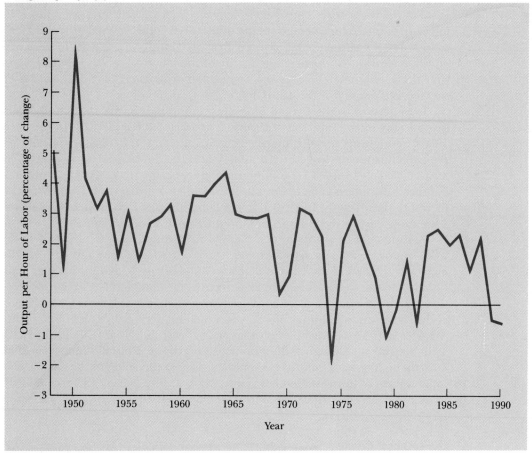

prove this. The group of students that took the SAT test in 1963 scored an average of 478 on the verbal test and 502 on the math test. The group of students that were tested in 1980 scored an average verbal score of 424 and average math score of 466. If these test scores do indicate education quality, this decline might be expected to have significantly affected the nation's productivity in the mid-1970s as the teenagers of the 1960s entered the mainstream labor market. By the early 1980s, test scores had started to rise again. If this rise reflects improved education, then this improvement may be reflected as a rise in the productivity of labor.

Changes in the Size and Composition of the Work Force. The increased working-age population in the late 1960s and early 1970s that resulted from the baby boom generation (people born between approximately 1946 and 1962) was a large pool of young, inexperienced workers. The average quality of the labor force may have fallen at that time. By the 1980s, however, the baby-boom segment of the labor force consisted of experienced workers employed in better jobs, which raised the average quality of the labor force. In the 1970s and 1980s more women entered the labor force. Because many of these women were new and thus untrained, the average quality of the labor force was reduced. Over time, as these women gained experience and skills, their participation raised the average quality of the labor force.

Immigration to the United States was quite high in the 1970s and 1980s, second only to the influx in the period between 1900 and 1920. In the early 1900s, immigrants came primarily from Europe. In the 1970s, the flow of people from Europe declined by 0.5 million and the flow from Latin America increased sharply. Almost 1.3 million immigrants came from Mexico alone, and another 0.5 million came from the West Indies. Immigration from Asia also increased significantly. In 1980 almost 1.8 million new U.S. residents were from Asia, mostly from the Philippines, South Korea, and Vietnam.

As is true of migrants in general, the new immigrants tended to be relatively young, primarily ages 20 to 49. During the late 1960s and early 1970s, many immigrants to the United States were relatively skilled individuals from low-income countries. More than 22 percent of the immigrants had four or more years of college education, a higher percentage than existed in the United States at the time. Among immigrants 25 years old and over, 6.9 percent from Latin America and 37.4 percent from Asia had at least four years of college. Since 1975, however, although skilled immigration to the United States from both low-and high-income countries remained close to the levels of the early 1970s, immigration of the unskilled has grown dramatically. Nearly 13 percent of the immigrants arriving since the mid-1970s have less than five years of elementary school education.

Technological Change. Innovation increases productivity so when productivity declines, an obvious candidate for the source of this decline is a reduction in the development of new technology. The pace of technological innovation is difficult to measure but a decent indicator is the size of expenditures on research and development. Research and development expenditures grew relatively rapidly in the early 1960s and again throughout the 1980s in the United States, but grew at a relatively slow rate and actually declined for five years in the late 1960s and 1970s.

Energy Prices. The OPEC oil cartel raised the price of oil substantially in 1973–1974 and 1979. The timing of the dramatic increase in oil prices coincides with the drop in productivity growth in the United States. A glance back at Figure 14-6 shows that output per labor hour actually fell in 1974 and 1979. An oil price rise shifts the AS^{sr} curve up and induces a supply shock, but does not necessarily cause the AS^{lr} curve to shift in (or not shift as far out as it other-wise would have). For this shift in the AS^{lr} curve to occur, the quantity of oil or other resources must decline. One way for the oil price rise to affect the long-run aggregate supply curve is through the capital stock. A rise in energy prices may make old, energy-inefficient capital goods obsolete. For instance, many oil-burning electric power plants became obsolete after the oil price hikes of the 1970s. Like any other decline in the value of the capital stock, this change reduces economic growth. Because most measures of the capital stock do not account for this energy obsolescence, the obsolescence would be included in the decline in total factor productivity.

Whether any or all of these factors played a role in the U.S. experience is hard to say. Their potential role did, however, stimulate a great deal of con-cern over the government's policies. Each *Economic Report of the President* in the 1980s devoted considerable attention to government policies to stimulate eco-nomic growth. The United States is not alone in being concerned about eco-nomic growth. All countries devote considerable attention to the policies that might best stimulate economic growth.

▼
Policies of Growth

Every country is unique, with a unique history and endowment of resources. The differences that seem to explain the different rates of economic growth and progress stem more from political or social factors than from endowments. Let's now discuss some of these political factors and some of the strategies that countries have used to enhance growth.

Political Factors

One of the most important functions a government performs in stimulating economic growth is providing a political environment that encourages saving and investment. People do not want to do business in an economy weakened by wars and demonstrations. A country that guarantees private property and the rights of property owners to do what they want with their property en-courages private investment and development. People do not start new busi-nesses or build new factories if they believe that a change in government could result in confiscation of their property. Countries that expropriate foreign-owned property without compensating the owners have difficulty encourag-ing foreign investment. The loss of foreign investment is particularly impor-tant in developing countries, which suffer from a lack of saving. If domestic residents are not able to save because they are living at or below subsistence level, foreign savings are a crucial source of investment. Without that invest-ment, economies of developing countries cannot grow.

Every politician wants more economic growth, all things being equal. But political pressures often force a government to forgo growth for more immediate objectives. In many developing countries, the strongest supporters of the political leaders are those working for the current government. As a result, governments are often overstaffed and inefficient. To maintain political support, governments often subsidize food and housing, and when they try to reduce or do away with these subsidies the governments face problems. When Egypt lowered its food subsidies to provide more funds for growth, widespread rioting ensued. When Venezuela reduced subsidies on transportation, rioting forced a return to subsidies. As the economies of Eastern Europe and the Soviet Union move away from a system of subsidies and government ownership to private property without subsidized production, many citizens must bear hardships they wouldn't have faced in the prior system, so pressure for a return to the old system rises.

When population rises faster than GNP (or GDP), the standard of living of the average citizen does not improve. With the exception of China, where population growth is tightly controlled (one child per couple), population growth in the developing countries is proceeding at a pace that will double the population in about thirty-two years. Rapid population growth reduces the amount of capital per worker and lowers labor productivity. Too rapid a population growth undoubtedly has had a negative effect on the development of many countries, but the actual impact of population growth is hard to measure. A larger population means a larger labor force and thus a greater potential for economic growth. So generalizations about levels of population growth are hard to make, and economic policies directed toward population growth are questionable in terms of their impact.

Policies Within Industrial Nations

The policies that industrial nations use to encourage more rapid economic growth fall into two general classes, those directed toward the fundamental growth equation and those dealing with other countries. Policies directed toward the fundamental growth equation include policies to increase labor quality (education and training programs for instance), policies to increase the innovation rate (patent policies and special tax programs such as accelerated depreciation or investment tax credits), and policies to encourage saving (IRAs and other tax-free saving programs). These are called **supply-side policies** because they are directed toward the aggregate supply curve.

In previous chapters, we discussed the **demand-side policies** directed toward business cycles. These policies are primarily directed toward the aggregate demand curve but they may have an impact on total factor productivity and thus aggregate supply. For instance, tightening the money growth may raise interest rates and reduce inflationary pressures. But higher interest rates discourage investment in physical capital, lead to a more rapid depletion of natural resources, and lead to less investment in human capital. A government budget deficit may affect interest rates and the use of savings funds. If so, budget deficits may discourage investment in physical and human capital and negatively affect economic growth.

During the early Reagan administration, 1982–1984, policymakers successfully argued for the need to dramatically reduce tax rates. They asserted that lower tax rates would stimulate economic growth and that the resulting higher income and profit levels would mean more government revenue and would not increase the government budget deficit. The idea was to shift the long-run *AS* curve further outward than the *AD* curve was increased. The results of this so-called *supply-side economics* were mostly disappointing for the Reagan policymakers. Although the economy grew — in fact, the longest boom phase of a business cycle since World War II took place after 1982 — the government's revenues from the economic growth were not enough to make up for the lower taxes. The government began running very large deficits. Thus, while the tax policies surely encouraged economic growth, the record-high budget deficits discouraged economic growth. The net result of the Reagan supply-side policies is controversial among economists.

The second approach the industrial economies take regarding economic growth involves their trade policies. Over the past three decades, most industrial countries have moved toward lower tariffs and other barriers to trade. Countries have focused on exporting goods and services in which they have a comparative advantage, and importing goods and services in which they have a comparative disadvantage. In recent years, the success of the Japanese economy has led some to rethink these free-trade policies. A new view of international trade called **strategic trade** argues that trade by comparative advantage is a mistake. Proponents of this view argue that international trade largely involves firms that pursue *economies of scale* — that achieve lower costs per unit of production the more they produce. So the government should use tariffs or subsidies to give domestic firms with potential economies of scale an advantage over foreign rivals. Once economies of scale have been achieved, the industry will dominate the world market and tariffs and subsidies will be unnecessary.

Strategic trade policy is aimed at gaining the economies of scale advantage by stimulating production in domestic industries capable of realizing economies of scale. The government must forecast which industries will experience economies of scale and then direct their subsidies and tariff policies toward those industries before other governments do the same. According to the proponents of strategic trade, Japan has accomplished this very well. The Japanese Ministry of International Trade and Industry (MITI) has for several decades selected industries for special subsidies and protection and has then seen them grow and take over the worldwide industry — automobiles and consumer electronics are excellent examples. In the industrial world today, debate is raging over whether to pursue free trade or strategic trade.

Strategies for Developing Countries

In the absence of government policy that directs production, we expect countries to concentrate on producing things for which they have a comparative advantage. However, many countries whose leaders believe that growth requires industrialization have pursued a policy of industrialization by subsidizing inefficient domestic producers. The idea is to identify domestic markets being supplied mainly by imports and then to impose tariffs or quotas on the imports. This provides a chance for a domestic industry to produce and sell the goods. Once the "infant" industry matures and price and quality become competitive with foreign goods, the import barriers are no longer needed. This is called **import substitution**. In fact, this strategy has not been productive. Industries protected by tariffs or quotas have no incentive to become efficient.

Another strategy focuses on taking advantage of those domestic industries that can compete effectively with producers in the rest of the world. Governments subsidize domestic firms to use the most abundant resources within a country to produce products that the country might be able to produce better than others. Because the abundant resource in most developing countries is labor, the industries focused on are labor intensive. This kind of growth strategy is called **export substitution**.

Most developing nations have taken the import substitution route. Hong Kong, Korea, and Singapore are the only countries that have taken the export substitution approach aggressively. As might be expected, these export substitution countries have grown much more rapidly than the other developing nations.

▼   ▼   ▼   ▼   ▼   ▼   ▼   ▼   ▼   ▼   ▼
Conclusions

Economic growth means more output and income per person. This result usually implies a higher standard of living. It definitely means more income with which to purchase health care and clean water and better nutrition. Thus, economic growth is a crucial element of economics and economic policy. The questions of what causes economic growth, why some economies grow faster than others, and what policies should be implemented to foster growth, do not have easy, straightforward answers. In fact, in most cases what is good for economic growth is bad for business cycles and vice versa.

Few developing countries have opted for outright competition and use of abundant resources. Instead, most have tried to protect their inefficient industries in an attempt to force the country to become industrialized. The results have not been productive; growth has not risen as a result of import substitution policies.

▼   ▼   ▼   ▼   ▼   ▼   ▼   ▼   ▼   ▼   ▼
Summary

1. What is economic growth?
Economic growth is an increase in real GNP or GDP per person.
2. What factors contribute to economic growth?
Economic growth is composed of three parts: the growth of total factor productivity, the growth of the capital stock, and the growth of the labor force.
3. What policies affect economic growth?
Any policy that affects one of the three components of the fundamental growth equation affects economic growth. Short-run business cycle policies affect economic growth by affecting interest rates and thus the rates of saving and of resource use. Policies oriented toward investment and saving may influence the rate of capital formation. Policies oriented toward human capital formation (training, education) may influence the rate of increase of labor — the rate of increase in labor quality. Policies directed toward technological innovation, research and development, and productivity influence economic growth. Energy policies influence economic growth. Political factors such as government stability and confidence in government influence investment, saving, and research and development. International trade policies influence economic growth.

▼
Key Terms

economic growth   334
roundabout production   341
total factor productivity (TFP)   346
Cobb-Douglas function   347
fundamental growth equation   347

supply-side policies   352
demand-side policies   352
strategic trade   353
import substitution   354
export substitution   354

▼
Problems and Exercises

1.   Why do differences in the rate of economic growth lead to differences in living standards? If the growth rate of Japan is 5 percent per year and the growth rate of the United States is 1 percent per year, and if both countries are the same size today in terms of output per person, how many years will it take for Japan's economy to become double that of the United States?

2.   If the production function for the economy is as described in the chapter, what happens to real GNP when labor and capital each double? What happens when labor and capital do not change but total factor productivity doubles?

3. Why are the observed shares of capital and labor income used as estimates of the weights of capital and labor in the fundamental equation of growth? Would it make any difference if the observed shares were the opposite of those given in the chapter?

4. How would each of the following affect economic growth, and through what channel?

    a.   An increase in the rate of immigration

    b.   An increase in the rate of immigration of unskilled workers

    c.   A shift to a tighter monetary policy and an easier fiscal policy

    d.   A shift to a tighter fiscal policy and an easier monetary policy

    e.   A change from a fixed to a flexible exchange rate system

5. Using the *AD–AS* framework and using the fundamental equation of growth, explain how the oil price shocks of the 1970s and the 1990s affect economic growth for

    a.   An industrial oil-importing country

    b.   A developing oil-exporting country

6. Explain the import substitution and export substitution strategies of growth.

7. Explain why there are different growth policies in industrial countries than in developing countries. Don't all face the same fundamental equation of growth? Why or why not?

Chapter 15

Business Cycles

What to Expect

Today, macroeconomics is the study of both business cycles and growth. In the early 1960s, business cycles had ceased to be an active area of research. A National Bureau of Economic Research (NBER) conference in the 1960s was entitled "Is The Business Cycle Obsolete?" and most economists at the time were proclaiming the death of the business cycle. The severity of the 1974–1975 and 1981–1982 recessions demonstrated most clearly that the business cycle had risen from the ashes with a vengeance. Most macroeconomic research in the past decade has turned again to the business cycle. This chapter looks at business cycles. It describes the common patterns among cycles and defines the causes of cycles and the behavior of variables over the cycle. The following questions are considered in this chapter:

1. What is a business cycle?

2. What is a propagation mechanism, and what is an impulse?

3. What do economists disagree about in business cycle theory?

4. Has the business cycle changed over time?

▼
The AD–AS Model and the Business Cycle

A business cycle is the expansion and contraction of real output over time; that is, the deviations of real output from the long-term growth trend rate of output. A business cycle is just the result of the AD and AS^{sr} curves shifting about the potential output level, Y_p or AS^{lr}. The issues of concern in macroeconomic research about business cycles today include the causes of such shifts in AD or AS, the adjustment path from the original equilibrium position to a new equilibrium position, and the implications of these two issues for economic policy. Let's use the $AD–AS$ diagram to illustrate a few concerns macroeconomists have about business cycles. We'll begin with an AD shock and then look at an AS shock.

AD Shocks

Assume that the monetary authorities unexpectedly increase the growth rate of the money supply above the rates that have prevailed for the past several periods. The behavior of the economy after such a shock depends on the assumptions made regarding information, the adjustability of wages and prices, and the exchange rate regime under which the country operates. Let's begin with the case where wages are sticky, fixed for a three-year period by long-term contracts, and where exchange rates are flexible. The monetary surprise means that individuals have more money than they want to hold. To get rid of the excess, they buy other assets and make expenditures. Buying financial assets drives their prices up and their rates of return or interest rates down. The lower interest rates, in turn, increase investment and cause foreign exchange to flow out of the United States. Thus the AD curve shifts out because consumption and investment rise and because the value of the dollar falls, leading to increased net exports. This is shown in panel A of Figure 15-1. Additional sales mean that inventory levels are reduced. As firms realize stock-outs or decreases in their desired inventory levels, they raise prices and gear up for greater production. The demand for labor rises but because wages are fixed the cost of labor does not rise in proportion to the price increases. So firms experience an increase in profits. Because output rises more than the number of workers employed, labor productivity rises. All this change is illustrated by the move from point a to point b in Panel A. In terms of business cycle dynamics, we see that the monetary shock causes the economy to rise above its trend growth path, in panel B.

   As the long-term contracts expire and new negotiations take place, the nominal wage increases. The higher costs of production mean that firms reduce their work force and production levels. The economy moves from point b to point c in panel A and along the colored line in the declining growth period in panel B. Depending on the size of the adjustment, the economy may overshoot the long-run equilibrium or growth path and fall to point d. It then adjusts back to the long-run AS curve over time.

FIGURE 15-1   *Demand shocks. In panel A, the economy is in equilibrium at point* a. *Panel B shows the dynamic version of panel A; the long-term growth trend is pictured as the black line. The monetary authorities unexpectedly increase the rate of growth of the money supply above the rates that have prevailed for the past several periods. Wages are fixed for a three-year period by long-term contracts, and exchange rates are flexible. The monetary surprise means that individuals have more money than they want to hold. To get rid of the excess, they buy other assets and make expenditures. The* AD *curve shifts out because consumption, investment, and net exports rise. As inventory levels are reduced, firms raise the price and gear up for greater production. This change is illustrated by the move from point* a *to point* b *in panel A. In terms of the dynamics of the business cycle, we see that the monetary shock causes the economy to rise above its trend growth path, in panel B.*

As the long-term contracts expire and new negotiations take place, the nominal wage increases. The higher costs of production mean that firms reduce their work force and production levels. The economy moves from point b *to point* c *in panel A and along the colored line in the declining growth period in panel B. Depending on the size of the readjustment, the economy might overshoot the long-run equilibrium or growth path and fall to point* d. *It then adjusts back to the long-run* AS *curve over time.*

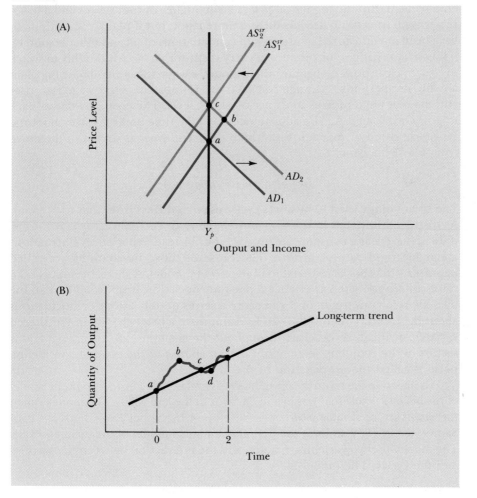

AS *Shocks*

Let's now consider a supply shock. The supply shock we'll discuss is an increase in the price of oil. Oil price changes are not the only source of supply shocks, because the *AS* curve also shifts as the result of productivity changes, technological changes, or changes in the available quantity or quality of resources. Nevertheless, an oil price change provides a good illustration of *AS* shocks. The higher oil price increases the costs of doing business, inducing firms to reduce production and to substitute away from oil to other resources. We'll assume that exchange rates do not change (by assuming that all oil-importing countries are affected equally and that oil-exporting countries use their foreign exchange to purchase assets in the oil-importing countries). Thus, the result of the oil shock is that the short-run *AS* curve of Figure 15-2A shifts to the left.

If wages are sticky, then employment and output fall. The economy moves from point *a* to point *b* in panels A and B. At point *b*, there is involuntary unemployment. But the higher oil prices mean higher output prices and a lower real wage. Firms try to use less oil and more labor, but if plant and equipment have been manufactured to use certain combinations of oil and other resources, it is costly to change. For instance, it's very costly for an electrical utility to switch to coal, nuclear power, or some other resources when it has an oil-burning plant already in operation. As wage contracts are renegotiated, the wage rate rises and the real wage returns to its pre-oil shock level. The economy moves back to point *a* in panel A. The adjustment may take time and may overshoot the long-term trend or may move slowly to the trend line, as shown in the move from *b* to *a'* in panel B.

Impulse and Propagation

The terminology used in business cycle research differs from that used so far. As discussed in detail in the previous chapter, an economy grows over time; it doesn't grow at a constant, steady pace, but instead experiences fluctuations about its trend rate of growth. The cause of those fluctuations are called **impulses** — the shocks referred to in the *AD–AS* model. A shock or impulse can cause an economy to experience a one-time deviation from trend and an immediate return to trend, or it can cause a series of oscillations or fluctuations about the trend. The impulse can lead simply to a brief change in the altered variable, or it can reverberate throughout the economy, affecting the various sectors of the economy sequentially. The response of the economy to the impulse is called the **propagation** of the impulse.

To illustrate the terminology of business cycles, let's consider a simple model of the business cycle that was briefly in favor in the late 1930s. The model, called the *multiplier–accelerator model,* was developed by Nobel Prize laureate Paul Samuelson in 1937 and was the first mathematical model of the business cycle. The model has two variables, *C* and *I,* and the interaction between the two creates the cycles. The model is

FIGURE 15-2   *Supply shocks. A higher oil price increases the costs of doing business, inducing firms to reduce production and to substitute away from oil to other resources. The short-run AS curve of panel A shifts to the left. If wages are sticky, then employment decreases and output falls. The economy moves from a to b in panels A and B. At point b, there is involuntary unemployment. The higher oil prices mean higher prices and a lower real wage. As wage contracts are renegotiated, the wage rate rises and the real wage returns to the level it was before the oil shock. The economy moves back to point a in panel A. The adjustment may take time and may overshoot the long-term trend or may move slowly to the trend line, as shown in the move from b to a′ in panel B.*

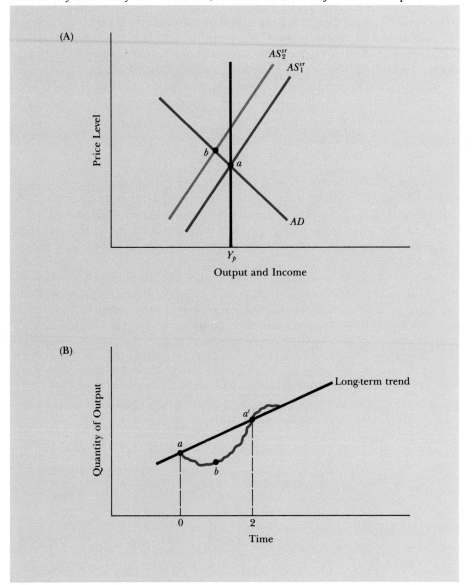

(1) $Y_t = C_t + I_t + G_t$

(2) $C_t = C_0 + c_y Y_{t-1}$

(3) $I_t = a(C_t - C_{t-1})$

(4) $G_t = G_0$

where the subscript t refers to the current time period and $t - 1$ refers to the previous time period. Thus, consumption this year depends on income last year, and investment this year depends on the change in consumption from last year to this year. The coefficient a in the investment function is called the *accelerator*, and the coefficient c_y is the MPC, marginal propensity to consume. Let's assume that c_y is 0.50. A \$1 change in income in one period causes a \$0.50 change in consumption in the next period. Also, assume that firms want a desired ratio of capital to the production of consumption goods of 1; that is, a is 1. Thus an increase of \$1 in consumption in any period induces \$1 of investment in the same period.

Solving the equations 1–4 for Y yields

(5) $Y_t = C_0 + c_y(1 + a)Y_{t-1} - ac_y Y_{t-2} + G_0$

The pattern of Y is described by equation 5. The path Y takes depends on the values of the MPC and the acceleration coefficient. The equilibrium situation occurs when $Y_t = Y_{t-1} = Y_{t-2}$, which is $(C_0 + G_0)/[1 - c_y]$. However, when Y is disturbed from this equilibrium, then it may take on one of several different patterns in moving to its new equilibrium. If $C_0 = 50$ and $G_0 = 0$, the initial equilibrium is $Y = 100$.

In Table 15-1, we have subjected the model to a permanent \$100 increase in government purchases (the impulse). The new equilibrium is $Y = 300$. The business cycle occurs as the economy moves from the level of $Y = 100$ to $Y = 300$. In the first period, consumption and investment do not change. Consumption depends on income in the previous period, and income in period

TABLE 15-1   *Multiplier–Accelerator Model of the Business Cycle*

Period	Government Purchases	Change in Consumption ($\Delta C_t = 0.5\Delta Y_{t-1}$)	Investment ($I = \Delta C_t$)	Resulting Income Change
1	100	0	0	100
2	100	50	50	200
3	100	100	50	250
4	100	125	25	250
5	100	125	0	225
6	100	112.5	-12.5	200
7	100	100	-12.5	187.5
8	100	93.75	-6.25	187.5
9	100	93.75	0	193.75
10	100	96.87	3.125	200

0 has not been altered. Investment depends on the change in consumption, which is zero. In the second period, consumption increases by the MPC times the increase in income of $100 and investment increases by 1 times the increase in consumption. For each period thereafter, consumption and investment change according to the change in income in the preceding period. You can see that the $100 increase in government purchases leads to oscillations of income. The increase in government purchases increased income beginning in period 1. By period 5, the change in income begins to fall and continues falling until period 9. Then the change in income begins to rise again, as do consumption and investment.

Given the assumed values for the MPC of 0.50 and the acceleration coefficient of 1, oscillations in Y will be dampened. The path resembles that labeled as path A in Figure 15-3. This is not the only possible outcome of this model. If the acceleration coefficient is significantly smaller than the MPC, there are no oscillations and the model yields a gentle or asymptotic approach to the new higher equilibrium level of income, as illustrated by path B. If the product of the MPC and the acceleration coefficient exceeds 1, the oscillations become explosive (path C); and if the acceleration coefficient is high enough, aggregate demand simply explodes without oscillating (path D).

The impulse in the multiplier–accelerator model is an exogenous event, something like a government purchases increase. The propagation mechanism of the multiplier–accelerator model is specified, however; it is the interaction of consumption and investment. The propagation mechanism is not enough to generate periodic or recurrent cycles. The model needs to be shocked on a regular basis—to have impulses that occur every so often—to start the process. So the model has many limitations as an explanation of the economy's behavior. Nevertheless, it's useful for illustrating the impulse–propagation terminology of business cycle research.

▼
Business Cycle Facts

The story of business cycles is necessarily long. The average cycle for the industrial countries lasts about four years. Thus, to study cycles, economists have had to examine and compare the movement of economic variables over many decades. Most economists have separated their examination of business cycles into two periods, the period before 1919 and the period since 1945. The reason for this demarcation generally rests with the role of the world wars. The world before 1919 seems very different from the world after 1945; and the period in between—World War I, the Great Depression, and World War II— seems altogether different. Whatever the basis for the division, there does indeed seem to be a clear distinction between the postwar period (1945 to the present) and the prewar period.

FIGURE 15-3   *The Multiplier–Accelerator model. We have subjected the model to a permanent $100 increase in government purchases (the impulse). The business cycle occurs as the economy moves from the level of Y = 100 to Y = 300. The path depends on how much consumption and invest-ment change in each period. Along path A, consumption increases by the MPC of 0.5 times the increase in income of the preceding period, and investment increases by 1 times the increase in con-sumption. The $100 increase in government purchases leads to oscillations of income. The increase in government spending increases income beginning in period 1. By period 5, the change in income begins to fall and continues falling until period 9. Then, the change in income begins to rise again, as do consumption and investment. If investment is less volatile, the business cycle is dampened— such as path B illustrates. The greater the changes in investment, the greater the oscillations in income—leading to path C or path D.*

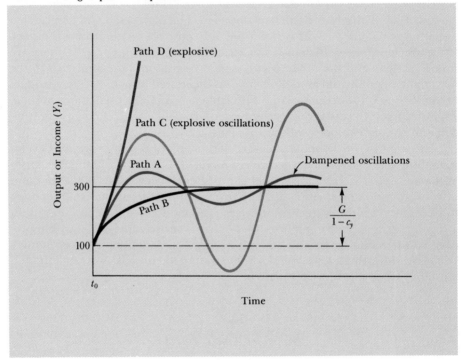

Amplitudes and Frequency

Both continuity and change appear in the most basic measures of the cycle from 1846 to the present. Although a cycle seems to have occurred about once every four years in the United States, the amplitude of cycles after 1945 is signifi-cantly smaller than before 1945. The average increase of real GNP and em-ployment in pre-1945 expansions was roughly double that in post-1945 expansions. As for contractions, the pre-1945 decline in industrial production was about double that in the postwar period, while the decline in employment was more than four times as great. You can get some idea of the difference in Figure 15-4, which shows the growth rate of U.S. real GNP from 1910 to 1990.

FIGURE 15-4   *The changing U.S. business cycle. The growth rate of U.S. real GNP from 1910 to 1990 is shown. According to this picture, the size of the cycles is significantly smaller after 1945 than before. Even abstracting from the Great Depression, cycle fluctuations were much larger before 1945 than since.*

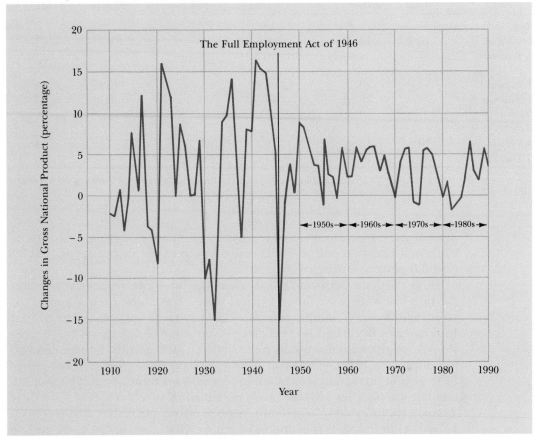

Sources: U.S. Bureau of the Census, *Historical Statistics of the United States, Colonial Times to the Present,* bicentennial ed. (Washington, DC: U.S. Bureau of the Census, 1975), Series F-31; *Economic Report of the President, 1991* (Washington, DC: U.S. Government Printing Office, 1991).

According to this picture, the size of the cycles is significantly smaller after 1945 than before. Even abstracting from the Great Depression, cycle fluctuations were much larger before 1945 than since.

Not only were postwar U.S. recessions much shallower, they were shorter; from 1846 to 1945, recessions were two-thirds as long as expansions, but from 1945 to 1982 they were only one-fourth as long. Another major change was in the cyclical behavior of inflation. Average U.S. inflation rates were similar in expansions before and after 1945 but were much higher in postwar contractions than in prewar contractions. You can see this in Table 15-2. In Table 15-2, rows 3 and 4 show how the amplitude of prices has changed from the prewar to the postwar period. In the prewar period, prices rose an average of 12.1

TABLE 15-2   *U.S. Business Cycle Facts: Before and After World War II*

Period	Number of Cyclical Movements		Average Duration in Quarters		Average Percentage Amplitude	
	1. Rise	*2. Fall*	*3. Rise*	*4. Fall*	*5. Rise*	*6. Fall*
Real GNP						
1. Prewar	12	12	8.9	3.2	17.3	− 5.1
2. Postwar	7	8	16.3	2.6	20.9	− 2.5
Price						
3. Prewar	11	10	6.6	6.9	12.1	− 11.8
4. Postwar	4	5	12.5	5.0	8.7	− 4.8
Interest						
Rate						
5. Prewar	10	10	9.1	6.0	2.7	− 2.8
6. Postwar	9	9	11.2	5.1	4.3	− 3.4

Source: Victor Zarnowitz, "Facts and Factors in the Recent Evolution of Business Cycles in the United States," National Bureau of Economic Research Working Paper No. 2865, February 1989.

percent during expansions and fell nearly 11.8 percent during contractions, while in the postwar period prices rose 8.7 percent during expansions but fell only 4.8 percent during contractions.

Along with the persistent rise in prices has come a persistent rise in wages; the nominal wage is much less cyclical than it was in the prewar period. Interestingly, however, interest rates have become more rather than less cyclical. Interest rates fluctuated in a relatively narrow range during 1875–1918; followed a pronounced downward trend between 1920 and 1934; remained very low during the 1930s, World War II, and the immediate postwar years; moved in large and increasing swings around an upward trend from 1950 to 1981; and fell sharply after 1981 and have remained relatively constant since then. You can see in Table 15-2, columns 5 and 6, rows 5 and 6, that the percentage by which interest rates rose and fell during cycles increased from the prewar period to the postwar period.

Causes of Differences

The two major contrasts between the prewar cycle and the postwar cycle are

1. The postwar period was more stable.
2. There were persistent rising prices in the postwar period.

What has caused the stability in the postwar period? Many have claimed that the increased size of the federal government, particularly the stabilizing role of government transfer payments and personal income tax (see Chapter 12 for details), has led to more stability. Real disposable personal income does not decline as much as real disposable personal income declined before 1945. The multipliers in the prewar period have been between 4 and 5, whereas in the postwar period they were 2 or less.

Not only has the size of government increased, but the Employment Act of 1946 committed government to full employment. This tended to increase the confidence of the private sector that deep recessions would not be tolerated. As a result, individuals and firms did not react to bad economic news as dramatically in the postwar period as they did in the prewar period.

Changes in the impact of monetary policy can be divided among the roles of changing government regulations, private institutions, and discretionary monetary policy. Some of the worst business declines of the pre-World War I and the interwar periods were associated with major financial crises. Typically, these events followed a speculative boom and collapse of prices of certain assets and involved an abrupt curtailment of credit. A number of severe business contractions were associated with banking panics; that is, great surges in bank failures, runs on banks, and fears of further failures. Many crises spread either from Europe to the United States or from the United States to Europe and turned into worldwide recessions. However, no such financial crises have occurred since 1933. Federal insurance of bank deposits, effective since the beginning of 1934 with the founding of the Federal Deposit Insurance Corporation (FDIC), prevented bank panics by reducing both bank failures and the depositors' fears for safety of their money. The FDIC assumed responsibility for losses of insolvent banks, and the public soon learned that it no longer was at risk. However, despite its evident benefits, federal deposit insurance is by no means an unmixed blessing, because it reduces the banks' need to be careful and the depositors' incentives to be watchful. It can be blamed for at least a portion of the current savings and loan and banking problems.

In addition to structural changes involving financial markets and the size of government, other changes in the private sector have played a role in changing the business cycle. Jobs have shifted away from the cyclically volatile industries since the 1920s. From 1920 to 1981, the "blue-collar" operative and laborer categories were cut in half, while the "white-collar" categories nearly doubled. Employment in service industries has increased much faster than employment in the production of goods since 1929. The share of the generally cyclical industries peaked at slightly more than 40 percent in 1948–1953 and has declined since to near 30 percent. The rest of the private sector, consisting of trade, finance, insurance, real estate, and services, gained steadily. Together with the government, these industries accounted for about 23 percent in 1869, 44 percent in 1929–1937, and 64 percent in 1980. Thus, an increasing percentage of employment occurs in the more recession-proof industries.

The Contribution of the Components of Spending to Cycles

During the period following the Great Depression, economists were concerned with the primary causes of the Depression; in other words, they wanted to know what the impulse had been and then why it had been propagated. Many attributed the impulse to spending, either investment or consumption. Others attributed the cause to monetary factors. Still others looked to productivity shocks. In a typical cycle, money growth, consumption, investment, and labor productivity all behave procyclically, and it is difficult to separate their influences.

It appears that consumer expenditures do nothing but rise. However, real consumer expenditures on durable goods fluctuate a great deal. In contrast, consumption of nondurable goods and services shows relatively small cyclical movements, rising and falling about one-third as much as durables, as shown in Figure 15-5. The main reason for the difference is that durable goods are accumulated and render services over time; their purchases are postponable. Services are consumed immediately and are not storable. Nondurables fall in between; they don't have to be consumed immediately but are not storable for a long period of time.

U.S. gross private domestic investment is shown in Figure 15-6A. Panel B shows business fixed investment and housing (residential investment). You can

FIGURE 15-5   *Consumption. Personal consumer expenditures do not seem to fluctuate much. However, real consumer expenditures on durable goods do fluctuate. In contrast, consumption of nondurable goods and services shows relatively small cyclical movements, rising and falling about one-third as much as durables.*

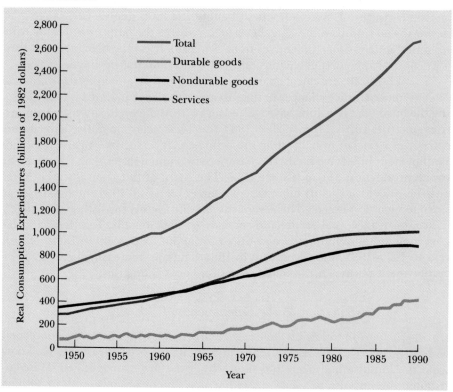

FIGURE 15-6 *Investment. Gross private domestic investment is shown in panel A, and business fixed investment and housing (residential investment) plus changes in business inventories are shown in panel B. Inventory investment is the most volatile of the spending components. In both the pre- and postwar periods, inventory changes have played a major role in business cycles.*

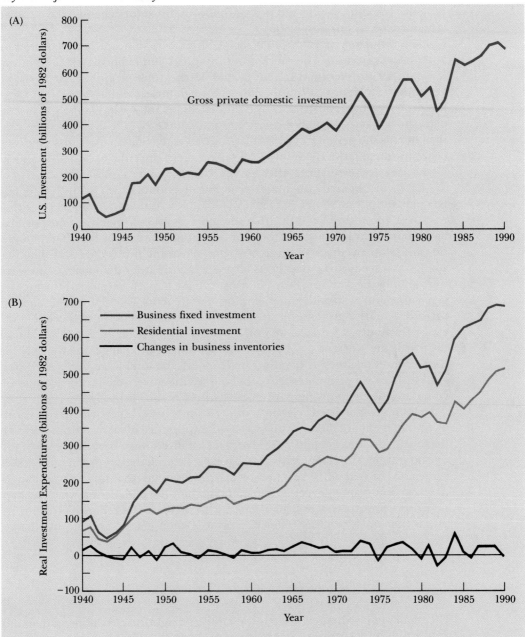

see that the cyclical swings in business investment exceeded those in consumer durables and housing early on, but in the postwar period movements in business investment and consumer durables and housing have been more nearly equal. Inventory investment, however, is the most volatile of the spending components. In both the pre- and postwar periods, inventory changes have played a major role in business cycles.

The influence of the foreign sector also varies, but not between the pre- and postwar periods. The ratio of both imports and exports to U.S. GNP was lower in 1950–1969 than in any period before 1929 or after 1970 as shown for imports in Figure 15-7A. Also, direct foreign investment in the United States has grown tremendously since the mid-1970s, as shown in Figure 15-7B. Foreign shocks were a much more important source of U.S. cycles before 1914 than during the period from 1914–1973. The United States was virtually a closed economy during the 1950s and 1960s. And then, since the early 1970s, shocks in the foreign sector have affected the U.S. economy significantly.

Labor productivity fluctuates procyclically; hours of labor input fluctuate less than output, as shown in Figure 15-8. Thus, as output rises and labor input rises less, the ratio of output to labor input rises; conversely, as output falls and labor input falls less, the ratio of output to labor input falls. The fluctuations of labor productivity have been greater in the postwar period. The reason for this seems to be that firms lay workers off rather than spread out work time among the workers. Firms do this, at least in part, because of the greater generosity and availability of unemployment benefits. Unemployment benefits provide a subsidy to those firms that lay off workers relative to those that decrease the hours of work for all workers but don't lay them off. If a firm chooses to spread the work out, the total wage bill does not change but the average income level declines. If firms lay workers off, the total wage bill is no different but because of the income provided by the government, the average income level is higher. The path of real wages is shown in Figure 15-9.

The more persistent rise in wages and prices and increased fluctuations of employment are linked. The increased importance of labor unions between the late 1930s and the mid-1970s led to centralized wage bargaining and multiyear contracts in many industries. Today's wage changes were in many cases agreed on last year or the year before; this process tends to insulate wage changes from current market forces and to increase their dependence on what has happened previously. However, it also tends to increase the reliance on labor input as the adjustment mechanism firms use when market conditions change.

▼
Business Cycle Controversies

The theory of business cycles may look quite straightforward: either a demand or a supply shock causes the economy to move away from equilibrium for a period of time whose length depends on sticky wages and other aspects of the

FIGURE 15-7   *The foreign sector. The ratio of imports to U.S. GNP was lower in 1950–1969 than in any period after 1970, as shown in panel A. Also, direct foreign investment in the United States has grown tremendously since the mid-1970s, as shown in panel B. The United States was virtually a closed economy during the 1950s and 1960s. Since the early 1970s, foreign sector shocks have affected the U.S. economy significantly.*

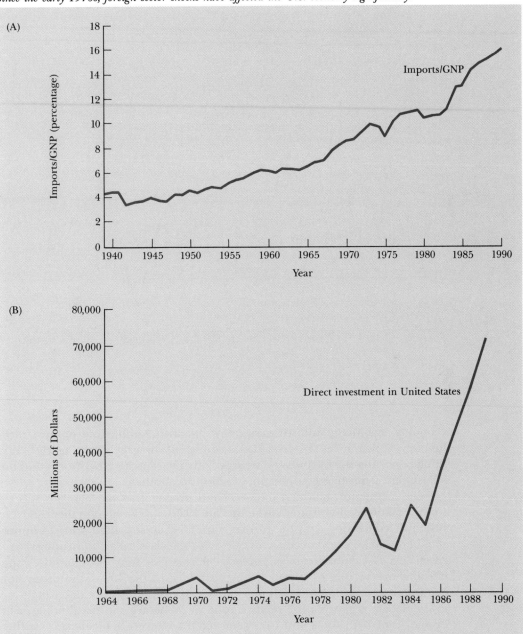

FIGURE 15-8   *Labor productivity. Labor productivity fluctuates procyclically; hours of labor input fluctuate less than output. Thus, as output rises and labor input rises less, the ratio of output to labor input rises; conversely, as output falls and labor input falls less, the ratio of output to labor input falls. The fluctuations of labor productivity have been greater in the postwar period.*

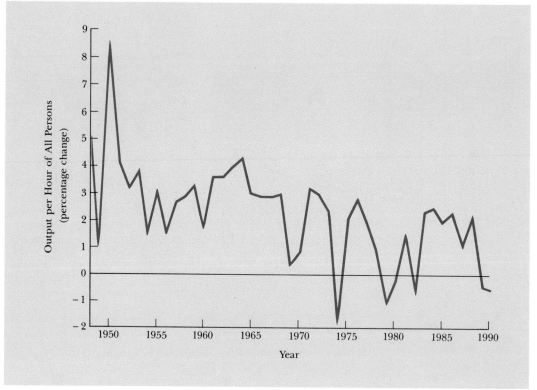

economy, eventually adjusting to a new long-run equilibrium point. Unfortunately, appearances are deceiving. Economists disagree about nearly everything regarding the business cycle, especially the causes of the shocks and the adjustment from one equilibrium position to another.

The distinction between impulses and propagation mechanisms was introduced into economic analysis in the late 1920s. Pre-Keynesian theories were primarily concerned with the propagation mechanism, attempting to understand how cycles could occur in the world of the classical, equilibrium system. After Keynes, economists began to focus more on the sources of impulses; specifically, on the role of money in the economy. In the 1960s, the profession lost interest in business cycle theory per se as economists became caught up in the debate regarding the relative roles of monetary and fiscal policy. The oil shocks of 1973–1974 and 1979 renewed the interest in business cycle fluctuations. Another effect of the supply shocks of the 1970s was to shift the blame away from government as the sole source of shocks. The monetary-fiscal con-

FIGURE 15-9   *Real wages. Real wages have shown a persistent rise in the postwar period. The percentage change has not fallen below zero in the last two decades—although they have slowed, wages and total labor compensation have continued to rise even during recessions.*

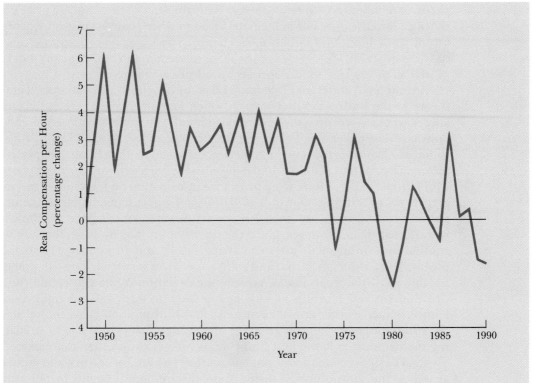

troversy of the 1960s had attributed the source of economic fluctuations to monetary policy decisions of the Federal Reserve Board and the fiscal policy decisions of successive administrations. But the oil shocks of the 1970s, and again in 1990 and 1991, were clearly an external phenomenon that forced on the Fed a decision whether or not to accommodate. In turn, this realization led to a broader perspective on the nature of monetary shocks. They are now viewed not just as external shocks but as part of the propagation mechanism, as monetary authorities react to changes in interest rates, inflation, unemployment, and federal deficits.

Business Cycle Theories

Today there are two basic views of the business cycle: the **equilibrium** or **real business cycle**, often called the **neoclassical business cycle**, and the **disequilibrium** or **neo-Keynesian business cycle**. We've discussed these two views before in terms of the *AD–AS* framework; the neoclassical and neo-Keynesian approaches. The neo-Keynesian business cycle relies on sticky wages and/or prices to create the propagation mechanisms. The sticky wages and/or prices resulting from long-term contracts create disequilibrium situations—excess capacity or involuntary unemployment. With the sticky wages and/or prices, a shock or impulse does not immediately lead to price changes; instead, quantities of labor input and output must change. The impulses of importance in the Keynesian business cycle are the large monetary and real demand shocks as well as the supply shocks such as an oil price change.

A completely different direction is taken by neoclassical economists. Their theory of the business cycle is one in which market clearing or equilibrium always occurs. According to the equilibrium business cycle, the underlying impulse could be either a monetary or a real ("productivity") shock, and the propagation mechanism is the result of imperfect information. In the case of imperfect information, output responds to the impulse for the length of time that agents, with rational expectations, need to acquire information on the value of the aggregate shock. Firms and/or individuals do not adjust immediately to the impulse because they do not know with certainty what has occurred and how it has affected them. However, given the information they do have, they are in equilibrium—individuals are maximizing utility and firms are maximizing profits. Thus, although output and employment can vary from long-run potential output or the trend rate of growth, the deviation is not a disequilibrium situation. Instead, it results because people *choose* to work less and enjoy more leisure, which also reduces their income and consumption. This choice may be mistaken in hindsight, but given the information that people had when making the decision, it is the best (utility-maximizing) choice they can make.

Real business cycle theory emphasizes the substitution of work and leisure as well as the substitution of saving and consumption. It begins by pointing out that an increase in government purchases increases the demand for goods. To achieve equilibrium in the goods market, the real interest rate must rise, which reduces consumption and investment. The increase in the real interest rate also causes individuals to reallocate leisure across time. In particular, at a higher real interest rate working today becomes relatively more attractive than working in the future; workers can earn more income today and buy assets or make deposits with that income, generating the higher interest earnings. So today's labor supply increases. This increase in labor supply causes equilibrium employment and output to rise.

Although neo-Keynesian theory also predicts a rise in the real interest rate in response to a temporary increase in government purchases, the effect of the real interest rate on labor supply does not play a crucial role. Instead, the increase in employment and output is due to the reduced amount of unemployed or underused labor. In the neo-Keynesian theory, the labor market is in a state of disequilibrium.

Thus, the real business cycle theorists must explain why people willingly alter their consumption and leisure activity and do so relatively quickly. Keynesian theorists, in contrast, must explain how an economy can get bogged down in a disequilibrium situation for a rather long time.

One Impulse, None, or Many?

Research on business cycles centers on two questions. The first question concerns the number of impulses. Monetarists often single out monetary shocks as the main source of fluctuations. Other economists argue that there are many, equally important sources of shocks, and that the shocks may be quite small but accumulate to cause relatively large fluctuations in output and employment.

The second question concerns propagation—the way the shocks lead to large fluctuations. Are fluctuations in economic activity caused by an accumulation of small shocks, where each shock is unimportant if viewed in isolation but together are important? Or are fluctuations due to infrequent large shocks? The first view agrees with the equilibrium business cycle approach: small technological shocks by themselves may have small effects, but when they accumulate and reverberate throughout the economy they lead to large fluctuations in output and employment.

In contrast, the neo-Keynesians feel that infrequent, large, identifiable shocks dominate all others. Particular economic fluctuations can be ascribed to particular large shocks followed by periods during which the economy returns to equilibrium. Such a view is implicit in the description of (1) periods such as the Vietnam War expansion, (2) the oil price shocks, and (3) the actions of the Fed. This view dominates the neo-Keynesian theories. The large shock leads to disequilibrium that takes a long time to correct and that may require governmental corrective action. As seen in previous chapters, the reasons given for the disequilibrium include long-term contracts and the costs of changing prices.

In the analyses of real business cycles, a monetary growth rate increase either has very temporary effects on output and employment or *absolutely no effects,* depending on whether the increase is a surprise or not. The money growth rise may lead to a deviation from the trend as individuals try to reduce their real balances and adjust their hours of work and leisure, and as firms adjust their production and employment levels. But as soon as it is realized that the monetary growth occurred, then wage and price levels are adjusted and production and employment return to their long-term growth paths. According to the real business cycle theory, whenever a shock or impulse affects the real interest rate, individuals alter their work and leisure allocation, choosing to work more now and enjoy more leisure time in the future as the real interest rate increases. By working more now, they earn more income now and with that income they can earn more interest. The higher the interest rate, the greater the substitution from leisure to work. The increased labor supply enables firms to increase output, and the economy expands. As wages and prices rise and real interest rates fall, workers choose to put in fewer hours and firms decrease production. The economy then returns toward the path taken by the long-term growth trend.

According to the real business cycle view of an oil shock, there is no involuntary unemployment. The higher price of oil means that profit rates decline; firms try to reduce output while at the same time substituting from oil to labor inputs. With their costs rising, firms pass along some increases in the form of higher prices. The higher price level raises the nominal interest rate but the real interest rate declines. This induces workers to substitute more leisure for labor. In the recession, workers voluntarily choose to work less. Depending on how the oil shock affects the sectors of the economy and the geographic areas of the economy, the adjustment back to the long-run trend may be smooth or may contain fluctuations.

Because the real business cycle theory describes economic fluctuations as a changing equilibrium, it implies that these fluctuations are **efficient**. The term *efficient* means that given the tastes of individuals and the technological possibilities facing society, the levels of employment, output, and consumption cannot be improved. Attempts by government to alter the allocations of the private market, such as policies to stabilize employment or to accommodate the oil shock, at best are ineffective and at worst can do harm by impeding the adjustment back to the long-term trend rate of growth. With the Keynesian business cycle theory, however, government policy can play a very important stabilizing role. The disequilibrium situation is inefficient and requires appropriate monetary and/or fiscal policy.

Evidence and the Solow Residual

It is difficult to distinguish the neoclassical and neo-Keynesian business cycles by examining actual business cycle data. One of the major arguments about the real business cycle is that technological shocks cause the cycles. Yet advocates of real business cycle theories have trouble convincing skeptics that the economy is subject to such large and sudden changes in technology. Recently, the debate over this issue has centered on the fundamental growth equation discussed in Chapter 14. The equation states that economic growth depends on the growth of resources (labor and capital) and technological changes:

$$\% \ \Delta \ Y \ = \ \%\Delta \ TFP \ + \ 0.3 \ (\% \ \Delta \ K) \ + \ 0.7 \ (\% \ \Delta \ L)$$

where *TFP* is total factor productivity or technological change, $\%\Delta Y$ is real output growth, $\%\Delta K$ is capital growth, and $\%\Delta L$ is labor force growth.

As noted in Chapter 14, ignoring technological change, about 25 percent of the growth in output is not accounted for by resource growth:

$$\% \ \Delta \ Y \ > \ 0.3 \ (\% \ \Delta \ K) \ + \ 0.7 \ (\% \ \Delta \ L)$$

The difference between output growth and the growth of resources is referred to as the **Solow residual**, named after economist Robert Solow.

$$\text{Solow residual} = \% \, \Delta \, Y - 0.3 \, (\% \, \Delta \, K) + 0.7 \, (\% \, \Delta \, L)$$

The Solow residual is then the proportion of economic growth that might be attributable to technological changes.

Advocates of the real business cycle have argued that because the Solow residual fluctuates and is large, it can account for a large proportion of the fluctuations in output. You can see in Figure 15-10 that the Solow residual does fluctuate a great deal and does fluctuate with fluctuations in output.

The critics of real business cycles have attacked the Solow residual on several grounds. First, it is argued that capital and labor are mismeasured so that the residual is much smaller than has been suggested. Second, it is argued that under conditions of market power (or imperfect competition), the residual does not exist or is very small. The argument stems from the fundamental equation of growth, which is derived by assuming perfect competition where factor payments are equal to factor marginal revenue products. When perfect competi-

FIGURE 15-10   *The Solow residual. Advocates of the real business cycle have argued that because the Solow residual fluctuates and is large, it can account for a large proportion of the fluctuations in output. You can see that the Solow residual does fluctuate a great deal and does fluctuate with fluctuations in output.*

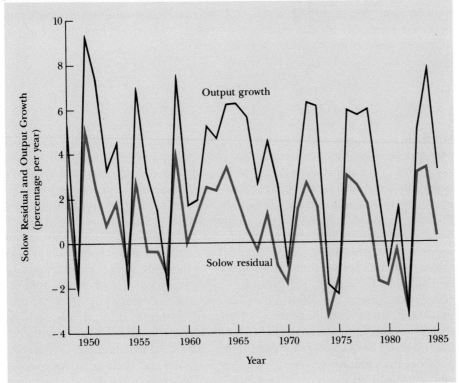

tion does not hold in resource and output markets, then factor payments are not equal to factor marginal revenue products. In this case, the Solow residual given by the fundamental equation is too large by the amount of the deviation between factor payments and factor marginal revenue products. If the residual is very small, then technological changes accordingly account only for a small portion of the output fluctuations characteristic of business cycles.

Proponents of real business cycles argue that fluctuations in employment over the cycle are fully voluntary. The critics argue that for the substitution to occur at the rate suggested by the real business cycle, labor supply must be very elastic, with a wage elasticity of about 2. Evidence has shown an elasticity of less than 0.5.

The neo-Keynesian economists must argue for rigidities in wages and prices so that involuntary changes in employment and output occur. Critics of this theory argue that the logic of disequilibria is disturbing; people don't let themselves be continually thrown involuntarily into and out of employment; and contracts and other institutional features of the economy adapt to offset the involuntary nature of business cycles. In addition, the Keynesian focus on a few large shocks is criticized as not accounting for most fluctuations of the economy.

So where is the research on business cycles today? We are in the middle of debate and controversy. Neoclassical and neo-Keynesian business cycle theorists are searching for the evidence to provide a knockout blow to the opponents. To date, none has been found.

▼
Reading and Interpreting Data

Students of business cycles become Fed watchers as well as fiscal policy and foreign exchange watchers. They must follow the patterns or trends that arise in important economic data. Fortunately, many of the data are provided in very accessible sources. The U.S. Departments of Commerce and Labor publish a great deal of economic data. These data are reported in several sources. The *Economic Report of the President* (Washington, DC: U.S. Government Printing Office) is available in January or February of each year. It includes the annual reports of the president and the Council of Economic Advisers as well as data tables. The data are presented in quarterly or monthly form for a short period and annually for most of the post-World War II period. The monthly publication *Economic Indicators* (Washington, DC: Council of Economic Advisers) provides the most recent data on total output, unemployment, prices, money, federal finance, and international statistics. Historical series are not presented. The *Business Conditions Digest* (Washington, DC: U.S. Department of Commerce) provides information on many economic variables and their behavior over recent months. The *Survey of Current Business* (Washington, DC: U.S. Department of Commerce) publishes monthly the most recent national income data and data related to general business conditions. The *Monthly Labor Review* is published monthly by the U.S. Department of Labor. In addition to articles summarizing various developments in the U.S. labor market, detailed monthly labor and productivity data are published. Data on hours worked, labor turnover, unemployment rates, employment status, and earnings are presented. The *Federal Reserve Bulletin* (Washington, DC: Board of Governors of the Federal Reserve System), published monthly, provides detailed data on monetary aggregates, interest rates, the financial position of commercial banks, and federal finances. The *International Financial Statistics* (Washington, DC: International Monetary Fund) is a monthly publication that provides data on all aspects of domestic and international finance. It shows for member nations the current annual, quarterly, and monthly data related to exchange rates, international liquidity, money and banking, trade, prices, and incomes. The *Main Economic Indicators* is published in Paris by the Organization for Economic Cooperation and Development (OECD). The OECD compiles monthly data on national income accounts, production, wages, prices, home and foreign finance, and international trade and payments for many countries.

Even more accessible are the reports that appear in the *Wall Street Journal* and other daily newspapers. Important Federal Reserve data are published every Friday in the *Wall Street Journal*.[1] The data appear in section C, "Money and Investing," under the title "Federal Reserve Data." The data presented include monetary aggregates and reserve aggregates. Items of particular interest to monetary policy watchers include free reserves, because this series indicates whether the Fed is tightening or loosening its monetary policy.

As we know from previous chapters, the Fed manipulates the banking system's reserves primarily by buying or selling U.S. government securities on the open market. When the Fed buys securities, the sellers deposit the proceeds of the sale in their banks, and the banking system's reserves grow. When the Fed *sells* securities, buyers withdraw funds from their banks to make the purchases, and bank reserves fall.

Trillions of dollars of U.S. Treasury securities are outstanding, and anyone (domestic and foreign corporations, individuals, state, local, and foreign governments, and private and central banks) can buy them. Billions of dollars are traded each day in New York City. The Fed uses U.S. Treasury securities rather than some other instrument to carry out its monetary policy activities because the Fed's activities are a very small part of the total government securities market. The Fed could just as easily deal in common stock or some other asset, but doesn't do so primarily because it doesn't want its actions to upset the stock market or some other asset market. The Fed purchased $240 billion

---

1   Michael Lehmann, *The Dow Jones Guide to Reading the Wall Street Journal* (Homewood, IL: Dow Jones-Irwin, 3d ed., 1990) provides an entire book on reading and interpreting the data given in the *Wall Street Journal*.

of U.S. government securities during the week of April 17, 1991. If the Fed had purchased $240 billion of common stock it would expand bank reserves just as surely as when it sold Treasury bills in the open market. However, because an individual company, even as large as General Motors, might have only $100 thousand trade during a week, the Fed purchases could swamp any other investors in the stock market.

Perhaps the best indicator of Fed's impact on the banking system is free reserves. The **free reserves** — or excess reserves minus reserves borrowed from the Fed — measure the extent to which the banking system is flush with or short of funds for lending. As noted, these data are reported each Friday in the *Wall Street Journal* under the heading "Federal Reserve Data." The data list includes a table that looks like Table 15-3. The notes in parentheses, "(sa)" or "(nsa)," represent whether the data are seasonally adjusted or not seasonally adjusted.

The free reserves indicate the impact of the Fed's actions on the banking system. The Fed supplies the banking system with reserves by buying securities, and it deprives the system of reserves by selling securities. If the Fed wants to slow the economy down, it sells securities and reduces the quantity of reserves. But if the Fed does this when the demand for loans is high, the banking system finds itself short of reserves. The banks then consider borrowing from the Fed at a Federal Reserve specified rate of interest, the *discount rate*. If borrowing exceeds excess reserves, the free reserves figure will be negative. This is a sign that bank lending is expanding at the same time the Fed is trying to restrain the banks and the expansion. Conversely, during a period of slack economic activity or a period in which the Fed is easing, the free reserves figure is positive. Thus, we usually find that free reserves are positive when the Fed pursues an expansionary policy and are negative when Fed policy turns contractionary.

The money supply is reported in each Friday's *Wall Street Journal* "Federal Reserve Data" as well. *M1, M2,* and *M3* are listed for the previous week and the previous four weeks.

Another indicator of Fed policy is interest rates. Key "Money Rates" are reported in the *Wall Street Journal*. The rates reported include the prime rate, the federal funds rate, the discount rate, the LIBOR rate (London Interbank Offered Rates), and the Treasury bill rate, among others. The federal funds rate is the rate banks charge one another for overnight loans of reserves in amounts of $1 million or more. The LIBOR rate is the rate charged on loans between major London banks; it is comparable to the U.S. federal funds rate but signals what is happening to world interest rates. In addition to the "Money Rates," short-term interest rates are reported daily in the *Wall Street Journal* under the heading "Markets Diary."

The federal funds rate was 5 ⅞ percent on April 19, 1991; the discount rate was 6 percent; the LIBOR rate on a one-month instrument was 6 ⅛ percent; and the Treasury bill rate on a thirteen-week instrument was 5.57 percent. Movements of these rates indicate the relative tightness or ease of the money markets and of Fed policy. A rising federal funds rate is a sign that the Fed is

TABLE 15-3   *Federal Reserve Data*

	Two weeks ended:	
	Apr. 17	Apr. 3
Total Reserves (sa)	49,502	50,022
Nonborrowed Reserves (sa)	49,279	49,810
Required Reserves (sa)	48,594	48,667
Excess Reserves (nsa)	907	1,355
Borrowings from Fed (nsa)	147	150
Free Reserves (nsa)	760	1,205
Monetary Base (sa)	308,883	312,090

Source: Wall Street Journal, April 19, 1991.

draining reserves from the banks with open-market operations, forcing some banks to borrow reserves from other banks. A falling federal funds rate suggests an easing of Fed policy. For instance, the federal funds rate fell during most of the first half of 1991, suggesting that Fed policy was easing in this period.

Every Tuesday, the *Wall Street Journal* reports key interest rates. The Tuesday report includes long-term as well as short-term rates. For instance, rates for Treasury bills (one year), Treasury notes (three, five, and ten years), and Treasury bonds (thirty years) are all reported for the current and previous weeks. The relationship between these Treasury instruments of different lengths is indicated daily in a chart showing the treasury yield curve. An example of a yield curve is shown in Figure 15-11. It measures interest rates on the vertical axis and time on the horizontal axis. A yield curve can take on several different shapes. The traditional curve shows interest rates rising as the maturity length rises, as shown in panel A of Figure 15-11. In some periods, however, the yield curve may be humped or may even slope downward, as shown in panel B. When this occurs, it is often interpreted as an attempt by the Fed to tighten monetary policy using short-term Treasury securities. Whatever the reason, it means that investors think that rates will fall in the future.

Money and interest rate data are more accessible and reported more frequently than other economic data. The U.S. Department of Commerce publishes foreign trade data only once per month or once per quarter (four times a year). The *Wall Street Journal* regularly publishes two Department of Commerce reports dealing with the balance of payments and the balance of trade. The BOP figures for the previous quarter appear in the third week of the last month of each quarter. Monthly balance of trade figures for the previous month are also published in the third week of each month. Most of the time you will find the reports in text form as opposed to tables. For instance, a headline might read "Trade Deficit Falls" for an article dealing with current BOP data.

Foreign exchange rates are published daily in virtually every newspaper, including the *Wall Street Journal*. In the *Journal* under the title "Markets Diary" is a record of the dollar's value compared with an average or trade-weighted index of 15 currencies. In addition, under the title "World Value of the Dol-

FIGURE 15-11   *The yield curve. A yield curve measures interest rates on the vertical axis and time on the horizontal axis. A yield curve can take on several different shapes. The traditional curve shows interest rates rising as the maturity length rises, as shown in panel A. There are periods, however, when the yield curve may be humped or may even slope downward, as shown in panel B. When this occurs, it is often interpreted as an attempt by the Fed to tighten monetary policy using short-term Treasury securities. Whatever the reason, it means that investors think that rates will fall in the future.*

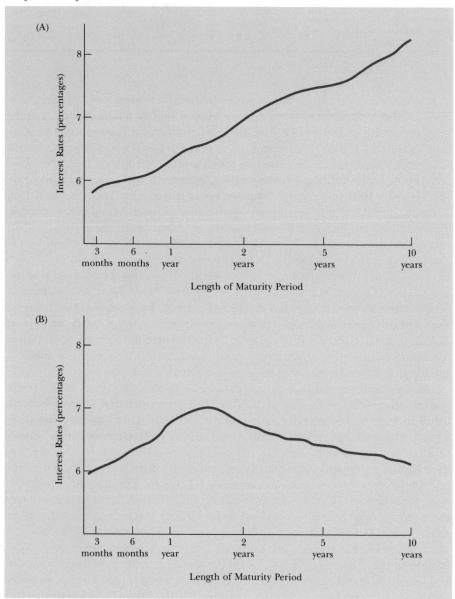

Source: N. Gregory Mankiw, "Real Business Cycles: A New Keynesian Perspective," National Bureau of Economic Research, Working Paper No. 2882.

lar," the exchange rate of the U.S. dollar to most trading partners is listed. This provides a broad view of the behavior of the dollar on foreign exchange markets. In addition, each day a table of exchange rates is reported. Along with the daily rates, futures rates are noted. A future rate is the rate for delivery of foreign exchange at some point in the future as contracted today. Because some buyers and sellers know they will deliver some goods and services in the future, they want to avoid any exchange rate risk (risk that exchange rates will change to the detriment of the customers), so they contract for the foreign exchange at a specified rate. The future rates give some indication of how investors feel about the behavior of the dollar or some other currencies vis-à-vis other currencies over the next month, three months, or year.

Fiscal policy data are reported in the daily newspapers in text form as well. Typically a heading such as "Federal Debt Hits New High" indicates that the article refers to federal finances. The Department of Commerce provides quarterly data and the historical data are reported in the *Economic Report of the President.*

▼   ▼   ▼   ▼   ▼   ▼   ▼   ▼   ▼   ▼   ▼

Conclusions

Macroeconomists are focusing on two aspects of economic behavior: growth and cycles. In this chapter, we looked at the business cycle. The study of cycles takes the form of examining the initial cause of a departure from potential output (the impulse) and the reasons why a cycle will continue after the impulse (the propagation mechanism). The debates over the impulse and propagation are not too dissimilar from the early debates between the classical and Keynesian economic schools. The debates continue because neither side has acquired the information that demonstrates unquestionable support for its arguments.

During the past century, business cycles have changed. They are now less volatile and contain rigidities in prices and wages that were not there in the pre-World War I period. Federal Reserve policy and fiscal policy are given credit (or criticized) for causing business cycles and for the greater stability observed, including the price and wage rigidities.

▼   ▼   ▼   ▼   ▼   ▼   ▼   ▼   ▼   ▼   ▼

Summary

1. What is a business cycle?
A business cycle is the movement of real GNP through a trough to a peak followed by the movement to another trough. A business cycle is actually a deviation from the trend or long-run growth path of the economy.

2. What is a propagation mechanism, and what is an impulse?
In the business cycle literature, the term *impulse* refers to the initial cause of the cycle—a demand or supply shock, for instance. The term *propagation mechanism* refers to the continuation of a cycle after the initial impulse occurs.

3. What do economists disagree about in business cycle theory?
Economists agree on almost nothing about business cycles. The current disagreement is very reminiscent of the debates between Keynesians and classicalists. The debate centers around whether the economy tends to automatically reach equilibrium at the potential output level (natural unemployment level) or remains mired in recessions for long periods of time.

4. Has the business cycle changed over time?
Yes, the business cycle has changed over time. Before 1920, the cycles were harsher than after 1945. In addition to the increased economic stability after 1945, prices have tended not to fall during recessions, as they did before 1920.

▼
Key Terms

impulses   360
propagation   360
equilibrium business cycle   373
real business cycle   373
neoclassical business cycle   373

disequilibrium business cycle   373
neo-Keynesian business cycle   373
efficient   376
Solow residual   376
free reserves   380

▼
Problems and Exercises

1.   Describe the basic differences between the real business cycle and the neo-Keynesian business cycle.

2.   Using the *AD–AS* diagram and the dynamic business cycle diagram, illustrate what is meant by an impulse and a propagation mechanism.

3.   With the multiplier–accelerator model, substitute the following values and solve for the dynamic behavior of Y.
   (1) $a = 0.2$, MPC $= 0.8$
   (2) $a = 0.2$, MPC $= 0.4$
   (3) $a = 2.0$, MPC $= 0.5$

4.   What is the Solow residual? Why do the real business cycle theorists claim that it supports their theory? How would you counter the claim that the residual is large?

5.   Describe how you, as the president's chief economic adviser, would tell him or her to proceed with respect to monetary and fiscal policy during a recession if you supported the Keynesian business cycle theory? If you supported the real business cycle theory?

6.   Does it matter which business cycle theory policymakers support when an oil price shock occurs, as when Iraq invaded Kuwait in 1990?

7.   Using the *AD–AS* model, illustrate the difference between the real business cycle impulse and the Keynesian business cycle theory impulse.

8.   In a Friday edition of the *Wall Street Journal,* find the Federal Reserve data and use these data to indicate what the Fed is doing in terms of monetary policy.

Part Six

Extensions

Chapter 16

Consumption

What to Expect

Back in the 1940s, the marginal propensity to consume provided the corner-stone for the Keynesian analysis of the economy, indicating that changes in expenditures can result in multiplied changes in output and income. Several implications arising from the Keynesian analysis of consumption and the marginal propensity to consume (MPC) did not appear to be supported by reality in the following decades. The multiplier did not seem to be as large as the consumption function suggested, and changes in government purchases did not result in multiplied changes in output and income, at least not very quickly. Economists began to reconsider the consumption function. They discovered that the consumption function specified by Keynes gave too much emphasis to the impact of current changes in income on consumption. As a result, they began to forge a new, more forward-looking consumption function, one that did not specify a large and immediate reaction by consumers to changes in current income. This chapter examines this new theory of consumption and its implications for monetary and fiscal policy and savings. The following questions are considered:

1. Does the simple consumption function, where consumption depends on current income, describe consumer behavior?

2. *What does it mean to say that consumers are "forward-looking?"*

3. *What are the determinants of saving?*

4. *What has been the pattern of national saving in the United States and in other countries?*

▼
The Simple Consumption Function

The consumption function that played the key role in Keynes's view of the economy describes consumer spending as dependent on disposable income in a form something like the following:

$$C = C_0 + c_y YD$$

With this consumption function, we find that the marginal propensity to consume (c_y) is constant and is less than 1. We also find that the saving-to-income ratio rises as income rises. In other words, the percentage of total income that is saved rises during expansions and falls during recessions, according to the Keynesian consumption function.

Short-Run Versus Long-Run Consumption Functions

Several important implications came from this consumption function. First, consumption rises (falls) by the MPC times the disposable income change whenever current disposable income rises (falls). Second, and related to the first, fiscal policy (and/or monetary policy) can rely on the MPC and thus the multiplier to expand changes in spending into larger changes in output and income. Third, because saving rises during expansions and because more saving means less spending, then income must eventually decline. This paradox of thrift created some problems for economists during and immediately after World War II. Many economists predicted that when the war ended the combination of less government spending and increased saving on the part of the public would cause the economy to stagnate. The behavior of the economy surprised economists as predictions were not supported by the economic statistics. The stagnation did not occur following World War II, and then in the 1950s and 1960s it became clear that the multiplier was not as large as had been predicted. Finally, in the early 1970s it was found that temporary tax changes seemed to have no effect on consumer behavior.

The real world did not seem to operate as the consumption function described. In fact, economists had discovered a puzzle: the data seemed to indicate two different consumption functions, a *short-run* function that looked much like the Keynesian function, and a *long-run* function that looked very different from the Keynesian function and described consumer behavior that was significantly different.

Consumption Data

Figure 16-1 shows two consumption (C) functions. The long-run line, labeled C^{lr}, is derived by plotting combinations of total real disposable income and total real consumption expenditures for each year from 1960 to 1990. The short-run line, labeled C^{sr}, is derived by plotting the consumption expenditures associated with each family income level during one particular year, such as 1985. There are differences between the two consumption lines. The long-run line, C^{lr}, nearly intersects the origin. Hence it has an algebraic form like $C = 0.90YD$, where there is no autonomous consumption and the MPC is 0.9. For the short-run line, C^{sr}, we get results more in conformity with the simple consumption model. The constant, autonomous consumption, is not zero and the MPC is about 0.8. Why the difference? Perhaps a simple example will illustrate.

Suppose the economy is composed of only five families and that their consumption and income levels in 1990 were as follows:

Family	Income	Consumption
A	$ 10,000	$ 13,000
B	20,000	18,000
C	30,000	23,000
D	40,000	28,000
E	50,000	33,000
Total	$150,000	$115,000
Average	30,000	23,000

If these consumption–income combinations are plotted, the 1990 consumption function will be that shown in Figure 16-2 as C_{1990}. In algebraic form, the data are represented by the equation $C = 8,000 + 0.5Y$. Now suppose that another study is conducted on these same five families in 1991, and their income and consumption levels are found to be as follows. This sample is plotted as C_{1991} in Figure 16-2.

Family	Income	Consumption
A	$ 20,000	$ 24,000
B	30,000	29,000
C	40,000	34,000
D	50,000	39,000
E	60,000	44,000
Total	$200,000	$170,000
Average	40,000	34,000

FIGURE 16-1   *The short-run and long-run consumption functions. The long-run line, labeled* C^{lr}, *is derived by plotting combinations of total income and total consumption expenditures for each year from 1960 to 1990. The short-run line, labeled* C^{sr}, *is derived by plotting the consumption expenditures associated with each family income level during one particular year, such as 1985. The long-run line has an algebraic form like* C = 0.90YD *where there is no autonomous consumption and the MPC is 0.9. For the short-run line,* C^{sr}, *results are more in conformity with the simple consumption model. The constant, autonomous consumption, is not zero, and the MPC is about 0.8.*

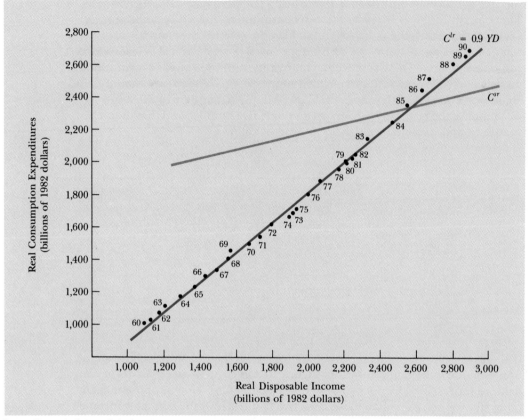

Source: Economic Report of the President, 1991 (Washington, DC: U.S. Government Printing Office, 1991).

The 1991 consumption line lies above the 1990 line in Figure 16-2. Algebraically, although the MPC is the same in both equations, the constant or autonomous part of consumption increased from 1990 to 1991. The algebraic form for the 1991 data is $C = 14,000 + 0.5Y$. Over time, the autonomous part of consumption rises.

As the short-run consumption function shifts up over time, it traces out the long-run consumption function. The average income level in 1990 is $30,000 and consumption is $23,000; in 1991 average income is $40,000 and consump-

FIGURE 16-2 *Shifting short-run consumption functions. Two consumption–income samples are plotted, one survey of families in 1990 and one for families in 1991. The 1991 consumption line lies above the 1990 line. Over time, the autonomous part of consumption rises. As the short-run consumption function shifts up over time, it traces out the long-run consumption function. The average income level in 1990 is $30,000 and consumption is $23,000; in 1991 average income is $40,000 and consumption is $34,000. Connecting these two combinations traces out the long-run consumption function.*

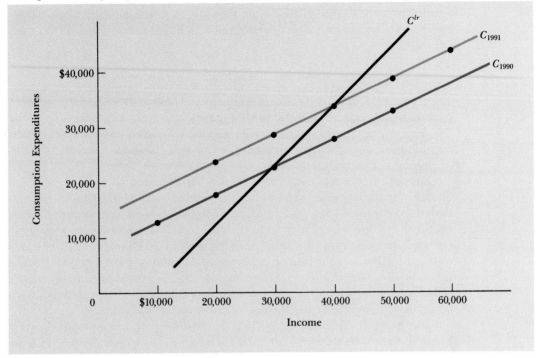

tion is $34,000. By connecting these two combinations, we trace out the long-run consumption function.

The discovery of the long-run and short-run consumption functions meant that economists had to reconsider the theory of consumption to make it consistent with both the short-run and the long-run consumption patterns. The simple consumption function was consistent only with the short-run pattern. Economists had to discover why the short-run consumption function shifted up over time. The new theory that emerged led to three basic conclusions: First, consumers tend to form expectations of their future income streams and to make expenditures on the basis of these expectations. In other words, consumers are forward-looking. Second, consumption does not change as current income changes to the extent that the simple consumption function predicted. Third, the multiplier is smaller than economists had previously thought.

▼
The Permanent Income and Life Cycle Theories

The main theme of the modern theory of consumption is that individuals are forward-looking, forming expectations of their future income and wealth and consuming accordingly. There are two versions of this modern theory, but their implications are so similar that often they are not distinguished. The brief discussion here focuses more on their common elements than on their differences.

The Permanent Income Theory

The first theory of consumption we consider is Milton Friedman's **permanent income hypothesis**. According to this theory, the most important input into the decision to consume nondurable goods and services and the services of durable goods is permanent income. The following example illustrates the idea of permanent income.

Suppose that a real estate salesperson has averaged an annual income of $20,000 for the few years she has been in the business. Her actual income has varied from a low of $8,000 to a high of $50,000. In addition, suppose she expects her average annual income to increase to $80,000 over the next few years. On what income would she base her consumption decisions? It would be most unlikely for her to consume on the basis of $10,000 or even $20,000, because she expects a large increase in her income. She is much more likely to consume on the basis of her expected income although her expectations might be tempered somewhat by her current and recent past income.

Similarly, if she is earning $80,000 and one year her income drops to $25,000, she probably won't cut back spending to the extent she would if she based her decisions solely on current income. Instead, she is more likely to maintain her lifestyle and to consume nearly the amount she had been spending in previous years by borrowing or drawing down savings.

On what basis does a person form expectations of future or permanent income? If someone has been in the work force for some time and has come back to school for a refresher or an additional degree, that person probably relies heavily on the income of the latest job to forecast future income. A full-time student might forecast his or her income on the basis of salaries of people currently in the chosen profession or of the college-educated population in general. In addition, he or she might look at future prospects of the chosen occupation and perhaps at monetary and fiscal policy and political developments. In other words, a full-time student most likely does not look solely at current income. So current income is unlikely to determine current consumption. In fact, a full-time student is probably consuming more than his or her current income today. The student is consuming more on the basis of permanent income—the level of income he or she expects to earn during the next several years.

The Life Cycle Theory

The other main theory of consumption behavior is known as the **life cycle theory**. It too focuses on the long run and on expectations. It emphasizes how people respond to the earnings and consumption streams they expect to experience over their lifetimes. The life cycle theory can be illustrated in Figure 16-3. Panel A plots the wage and age profile of full-time workers for one year. Income rises as age rises until about age 50 to 55 and then declines when retirement occurs.

Based on the pattern of Figure 16-3, how will someone of any given age decide how much of his or her income to consume? Will people consume little in their early years, increase consumption until about age 50, and then reduce consumption until death in order to follow the path of income? Most likely not. People just don't behave that way. They tend to increase their consumption moderately over the years, spending more than their income in the early years and saving more in the middle-aged years. In other words, people tend to use the entire life cycle of their income to determine their consumption rather than the income of any one year. We have sketched a typical consumption pattern on top of the age–earnings profile in panel B of Figure 16-3. The colored area is savings, and the gray areas are dissavings.

The life cycle theory suggests that if people had perfect information about their life spans they would consume their savings to the point that the day they die the amount of income left would be exactly zero except for any bequests they planned to leave. In recent years, people have continued to accumulate wealth and to save during their retirement years. Why? One explanation is that uncertainty is associated with the length of life, and people try to have a buffer for major or catastrophic events. People who want to leave bequests to their offspring may continue accumulating wealth because they don't know how long they will live. If they guess wrong and consume everything before death, they have nothing to leave their survivors.

The life cycle theory emphasizes an important role for wealth. If two people have identical income streams over their lives but one has more wealth than the other, their consumption patterns will not, in all likelihood, be the same. The person with wealth does not have to accumulate as many assets (save as much) during the middle portion of life in order to finance the retirement years (or leave an inheritance) as does the person without this wealth. As a result, we can expect the more wealthy individual to consume a higher proportion of any given income level than the less wealthy individual.

Household wealth consists of (1) short-term financial assets such as cash holdings, checking and savings accounts, and some types of bonds; (2) long-term financial assets such as stocks, long-term bonds, pension funds, and insurance policies; (3) real assets such as the real market value of consumer durables net of the debt on these durables, and houses and other real estate net of mortgage debt; and (4) human capital that household members acquire. An increase in any of these is an increase in wealth.

FIGURE 16-3   *The life cycle theory. Panel A shows the wage and age profile of full-time workers for one year. Income rises as age rises until about age 50 to 55 and then declines when retirement occurs. In panel B, the wage and age profile is put together with a consumption pattern. According to this pattern, people tend to increase their consumption moderately over the years, spending more than their income in the early years and saving more in the middle-aged years.*

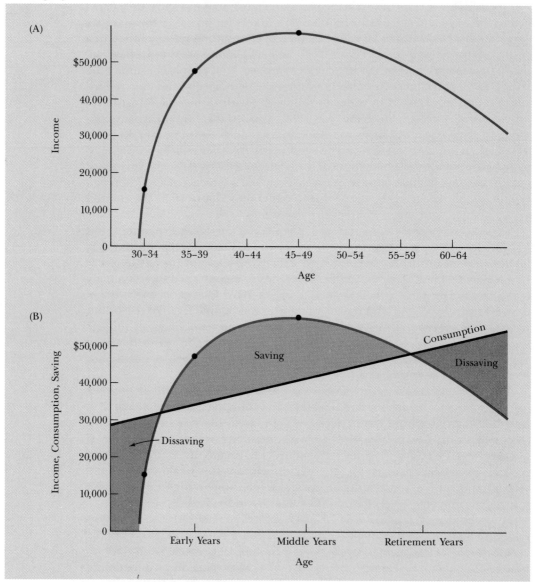

Source: U.S. Bureau of the Census, *Current Population Reports,* Series P-60, no. 154 (Washington, DC: U.S. Government Printing Office, 1989).

The life cycle theory reconciles the long- and short-run consumption functions by making consumption behavior depend on individual lifetime income profiles and wealth. Changes in income or wealth that people expect to be long lived or permanent induce them to change their consumption. Changes in income they consider only temporary have little effect on consumption.

Implications for Monetary and Fiscal Policy

The permanent income and life cycle theories of consumption focus on the long-run view of income and wealth for determining consumption, not the year-to-year or month-to-month levels of income. Both theories imply that income fluctuations that are considered only temporary have little effect on consumption.

What implications do these modern theories of consumption behavior have for monetary and fiscal policy? Their most immediate impact is on the multiplier. According to the multiplier analysis, a given change in spending leads to a multiplied change in income. Now substitute the permanent income or life cycle consumption theories in the analysis. If government spending rises from $500 billion to $510 billion during the year, what will households do in response? Under the prior analysis, we would expect households to spend a proportion as given by the MPC and to save the rest, so that the multiplier process would be off to the races. With the permanent income and life cycle theories, however, the response of households to the government spending change depends on whether they perceive the change to be temporary or permanent and how they expect the change to affect their long-run income.

If households don't expect the $10 billion increase in government purchases to raise their permanent incomes, they don't alter their spending behavior. They save most of the increased income. Conversely, if households expect their permanent incomes to rise, they may spend all the additional income they receive.

Consider, for example, a situation in which a family learns that Congress has enacted a tax revision that will result in a one-year increase in disposable income. What will the family do with that increase? If it spends the entire amount, nothing is left for future years. The only way the family can increase its consumption permanently is to save the new income and then spend only the interest earned on that income. A family can, alternatively, spend a part of the principal or all the additional income and thus have less to consume in the future. What will it do? The answer depends partly on how important the future is to the family. If the time preference (preference for spending today versus tomorrow) is heavily in favor of today, the family will choose to consume more today. Conversely, if the preference is more in favor of tomorrow, the family will save.

In contrast, a tax change that increases disposable income permanently (or winning a lottery that pays a yearly sum of money for life or for twenty years) leads people to alter consumption substantially. When the family learns that the tax revision will increase its disposable income by $2,000 each year, it doesn't have to worry quite so much about the impact of consuming the $2,000 today, because there will be another $2,000 tomorrow. Nevertheless, the time preference affects the actual amount consumed and saved. Most likely, the family will increase its annual consumption but won't consume the current equivalent of the entire additional $2,000 per year.

When an income change is temporary, consumption changes very little, in contrast to when an income change is permanent. How much less and how much more depend on the time preference. In general, however, the marginal propensity to consume out of current income is larger if the income change is expected to be more permanent. If a family receives an unexpected temporary increase in its disposable income, it raises its consumption by the interest earned on that increment plus a little bit more, depending on its rate of time preference. For example, a $2,000 tax cut that is expected to last only one year means, at 10 percent, an interest earnings of $200. With an MPC of 0.9, this additional $200 may induce additional consumption of $180. This is an MPC of only $180/$2,000 = 0.09 out of the current income change of $2,000. Now compare this to the Keynesian consumption function, where the $2,000 tax cut would have resulted in additional spending of an amount closer to $1,800, based on an MPC of 0.9.

An Example

To show how changes in current income may have only small impacts on current consumption, let us suppose that permanent income consists of a weighted average of past income levels. We'll denote permanent income as Y^p, actual income this period as Y_t, actual income last period as Y_{t-1}, and so on. For example, we'll specify that permanent income depends on a weighted average of past income levels:

$$Y_t^p = 0.4Y_t + 0.3Y_{t-1} + 0.2Y_{t-2} + 0.1Y_{t-3}$$

The farther the income is in the past, the less important it is in influencing permanent income, as shown by the declining weights, 0.4, 0.3, and so on.

Suppose income has been $20,000 for several periods. Then

$$Y_t^p = 0.4(\$20,000) + 0.3(\$20,000) + 0.2(\$20,000) + 0.1(\$20,000)$$
$$= \$20,000$$

Now, suppose that income this period increases from $20,000 to $30,000. Then permanent income rises to $24,000:

$$Y_t^p = 0.4(\$30,000) + 0.3(\$20,000) + 0.2(\$20,000) + 0.1(\$20,000)$$
$$= \$24,000$$

If the consumption function is $C_t = 0.9Y_t^p$, then $C_t = \$21,600$. If current consumption depended on current income only, $C_t = 0.9Y_t$, then consumption would have been $27,000.

The weights — 0.4, 0.3, and so on — were picked arbitrarily to illustrate how permanent income would adjust only a little to an unexpected increase in current income. Some studies have shown that the MPC out of current income may be as low as 0.1 and no more than half of the MPC out of permanent income.

AD–AS *and Consumption*

The main conclusion of the forward-looking permanent income hypothesis and life cycle theory of consumption is that the marginal propensity to consume out of current disposable income is much smaller than the simple consumption function implied. The smaller MPC not only leads to a flatter *AD* curve but also implies that any given increase in the autonomous components of spending is met with a smaller multiplied effect on income. For instance, if the MPC out of current income is 0.09 instead of 0.9, then the multiplier is 1.01 rather than 10. The smaller multiplier effect means that any change in autonomous spending has a much smaller impact on the economy than the simple consumption function implied. Thus, modern theories of consumption predict smaller fluctuations of output and prices than does the simple consumption function.

Because consumption is determined on the basis of the anticipated income stream over an individual's lifetime rather than just today's income, the impact of economic policy directed toward current income is greatly tempered. In sum, economic events that affect current income, but not the long-term income stream, do not tend to have very large effects on consumption. The life cycle and permanent income theories imply that consumption plays a small role in the business cycle, contributing significantly to neither the impulse nor the propagation of the cycle.

▼
Saving

Of course, when we are talking about consumption, we also are implicitly considering saving. Families choose to allocate their expected lifetime income between consumption and saving each period in a way that maximizes their utility. Depending on its rate of time preference (preference for spending today versus tomorrow) and the interest rate, a family chooses to spend a portion of its income today and save a portion.

As noted in Chapter 14, the U.S. saving rate is lower than that of other industrialized nations. Although international comparisons are always difficult to make, Table 16-1 shows the personal saving rates for the United States, Japan, the United Kingdom, and West Germany. The U.S. personal saving rate was 5.1 percent in 1985, compared with 22.5 percent in Japan, 11.9 percent in the United Kingdom, and 13.0 percent in West Germany. In 1990 these rates

TABLE 16-1   *Personal Saving Rates*

	United States	Japan	United Kingdom	West Germany
1970–1974	8.5	20.6	10.1	14.9
1975–1979	7.5	22.7	12.4	14.2
1980–1984	6.6	21.0	12.9	13.6
1985–1989	5.1	22.5	11.9	13.0

Source: C. Alan Garner, "Tax Reform and Personal Saving," *Economic Review* (Federal Reserve Bank of Kansas City, February 1987), pp. 8–19; *Economic Report of the President, 1990* (Washington, DC: U.S. Government Printing Office, 1990).

had altered only a little. These differences may be based on differences in social security benefits, taxes, population age, and rates of time preference. Whatever the explanation, the low and apparently declining saving rate in the United States has been the focus of a great deal of attention in recent years.

Although substantial difficulties arise in measuring the rate of saving, by any measure the national saving rate in the United States is the lowest of the industrial countries. The lower rate of saving appears to be concentrated more in the federal government than in the other sectors. Yet businesses, governments, and households all save at lower rates than do their counterparts in other industrialized economies.

The private saving rate has declined only slightly in the 1980s, but the composition of saving has shifted. During the period 1980 to 1988, the household saving rate fell by more than 1 percentage point relative to the 1950–1979 period, but this decline was almost fully offset by a rise in business saving. The government borrowing (or dissaving) rate has risen by more than 2 percentage points between the 1950–1979 period and the 1980s, although state and local governments ran surpluses. In the 1980s, federal government deficits were the principal reason for lower gross national saving in the United States.

The decline in household saving in the 1980s may be due to the large rise in household wealth attributable to increases in the value of household assets. For example, the stock market boom doubled the value of corporate stock owned by households between 1981 and 1988. Increases in wealth that are not spent are conceptually equivalent to new saving, but are not included in the national income and product accounts. Also, many types of personal saving are taxed twice, once when the income is earned and again when the returns on the saving are received. Returns to corporate equity or dividends are taxed at both the corporate and individual levels.

One source of change in household saving is a change in the age structure of the population. Because of the pattern of births in the United States, the age structure has changed. The baby boom generation—people born between 1946 and 1965—is a large fraction of the total U.S. population. Because young people typically save relatively little of their income, as the baby boom generation moved into their 30s and 40s during the 1980s U.S. saving rates fell. However, as the baby boom generation moves into the 50s and 60s in the decade of the 1990s and beyond, the household saving rate is likely to increase.

Foreign Saving Flows

Saving means that not all income created is consumed—some is used for capital creation; that is, for investment. As Table 16-2 shows, from 1950 to 1979 gross national saving—the sum of household, business, and government saving—exceeded gross private domestic investment in the United States, leaving an average of 0.3 percent of GNP available for net U.S. investment abroad. This pattern changed in the 1980s. Between 1980 to 1988, gross private domestic investment exceeded national saving by 1.6 percent. That 1.6 percent had to come from foreign saving.

Between 1980 and 1988, the share of GNP devoted to gross investment was essentially the same as had been the case from 1950 to 1979, but national saving's share of GNP fell more than 2 percentage points. The difference was provided by increased net inflows of foreign saving into the United States. Foreign individuals and institutions use their savings to purchase assets in the U.S. capital market to take advantage of available high returns. In 1988, the flow of foreign saving into the United States totaled $219.3 billion. Similarly, some U.S. domestic saving is directed toward investment opportunities in other countries; in 1988, this amounted to $82.1 billion. The difference, $137.2 billion in 1988, is the net capital inflow.

Foreign saving in the United States takes two forms. One is foreign direct investment (FDI), defined as development of a new business or acquisition of at least a 10 percent interest in a domestic company or tangible asset, such as an office building. The other form is purchases of financial instruments such

TABLE 16-2   *The Changing Finance of Investment, 1950–1988 (percentage of GNP)*

	1950 to 1979	1980 to 1988
Gross Private Domestic Investment	16.0	15.8
EQUALS:		
National Saving	16.3	14.1
Private	16.8	16.7
Household	5.0	3.8
Business	11.8	12.9
Government	− .4	− 2.6
Federal	− .6	− 3.9
State and Local	.2	1.3
PLUS:		
Net Foreign Capital Inflows	− .3	1.6

Note: Detail may not add to totals because of rounding.
Source: U.S. Department of Commerce, Bureau of Economic Analysis; *Economic Report of the President, 1990*, (Washington, DC: U.S. Government Printing Office, 1990), p. 123.

as stocks or bonds. Of total foreign investment in the United States in 1988, $58 billion, or 26.7 percent, was FDI. The growth of FDI since the early 1970s is shown in Figure 16-4.

Net foreign capital inflows in the 1980s have helped to sustain U.S. investment and thus contributed to economic growth, despite the low U.S. national saving rate. Nonetheless, increases in the national saving rate would further enhance economic growth in the United States.

Policy Toward Saving

National saving reflects the actions of the three principal sectors of the economy. Household saving is the result of the spending decisions by households; business saving reflects decisions by firms to retain after-tax profits; and government saving is the outcome of the political debate over revenue measures and spending priorities.

Ricardian Equivalence and the Budget Deficit. Most economists argue that the single most direct way for the government to increase national saving is to reduce the federal budget deficit. Some economists argue that reducing federal deficits would not succeed in raising national saving because private savers would recognize the increased government saving and feel a corresponding reduction in their own need to save — the Ricardian equivalence argument. According to Ricardian equivalence, private saving adjusts to offset changes in government saving. Most economists do not agree with this very strict Ricardian view. They believe that even if some private saving is offset, reducing the deficit adds to total national saving.

Social Security. The oldest population segment of the United States, people aged 65 or more, numbered 30 million in 1989 and represented more than 12 percent of the U.S population — about one in every eight Americans. The oldest group itself is getting older. In 1986, the 65–74 age group (17.3 million) was eight times larger than in 1900 but the 75–84 age group (9.1 million) was twelve times larger and the 85 plus group was twenty-two times larger. A child born in 1986 could expect to live seventy-five years, about twenty-eight years longer than a child born in 1900. The percentage of the U.S. population over age 65 is expected to continue to grow. This growth will slow somewhat during the 1990s because of the relatively small number of babies born during the Great Depression of the 1930s, but the most rapid increase ever is expected between the years 2010 and 2030, when the baby boom generation reaches age 65. The aging of the population has several implications for the economy: (1) a decline in the saving rate, (2) an increase in the demand for health care, and (3) more demands for social security and changes in retirement policies.

The earlier a person retires, the less likely saving will occur and the more likely demands for retirement benefits will rise. At what point does a worker

FIGURE 16-4   *Foreign saving. Foreign saving in the United States takes two forms. One is foreign direct invest-ment (FDI), defined as development of a new business or acquisition of at least a 10-percent interest in a domestic company or tangible asset, such as an office building. The other form is purchases of financial instruments such as stocks or bonds. Of total foreign investment in the United States in 1988, $58 billion, or 26.7 percent, was FDI. The growth of FDI since the early 1970s is shown.*

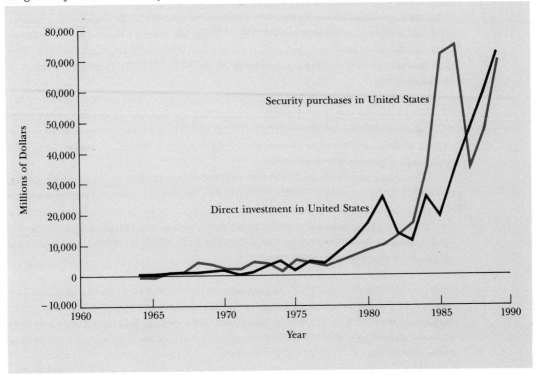

retire? It is the point at which the marginal benefits of increased leisure just offset the marginal benefits of additional income. To determine this point, a person looks into the future and calculates the present value of future income streams and the present value of planned future consumption streams and de-termines the age at which he or she will have accumulated enough savings to ensure that the consumption value does not exceed the income value plus sav-ings. Old-age, Survivors, and Disability Insurance (OASDI), also known as so-cial security, had been established in 108 countries by the beginning of 1975. Some of the oldest plans are those of Germany (1889), the United Kingdom (1908), France (1910), Sweden (1913), and Italy (1919). The United States did not enact a national retirement program until 1935.

The social security system in the United States is financed by a payroll tax levied in equal portions on the employer and the employee. The tax has risen considerably since its beginning of 1 percent of the first $3,000 of earned income. Today the tax rate is 15.3 percent of the first $53,400 of earned income. The system is a "pay-as-you-go" plan. This means that current revenue from social security taxes are used to provide benefits to current social security recipients. As a result, the financial viability of the system depends on the ratio of those working to those retired. During the past twenty-five years, three changes have affected the viability of the system. First, life expectancy has increased. Second, birthrates have fallen. Third, labor force participation of men over age 65 has dropped from 45 percent in 1950 to 20 percent in 1980. The retirement age has fallen, particularly since 1935 and the implementation of social security.

The effect of the social security program on personal saving has been the object of intense study and controversy among economists. Some economists believe that individuals consider social security to be a substitute for personal saving and thus reduce their personal saving when social security rises—the Ricardian equivalence idea again.

The substitution of social security for private saving would not be as important for the economy if the government used accumulated savings to pay for social security. But until recently, social security ran on a pay-as-you-go basis, with current workers' payroll taxes paying current retirees' benefits. As a result, no government saving was available to offset any reduction in private saving that might have occurred.

Role of the Real Interest Rate. Government policies affect saving through the interest rate. The real interest rate is the return in terms of purchasing power that lenders expect to get when they make a loan. The real interest rate is also the amount of purchasing power borrowers expect to give up when they pay back their debt. Borrowers are choosing to consume today in exchange for sacrificing consumption tomorrow (and conversely for lenders). In other words, the real interest rate is the relative price between current consumption and future consumption. Typically, the higher the real interest rate, the lower today's consumption is, because people have more incentive to defer spending. Borrowers face high costs of consuming today, and lenders face high rewards for not consuming today. This tends to make consumption inversely or negatively related to the real rate of interest. Saving, in contrast, tends to be positively related to the real rate of interest.

Although this result seems relatively straightforward, there is an offsetting effect. Incomes rise when interest rates rise because interest earnings rise. This tends to cause an increase in consumption. The net effect appears to be that consumption is negatively related to the interest rate, but the evidence isn't clear-cut. A higher real interest rate is likely to induce a flow of foreign savings into the domestic economy but may have only small effects on domestic saving.

Another reason why it is difficult to assess the impact of the interest rate on saving is that income and interest rates tend to move together over the business cycle. As income rises, so does the interest rate and so does saving. Which causes saving to rise, the rising interest rate or the rising income level?

Role of the Rate of Time Preference. Economists commonly assume a positive rate of time preference. In other words, it is almost taken for granted that people are impatient, preferring to do things, receive things, and so on, today rather than tomorrow. The rate of time preference plays a crucial role in the decision to save. Of two identical people, the person who has the higher rate of time preference tends to consume more and save less than the one with the lower rate of time preference. Younger people tend to have higher rates of time preference (preferring things today) than older people. Thus, if a society is composed largely of young people it tends to consume a relatively higher percentage of its income than does a society composed largely of older people. As noted, policies designed to increase pension benefits or government-provided pensions tend to reduce the incentive for people to save for retirement. A society composed heavily of older people with a governmentally provided retirement program tends to save less than a generally younger society or a society that does not have such a program.

Business Saving. Corporate saving typically accounts for well over half of gross private saving. Businesses save out of earnings by retaining and reinvesting some profits within the business rather than paying them out as dividends or share repurchases. The impact on business saving of a particular policy therefore depends crucially on its effects on the level of earnings and on the incentive to pay them out. Double taxation of corporate dividends provides an incentive for businesses to "save" rather than distribute earnings as dividends. Double taxation results because the corporation pays a corporate income tax and then distributes remaining earnings to shareholders, who then pay a personal income tax. In this sense, the higher the personal income tax, the greater the incentive for the corporation to save. As is typical, fiscal policy may have conflicting parts: reducing the personal tax rate to induce more saving and consumption and raising the personal tax rate to induce more business saving.

▼　　▼　　▼　　▼　　▼　　▼　　▼　　▼　　▼　　▼　　▼
Conclusions

According to the modern theory of consumption, consumption is more stable and less dependent on current income than the earlier theory had argued. The MPC out of current income is quite low, which implies that the multiplier effect of a temporary income change is quite low. To affect output and income through the multiplier, policy must be long term and expected to remain in effect for a long period of time. The U.S. saving rate has declined and is lower than in other industrialized nations. Possible reasons include the aging of the population, the effect of the social security system on early retirement, and the Ricardian equivalence idea that people reduce private saving because of social security. Like consumption, saving is a forward-looking or long-term decision. People decide to save today based on expectations regarding lifetime earnings and consumption streams. Policies that affect these streams permanently have a greater impact on saving than do policies that have only temporary effects.

▼   ▼   ▼   ▼   ▼   ▼   ▼   ▼   ▼   ▼
Summary

1. Does the simple consumption function, where consumption depends on current income, describe consumer behavior?
The simple consumption function describes only one aspect of consumer behavior. Over time individuals consume according to their permanent or life cycle view of income, not just current income. However, at any one point in time, consumers in society with different income levels consume different amounts. This one-point-in-time picture of consumption and income looks very much like the simple consumption function, but appearances can be deceiving: the simple consumption function does not describe how consumers behave.

2. What does it mean to say that consumers are "forward looking"?
Consumers look at what they believe will be their earnings over many years, perhaps their lifetimes, to determine how much to consume. They look not just at current income, but future expected income, retirement plans, inheritance plans, medical care needs, and many other items, in forming their judgments of how to spend their income.

3. What are the determinants of saving?
Saving depends on expectations of income, retirement, medical care, and other anticipated events as well as current and past income levels. Saving, like consumption, is a long-term proposition. People are forward-looking in their consumption and in their saving decisions.

4. What has been the pattern of national saving in the United States and in other countries?
The saving rate in the United States declined during the 1970s and 1980s and is lower than the saving rates in other industrialized nations.

▼
Key Terms

permanent income hypothesis 394   life cycle theory 395

▼
Problems and Exercises

1. Saving is generally thought to depend not only on disposable income but also on interest rates. Usually we think that higher interest rates raise the quantity of saving in the economy. However, with a higher interest rate a smaller amount of

savings is necessary to get the same future purchasing power. Use this fact to explain why saving may be negatively related to the interest rate.

2. Describe why the simple consumption function became discredited.

3. Describe why consumption is much more stable in the face of demand shocks, according to the modern consumption theories, than the Keynesian function implied.

4. According to the life cycle theory of consumption, what would be the effect of a reduction in the average retirement age?

5. What is the main policy implication of the modern consumption theories?

6. Why would it matter whether investment was financed by the flow of saving from the domestic economy or from foreign economies?

Chapter 17

Investment

What to Expect

In the Keynesian view, investment fluctuations are the primary cause of business cycles. These fluctuations are unpredictable—the results of "animal spirits" in businesses. Investment no longer is blamed for all business cycles, but remains an important part of the economy's behavior. Investment is the foundation of economic growth. The prospects for long-term economic growth depend on the rate of investment in physical and human capital. The investment rate in the United States has been lower than that of other major industrialized countries for several decades. This chapter considers the determinants of investment and the role of investment in the economy. Investment consists of three very distinct components: business fixed investment, residential investment, and inventory investment. Each of these components is discussed and then combined to develop a theory of investment. The following questions are considered:

1. What is the pattern of investment in the United States?

2. What are the determinants of investment?

3. Is investment volatile?

4. What are the differences among fixed investment, inventory investment, and residential investment?

▼
An Overview of Investment

Although the United States has devoted substantial resources to investment, the U.S. investment rate is low by international standards. Gross fixed domestic investment, as a percentage of GNP in the United States, is the lowest of the six major industrialized countries shown in Figure 17-1. Between 1975 and 1987, while the other countries devoted an annual average of 22.5 percent of their GNP to national investment, the United States invested only 17.3 percent.

The comparatively low rate of investment in the United States is not a recent phenomenon. As shown in Figure 17-2, real capital purchases have fluctuated around 16 percent of real GNP for the entire postwar period. It appeared that this was changing during the long expansion between 1982 and 1990. However, depreciation makes this picture deceiving. Real net investment (gross investment less depreciation) as a fraction of real net national product has remained below the postwar average for the decade of the 1980s, as shown in Figure 17-3.

The behavior of investment as an economic variable is not easy to describe. Forecasts of GNP have gone astray more because of erroneous predictions of investment spending than because of errors in forecasting any other economic variable.

Investment is actually business spending on three different types of products: (1) on plant (structures) and equipment, known as **business fixed investment** (or fixed nonresidential investment); (2) on inventories, called **inventory investment**; and (3) on the construction of apartments and houses, termed **residential investment**. The reasons for investing vary according to the type of investment to be undertaken. Moreover, the costs, the rates of return, and the impacts of fiscal and monetary policy vary among the types of investment.

Figure 17-4 traces out the structure of U.S. investment spending since 1960. The most striking observations in this chart are the growth in equipment purchases relative to structures, the fluctuations in residential investment, and the relative stability of gross investment as a proportion of GNP over the past twenty years. Also, depreciation (capital consumption allowance) has risen since 1960 from about 60 percent of GPDI to about 66 percent. This is related to the shift in investment from structures to equipment. Equipment has higher depreciation rates because of its shorter service life. Finally, inventory investment is a very volatile component of investment.

The pattern of investment spending on structures and equipment is particularly worrisome to economists. Many fear that a continued downward trend

FIGURE 17-1   *Gross fixed investment as a percentage of GNP in several countries. Gross fixed domestic investment, as a percentage of GNP in the United States, is the lowest of the six major industrialized countries. Between 1975 and 1987, while the other countries devoted an annual average of 22.5 percent of their GNP to national investment, the United States invested only 17.3 percent.*

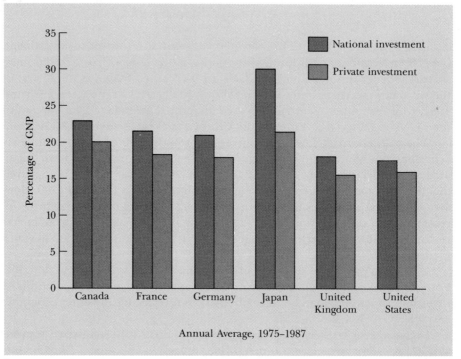

Source: Economic Report of the President, 1990 (Washington, DC: U.S. Government Printing Office, 1990), p. 128.

of long-term capital accumulation will spell further productivity declines, inflationary problems, and unemployment. The reason for this concern is that long-term capital has been the foundation of productivity — the buildings and the factories in which labor has been able to create increasingly more output. Short-term capital, in contrast, has been associated with the peripheral aspects of production — the autos, typewriters, filing cabinets, and such — that have not generated the output gains associated with long-term capital.

Capital accumulation has both demand-side and supply-side effects on the economy. On the demand side, investment is simply business spending and one component of aggregate demand. On the supply side, investment adds to the capital stock and thereby increases the productive capacity of the economy. The purchase of equipment is business spending, just as is the purchase of structures. So $1 million spent on either is $1 million of demand. Yet $1 million spent on one type of capital may increase the productive capacity of the economy substantially more than will $1 million spent on some other type of capi-

FIGURE 17-2   *U.S. investment rate over time. The comparatively low rate of investment in the United States is not a recent phenomenon. As shown, real capital purchases have fluctuated around 16 percent of real GNP for the entire postwar period. During the long expansion between 1982 and 1990, however, U.S. real gross investment exceeded that 16 percent figure.*

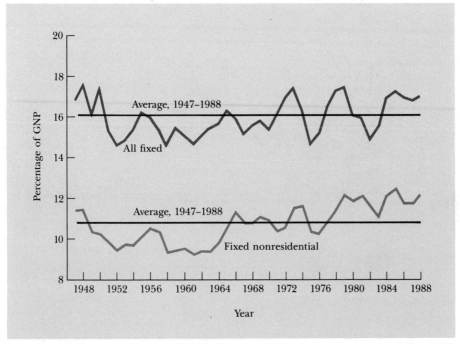

Source: *Economic Report of the President, 1991* (Washington, DC: U.S. Government Printing Office, 1991).

tal. Hence it is the supply side of the economy that economists worry about when they see a U.S. trend toward investment in short-lived capital and away from investment in long-lived capital.

What induces firms to acquire more capital? Can economic policy affect this decision? Let's begin to answer this question by outlining the factors involved in a firm's investment decision. Then we'll examine the impact of policy on investment.

▼
Theory of Business Fixed Investment

To lay some groundwork for determining what induces a firm to undertake investment expenditures, let's assume that units of capital can be acquired or discarded easily, much as people can rent lawn and household equipment from local rental stores. In fact, a good deal of capital is rented, so this assumption is not unrealistic. Furthermore, suppose a firm has determined the size of its

FIGURE 17-3 *Depreciation and net investment. Depreciation of the U.S. capital stock has been high. Real net investment as a fraction of real net national product has remained below the postwar average for the decade of the 1980s, as shown.*

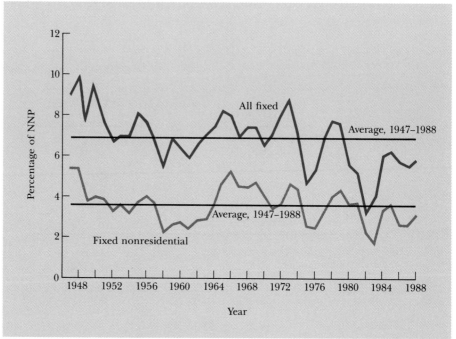

Source: *Economic Report of the President, 1990* (Washington, DC: U.S. Government Printing Office, 1990).

labor force—say, two workers—for the day. Then the firm will rent an additional unit of capital only as long as that additional unit costs less than the revenue it produces. However, with the usual assumption of a diminishing marginal product, at some point the cost of an additional unit is greater than the additional revenue that unit brings in. The firm doesn't rent additional units of capital beyond that point. Under these circumstances, more capital is rented as the rental cost decreases. This is illustrated graphically in Figure 17-5. The return to each additional unit of capital, called the **marginal revenue product (MRP)**, is shown by the downward-sloping line. The desired stock of capital (K_1^D) is determined by the intersection of the rental cost line (RC_1) and the MRP curve. If the rental cost decreases, the desired quantity of capital increases, as shown by the intersection of the MRP curve and the lower rental cost line (RC_2).

The User Cost of Capital

The practice of accumulating capital is more complicated than simply renting it on a daily basis. When a capital good is general in its use (computers, bulldozers, and so on), rental markets often develop. Figure 17-5 provides a good

FIGURE 17-4   *U.S. investment. The structure of U.S. investment spending since 1960 is shown. The most striking observations in this chart are the growth in equipment purchases relative to structures, the fluctuations in residential investment, and the relative stability of gross investment as a proportion of GNP over the past twenty years. Two other points regarding investment are first, depreciation (capital consumption allowance) has risen since 1960 from about 60 percent of GPDI to about 66 percent. Second, inventory investment is a very volatile component of investment.*

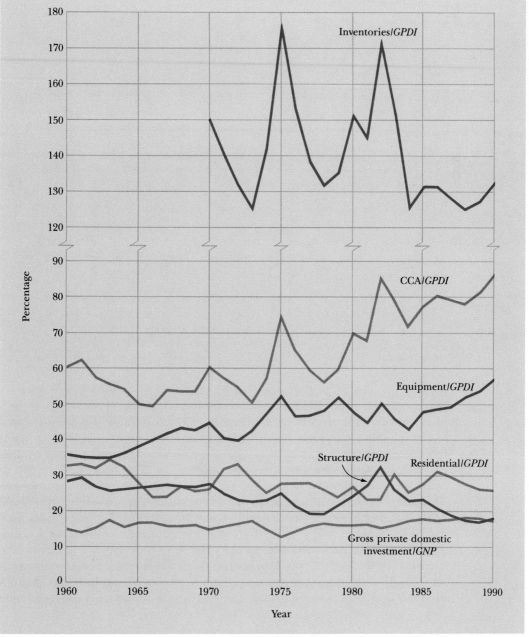

FIGURE 17-5   *The optimal stock of capital. The return to each additional unit of capital, called* the *marginal revenue product (MRP), is shown by the downward-sloping line. The desired stock of capital (K_1^D) is determined by the intersection of the rental cost line (RC_1) and the* MRP *curve. If the rental cost decreases, the desired quantity of capital increases, as shown by the intersection of the* MRP *curve and the lower rental cost line (RC_2).*

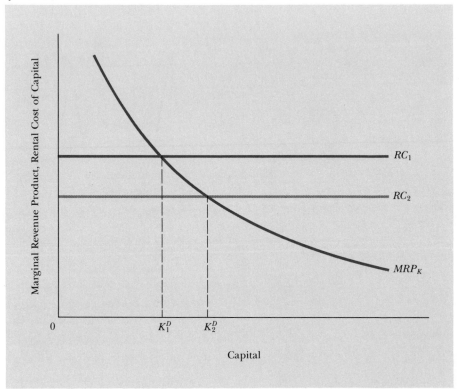

representation of the investment decision in such a case. However, most capital is not generally suitable for daily rental markets because it is often tailored to an individual company's needs. Most often, firms can vary the quantity of labor they use much more easily than they can vary the quantity of capital.

The typical process a firm goes through in deciding how much capital to acquire can be characterized as follows. A firm decides how much output to produce over the next year or so. It then acquires the necessary capital and labor (the mix of which depends on expected factor prices), perhaps by signing labor contracts and seeking to increase or decrease its capital stock. Once it has acquired a particular capital stock, the firm is pretty well committed to produce its planned output. However, if demand increases and the firm realizes that the output it is producing is temporarily insufficient to meet the new demand, it will use existing inventories and/or vary the number of labor-hours it uses, combining more or less of those with the fixed quantity of capital. However, should the firm believe the increased demand it has experienced will be long lived, it will then alter its capital stock.

What is the appropriate measure of rental costs? Firms do not often acquire capital for short time periods only and then return the capital. Once acquired, capital yields a flow of services for several years. Thus, the price of capital services to the firm is not simply the acquisition price of the capital equipment but instead the cost per unit of services, called the **user cost of capital**: the opportunity cost a firm incurs when its resources are tied up in capital. The firm forgoes interest it could earn on alternative assets.

In addition, a firm must take into account the speed at which capital wears out or becomes obsolete. Funds tied up in capital can't be used elsewhere. The difference between the rate of return on those funds and the rate of return that could be obtained from some other use of the money provides the incentive for undertaking a capital purchase. Funds tied up in obsolete or worn-out capital create a cost because they don't generate a return and can't be used in an alternative manner. The firm's cost of capital (u) must therefore include the sum of the interest rate (r) and the rate at which capital wears out or becomes obsolete (the rate of depreciation, d).

Another factor that influences a firm's decision to purchase capital is the tax consequence of the purchase. Suppose that for each dollar spent on capital the firm can reduce its annual tax liability by some specific amount. Then the user cost is reduced by that amount. In particular, tax laws allow firms to offset taxable income with a certain proportion of their depreciation (δ) as well as a proportion of their interest charges (γ). These tax laws serve to reduce the user cost of capital. The user cost is the sum of all these factors, and in symbols is

$$u = r + d - \delta d - \gamma r$$

In addition, firms are often allowed to deduct from taxes a certain fraction of their investment expenditures, called an **investment tax credit (ITC)**. This tax credit reduces the user cost of capital by τ. The user cost of capital can be symbolized as

$$u = (1 - \tau)(r + d - \gamma r - \delta d)$$

The user cost of capital provides a very convenient way to examine the impact of economic policy on investment. For example, over the last two decades, the U.S. tax system has treated structures and equipment differently. The investment tax credit first introduced in 1962 applied only to equipment until 1981. The ITC was repealed in 1969, only to be readopted in 1971, and liberalized in 1975, 1976, and 1981. In 1986, the ITC was abolished. The tax credit had the effect of reducing the user cost of short-lived capital equipment relative to that of longer-lived equipment and structures. In the 1970s and early 1980s, the effective tax rate (the rate actually paid after deductions and other adjustments) for equipment was the lowest for pieces of equipment having asset

lives from six to ten years; about half as much as the rate for pieces of equipment having lives of twenty to thirty-five years. No wonder that firms invested
in short-lived assets rather than in long-lived ones.

Tax Laws and Investment

Federal income tax law has long required the cost of most machinery and other
assets employed by businesses in the production of goods and services to be
depreciated over a period of years, representing the anticipated useful life of
the assets as recognized by the Internal Revenue Service. **Depreciation** is the
process by which the cost of an asset is allocated to the years of its anticipated
useful life. By increasing the rate at which capital can be depreciated (the accounting rate of depreciation), called **accelerated depreciation**, the user cost
is decreased.

Tax law has differentiated among assets depending on the length of their
service lives. For example, the Capital Cost Recovery Act of 1981 increased the
rate of depreciation on all forms of capital. However, long-term assets were
to be depreciated over a period of ten years and allowed a 10 percent ITC,
equipment was to be depreciated over five years and allowed the same 10 percent ITC, while autos, taxis, and light-duty trucks were to be depreciated over
three years and have a 6 percent ITC. Depending on the capital's actual expected service life, the user cost from one type of capital may have changed
more than for other types.

Tax laws that differentiate among assets based on their service lives draw
criticism from many economists. The law results in widely divergent tax rates
on various kinds of investment, thereby shifting investment away from its most
productive uses into less productive, but tax-favored, areas. For investment in
new equipment, the effective tax rates may actually be negative. In other words,
instead of taxing the income from such investments the government subsidizes
it. This happens because the depreciation writeoffs plus the investment tax
credit may produce tax savings greater than the immediate expensing of the
entire cost of the asset. The lowest tax rates—that is, the largest tax subsidies—
are often granted to short-lived equipment. The bias in favor of short-term
equipment is exacerbated rather than diminished by this type of tax law. It leads
to an even more rapid accumulation of short-term equipment at the expense
of long-lived assets.

Lags in the Investment Process

Much of the capital that businesses acquire can't be put into place for several
months or years after it has been obtained. The expansion of a building, a new
production line, a new system of computers, a new fleet of airplanes, and so
on, all require significant periods of time before they are up and running. The
theory we've discussed seems to imply that the capital is acquired and immediately used once the decision is made to buy additional capital. In fact, much

of this year's investment is the result of decisions made in previous years. Economists have discovered that only about a third of all capital is put into place during the year in which the firm decides to acquire the capital.

An implication of delays or lags in investment is that the marginal revenue from capital is not always equal to its user cost. This idea was developed into a theory of investment, called the **q-theory**, by James Tobin. The q-theory is a rather simple or straightforward comparison of the cost of new capital (replacement cost) and the cost of existing capital (the market value of the firm). The q-theory does not really alter the theory of investment just described. Instead, it suggests that whenever the marginal revenue on new capital is greater than the user cost, the firm will invest in new capital; and conversely, when the marginal revenue on new capital is less than the user cost, the firm will purchase existing capital. The ratio of the market value of the firm to the marginal revenue on new capital is called q. Hence, Tobin notes that when q is greater than 1, new investment occurs, and when q is smaller than 1, acquisition of existing capital occurs. A firm can buy existing capital by buying shares of its own stock.

The value of q is the value of existing capital divided by the value of replacement capital. The idea is that the market value of the firm is greater than the price of its capital whenever the marginal revenue of the firm is greater than the user cost, and this leads to new investment.

The value of the q-theory of investment is that it is relatively easy to measure because data on the value of firms' stocks are widely available. The q-theory is really no different from the first theory of fixed investment presented in this chapter.

Summary of the Theory of Business Fixed Investment

Although questions remain about the relative importance of alternative economic variables in the investment decision, economists believe that they have isolated the main variables involved. Interest rates, depreciation rates, and tax policies have major impacts on investment. Expectations are also very important. Expectations of revenue or sales and of economic policy, the rate of depreciation allowed for tax purposes, the tax credit available on capital expenditures, the proportion of interest expenses that may be claimed against taxes and, of course, interest rates and monetary policy all play a role in the firm's investment decision.

▼
Residential Investment

The most interest-sensitive component of investment is residential investment. The 1979–1981 and 1985–1986 periods offer very good examples of this interest sensitivity. As mortgage rates rose from 9 to 15 percent, residential investment fell to its lowest level in over twenty years. The interest sensitivity comes about primarily because of the institutional features of the U.S. economy's mortgage market. These features have caused funds to flow away from the housing sector whenever interest rates rose. This, in turn, has caused the quantity of new housing constructed to drop significantly. Figure 17-6 shows the pattern of U.S. residential investment and the conventional mortgage rate from 1960 to 1990. The relationship between housing construction and interest rates is clear.

Residential investment measures the construction of single-family and multifamily dwellings and is the addition to the existing stock of housing. Theoretically, the main difference between residential and fixed investment is the source of demand. The demand for fixed capital originates in the business sector, whereas the demand for residential capital (housing) arises from the consumer sector. This theoretical difference, combined with the institutional features of the mortgage market, makes the residential component of investment entirely distinct from the other components. To analyze residential investment, let us first describe the theory of residential investment and then link that to the institutional features of the mortgage market.

Theory of Residential Investment

The theory of residential investment maintains that new housing is constructed until the expected return on housing equals its user cost. The principal determinants of residential investment can perhaps best be described by examining which factors determine the value of the stock of housing, and then by describing the factors that determine the value of the addition to this stock.

The demand for housing depends on wealth: the greater the wealth, the greater the demand for housing. In addition, the quantity of housing demanded depends on the expected return on, and the opportunity or user cost of, housing. Hence the lower the expected return on other assets — or, conversely, the greater the expected net return on housing — *ceteris paribus,* the greater the quantity of housing demanded.

Housing, like other durable goods, is bought for the services it renders. If a house is rented, the return on the investment (the purchase of the house) is the rent minus maintenance costs. If the homeowner lives in the house, the return on the investment is implicit — it is equal to the rent that would have to be paid to live in a comparable house. The costs of housing consist of the interest cost plus taxes and depreciation, minus the tax benefits of home ownership. The sort of decrease in the return to housing that would result from, say, an increase of the mortgate rate makes housing a relatively less attractive investment. Hence the quantity of housing demanded decreases as the mortgage rate rises, *ceteris paribus.*

The price (or cost) of housing, which includes the value of the property, mortgage interest rates, expected appreciation, and tax benefits and costs, is determined by the intersection of the demand for and supply of housing curves,

FIGURE 17-6   *U.S. residential investment. Residential investment grew rapidly from 1975 to 1978. This was a period of high inflation and rapid bracket creep. When inflation fell in the early 1980s, housing's advantage was reduced. Housing starts fell in the early 1980s and then recovered in the mid-1980s. By 1990, the economy had again fallen into a recession and housing starts had declined significantly.*

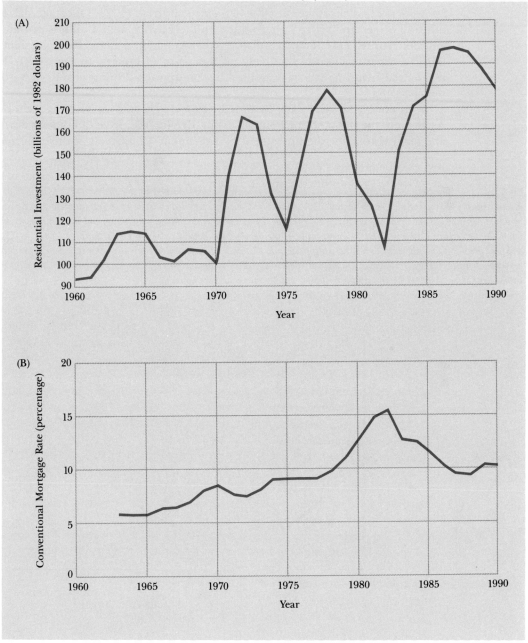

Source: Economic Report of the President, 1991 (Washington, DC: U.S. Government Printing Office, 1991).

as shown in Figure 17-7. The quantity of housing supplied consists of the existing stock of houses (not just new houses) shown by the vertical supply curve. Investment in new houses—what we call *residential* investment—occurs when the net return on houses rises. For example, should the demand for housing rise, say to D_1, a shortage (of $Q_1 - Q_0$) exists at price P_0. The shortage drives housing prices up. With a larger return on their investment, builders produce additional units. This new construction is residential investment. Hence, residential investment depends positively on the price of houses. In Figure 17-7B, residential investment is represented by the upward-sloping supply curve of new housing.

If interest rates rise, *ceteris paribus,* the expected return on housing declines. As a result, the demand for housing drops, driving the price of housing down and leading to a decline in residential investment. Conversely, if the expected

FIGURE 17-7   *The housing market. The price (or cost) of housing is determined by the intersection of the demand for and supply of housing curves, as shown. The quantity of housing supplied consists of the existing stock of houses (not just new houses) shown by the vertical supply curve. Investment in new houses, or residential investment, occurs when the net return on houses rises. For example, if the demand for housing rises to D_1, a shortage (of $Q_1 - Q_0$) exists at price P_0. This shortage drives housing prices up. With a larger return on their investment, builders produce additional units. Hence, residential investment depends positively on the price of houses. In panel B, residential investment is represented by the upward-sloping supply curve of new housing.*

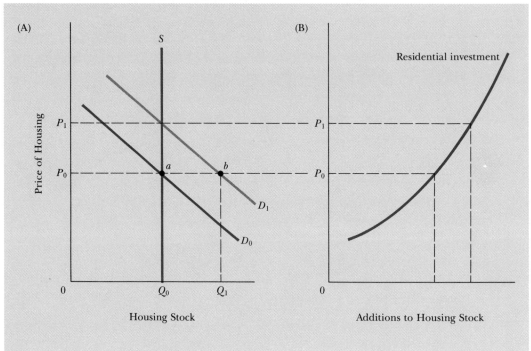

return on housing increases, the demand rises, driving up the asset price and stimulating residential investment. So residential investment depends on demand for housing and is influenced by the same factors that influence this demand – the interest rate, other costs, and the expected return.

Institutional Features of the Mortgage Market

The mortgage interest rate is an important determinant of residential investment. The mortgage rate is, in turn, influenced by several institutional features of the U.S. economy. For example, most mortgage lending in the United States during the past fifty years has been undertaken by savings and loan associations (S&Ls). In 1979, 46 percent of mortgage debt outstanding on one- to four-family nonfarm properties was held by S&Ls. Obviously, residential housing demand is very sensitive to developments pertaining to the S&Ls.

The commitment of S&Ls to mortgage credit has been encouraged over the years by federal tax incentives and state laws. Under federal tax laws instituted in 1962 and 1967, S&Ls had to maintain at least 82 percent of their assets in specified items, including housing-related loans, to be eligible for favorable tax treatment. This commitment placed S&Ls in a precarious position each time interest rates rose. Because their assets were primarily long term (mortgages have a contract life of twenty-five to thirty years), their rates of return on these assets fluctuated very little. Their liabilities – primarily savings deposits – were almost entirely short term. So during tight money periods the cost of liabilities rose, while the return on assets did not. The S&Ls then faced a two-edged sword. They could raise new mortgage rates enough to recoup current losses in the near future, or they could refuse to pay higher rates of interest on deposits. In the first case, the quantity of housing and mortgages demanded would fall. In the second case, depositors would withdraw their deposits and use them to buy higher-yielding assets, a process called **disintermediation**. This in turn would mean fewer funds available for mortgages.

After 1966, the government put a ceiling on the interest rate that financial institutions could pay on savings deposits. This ceiling, called Regulation Q, was supposed to protect the S&Ls. But it didn't. Instead, it enhanced the process of disintermediation. Disintermediation occurred in 1966, 1969, and 1973, precipitating recessions in each of those years. As other saving opportunities drew funds from the S&Ls, the federal government was left with two choices. It could close the insolvent institutions and require the remaining ones to come up with more capital to protect their mortgages. Or it could allow the insolvent institutions to stay open and reduce the capital requirements to keep them from going bankrupt. Congress chose the second option. In 1980 Congress took two steps to help the S&Ls hold onto deposits. First, it raised the insurance limit from $40,000 to $100,000 on each account. Second, deposit interest rate ceilings were relaxed (Regulation Q was rescinded) to let S&Ls and banks compete with the other savings options.

The gamble by the government that interest rates would fall was success-ful. The S&Ls were still in business in the 1980s. At that time Congress could have solved the remaining problems by requiring additional capital backing and reducing insurance limits. It did not, and the S&Ls were free to expand their loan portfolios while at the same time being assured that depositors' ac-counts were government insured. The S&L profits were based on increasing the number of loans and the total amount of credit provided while drawing increasing amounts of deposits. As a result, risky speculative loans were made, on the basis of inflated appraisals. A major segment of the S&L industry wasted billions of dollars on high-risk ventures and outright fraud. When the institu-tions began failing, the federal government had to intervene to support the insured deposits. Over $500 billion of taxes were allocated to protect the S&Ls and their depositors.

Who got those $500 billion of taxpayer losses? Some went to crooks. A great deal went to real estate developers. Most went to the U.S. homeowners who bought houses with mortgages at low interest rates before inflation pushed up interest rates and house prices. They reaped huge capital gains.[1]

Tax Benefits of Homeownership

Individuals are allowed to deduct mortgage interest expenses from taxable in-come in determining their income tax. In the late 1970s, as inflation pushed people into higher tax brackets and drove up mortgage interest payments, bor-rowers could deduct larger interest expenses even if the real cost of borrowing was unchanged. In other words, the higher the anticipated future inflation, the cheaper it was to borrow, given the current U.S. tax system. Morever, as infla-tion pushed people into higher brackets (bracket creep), borrowing became even less costly. For example, bracket creep increased the marginal tax rate for the median-income family from 17 percent in 1965 to 24 percent in 1980. The interest expenses became 7 percent less costly simply because of bracket creep.

As is evident in Figure 17-6, residential investment grew rapidly from 1975 to 1978. This was a period of high inflation and rapid bracket creep. With in-flation falling in the early 1980s, housing's advantage was reduced. Housing starts fell in the early 1980s and then recovered in the mid-1980s. By 1990, the economy had again fallen into a recession and housing starts had declined significantly.

1   For more detail on the S&L debacle, see George Bentson, "How the Industry Got into Trouble," *New York Times*, April 23, 1989.

▼
Inventory Investment

The reason why residential investment fluctuates is well known, but we can't say the same for inventory investment. Inventory investment, the change in inventories, fluctuates more than any other component of demand. Figure 17-8 shows the wide fluctuations of inventory investment since 1964. Indeed, fluctuations in inventory accumulation accounted for over 70 percent of the decline in real GNP experienced in the five recessions between 1948 and 1961. Yet a single unified theoretical explanation of inventory investment has been hard to find.

Inventories serve as a buffer. Firms can meet short-run or temporary fluctuations in demand without having to alter their long-run contracts with suppliers, by allowing inventories to accumulate or decumulate. Inventories may be allowed to fluctuate if firms find it too costly to buy inputs instantaneously, if firms expect difficulties in getting inputs in the future, or if the prices of supplies are expected to change. Finally, inventories of finished products may

FIGURE 17-8   *U.S. inventory investment. Inventory investment — the change in inventories — fluctuates more than any other component of demand. The wide fluctuations of U.S. inventory investment since 1964 are shown. The 1990–1991 recession was not the classical inventory recession. Firms kept their inventories low throughout the late 1980s and were able to avoid large inventory accumulations when the economy turned down. As is evident in this figure, inventory changes were smaller than in previous recessions.*

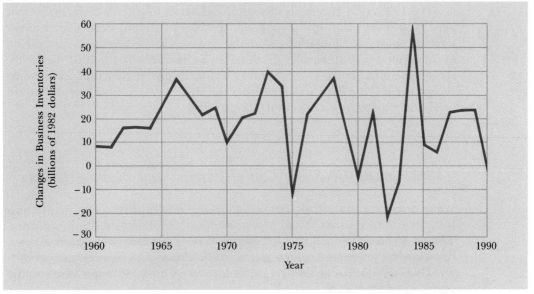

Source: Economic Report of the President, 1991 (Washington, DC: U.S. Government Printing Office, 1991).

accumulate when sales are not what they were expected to be. In earlier chapters, these were called *unanticipated* or *unintended inventory accumulations.* Because a firm must tie up its money when it holds inventories, the opportunity cost of this money should be important. As the opportunity cost rises, inventory investment should fall. Increased uncertainty, either about the demand for a firm's products or about the supply of inputs, should also induce a rise in inventory holdings.

The behavior of inventory investment has not changed for several decades. As demand or final sales begin to decline, firms trim their staffs and cut production. However, it takes some time before firms cut back production to meet the lower demand. As a result, inventories continue to accumulate. Eventually, as the inventory stock declines to the firm's desired level, production is increased to meet sales. Output, income, and employment all start increasing again. Changes in inventories indicate where the economy is headed. An unintended accumulation of inventories signals a decline in output, and a decline in inventories signals a business upturn.

In the recessions of the 1960s, 1970s, and early 1980s, the pattern just described typically followed a period of tight money. The monetary policy led to a rise in interest rates, causing disintermediation and a subsequent decline in residential investment. Inventory investment increased as production outpaced sales. Firms decreased production, and the recession began. As demand picked up relative to production, firms reduced their inventories to the desired level. At this point, production began to increase, bringing increases in employment and income.

The 1990–1991 recession was not the classical inventory cycle. Firms had kept their inventories low throughout the late 1980s and were able to avoid large inventory accumulations when the economy turned down. In fact, the ratio of inventory to final sales declined throughout the last half of the 1980s. As is evident in Figure 17-8, inventory changes were smaller than in previous recessions. It is too early to tell whether the 1990–1991 cycle was an aberration or is a new pattern for inventory investment.

▼
Investment, GNP, the Cost of Capital, and Business Cycles

We've discussed how a firm determines its optimal capital stock—that is, how it decides to purchase capital, produce housing, and accumulate inventories. The desired level of capital, K^*, depends on such factors as interest rates, depreciation rates, tax laws, expected profit, and expected sales and production. We can summarize these relationships in a simple equation based on the user cost of capital as

(1) $$K^* = v(W/u)Y^*$$

Equation 1 states that the desired capital stock (K^*) depends in some particular way (v) on the price of labor (W) relative to the cost of capital (u) and on the expected level of sales (Y^e). For example, if $v = 0.8$, then whenever output is expected to rise by 10 percent, everything else held constant, the desired capital stock rises by 8 percent. Also, if the user cost of capital rises (everything else held constant), firms tend to substitute labor for capital as the desired level of capital declines, and vice versa for the wage rate of labor.

Investment is the addition to the capital stock, the amount of new capital necessary to bring the existing capital stock to the desired level:

$$I_t = K_t^* - K_{t-1}$$

Substituting from equation 1 for the optimal capital stock, we get

(2) $$I_t = v(W/u)Y_t^e - K_{t-1}$$

Equation 2 shows that investment depends positively on the wage rate, negatively on the user cost of capital, and positively on expected sales. The expression also shows that investment depends on the speed with which the capital stock is adjusted to the desired level of capital. The more costly it is for a firm to change its capital stock, the more time is involved in adjusting it, the less likely it is that investment will change in response to short-run events. In addition, the more a firm forms its expectations on the basis of long-term (permanent) developments, the less volatile investment in that firm should be.

The lags that occur in the investment process are taken into account by a specific form of equation 1 known as the *accelerator model of investment.* The accelerator form, sometimes called the *flexible accelerator form,* of investment specifies that firms adjust their actual capital stock to their desired capital stock over time.

Accelerator

In its simplest form, the accelerator model assumes that a firm adjusts its actual capital stock to its desired stock each period and that the actual stock depends in a fixed way on actual output or sales.

$$K_t = vY_t \text{ and } K_{t-1} = vy_{t-1} \text{ so that } I_t = vY_t - vY_{t-1} = v(\Delta Y)$$

Thus the level of investment depends on the change in the level of output, ΔY. As a result, changes in investment depend on the rate of change (changes in the change) in output. When output accelerates, investment is positive, and when output decelerates, investment is negative. Thus a rise in output from one period to another induces firms to invest but unless output continues rising at ever more rapid rates, investment will diminish and eventually subside totally.

The accelerator theory of investment can account for a significant amount of the fluctuations in GNP once some shock changes the growth rate of output. Suppose that for some reason the growth rate of output, which has been rising at a steady pace of 3 percent, accelerates to 4 percent. Investment in-creases by the accelerator (v) times the change in output, and adds to aggregate demand. Output then rises again, pulling investment up with it. Eventually, however, the growth rate of output begins to slow, and as it does, investment subsides. Moreover, as investment declines, aggregate demand declines, lead-ing to a more rapid slowing in output. In other words, GNP goes through an entire business cycle, due simply to an initial increase in (shock to) aggregate demand.

The role of interest rates and other variables are included in the accelera-tor model of investment. The value of v depends on these other variables. So investment may not have the same exact pattern during each cycle, but follows the general patterns noted earlier.

▼   ▼   ▼   ▼   ▼   ▼   ▼   ▼   ▼   ▼   ▼
Conclusions

Investment, like consumption, depends more on events that are expected to be long lived or permanent than on short-run developments. The decision to acquire capi-tal is sensitive to expectations regarding relative prices and interest rates as well as the expected level of sales. Investment depends positively on changes in GNP and negatively on the interest rate. More output (or a higher expected level of out-put) requires firms to invest in new plant and equipment, induces families to buy new houses, and tends to increase inventory accumulation. The accelerator describes the manner in which these activities depend on output. An initial increase in the growth rate of output (or anticipated increase in output) leads to an increase in investment. Once the initial increase subsides or the rate of growth of GNP reaches a steady-state level, investment subsides. Investment also depends negatively on in-terest rates. Higher interest rates tend to make businesses use other factors of production rather than acquire additional plant and equipment, tend to induce families to forgo or delay purchases of houses, and tend to induce firms to reduce the amount of inventories they accumulate.

▼   ▼   ▼   ▼   ▼   ▼   ▼   ▼   ▼   ▼   ▼
Summary

1. What is the pattern of investment in the United States?
Business fixed investment is relatively stable, while residential investment and in-ventory investment change significantly. Investment in the United States has been lower than in most other industrialized nations for the past several decades.
2. What are the determinants of investment?
Investment depends on interest rates, the expected rate of growth of sales or out-

put, on tax policies, on the cost of substitute inputs, and on expected profits. These are captured in the user cost of capital. The higher the user cost of capital, the less investment occurs. Each component of investment depends more or less heavily on these variables. For instance, residential investment depends heavily on interest rates, while inventory changes depend heavily on expected sales.

3. Is investment volatile?

Investment is relatively stable; the inventory component of investment is the only one that might be called *volatile* and for at least the 1990–1991 recession, it too remained reasonably stable.

4. What are the differences among fixed investment, inventory investment, and residential investment?

Fixed investment is the purchases of equipment and non-residential structures. Inventory investment is the inventory stocks that firms hold. Residential investment is the housing that firms construct.

▼
Key Terms

business fixed investment   409
inventory investment   409
residential investment   409
marginal revenue product
  (MRP)   412
user cost of capital   415

investment tax credit (ITC)   415
depreciation   416
accelerated depreciation   416
q-theory   417
disintermediation   421

▼
Problems and Exercises

1.   What is the user cost of capital? (Explain.)

2.   Many people use U-Haul trucks (or Ryder or some other company) to move from one place to another. When they do, they must pay a rental price for the truck. What factors determine the rental price of the trucks? Is this rental price related to the user cost of capital? If so, how?

3.   What is the effect of increasing the rate at which capital can be depreciated?

4.   Why is it important whether or not investment (or the private sector in general) is uncontrollably volatile or unstable?

5.   What is an inventory cycle? What economic events can lead to an inventory cycle? Would you describe the 1990–1991 recession as an inventory cycle? Why or why not?

6.   What is meant by the statement that the U.S. tax system biases investment in favor of less productive tax-favored areas?

Chapter 18

Government: Public Choice and Economic Policy

According to virtually any measure, government in the United States has been a growth industry since 1930. The number of people employed by the local, state, and federal governments combined grew from 3 million in 1930 to 17 million in 1990. Annual expenditures by the federal government rose from $3 billion in 1930 to over $1 trillion in 1990. In 1929, government spending constituted less than 2.5 percent of total spending in the economy. By 1990, it had increased to nearly 25 percent. The number of rules and regulations legislated by the government is so large that it is measured by the number of volumes of books needed just to list them. The United States is far from alone in its growth of government. In fact, the government constitutes a smaller percentage of GDP in the United States than in most other nations.

Why is the government such an important part of our lives? According to most economists, the private market usually allocates resources in the most efficient manner possible. If indeed the private market system is efficient, then the role of government is limited to instances when the private market fails. If the private market fails to allocate resources efficiently, then the role for government is to offset the costs on society from the market failure. Has government grown only because of private market failure? This chapter discusses market failures and the role of government. Various theoretical justifications are given for government involvement in the private economy, but these justifications do not describe the extent of intervention that actually occurs. Monetary and fiscal policy are discussed in light of political realities. The following questions are considered:

1. *Why does the government intervene in the private economy?*

2. *What does the government seek to accomplish when it intervenes in the private economy?*

3. *Who or what is the government?*

4. *What do political markets imply for monetary and fiscal policy?*

▼
Justifications for Government Activities

When consumers or producers do not bear the full costs or benefits of the transactions they undertake, a **market failure** is said to have occurred. Market failures provide a rationale for government action. Three sources of market failures exist: externalities, lack of private property rights, and public goods.

Externalities

A business firm knows how much it costs to employ workers, and it knows the costs of purchasing materials or constructing buildings. Someone who buys a new car or pays for a pizza knows exactly what the cost will be. Such costs are private costs; they are borne solely by the people involved in the transactions that created the costs. They are internal, in the sense that the firm or household must explicitly take account of them. Many environmental problems arise because the costs of an individual's actions are not borne directly by that individual. When a firm pollutes the air or water or when a tourist leaves trash in a park, the costs of these actions are not easily determined and are not borne solely by the individual firm or person who created them. The cost is external to the activity and is called an **externality**. When external costs are added to private costs, the result is social costs:

Social costs = private costs + external costs

When private costs differ from social costs, individual decision makers are ignoring externalities. They are not internalizing the externality. The full opportunity cost of using a scarce resource, for example, is borne not by the producer or the consumer but by society.

The environment is not the only area in which externalities occur. Externalities occur any time individual actions create costs (or benefits) that are not borne by the individuals involved in the action. Externalities need not be negative. A positive externality may result from an activity in which benefits are received by consumers or firms not involved directly in the activity. For instance, a literate population can provide benefits to society as a whole that exceed the benefits received by people who acquire an education.

If social costs exceed private costs, then the cost to someone of undertaking some activity is less than the full opportunity cost of the activity to society, and in society's view, *too much* of the activity is undertaken. For instance, those who pollute do not bear the entire costs of the pollution and therefore pollute more than they otherwise would. Although chlorofluorocarbons from air-conditioners and aerosol sprays damage the ozone layer, the people producing aerosol cans and those buying aerosol sprays do not pay for the damage to the ozone layer. As a result, more aerosols are produced and consumed than would be the case if the external costs (externalities) were part of the production cost or consumption cost. Social benefits exceed private benefits when external benefits are created. From society's viewpoint, too little education would take place if individuals bore all the costs of education, because people would acquire additional education only to the point where the additional *private* benefit justified the additional cost. These situations represent market failures because the price of the good and the equilibrium quantity produced and consumed do not reflect the full costs of producing and/or consuming the good.

Private Property Rights

Market failures may result because of the absence of well-defined private property rights. No one has a private property right to the ocean or air. No one owns the fish in the sea; no one owns the elephants that roam the African plains; and during the past hundred years no one owned the American buffalo or bald eagle. Because no one owns these natural resources, a too-rapid rate of use or harvest occurs. Without private property rights, no one can produce the resources and control their sale in order to maximize profits over the long run. The private costs of consuming the resource are less than the social costs. As a result, a private market failure results. The economies of eastern Europe and Russia were based on a lack of private ownership. The result was market failure and the misallocation of resources that eventually led to the collapse of the system.

Public Goods

According to the principle of mutual exclusivity, the owner of private property is entitled to enjoy the consumption of private property privately. The principle of mutual exclusivity says, "if you own a good, I cannot use it; and if I own a good, you cannot use it. When I buy a pizza, it is mine to consume as I wish. You have no right to the pizza unless I provide that right." A **public good** is a good for which the principle of mutual exclusivity does not apply: "If you use a public good, I may also use it."

National defense, police protection, the legal system, and the air waves are public goods. The air waves illustrate the characteristics of a public good quite well. A television station broadcasts on a certain frequency, and anyone can pick up that station for free. It doesn't matter whether one person or a million people tune in the station—the signal is the same, and additional users don't deprive others of any of the public good. If your neighbor tunes in to the channel you are watching, you don't receive a weaker signal.

When goods are public, people have an incentive to be **free riders**— consumers or producers who enjoy a good without paying for it. If national defense were private, you would not be protected by the armed forces unless you paid a fee. Because national defense is a public good, however, you are protected whether or not you pay for it as long as others pay. Of course, because each person has an incentive not to pay for the public good, very few voluntarily do and the quantity of the good produced is too small from society's viewpoint. This is a market failure.

Resolution of Market Failures

Externalities, lack of private property rights, and public goods all lead to private market failures. The problem is that the private market and individuals have no incentive to correct the failure. Society as a whole loses, but single individuals cannot and will not bear the additional costs to ensure that the "right" amount of the good is produced and consumed. As a result, the government is asked to step in and resolve the problem, to assign property rights, impose taxes or subsidies, regulate an activity, or produce public goods and services. Market failures thus provide one justification for government intervention in the economy.

▼
Income Distribution and Poverty

In a market system, incomes are distributed according to the ownership of resources. Those who own the most highly valued resources have the highest incomes. One consequence of a market system, therefore, is that incomes are distributed unequally. Many people argue that the government should reduce income inequality and eliminate poverty. In some cases, the arguments are couched in terms of market failure; in most cases, they are couched in normative terms—compassion, humanitarian concerns, and so on.

Inequality

To compare income distributions, economists use a graph known as the **Lorenz curve**. Equal incomes among members of a population can be plotted as a 45-degree line that is equidistant from the axes, as in Figure 18-1. The horizontal axis measures the total population in cumulative percentages. As we move along the horizontal axis, we are counting larger and larger percentages of the population. The numbers end at 100, which designates 100 percent of the population. The vertical axis measures total national income in cumulative percentages. As we move up the vertical axis, the percentage of total national income being

FIGURE 18-1   *The Lorenz curve. This Lorenz curve is for the United States in 1987. The bottom 20 percent of the population has 5 percent of total national income, seen at point a. Point b indicates the bottom 40 percent of the population has 17 percent of the national income (5 percent received by the first 20 percent of the population plus 12 percent received by the second 20 percent). The third 20 percent accounts for another 18 percent of national income, so point c is plotted at a population of 60 percent and an income of 35 percent. The fourth 20 percent accounts for another 25 percent of the national income, shown as point d, where 80 percent of the population owns 60 percent of the income. The richest 20 percent accounts for an additional 40 percent of national income, shown as point e. At point e, 100 percent of population and 100 percent of national income are accounted for.*

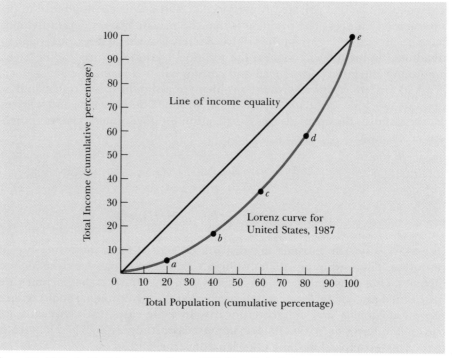

Source: World Bank, *World Development Report, 1989* (New York: Oxford University Press), Table 30.

counted rises to 100 percent. The 45-degree line splitting the distance between the axes is called the *line of income equality.* At each point on the line, the percentage of total population and the percentage of total national income are equal. The line of income equality indicates that 10 percent of the population earns 10 percent of the income, 20 percent of the population earns 20 percent of the income, and so on, until we see that 90 percent of the population earns 90 percent of the income and of course 100 percent of the population earns 100 percent of the income.

Points off the line of income equality indicate an income distribution that is unequal. Figure 18-1 shows the line of income equality and a curve that bows down below the income equality line. The bowed curve is a Lorenz curve. The Lorenz curve in Figure 18-1 is for the United States in 1987, the latest year for which data are available. The bottom 20 percent of the population has 5 percent of total national income, seen at point *a.* The second 20 percent accounts for another 12 percent of national income, shown as point *b,* where the bottom 40 percent of the population has 17 percent of the national income (5 percent received by the first 20 percent of the population plus the additional 12 percent received by the second 20 percent). The third 20 percent accounts for another 18 percent of national income, so point *c* is plotted at a population of 60 percent and an income of 35 percent. The fourth 20 percent accounts for another 25 percent of the national income, shown as point *d,* where 80 percent of the population receives 60 percent of the income. The richest 20 percent accounts for an additional 40 percent of national income, shown as point *e.* With the last 20 percent of the population and the last 40 percent of national income, 100 percent of population and 100 percent of national income are accounted for. Point *e,* therefore, is plotted where both income and population are 100 percent.

The farther the Lorenz curve bows down away from the line of income equality, the greater is the inequality of the distribution of income. In developed countries, the richest 20 percent of households receives about 40 percent of all household income while the poorest 20 percent receives only about 5 or 6 percent of all household income. That distribution, however, is much more equal than the typical distribution found in less developed countries. In less developed countries, the richest 20 percent of the population receives more than 50 percent of total household income while the poorest 20 percent receives less than 4 percent of total household income. In Figure 18-2 are Lorenz curves for a typical developed and for a typical less developed country. You can see that the Lorenz curve for the less developed country bows down below the developed country curve.

Poverty

A Lorenz curve does not indicate who the poor are or what their quality of life is. It is a relative measure. It indicates only the degree to which incomes are equally distributed. To understand the outcomes of market and other sys-

FIGURE 18-2 *Lorenz curves for different countries. The farther the Lorenz curve bows down away from the line of income equality, the more unequal the income distribution. In developed countries, the richest 20 percent of households receives about 40 percent of all household income, while the poorest 20 percent receives only about 5 or 6 percent of all household income. The typical distribution found in less developed countries is even more unequal — the richest 20 percent of the population receives more than 50 percent of total household income while the poorest 20 percent receives less than 4 percent of total household income. The Lorenz curve for the typical less developed country bows down below the curve for the typical developed country.*

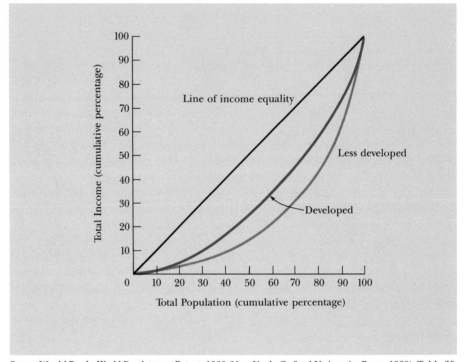

Source: World Bank, *World Development Report, 1989* (New York: Oxford University Press, 1989), Table 30.

tems, economists look not only at income distribution but also at the number of people living in poverty.

Poverty is an arbitrary measure of the quality of life. A 1955 study found that the average family in the United States spent about a third of its income on food, so in the 1960s, when the government decided to begin measuring poverty, it calculated the cost of buying food that met a predetermined nutritional standard and multiplied that cost by 3. That is where it drew the **poverty line**. Since then, the official poverty-line income has been adjusted for family size and for inflation. In 1987, a family of four whose income, including cash and in-kind transfers, fell below $11,611 was defined as living in poverty. In 1989 the cutoff was $12,675.

In 1990, nearly 30 million U.S. residents received incomes that were lower than the cutoff. As large as this number is, the incidence of poverty in the United States has declined since 1960, when poverty information was first collected. Figure 18-3 compares the number of people living in poverty from 1960 to 1988. From 1960 to the late 1970s, the incidence of poverty declined rapidly. From the late 1970s until the early 1980s, the incidence of poverty rose; it then began to decline again after 1982. Small upswings in the incidence of poverty occurred in 1969 and 1974, and a large rise occurred between 1978 and 1982.

Poverty and Recession

A major factor accounting for the incidence of poverty is the health of the economy. Each recession since 1960 has had important impacts on the numbers of people thrown into poverty. Between 1960 and 1969, the U.S. economy grew quite steadily and the incidence of poverty declined. Although the recession of 1969–1970 was relatively mild, the U.S. unemployment rate rose from 3.4 to 5.8 percent, and the total number of people unemployed rose from 2,832,000 to 5,016,000. When the economy once again began to expand, the poverty rates again dropped. The 1974 recession brought on another bout of unemployment that threw people into poverty. The 1974 recession was relatively serious, causing the unemployment rate to rise to 8.3 percent by 1975 and the number of unemployed to rise to 7,929,000. Once again, the poverty rate declined as the economy picked up after 1975. The recession of 1980–1982 threw the economy off track again. In 1979, the total number of people unemployed was 6,137,000; by 1982, a whopping 10,717,000 were without jobs. As the economy came out of this recession, the poverty rate began to decline and went on declining as the economy continued to grow throughout the 1980s. But as the economy entered recession in late 1990, unemployment rose and thus the incidence of poverty increased again.

The primary characteristic of those who fall below the poverty line is the lack of a job. In 1989, almost half of all poverty households were headed by people 65 years of age and over. Another 12 percent were headed by disabled people. Another 7 percent were headed by women with children under 6. Nonworking students constituted 5 percent of the poverty group. Those not working accounted for nearly three-fourths of the poverty group. Some people who work fall below the poverty line, but they work less than full time, or else their jobs pay so little that their income does not exceed the poverty cutoff line. For instance, a job paying $4.65 per hour for forty hours a week and 50 weeks a year yields an income of $9,300 — fully $2,000 below the poverty level. The health of the economy and poverty are inextricably linked.

Resolution of the Poverty Problem. Why are economists and others concerned with income inequality and poverty? One reason might be normative. People may have compassion for those who have less than they do, or people may not like to see the squalid living conditions endured by some in poverty. In other

FIGURE 18-3   *The incidence of poverty. The number of people living in poverty from 1960 to 1988 and the percentage of the population in poverty are shown. Nearly 30 million U.S. residents received incomes that were lower than the cut-off point in 1990. As large as this number is, the incidence of poverty in the United States has declined since 1960, when poverty information was first collected. From 1960 to the late 1970s, the incidence of poverty declined rapidly. From the late 1970s until the early 1980s, the incidence of poverty rose; it then began to decline again after 1982. Small upswings in the incidence of poverty occurred in 1969 and 1974, and a large rise occurred between 1978 and 1982.*

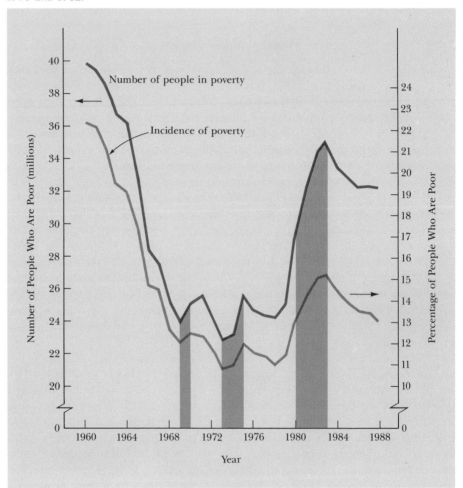

Source: U.S. Bureau of the Census, *Current Population Reports,* Series P-60, no. 161 (Washington, DC: U.S. Government Printing Office, 1988).

words, the existence of poverty may mean lower levels of utility for members of society not in poverty. If increases in poverty mean decreases in utility, then people will want less poverty. They will be willing and able to buy the existence of less poverty, by allocating part of their income or their time to alleviating the problem. But the existence of poverty is a public good—or rather, a public bad. One person alone can't have much effect on the incidence of poverty and everyone has an incentive to take a free ride on the efforts of others. From society's viewpoint, there is too much poverty. So, the government is called on to reduce the incidence of poverty.

Another reason for concern about income inequality and poverty might be positive. Perhaps the inequality is a result of inefficiency, and correcting the situation that creates the inefficiency will improve the functioning of the economy. For instance, if inequality is partly the result of a market failure—say due to the positive externality of education—then the economic system will function more efficiently after the market failure is corrected. If education provides benefits for society that are not taken into account in individual decisions to acquire education, then too few people acquire education. People who would have acquired education if the positive benefits for society had been subsidized but did not, are wasted resources. These people would have earned more income; fewer would have fallen into poverty, and the distribution of income might have been more equal. In this sense, the number of people in poverty and the existence of income inequality indicates that allocative efficiency has failed to occur.

Similarly, externalities are associated with business cycles and recessions. It is not just the inefficient who are forced into bankruptcy. People are thrown out of jobs and into poverty who had nothing to do with creating the conditions of the firm or industry; the very young and the aged, those without education and training and women and minorities are most susceptible. The externalities of recession may mean a market failure that requires government action. The externalities associated with business cycles—increased poverty—may provide a justification for fiscal and monetary policy.

▼
Natural Monopolies, Imperfect Information, and Unfair Practices

Other areas in which the government is asked to intervene in the private market include natural monopolies, problems with gathering and using information about products and services, and unfair trade practices on the part of firms.

Natural Monopoly

A **natural monopoly** occurs when a firm can become increasingly more efficient as it grows—producing a larger quantity at a lower cost per unit—throughout the range of market demand. The natural monopoly leads to an industry composed of one large firm—a firm with the ability to set price and extract above-normal profits. The private market supports this formation when there are economies of scale. For the firm to be forced to act as would a perfectly competitive firm, the natural monopoly must be regulated (or in some countries nationalized) by government.

Imperfect Information

Another area in which the private market may not result in the most efficient or perfectly competitive solution is when consumers and/or producers don't have complete or correct information. Often the government is called on to ensure that incorrect or improper decisions are not made when information is imperfect, to protect consumers from fraudulent ads, and to ensure that claims made by producers are valid.

Antitrust

The government also sets ground rules by which firms must play. Unfair practices and attempts to run competitors out of business are not condoned, and in some instances are considered illegal. Such governmental *antitrust* actions are captured in laws such as the Sherman Antitrust Act, the Clayton Act, and the Federal Trade Commission Act.

▼
What Does the Government Maximize?

Theoretically, the government is called on to intervene in the economy to correct problems associated with externalities, public goods, natural monopolies, imperfect information, income inequality, and the lack of well-defined property rights. The government does not intervene only in such cases, however. As noted in the introduction to this chapter, the government's activities are significantly greater than these theoretical justifications imply. Some have argued that the government intervenes whenever necessary in order to protect the public interest. Others argue that special interest groups receive government support, whether or not that support is in the public interest.

The Public Interest

The argument that the government must regulate certain industries or must restrict certain behavior arises from the view that such action benefits the general public. It is argued that the government regulates nuclear power, airlines, and pharmaceuticals because public safety depends on this regulation. People argue that government must intervene to protect farmers from destructive competition. Interest rates are often controlled to protect low-income people from exploitation by banks. Rent controls on apartments are intended to ensure that low-income people can afford housing. Even in the case of monetary and fiscal policy, government action is defended as being in the public interest. According to the **public interest theory** of government, government activities are designed to maximize society's welfare. The public interest theory justifies very active policymaking—minimizing recessions by increasing deficits and monetary growth and then offsetting inflation by decreasing the deficit and monetary growth. The public interest view is the basis of Keynesian policymaking—Keynes envisioned government as a benevolent dictator who would know what is best for the general public and would implement fiscal policy to direct the economy toward that result.

The Capture Theory

If government operates solely in the public interest, then why in so many cases do regulatory agencies or government bureaus seem to side with an industry against the general public? Why did senators intervene in the savings and loan regulatory process in the 1980s to help one of the biggest S&Ls even though the intervention cost the general public billions of dollars? Why are foreign auto manufacturers restricted in selling their cars in the United States when a higher quantity and lower price would benefit the consumer? And why are the prices of sugar, meat, and dairy products in the United States kept higher than world prices?

Not all government actions are in the public interest. So what accounts for the government intervention in the economy? One answer is that the regulatory bodies or government agencies are "captured" by special interest groups. In other words, special interest groups control the agencies that are supposed to regulate the special interest groups. For instance, a key part of the Clean Air Act of 1977 required new power plants to install expensive scrubbers to cut down on sulfur dioxide emissions even though using low-sulfur coal would have achieved the same emission reduction goal at a fraction of the cost. Lobbying by producers of high-sulfur coal and by the United Mine Workers Union resulted in the scrubber requirement.

The view that government intervention occurs because special interests dominate the decision making is known as the **capture theory** of government. In contrast to the view that government operates in the general public interest, the capture theory argues that the government operates for the benefit of special interest groups; that the government maximizes the welfare of special interest groups. In this case, the optimal monetary and fiscal policies would depend on the objective of the special interest group. If the group wanted lower taxes, lower unemployment, and more rapid growth, then we'd see larger deficits and money growth irrespective of the phase of the business cycle.

Public Choice

The capture theory may be valid in many cases, but it certainly does not hold in all. In many instances, an industry has suffered relatively more than the public, or one industry group has suffered while another benefited from government intervention. In the Clean Air Act case, for instance, the scrubber requirement helped the United Mine Workers and producers of high-sulfur coal but hurt the producers of low-sulfur coal. Cigarette manufacturers do not support nonsmoking areas in buildings or on airplanes, and not all pharmaceutical firms support the multiyear delays they face in introducing a new drug. A third view of government behavior, the **public choice theory**, incorporates aspects of public interest and capture theories. The public choice theory of government is based on the idea that government is nothing more than the many people who work for the government, each trying to maximize his or her own utility. In this view, the government is a complex organization comprising many individuals, each with a different objective.

The public choice theory of government is the most widely accepted theory of government among political scientists and economists. It incorporates the public interest and capture theories—depending on the relative political power of the groups, the public interest might win or the special interest group might win. From case to case, results may differ.

Do Politicians Really Act in Their Own Self-Interest? The public choice theory of government assumes that in a democratic political system the central objective of politicians is to get elected. Accordingly, to a politician votes are like dollars to a private firm. Do elected officials really act this way? A great deal of evidence suggests they do.

The voting records of members of Congress reflect the necessity of responding to constituent interests as an election nears. U.S. representatives and senators behave differently during their terms in office because the lengths of their terms differ. Senators, with a six-year term, are more independent than Congressional representatives, who must run for re-election every two years. Senators have more time in which to pursue their own interests independently of their constituents' interests. Senators thus align their voting records with the concerns of their constituents in the years before an election, but they follow their own objectives immediately after an election. Senators have cyclical voting records, as shown in Figure 18-4. They vote a more conservative line as an election nears if they are from a conservative state, or they vote a more liberal line as an election nears if they are from a liberal state. Once the election is over, they vote as their own self-interest dictates.

The executive branch also responds to the political market in making its policy decisions. A dramatic illustration of this was pointed out by author Gore Vidal in his historical novel, *Lincoln.* Vidal noted that President Lincoln used troop deployment to ensure his re-election in 1964. Units from states in which his election was in question were moved to the rear or out of the fighting in the hope that they and their friends and families would support Lincoln or at least would not have reasons *not* to support him. Troops from states in which his re-election was virtually either a certainty or an impossibility, saw front-line action.

FIGURE 18-4   *Cyclical voting behavior. The voting records of members of Congress reflect the necessity of responding to constituent interests as an election nears. Senators thus align their voting records with the concerns of their constituents in the years before an election, but they follow their own objectives immediately after an election. Senators have a cyclical voting record.*

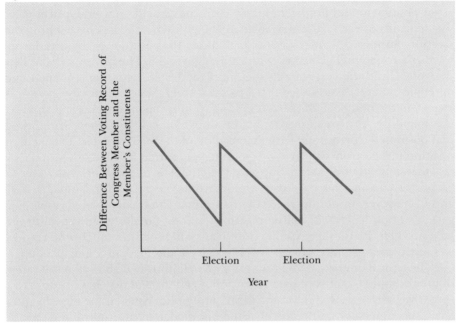

Political Markets and the Median Voter. One crucial aspect of the development of a public choice perspective of economic policy is recognition of the limitations of the single, well-informed rational actor model that underlies much of macroeconomic analysis. The mechanism of collective decision making can lead rational individuals to generate outcomes that would be irrational if viewed from the perspective of a single individual. Individuals do not have the incentive to acquire and assimilate information about the issues confronting them because each individual's influence over the outcome is relatively small. This is why many voters may be relatively, but rationally, uninformed.

In the political market, there is one vote per person, not one vote per dollar. Politicians need only formulate policies that a majority of voters support. In the political market, voters do not purchase one good at a time, as they do in the marketplace; instead, they must choose a **full-line supply** of products when they cast their votes. A full-line supply is the entire bundle of policies offered by a candidate. Voters cast a vote for a candidate knowing that the candidate will take stands on many issues. An individual who agrees with a candidate's environmental policies but not with the candidate's support for income redistribution does not vote yes for the environmental policy and no for the income distribution policy. He or she votes yes or no for the candidate's entire bundle of policies.

A politician does not try to satisfy each constituent, as would a firm meet the demands of each customer; instead, the politician focuses on winning the election. Suppose all voters are aligned along the continuum of attitudes toward environmental protection shown in Figure 18-5. The horizontal axis lists the voters, and the vertical axis measures the level of government spending on environmental issues supported by each voter. Voter *D,* labeled *median,* is exactly in the middle: half the voters support more spending and half support less spending. The greatest support for a position can be gained by defining that position to correspond with the position of the **median voter**. The median position differs from the level of spending supported by each other voter by less than any other position. Suppose the choice is to go along with voter *C.* Candidates would pick up more support from voters *A* and *B.* Voters *D, E, F,* and *G,* however, would decrease their support. The median voter result suggests that politicians will define positions and set policies that appeal to the median voter. It also suggests that politicians will not differ much with respect to their positions and policies—each will have the median voter in mind.

The typical or median voter may not be well informed about the full range of the costs and benefits of particular policy actions and may have little direct incentive to become well informed about most policy issues. If the median voter has a short memory and relatively little knowledge of macroeconomic analysis, vote-seeking incumbent politicians have incentives to generate business cycles using unanticipated policy changes. In the short run, unanticipated changes in macroeconomic policies tend to influence employment and output more quickly than prices. Thus, unless fully anticipated by the public, an economic expansion shortly before an election yields a high portion of its political benefits (employment expansion) before the election while most of the costs (inflation) come after. If a substantial proportion of voters react primarily to the current state of the economy, then this would be a vote-gaining strategy. A misinformed median voter provides a basis for the political business cycle.

The Political Business Cycle. As an illustration of how the public choice theory might affect macroeconomic policymaking, let's analyze how economic policy might be determined under conditions where voters have short memories and are not fully informed of the policies undertaken by the government. Consider the situation where the political party in power wants to get re-elected—it maximizes votes. Voters determine whether to support the incumbents on the basis of unemployment and inflation. The higher the unemployment rate or the inflation rate, the less likely it is that the voter will support the incumbent party. The voter's desires are shown as the set of curves labeled *V* in Figure 18-6. These curves are called *isovote curves;* any combination of inflation and unemployment that lies on say V_3 yields the same number of votes to the incumbent party.

FIGURE 18-5   *The median voter. Suppose all voters are aligned along the continuum of attitudes toward environmental protection. The horizontal axis lists the voters, and the vertical axis measures the level of government spending on environmental issues supported by each voter. Voter D, labeled* median, *is exactly in the middle: half the voters support more spending, and half support less spending. The greatest support for a position can be gained by defining that position to correspond with the position of the median voter. The median position differs from the level of spending supported by each other voter by less than any other position.*

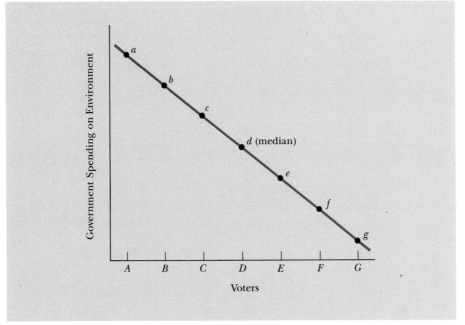

The incumbent party is assumed to be able to set its desired unemployment rate through monetary and fiscal policy, but is constrained by the short-run and long-run aggregate supply curves—the Phillips curve. The short-run Phillips curve is shown in Figure 18-6 as the *PC* lines. The long-run curve is the vertical line labeled PC^{lr}.

Suppose an election is approaching and the economy is at point *a*. If the incumbent policymakers believe the odds of re-election (along V_2) are too low, an expansionary demand policy may be enacted. With such a policy, the unemployment rate falls if workers underestimate the accompanying price increase. The policymakers' goal is to reach the lowest voter preference curve possible, because the lower the curve, the higher the odds of re-election. However, the party is constrained by the economy to move along the short-run Phillips curve PC_1. So the incumbents must choose the inflation–unemployment combination along PC_1 that puts them on the lowest voter preference curve. This is shown at point *b*, where the short-run Phillips curve PC_1 just touches the voter preference curve V_1. If the policymakers can move to this point just before the election, their chances of re-election will improve.

FIGURE 18-6   *The political business cycle. Voters' reactions to inflation and unemployment are shown as the set of isovote curves labeled V; any combination of inflation and unemployment that lies on, say V_3, yields the same number of votes to the incumbent party.*

    Suppose the economy is at point a. If the incumbent policymakers believe the odds of re-election (along V_2) are too low, an expansionary demand policy may be enacted. With such a policy, the unemployment rate falls if workers underestimate the accompanying price increase. The policymakers' goal is to reach the lowest voter preference curve possible, because the lower the curve, the higher the odds of re-election. However, the party is constrained by the economy to move along the short-run Phillips curve, PC_1. Thus, the incumbents must choose the inflation–unemployment combination along PC_1 that puts them on the lowest voter preference curve. This is point b, where the short-run Phillips curve PC_1 is just tangent to the voter preference curve V_1. If the policymakers can move to this point just before the election, their chances of re-election improve.

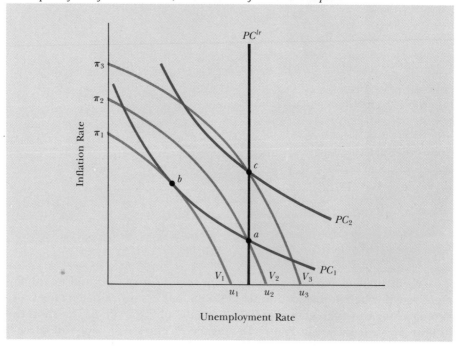

    The inflation and unemployment rate combination represented by point *b* is not sustainable. Workers eventually realize that prices are rising, and the short-run Phillips curve shifts to PC_2 as the economy moves to point *c*. Notice that point *c* lies on voter preference curve V_3 which is inferior to the tradeoff existing before the stimulative policy was instituted. The economic oscillations resulting from this behavior are known as **political business cycles**. This adjustment will likely occur after the election. However, it may not. Recall that the short-run curve PC_1 is relevant only as long as it takes workers to realize that their price forecasts were incorrect. If policymakers stimulate demand and move the economy from point *a* to point *b* only to have workers' price expectations adjust quickly and accurately, they may end up with a lower likelihood of re-election (at point *c*) than if they had done nothing. So for the incumbents timing is everything. Their policy change must be initiated early enough to lower the unemployment rate but late enough so that inflationary expectations have no time to adjust. A miscalculation may cost them the election.

Pro-Inflation Bias. The public choice literature suggests ways in which the distribution of effective political power may deviate substantially from the "one person, one vote" and median voter result. For instance, a divergence between individual and group interests often results in small, well-organized special interest groups winning out in the political process against the interests of large but unorganized groups. Thus, while a simple median voter model predicts that government policies with widely dispersed benefits and costs concentrated on a few voters are likely to achieve a majority vote, policies that have concentrated benefits and widely dispersed costs are more successful if the special interest group receiving the benefits is more effectively organized than the large group. This might help to explain the persistence of inflation the United States has experienced since the 1960s. In general, the distribution consequences of inflation in comparison with unemployment are difficult to determine. They vary depending on the particular causes of the inflation and the degree to which inflation is anticipated or not. Unemployment significantly strikes smaller groups (such as a particular industry or a particular type of worker), while inflation affects everyone but typically not too seriously. So it shouldn't be too surprising that we find much less difference across income groups in attitudes toward inflation than toward unemployment. And it shouldn't be surprising that we find a proinflationary bias in economic policy.

Public Choice and Monetary Policy. The Keynesian assumption that the government consists primarily of experts motivated by "the public interest" is the basis of many independent regulatory commissions and the structure of the Federal Reserve system. The fear that democratic politics will hinder the experts leads to the idea of having independent agencies wherein experts can pursue the public interest free of the pressures of political considerations.

The Federal Reserve system was begun in 1914. Its structure reflected many concerns of Congress. The system was set up to be decentralized; each district bank was to be like a distinct central bank for its region of the country. The Board of Governors was to be subservient to the district banks and the Congress. The Federal Reserve system was made to be self-sustaining; no general tax revenues are allocated toward its expenses. The Fed generates revenue for itself by holding government debt to maturity (this requires prior open-market purchases), taking capital gains on maturing securities (open-market churning), and by charging fees for services it provides. Between 1914 and 1933, district banks conducted their own open-market sales and purchases, paid expenses, and then sent any excess revenue to the Treasury. The Board of Governors had to petition the Treasury for part of these revenues. The Board was just a bit player compared to the district banks.

The situation changed with the passage of the Banking Acts of 1933 and 1935. These acts reflected the attitude that experts, independent of politics, would operate best in the public interest. The Board was allowed to obtain district bank revenues before they went to the Treasury. Also, the terms of Board members were lengthened, the secretary of the Treasury and the comptroller of the currency were removed from Board membership, and open-market operations were specified as the function of the Federal Reserve Open Market Committee (FOMC). These changes raised the independence and central power of the Board. Between 1933 and 1947, the Board had a great deal of latitude. But by 1947 the Board was feeling pressure from Congress. Fearing legislative sanctions, the Board began to submit its earnings above expenses to the Treasury, a practice that continues today.

These institutional arrangements meant that the Board had different powers at different times in U.S. history and that the Board's "independence" changed over its history. During the early period when the Board had to petition the Treasury for its revenues, the executive branch and Congress had an incentive to closely monitor the behavior of the Board. If they were unhappy with the Board, they could allocate fewer funds. After 1933 but before 1947, the Board had a great deal of independence and power. All system revenue flowed to the Board and was then allocated by the Board. From 1947 on, the Board submitted its excess earnings above operating expenses to the Treasury.

Given the institutional setting where the Board submits the excess revenues above costs to the Treasury, consider what would happen if the members of the Board wanted the Board to grow in size, stature, and power. The Board would have to be concerned only that its expenses grew too fast and that it could not submit about the same quantity of revenue to the Treasury. The Board could grow and carry larger expenses if it could increase revenue. Because the lion's share of the Fed's operating revenues come from open-market operations, the Fed's Board could grow if it increased open-market purchases. The Board has indeed grown in size and expenses since 1950. It is entirely possible that the desire of the Federal Reserve Board to grow may have biased monetary policy toward excessive monetary growth.

Fiscal Policy and Pork Barrel Politics

One major reason why political outcomes can deviate from median voter interests with a well-informed electorate is that most political decisions are based on decisions by elected or appointed officials rather than on direct referenda by the public. This suggests considerable scope for special interest groups to lobby for pork barrel measures. Suppose that farmers constitute only 5 percent of voters, but that for them the farm bill is an extremely important determinant of their vote. Voting against a general farm bill substantially affects the vote of farmers. The other 95 percent of the voters may gain from reduced farm support, but in a presidential vote it is unlikely that opposition to the farm bill would be very important in most people's votes.

The influence of small special interest groups has increased because of the way Congress operates. Congress has developed the tradition of giving committees substantial power in spending decisions. The memberships of these committees are largely self-selected on the basis of the interests of members of Congress. This enhances the idea of **log rolling**, or vote trading. Let's say a certain senator from Massachusetts who wants to provide his constituents additional benefits must convince a certain senator from Kansas that a boat-building project in Boston Bay is worthwhile. To do that, the Massachusetts senator offers to vote for a farm support bill the senator from Kansas wants in return for her support for the Boston Bay project. In this way, each senator can provide benefits to his or her constituents. The result is an increase in federal government spending and an increase in the government's role in the economy. Because senators and representatives can get benefits for a small group (such as in a single state) while shifting the costs of those benefits to the entire population, the political structure of fiscal policymaking is biased toward increased spending. By enlarging the numbers who pay for special benefits to future generations (bond financing), the costs imposed on each voter decrease further. So the political system includes a bias toward increased spending, deficits, and bond financing.[1]

Politics has rendered fiscal policy ineffective as a stabilization tool. Only the 1964 and 1968 tax changes were undertaken primarily for stabilization, and the latter took a year and a half to get through Congress. During Jimmy Carter's 1976 presidential campaign, he promised to produce a balanced budget by the end of his term. Yet Carter's budget was in substantial deficit in 1982. Comparing his budget to his campaign promises, President Carter lamented that "we have reached a point where uncontrollable spending threatens the effectiveness of the budget as an instrument of discretionary national economy policy." What constitutes uncontrollable expenditures? The Carter administration defined the following categories: interest on the national debt, funds obligated under contract, social security payments, railroad retirement, federal employees' retirement, unemployment compensation, Medicare, Medicaid, food stamps, and various other programs. These outlays are considered to be uncontrollable because of the political action that would be necessary to bring them under control. The outlays are indexed—payments increase automatically as inflation rises. The outlays are primarily entitlements. So if someone is 65 or if someone under 18 years of age is the survivor of a social security recipient, then that person receives payment automatically. He or she is "entitled" to the funds. As a result, over 40 percent of the budget becomes effective without any congressional review. An even more drastic way to insulate a program is to take it out of the budget entirely. The U.S. Railway Association, the Pension Guaranty Corporation, the Federal Financing Bank, and the Post Office are off-budget programs whose expenditures are over $20 billion per year.

---

1   Could you support this cost-shifting argument of the growth of government if you believed in Ricardian equivalence?

Government guarantees of credit have also grown tremendously in recent years. The provision of guaranteed credit has a history dating back to the Great Depression and the establishment of agencies such as the Federal Housing Administration (FHA). The loan guarantee was originally designed to aid home buyers. The programs were placed on an actuarially sound basis, which meant that the present value of revenues met or exceeded the present value of outlays. In the 1960s, however, these guarantees were extended through subsidies to borrowers such as students and low-income families, and guarantees have been provided for firms such as Lockheed and Chrysler and to cities such as New York. The federal budget lists more than thirty programs with guarantees near $1 trillion. Guarantees have particular appeal in the political process, because they provide benefits to constituents without direct costs to constituents. Guarantees are regarded by many as virtually costless because they show up in the federal budget only if the guarantee is exercised; such as in some of the FSLIC (savings and loan) guarantees.

Proposals for Reform

Proposals to reform the monetary system range from increasing the independence of the Fed to doing away with the Fed. Monetary growth rules are, in essence, proposals to do away with the Fed independence; money would be allowed to grow at a specified pace without any deviation or change by monetary authorities. This type of proposal is supported by monetarists, some new classical economists, and some public choice economists. Another means to reduce the Fed's independence is to return to the gold standard or some type of commodity standard: to restrict the money supply to the growth of the stock of gold or some other commodity. Proposals for reducing independence also include making the Fed part of the Treasury and/or giving the U.S. president control over the money supply. The argument is that voters could vote up or down on increasing monetary growth by voting for or against a presidential candidate. As we've seen, however, full-line supply and log rolling mitigate the impact of this idea. Moreover, in those nations where monetary policy is housed within the same office as fiscal policy, hyperinflation often results.

On the opposite side stand those who support a more independent Fed. One idea is to make the Fed a private profit-maximizing corporation that supplies money in competition with other private profit-maximizing corporations. Money would consist of the most used and trusted corporation's securities; there might be "IBMs" or "ATTs" instead of Federal Reserve notes. Critics of this approach counter that money creation is a natural monopoly, so only one money producer would emerge. This monopolist would reap huge monopoly profits from its control of the money supply.

Wide-ranging reforms of fiscal policy are also proposed. In most cases, the idea is to reduce the ability of Congress to create off-budget programs and entitlements. There have been calls for a balanced budget amendment that would require the government to run balanced budgets. The Gramm-Rudman-Hollings Act of 1985 sought to reduce deficits automatically unless Congress and the executive branch agreed to budget-reducing initiatives. The act was not effective, however. Congress passed expenditure bills designed to escape the automatic budget cuts. For instance, the Gulf War of 1990–1991 was placed "off budget" to escape Gramm-Rudman-Hollings restrictions.

▼   ▼   ▼   ▼   ▼   ▼   ▼   ▼   ▼   ▼   ▼
Conclusions

This chapter completes the discussion of economic policy and macroeconomics. Several rationales are used to justify (1) government interference in the private economy and (2) monetary and fiscal policy. Economic policy is complicated to create and manage, even when the reality of politics is ignored. Given the reality of voting, log rolling, full-line supply, and the rational interests of voters and politicians, the task of creating and managing economic policy may seem nearly impossible. Fiscal policy has become useless as an economic tool. Monetary policy is controversial. Some argue that monetary policy is heavily influenced by politics and is biased toward inflation. Some claim that giving the Federal Reserve discretion over monetary policy produces the political business cycle. Proposed solutions range from doing away with the Fed to letting the Fed become a private, profit-making firm.

▼   ▼   ▼   ▼   ▼   ▼   ▼   ▼   ▼   ▼   ▼
Summary

1. Why does the government intervene in the private economy?
Market failures provide a rationale for government intervention. The resolution of externalities, the provision of public goods, the regulation of natural monopolies, income redistribution, and problems created by imperfect information all offer roles for government to play. In addition, the government must provide a legal system to create and defend the private property system.

2. What does the government seek to accomplish when it intervenes in the private economy?
The answer depends on which theory of government you support. Under the public interest theory, the government carries out only those activities that are in the public interest. Under the capture theory, the government works for the special interests that control lobbying and other decision-making aspects of government. Under the public choice theory, government works to enhance the best interests of those in government.

3. Who or what is the government?
The government is simply the individuals who work for government.

4. What do political markets imply for monetary and fiscal policy?
Fiscal policy has become useless as an economic tool. Monetary policy is controversial. Some support doing away with the Fed. Others support increased Fed independence and power. Irrespective of theory, the facts indicate a proinflation bias in U.S. economic policy over the past several decades, and the best explanation for this bias seems to be the interaction of politics and economics.

▼
Key Terms

market failure   429

externality   429

public good   431

free riders   431

Lorenz curve   432

poverty line   434

natural monopoly   437

public interest theory   438

capture theory   439

public choice theory   440

full-line supply   441

median voter   442

political business cycles   444

log rolling   447

▼
Problems and Exercises

1.   Describe the three main theories of government.

2.   Explain what a market failure is. Why would the government be called on to resolve a market failure?

3.   Develop a theory to explain the behavior of prices in the United States in the past 200 years.

4.   In May 1991, President Bush was applying pressure on the G-7 nations to lower interest rates. Why would Bush want world interest rates lowered? The other countries rejected his pressure. Why would they not follow Bush's calls for lower interest rates?

5.   Using each theory of government, explain the objectives and practice of monetary and fiscal policy. What does each theory suggest would be done in a recession? How about in an inflationary period?

Glossary

A

accelerated depreciation An increased rate at which capital can be depreciated (the accounting rate of depreciation).

adaptive expectations hypothesis (AEH) The idea that people form their expectations of economic variables solely on the basis of previous values of those variables.

age–income profile The graphic curve that shows the relationship between age and income.

age–productivity profile A graphic representation of the relationship between age and productivity.

aggregate demand (AD) The sum of household, business, government, and foreign demand for domestic goods and services.

aggregate expenditures (AE) Total expenditures—by households, businesses, and government in the domestic economy plus foreign expenditures, at any given (fixed) price level.

aggregate production function The relationship between input combinations and output.

aggregate supply (AS) A curve showing the total quantity of output produced (real GNP) as a function of the price level.

arbitrage The process of buying a good in one market at a lower price than the good can be sold for in another market. The simultaneous buying and selling equalizes the price in the two markets.

B

balance of payments (BOP) The record of transactions among countries.

beggar-thy-neighbor policy Policy designed to improve domestic conditions by causing worsening conditions in other countries.

BOP curve The combinations of domestic interest rate and output level where the balance of payments (BOP) is in equilibrium.

bubble A situation in which a given economic variable progressively or cumulatively deviates from the path consistent with its fundamental long-run equilibrium, or PPP value.

business cycles Fluctuations in economic activity in which an expansion is followed by a contraction and then another expansion.

business fixed investment Business spending on plant (structures) and equipment.

C

capital controls Barriers to the free flow of money, erected by governments, that take the form of quotas on the amount of foreign exchange that can be bought or sold, or the form of restrictions on who can own what assets.

capture theory The view that government intervention occurs because special interests dominate the decision making.

ceteris paribus Latin phrase meaning "other things being equal" or "everything else held constant."

Cobb-Douglas production function A commonly used form of an aggregate production function where $Y = AK^bN^{1-b}$, where K = capital stock, N = labor supply, Y = output, b = capital's contribution to total output.

compensating wage differentials Wage differences that make up for the high risk or poor working conditions of a job.

consumer price index (CPI) Measures the cost of a "basket" of goods purchased by a typical urban household.

consumption The flow of expenditures on goods and services used to satisfy wants and needs during the current period. Household spending.

cooperative games When, for example, countries form their policies jointly, in consultation with each other.

cost-plus pricing Adding a fixed percentage margin to the average variable cost of an item.

cost–push inflation Inflation caused by rising costs of production.

crowding out What happens to private spending when private investment is reduced because of an expansionary fiscal policy.

cyclical unemployment Unemployment that is the result of business cycle fluctuations.

D

demand deposits Deposits payable when demanded by depositors.

demand–pull inflation Any event that can be represented as an outward shift of the aggregate demand (*AD*) curve.

demand shocks When random, or unpredictable, influences affect the demand curve.

demand-side policies Policies directed toward the aggregate demand curve.

depository institutions Intermediary between savers and borrowers; they accept deposits and make loans.

depreciation The process by which the cost of an asset is allocated to the years of its anticipated useful life.

depression A prolonged period of severe recession.

dirty float A floating exchange rate system in which there is some occasional intervention by national governments.

discount rate The interest rate banks pay to borrow funds.

discretionary fiscal policy A fiscal policy in which changes in taxation and government spending can be used to manipulate equilibrium.

disequilibrium business cycle The model that presumes market clearing or equilibrium always occurs. Also called the *neo-Keynesian business cycle*.

disintermediation If financial institutions are restricted in the rate of interest they may pay on deposits, then they may lose deposits during periods of high interest rates. Rather than place funds in a financial institution, individuals and businesses may choose to invest directly in such vehicles as Treasury bills and various types of bonds.

dissaving When individuals borrow or use part of their savings for consumption.

dual labor market The skilled–unskilled dichotomy of the labor market.

E

economic growth An increase in the output produced in the economy; also, measurable as an increase in real income, the year-to-year percentage change in real GNP or real GDP.

economic shock An unexpected change in aggregate demand or aggregate supply.

efficiency wages Wages set above the equilibrium wage, to motivate workers or to retain skilled workers.

efficient Given individuals' tastes and society's technology, efficient levels of employment, output, and consumption cannot be improved.

equilibrium business cycle The model that relies on sticky wages or prices to propagate the economic impulse. Also called *real business cycle* or *neoclassical business cycle.*

Eurocurrency market The international deposit and loan market. Also called *offshore banking.*

excess reserves The excess of a financial institution's vault cash and reserves at the Fed over its required reserves.

exchange rate The price of a unit of one country's currency in terms of another country's currency.

expansion The economic period between a trough and a peak that follows.

expected rate of return A rate calculated by dividing the expected annual dollar earnings less all expenses (except interest payments on borrowed funds) by the cost of the asset.

exports Sales by domestic firms to the rest of the world.

export substitution Growth strategy that focuses on giving domestic firms subsidies to use the most abundant resources within a country to produce products that they might thus be able to make better than other countries' firms.

externality A cost that is external to an activity, such as the costs of pollution that are not borne solely by the individual or corporate polluter.

F

fallacy of composition The error of attributing what applies to one, to the case of the many.

fallacy of interpreting association as causation The error of attributing a cause and effect relationship to unrelated or coincidental events.

federal funds Loans made from one depository institution to another for very short periods, typically overnight.

federal funds rate The equilibrium interest rate in the federal funds market. It is the rate which financial institutions pay to borrow from each other.

Federal Open Market Committee (FOMC) The policymaking body of the Federal Reserve system.

feedback effect In the *IS–LM* model, the change in aggregate expenditures that results from the influence of the money market (see Appendix to Chapter 5).

final good or service A good or service that is not resold in order to be used in the production of another product.

fiscal policy The deliberate manipulation of taxes and government expenditures in order to affect the level of national income, prices, unemployment, and other economic variables.

Fisher effect The relationship between nominal and real interest rates: the nominal interest rate equals the real interest rate plus the expected inflation rate.

fixed exchange rate system The situation when the exchange rate is set by law independent of demand and supply.

flexible exchange rate system A free market, where demand for and supply of a currency determines the exchange rate.

FOMC directive The mechanism for translating Federal Reserve policy into actions; each directive outlines monetary policy for six to eight weeks until the FOMC meets again.

foreign exchange Foreign money, including paper money and bank deposits such as checking accounts, denominated in foreign currency.

foreign exchange market intervention Action taken by the Fed (FOMC) to control the foreign exchange rate.

fractional reserve banking system A monetary system in which financial institutions keep only a fraction of their deposits in the form of reserves.

free reserves Excess reserves minus reserves borrowed from the Fed, held by depository institutions.

free riders Consumers or producers who enjoy a good without paying for it.

frictional unemployment Unemployment that is the result of (1) the movement of workers among jobs and (2) first-time job seekers.

full-line supply The entire bundle of policies offered to the voters by a candidate for political office.

fundamental growth equation The equation $y = a + 0.3k + 0.7n$; showing that economic growth, y, depends on productivity changes, a, and on changes in resources, capital, and labor.

G

GNP gap Potential gross national product minus real GNP; the difference between the two provides a measure of the output (and hence income) that is not produced due to unemployment; that is, the cost to society due to unemployment.

gold exchange standard A variation on the gold standard. Under the gold exchange standard, a country pegs the value of its currency to the value of the currency of some other country that is on the gold standard.

gold standard A monetary system according to which the value of a country's money is legally defined as a fixed quantity of gold. The country's monetary authority agrees to exchange domestic currency for gold at a specified rate.

government purchases Purchases of goods and services by the government; the second largest component of aggregate expenditures in the United States.

gross domestic product (GDP) A measure of the purely domestic output of a country.

gross national product (GNP) The value, at market prices, of all final goods and services produced in the economy during a given time period. It is a measure of the aggregate production of the economy during that time period.

H

high-powered money The sum of currency in circulation and reserves; vault cash plus deposits at the Fed.

human capital Skills, training, and job experience.

hyperinflation An extremely high rate of inflation.

I

implicit price deflator The broadest measure of prices, including all items measured in the gross national product.

imports Domestic purchases from the rest of the world.

import substitution Policies that protect, with tariffs on imports, industries that produce products now largely made by foreign producers.

impulse An economic shock that can either cause a one-time deviation or can set off a series of fluctuations around the trend.

inflation The rate at which the price level rises.

interest rate effect The result that higher price levels have on the rate of interest and thus on planned business and household purchases.

interest rate parity (IRP) A condition in which the return, or effective interest rate, tends to be the same on similar bonds (when returns are measured in terms of the domestic currency).

intermediate good Good used in the production of a final product.

intermediate target The monetary base and the money supply, which the Fed controls in order to affect GNP and price level.

international banking facilities (IBFs) Bookkeeping systems set up in existing bank offices to record international banking transactions.

international trade effect The effect of domestic prices rising while foreign prices and the exchange rate stay constant; domestic goods become more expensive, so foreign buyers buy less and thus the total demand for U.S. goods declines.

inventories Final goods or goods in process that have not been sold.

inventory investment Changes in the stock of raw materials and finished or semifinished goods held by business firms.

investment The flow of expenditure on additions to the stock of capital. Alternatively, the flow of expenditures on goods that are used as inputs to further stages of production.

investment tax credit (ITC) A reduction in income tax liability offered to businesses that undertake certain forms of investment spending.

***IS* curve** A negatively sloped curve showing all combinations of the interest rate and the level of income that are consistent with equilibrium in the goods market when the price level is fixed.

L

labor market The economic arena in which supply of and demand for labor is expressed.

law of one price The idea that arbitrage will eliminate all price differences on identical commodities sold in different countries. More precisely, arbitrage will continue until there are no more profits to be made from buying a commodity in the country where its price is low and selling it in the country where its price is high.

leakages The additional amounts of income that are not passed on as additional spending on domestic goods and services.

legal reserves The sum of vault cash and deposits in the depository institution's vault.

life cycle hypothesis A theory of consumption spending developed by Ando, Brumberg, and Modigliani. The theory is based on the hypothesis that economic units attempt to smooth out consumption over their lifetime despite the fact that income may vary widely.

liquidity trap A situation that exists when the demand for real money balances is perfectly interest elastic. In such a situation, a drop in the interest rate will not induce larger money holdings, and therefore the *LM* curve will be horizontal.

LM curve A positively sloped curve showing all combinations of the interest rate and the level of income that are consistent with equilibrium in the money market when the price level is fixed.

log rolling Vote trading among politicians.

long-run aggregate supply curve The graphical representation of aggregate supply after all adjustments in price and wage levels have taken place.

long-term contracts Contracts that specify wages and working conditions for more than one year.

Lorenz curve A graph used to compare income distributions.

Lucas supply curve The positive relationship between GNP and unexpected price rises.

M

M1 monetary aggregate The sum of currency and coin, traveler's checks of nonbank issuers, demand deposits at commercial banks, NOW and ATS account balances, credit union share draft balances, and demand deposits at mutual savings banks. This monetary aggregate is often taken to represent money in its role as a medium of exchange.

M2 monetary aggregate The sum of *M1* plus savings and small denomination time deposits at all depository institutions, overnight repurchase agreements, overnight Eurodollars, and money market mutual fund balances. This monetary aggregate is often taken as a measure of money in its role as a store of wealth.

M3 monetary aggregate The sum of *M2* plus large denomination time deposits at all depository institutions, term repurchase agreements at commercial banks and savings and loan associations, and balances of money market mutual funds of institutions.

macroeconomics The study of the economy as a whole or in the aggregate.

managed floating system The exchange rate system in which the government at times intervenes to cause the demand curve or the supply curve to shift, but normally allows the market to move freely; also called a *dirty float.*

marginal propensity to consume (MPC) The ratio of additional consumption expenditure to the change in national income that induced it.

marginal propensity to import (MPI) The change in imports divided by the change in income.

marginal propensity to save (MPS) The ratio of a change in saving to the change in national income that induced it. MPS = 1 − MPC.

marginal revenue product (MRP) The return on each additional unit of capital.

market failure When consumers or producers do not bear the full costs or benefits of the transactions they undertake.

mark-up pricing Adding a fixed percentage of margin to the average variable cost of an item.

median voter The voter in the position that differs from the level of spending supported by each other voter by less than any other position.

monetary accommodation The expansionary monetary policy in reaction to negative supply shocks.

monetary base The total of currency in circulation plus reserve deposits at the Federal Reserve Bank.

monetary policy The deliberate manipulation of the money supply and/or interest rates in order to affect the level of national income, prices, unemployment, and other economic variables.

monetization A situation that occurs when newly issued federal government bonds, issued to finance a budget deficit, are purchased by the Federal Reserve. As a consequence, the economy's money supply is increased.

money illusion The illusion that workers are under regarding money because they care more about the nominal (or money) wage, W, than the real wage, W/P.

money market The economic arena in which the demand for and supply of money is expressed; where the interest rate is determined.

money multiplier The value by which the monetary base is expanded into the money supply.

multiplier The ratio of the change in income to the change in the autonomous component of aggregate demand that caused it.

N

national debt The stock of government bonds that are outstanding; the result of past and current budget deficits.

natural monopoly The situation that occurs when a firm can become more efficient as it grows— producing a larger quantity at a lower cost per unit—throughout the range of market demand.

natural rate of unemployment The rate of unemployment that would exist at the natural output level.

neoclassical business cycle The model assuming that the market always clears; equilibrium always occurs. Also called *real business cycle* or *equilibrium business cycle*.

neo-Keynesian business cycle Model of cycle in which sticky wages or prices propagate economic shock. Also called *disequilibrium business cycle*.

net exports The component of aggregate expenditures that equals a country's exports minus its imports.

net national product (NNP) The value derived when depreciation is subtracted from GNP.

new classical economics A refinement of classical economic thought that updates the classical scheme and incorporates monetarist elements; assumes that people form rational expectations based on all available information, so forecast errors can't last very long.

new Keynesian theory The theory that says (1) wages and prices are not flexible in the short run; (2) the economy is not always in long-run

equilibrium; and (3) it takes a considerable period of time for the economy to adjust to demand changes.

nominal GNP The value of all final goods and services produced in the economy during the year.

nominal interest rate The interest rate actually observed in the market and quoted in mass media.

nominal wage The wage that is measured by the amount of dollars paid to a worker.

nonborrowed reserves Reserves at depository institutions that have not been borrowed; the FOMC's current indicator of money supply growth (short-run operating target).

noncooperative games A situation in which two countries want to implement macroeconomic policies that might be detrimental to each other; for example, the prisoner's dilemma.

nondiscretionary fiscal policy The idea that whenever income changes, tax revenues and the government's budget position will change without any overt action by policymakers. In other words, an automatic fiscal policy change takes place.

normative analysis Analysis that imposes the value judgments of one individual on the decisions of others.

O

off-budget spending Government projects and programs that are not listed on the budget. As such, financing of the projects need not face the annual review that other projects face.

offshore banking The international deposit and loan market. Also called the *Eurocurrency market*.

open economies Economies that trade goods and financial assets with the rest of the world.

open-market operation An operation in which the Fed writes a check on itself in order to purchase securities.

operational lag The time between the point when a policy is implemented and the point when it begins to take effect.

other checkable deposits (OCDs) Checking accounts other than demand deposits; include negotiable orders of withdrawal (NOW) accounts, credit union share draft accounts, and demand deposits at thrift institutions.

P

perfect capital mobility The situation where any interest rate differential, however slight, causes funds to flow from the rest of the world to the nation with the highest interest rate, thereby lowering interest rates in the nation into which funds are flowing.

permanent income hypothesis A theory of consumption spending developed by Milton Friedman. It postulates that economic units determine their present consumption based on their permanent income—the income that the unit expects to receive over the balance of its lifetime. More formally, permanent income is the current asset value of the lifetime income stream consisting of both labor and property income.

Phillips curve A curve showing an inverse relationship between the unemployment rate and the rate of inflation.

Pigou effect The idea, advanced by A. C. Pigou, that when the real value of people's money holdings increases, people will spend more. Thus changes in real money balances, M/P, affect the AD. A lower price level increases real wealth, M/P, and thus increases consumption.

policy coordination The cooperative, mutual implementation of economic policy by governments.

political business cycle The economic oscillation that results from politicians approaching reelection who enact expansionary policies (and thus produce price and wage rises).

positive analysis Analysis that does not impose the value judgments of one individual on the decisions of others.

potential output level The level the economy can produce if inputs are used efficiently and fully; no one is underemployed or involuntarily unemployed.

poverty line An arbitrary but official measure of poverty based on the income level necessary to purchase sufficient food to gain a specified nutritional level.

producer price index (PPI) Measures the cost of a basket of goods at the level of the first significant commercial transaction.

propagation The response of the economy to an impulse or economic shock.

public choice theory The view that government is nothing more than the many people who work in it, each trying to maximize his or her own utility.

public good A good that, once provided, is available to everyone at zero cost.

public interest theory The idea that government activities are designed to maximize society's welfare.

purchasing power parity (PPP) An extension of the law of one price to a multigood setting. The rate at which two currencies can be exchanged (the exchange rate) should reflect the relative purchasing powers of those currencies.

Q

q-theory A comparison of the cost of new capital (replacement cost) and the cost of existing capital (market value of the firm); whenever marginal revenue on new capital is greater than user cost, the firm will invest in new capital; when marginal revenue on new capital is less than user cost, the firm will purchase existing capital.

R

rational bubble When new investors enter the market expecting the original exchange rate movement to continue, the movement becomes self-sustained, leading to a persistent exchange rate deviation from PPP value.

rational expectations hypothesis (REH) The idea that people form their expectations regarding future values of economic variables by using all information that is available to them. This means that individuals will not systematically err in forming expectations.

real business cycles The interpretation of economic evidence to imply that changes in the money supply have no direct effect on real variables. It stems from the belief that the momentum observed in real variables and the business cycle in general is created by random disturbances and uneven and sluggish adjustments to these disturbances that cannot be offset by economic policy.

real interest rate The nominal interest rate adjusted for inflation. The real rate is defined as the nominal rate of interest minus the expected rate of inflation.

real value The nominal value of a variable deflated by the price level relative to some base year.

real wage The nominal wage divided by the price level.

recession The economic period between a peak and the trough that follows.

recessionary gap The situation where the economy's output level is less than its potential output level.

relative version of purchasing power parity (PPP) A version of the idea that the same amount of money may buy the same amount of goods in two markets; this version states that the percentage change of the exchange rate equals the difference between the percentage changes of the foreign and home price levels.

reserve requirement The fraction of deposits that banks must leave on reserve and not loan out, that is set by the Fed.

residential investment Additions to the stock of homes and apartment buildings.

Ricardian equivalence An argument asserting that because deficits must eventually be paid off, they won't affect current economic activity.

risk premium The extra return on foreign issue assets that must be offered to offset U.S. investors' risk of holding assets in regions experiencing political instability.

roundabout production Sacrificing current consumption to accumulate capital with which output can be produced.

S

saving Not consuming.

Say's law The classical view of *AD* and *AS:* that supply creates its own demand.

scientific method A five-part method of developing and testing a hypothesis: (1) recognize the problem, (2) make assumptions in order to cut away unnecessary detail, (3) develop a model of the problem, (4) present a hypothesis, and (5) test the hypothesis.

seasonal unemployment Unemployment that results from regular, recurring changes in the production requirements of certain industries.

short-run aggregate supply curve The graphical representation of aggregate supply derived under conditions where workers have not realized the true price level or for some reason the nominal wage has not adjusted to a new price level.

short-run operating target An intermediate, easily controllable target for Fed (FOMC) policy, that has a consistent, predictable relationship to the money supply.

Solow residual The difference between output growth and the growth of resources.

special drawing rights (SDR) A form of international money issued by the International Monetary Fund. SDRs are used by nations as a form of reserves for financing balance of payments deficits.

stagflation High rates of unemployment accompanied by high inflation rates or a simultaneously increasing rate of unemployment and inflation.

standards of living A measure of affluence or poverty; for example, per capita income.

sterilization A domestic open-market operation used to offset the expansionary effect of a foreign exchange market intervention by the FOMC; an open-market bond sale used to reduce the money supply.

sticky wages Wage conditions that do not immediately respond to demand and supply changes, such as paying efficiency wages.

strategic behavior Each firm or government taking into account the responses of its competitors to any action.

strategic trade A new view of international trade that suggests government should use tariffs to give domestic firms with potential for economies of scale an advantage over foreign rivals.

structural unemployment Affects those people in the labor force who do not have the appropriate training to obtain employment. Examples include makers of horse-drawn carriages after the invention of the automobile and dental care providers after the discovery of an anticavity drug.

supply shock Event that causes a reduction in the productive capacity of an economy. Such shocks reduce supply either by reducing the availability of factor inputs or by reducing the productivity of those inputs.

supply-side policies Policies directed toward the aggregate supply curve; for example, policies to increase labor quality, innovation rate, investment, and savings.

T

total factor productivity (TFP) Total output divided by total quantity of inputs.

total product curve (TP) The graphic representation of the aggregate production function; the mechanism through which inputs are combined to produce output.

tradeoff Policymakers interpreted the Phillips curve as showing the tradeoff between inflation and unemployment. According to this interpretation, any point along the curve could be attained through the use of monetary and fiscal policy.

twin deficits The government budget deficit and the deficit in the current account; the first is presumed to drive the latter.

U

unemployment rate Indicates the extent to which available labor resources are being used.

user cost of capital The implicit rental value of capital services.

V

velocity A rate at which the stock of money is used to purchase GNP. It is a measure of the speed with which the average dollar changes hands. GNP/M = velocity.

vicious circle Rising prices may evoke demands for nominal wage hikes and the monetary authorities may increase money supply to validate the hikes.

W

wealth effect A change in the real value of wealth makes spending change when the price level changes.

Author Index

Subject Index

TABLE C U.S. Money Supply and Interest Rates

Year	M1	M2	M3	Three-Month T-Bill Rate	Prime Rate	Federal Funds Rate
	Billions of Dollars			Percent		
1965	167.9	459.4	482.3	4.0%	4.5%	4.1%
1966	172.1	480.0	505.1	4.9%	5.6%	5.1%
1967	183.3	524.4	557.1	4.3%	5.6%	4.2%
1968	197.5	566.4	606.3	5.3%	6.3%	5.7%
1969	204.0	589.6	615.1	6.7%	8.0%	8.2%
1970	214.5	628.1	677.4	6.5%	7.9%	7.2%
1971	228.4	712.7	776.2	4.3%	5.7%	4.7%
1972	249.3	805.2	886.0	4.1%	5.3%	4.4%
1973	262.9	861.0	985.0	7.0%	8.0%	8.7%
1974	274.4	908.6	1070.4	7.9%	10.8%	10.5%
1975	287.6	1023.3	1172.3	5.8%	7.9%	5.8%
1976	306.4	1163.7	1311.8	5.0%	6.8%	5.0%
1977	331.3	1286.7	1472.6	5.3%	6.8%	5.5%
1978	358.5	1389.0	1646.6	7.2%	9.1%	7.9%
1979	382.9	1497.1	1803.2	10.0%	12.7%	11.2%
1980	408.9	1629.9	1987.5	11.5%	15.3%	13.4%
1981	436.5	1793.5	2234.2	14.0%	18.9%	16.4%
1982	474.5	1953.1	2441.9	10.7%	14.9%	12.3%
1983	521.2	2186.5	2693.4	8.6%	10.8%	9.1%
1984	552.1	2371.6	2982.8	9.6%	12.0%	10.2%
1985	620.1	2570.6	3202.1	7.5%	9.9%	8.1%
1986	724.7	2814.2	3494.5	6.0%	8.3%	6.8%
1987	750.4	2913.2	3678.7	5.8%	8.2%	6.7%
1988	787.5	3072.4	3918.3	6.7%	9.3%	7.6%
1989	794.8	3221.6	4044.3	8.1%	10.9%	9.2%
1990	825.5	3323.3	4094.0	7.5%	10.0%	8.1%

Source: *Economic Report of the President,* February 1991.